CW01213860

DOMENICO ITALO COMPOSTO-HART

About the Author

DOMENICO ITALO COMPOSTO-HART was born and raised in Chicago, Illinois. He studied Archaeology and Anthropology at Boston University and lived in Tokyo, Japan for over three years pursuing a career as a freelance musician. He currently teaches economics for the International Baccalaureate (IB) Diploma Programme at an international high school. He lives with his wife and sons in Barcelona, Spain.

ALSO BY DOMENICO ITALO COMPOSTO-HART

FICTION
Dark Legacy: Book I – Trinity
The Astor House of Old Shanghai
White Lion Rising

NONFICTION
Travels in the Land of Hunger

TRAVELS IN THE LAND OF HUNGER

A backpacker's earthbound journey from the East to the West

DOMENICO ITALO COMPOSTO-HART

DRAGON BONE BOOKS

DOMENICO ITALO COMPOSTO-HART

TRAVELS IN THE LAND OF HUNGER.

Copyright © 2004 – 2019 by Domenico Italo Composto-Hart.

Excerpt from *The Astor House of Old Shanghai* copyright © 2004, 2011, 2013, 2019 by Domenico Italo Composto-Hart.

Excerpt from *White Lion Rising* copyright © 2011 – 2019 by Domenico Italo Composto-Hart.

Cover illustration copyright © 2007 by Tiberius Viris.

All rights reserved.

Without limiting the rights under copyright reserved above, no part of this literary book may be reproduced, stored in or introduced into a retrieval system, or transmitted, in any form, or by any means (electronic, mechanical, photocopying, recording, or otherwise), without the prior written permission of the copyright owner.

This book includes works of fiction. Names, characters, places, and incidents are either the product of the author's imagination or are used fictitiously. Any resemblance to actual persons, living or dead, business establishments, events, or locales is entirely coincidental.

Cover illustration by Tiberius Viris, www.tiberius-viris.com.

Cover design by James T. Egan, www.bookflydesign.com.

Writers Guild of America, West

TRAVELS IN THE LAND OF HUNGER is a literary book registered under the WGAWEST Intellectual Property Registry.

Registration Number: 2012499

ISBN-13: 978-0-9850177-6-7 (hbk)

ISBN-13: 978-0-9850177-7-4 (hbk)

ISBN-13: 978-0-9850177-8-1 (pbk)

ISBN-13: 978-0-578-57271-0 (pbk)

ISBN-13: 978-0-9850177-9-8 (ebook)

First Paperback Edition

In Loving Memory of Manuel Cabello Zahonero.

(espiritu)

Insontes protego.

DOMENICO ITALO COMPOSTO-HART

For my sons, Leonardo and Valentino, and my nephews and niece, Billy Jr., Charles, Rubén, and Lucy.

May you travel far and wide into the world.

ACKNOWLEDGEMENTS

I would like to thank the people—and their culture and history—of the following countries that I visited during this journey: Cambodia, China, Denmark, Estonia, Finland, France, Germany, Hong Kong, Hungary, Italy, Japan, Laos, Macau, Malaysia, Mongolia, Myanmar, Norway, Poland, the Russian Federation, Serbia, Singapore, Slovakia, South Korea, Spain, Sweden, Thailand, and Vietnam.

I would also like to thank the following friends, family, and supporters: Marc & Debbie Forkins & the Forkins family; David & Tonya & Joaquin & Adriana Torres, Phil Annetta & Suzy Annetta, Thomas Lee, Emiko Watanabe, Mika Takemura, Aaron Deupree, Janusz & Magda Migasiuk & the Migasiuk family, David & Maura Cevoli, Martha Correa, Isid Spaho, David Magaña, Ali Jessie, Jason Pendell, all of my students and everyone at BFIS, Manu Maculet, S.J. Wist, Gavin Wilson, Wayne John Haag, Tiberius Viris, James T. Egan, Mitchell Tyler, George Jaros, Mike "Roy" Pearce, Andy Ciordia, and Ema Cojocaru.

Neil Peart (an intellectual guide in my adolescent years; a master of music, words, and travel), RUSH, and Living Colour.

Billy (for being a good friend and brilliant husband to my little sister), Billy Jr., Charles, and Lucy Cannon.

Antonio Bello & Catalina Jordán, Josep Jordán & Carme Carreras, Sara & Mireia Jordán, Jeronimo Bello & Jessy Ojeda & Rubén, and Júlia Via.

The Hart & Composto Clans (both here and beyond).

And most especially to my nuclear family who celebrates me when I am victorious and cradles me when I am defeated: Keki Cannon (the flame), Lucy Composto (the earth)—*my biggest supporting fan*, and Domingo Composto (the shaper); you are my sacred Trinity for I am because of you. And from three there are four, five, and six: to my beautiful wife, María del Carmen Bello Jordán (the light), who was with me when I fell into the darkness (twice); and to my sons, Leonardo (the lion) and Valentino (the brave), who are my shining stars and guiding lights.

CHAPTERS

LEAVING THE LAND OF PLENTY 17
Sayonara 日本 19
An Nyoung Ha Sae Yo South Korea 26
Singapore 46
Malaysia 63

ENTERING THE LAND OF HUNGER 87
Thailand 89
Myanmar (Burma) & Bangkok, Thailand 98
Chiang Mai, Thailand 134
Laos 144
Back in Bangkok 163
Cambodia 187
Vietnam 236
Hong Kong & Macau 273
The Middle Kingdom: Part I 285
The Astor House of Old Shanghai **301**
The Middle Kingdom: Part II 321
Mongolia 353

RETURNING TO THE LAND OF PLENTY 365
Russia 367
Estonia 377
Suomi 379
The Open-Mindedness of the Swedes 386
Oslo, Norway 391
Copenhagen, Denmark 396
Berlin, Germany 397
A Note from Bratislava, Slovakia 398
The Art of Burning Out & Finding Salvation in Barcelona 400
Catalunya 402
White Lion Rising 403
Notes 439
Index 471

TRAVELS IN THE LAND OF HUNGER

A backpacker's earthbound journey from the East to the West

DOMENICO ITALO COMPOSTO-HART

"Travel is fatal to prejudice, bigotry, and narrow-mindedness, and many of our people need it sorely on these accounts. Broad, wholesome, charitable views of men and things cannot be acquired by vegetating in one little corner of the earth all one's lifetime."

— Mark Twain, *The Innocents Abroad, or The New Pilgrims' Progress*

LEAVING
THE LAND OF PLENTY

SAYONARA 日本

Sunday, March 21, 2004

After three-and-a-half years I will be departing Japan on March 29 to travel for five months through the continents of Asia and Europe; a journey that I have been dreaming about since high school.

The road before me runs through South Korea, the nations of Southeast Asia, China, Mongolia, Russia, Scandinavia, and the states of Eastern and Western Europe. The goal is to make as much of the journey by land and sea–rather than by air–to gain a sense of the distances that separates the unique people, cultures, languages, cities, and countries that I will encounter. The road will be long, and at times arduous, as I travel alone through the lands of Eurasia, but one that promises much beauty, mystery, and adventure.

Domenico です

Posted by The Legacy Cycle at 2004-03-21T08:12:00-08:00

Monday, March 29, 2004

I said goodbye to Japan today after more than three years. I woke up at 5:30 a.m. in the small, narrow one-bedroom apartment of my Canadian friend of South Korean descent, Thomas Lee. I sat up from the futon, allowed my eyes to adjust to the dim morning light, looked to the window, and touched the tatami floor taking a deep breath. *It is done*, I thought. The life I had enjoyed in the Land of the Rising Sun was now at a melancholic end. My apartment–a few minutes' walk from Thom's place–was empty as I had either shipped all that was precious to me back to the U.S. or had given items and appliances (such as the rice cooker I found in the garbage a few days after I moved into my apartment a couple of years back) to friends. The electricity, water, and gas had been shut off on March 28.

    I quietly stood up and took a few steps to reach the bathroom that (like most apartment bathrooms in Japan) looked almost identical to a commercial airliner lavatory: cramped. I showered, brushed my teeth, put on my clothes, cleaned my glasses, and checked my bag. It was time to go.

    Thomas–now awake–approached me. I thanked him for his hospitality and friendship, and we said our goodbyes not knowing when we would see each other again.

    I walked down the steps from his apartment to the street and walked through the town of Shiki with my black travel backpack hanging from my right shoulder. I took my routine route to the Tobu-Tojo Line's Shiki Station feeling, along the way, the weight of my bag beginning to pain my shoulder and lower back.

    At the station, I saw the usual morning scene of uniformed school children as young as six smiling and talking as they waited for the next train, and salarymen (white-collar businessmen) dressed in dark business suits along with career women and office ladies lining up on the platform. Surprisingly, in all my years in Japan, I saw for the first time the white-gloved pushers; the railway station attendants who literally pushed passengers into beyond capacity trains. I began to line up knowing that the 20-minute train ride to Ikebukuro Station was going to be very unpleasant. Passengers began to glare at me in strong disapproval of my large backpack, which would occupy valuable maneuvering space.

    The train arrived, the doors opened, a person or two exited, and the mad rush of people and children began the impossible squeeze into the already packed train. I was able to get on, but there I stood with people pressed against all sides of my body. I gripped the leather handle of my bag that I held vertically against my right leg and saw the pushers shoving the last few people onto the train. The doors closed and the trained moved causing the weight of several people who lost their balance to push against me. In typical Japanese fashion, we all kept our heads down and avoided eye contact as we tried to bare the uncomfortable journey.

    Each stop brought welcomed fresh air as the train doors

opened to trade a few exiting passengers for those who wanted to enter.

After arriving to Ikebukuro Station, I joined the rush through the ticket gates hearing the rapid clicking sounds of all the passengers who were swiping their electronic train cards to exit. I made my way to the green Yamanote Line and took the train to Shinjuku Station arriving at 7:00 a.m., which was an hour before the Narita Express was to depart for the airport.

To my luck the train to Narita International Airport pulled into Shinjuku Station at 7:30. I was able to board the train to escape the brisk morning air. I sat down in my assigned seat and began reading the tidbits of South Korean history that my *Lonely Planet* travel guide had to offer. And then, at precisely 8:00 a.m., the train began to move.

After an hour, the Narita Express train slowed to a halt at the end of the line. I gathered my belongings and disembarked with a trio of young Occidental businessmen who had been sitting behind me. As soon as we reached the end of the platform to enter the airport the Narita Express train began to move, sped up, and left.

"Oh, no!" exclaimed one of the Occidental businessmen. "I forgot my laptop on the train!"

The eyes of his colleagues widened as they realized that they would have to make a choice between finding a way to retrieve the laptop on a train that was speeding back to Tokyo or taking their flight back home.

I kept walking toward the airport wondering what choice they made.

I followed the signs to the check-in counter turning right, and left, and walking down long, nearly empty halls, and noticed an unusually high number of police officers on patrol. I also noticed that all the garbage bins had a paper sheet taped over them with a written warning in Japanese that politely explained that due to possible terrorist activities the garbage bins had to be covered up so that no one could slip a malicious device into them. For obvious reasons I couldn't take this effort to dissuade "potential terrorists" seriously for how would a thin sheet of paper serve as a strong enough barrier to obstruct the insertion of a bomb into the bin?

I found this poor effort by the police amusing, and this warning of a potential act of terror highly unlikely. All ethnic minorities stick out like sore thumbs in Japan; a society that is very homogeneous. It would be practically impossible for al-Qaeda operatives or any other foreign terrorists to operate in Japan without gaining quick attention from the yakuza (transnational organized crime syndicates) or the police. Keep in mind that in 2003 there were approximately 1.9 million registered foreigners in Japan, which represented 1.5 percent of the total population.[1] And of these foreigners 32 percent were from South Korea, 24 percent were from China, 18 percent were from South America, and 10 percent were from the Philippines.[2] Gaikokujin from North America, Europe (excluding Russia), Australia, and New Zealand made up approximately 0.01 percent of the total population.[3] What about foreign residents from potentially hostile nations? In his 2002 State of the Union Address, United States President George W. Bush labeled Iran, Iraq, and North Korea as part of an "axis of evil" accusing the governments of these nations of sponsoring terrorism and "seeking weapons of mass destruction". In 2000 there were 6,167 legal Iranian residents living in Japan[4] and approximately 5,821 illegal residents.[5] Taken together there was a total of 11,988 Iranians living in the country, and out of a total population of approximately 127 million, Iranians composed only 0.0094393701 percent. I would assume that the number of legal and illegal Iraqis residing in Japan would be the same if not less than the Iranian resident population. The majority of Iranian migrants in Japan are benign as they only seek to work, save, and return home to buy an apartment or start their own business.[6] We need to also consider the extreme difficulty a foreign terrorist cell operating in Japan would have in acquiring materials to commit an attack on an island that is patrolled and protected not only by various law enforcement and military agencies, but also by the yakuza who maintain absolute control over the Japanese underworld. A terrorist cell would attract immediate attention in their first attempt to acquire harmful materials through the illicit trade networks that are overseen by the yakuza; Japanese gangsters would never tolerate any act of terrorism against their own population by a group of gaijin.

Where then was the threat in Japan? Considering the March 20, 1995 Tokyo subway sarin attack by the religious cult Aum Shinrikyo that resulted in 13 deaths, the most likely terrorist threat would come not from an organized group of foreigners, but from a Japanese fanatical group.

An economist should research and publish the wasted time and tax funds used in having the police tape up garbage bins in Narita International Airport as a means to deter acts of terrorism. But of course, people in a post-9/11 world feel better seeing the police in full force in public places taping up garbage cans. I wonder if it would not have been more time and cost efficient for the Japanese media to report the probability of a terrorist attack by an outside group to be highly unlikely to nearly impossible? But the media needs to sell and when the threat of something that will not happen is broadcasted over the airwaves, it sells.

With all this in mind I am reminded of the fax from the U.S. Embassy in Japan that I had read (and did not take seriously for all of the above reasons) in the faculty room of the Ikebukuro branch of Berlitz Japan on September 10, 2001:

U.S. Department of State, U.S. Embassy, Tokyo, Japan
Consular Section, Fax: 03-3224-5856

September 10, 2001

Please pass the following U.S. Department of State public announcement to American citizens. Further travel information is always available at http://travel.state.gov, on recorded telephone message at 1-202-647-5225 or by fax at 1-202-647-3000.

PUBLIC ANNOUNCEMENT – Worldwide Caution –
September 7, 2001

Over the last several months, the U.S. Government has learned that U.S. citizens and interest abroad may be at increased risk of a terrorist action from extremist groups. In addition, we have received unconfirmed information that terrorist actions may be taken against U.S. military facilities and/or establishments frequented by U.S. military personnel in Korea and Japan. We are also concerned about information we received in May 2001 that American citizens may be the target of a terrorist threat from extremist groups with links to Usama Bin Ladin's Al-Qaida organization. In the past, such individuals have not distinguished between official and civilian targets. As always, we take this information seriously. U.S. Government facilities worldwide remain at a heightened state of alert.

U.S. citizens are urged to maintain a high level of vigilance and to take appropriate steps to increase their security awareness to reduce their vulnerability. Americans should maintain a low profile, vary routes and times for all required travel, and treat mail and packages from unfamiliar sources with suspicion. In addition, American citizens are also urged to avoid contact with any suspicious, unfamiliar objects, and to report the presence of the objects to local authorities. Vehicles should not be left unattended, if at all possible, and should be kept locked at all times. U.S. Government personnel overseas have been advised to take the same precautions. In addition, U.S. Government facilities have and will continue to temporarily close or suspend public service as necessary to review their security posture and ensure its adequacy.

U.S. citizens planning to travel abroad should consult the Department of State's Public Announcements, Travel Warnings, Consular Information Sheets, and regional travel brochures, all of which are available at the Consular Affairs Internet website at http://travel.state.gov. We will continue to provide updated information should it become available. American citizens overseas may contact the American Citizens Services unit of the nearest U.S. Embassy or Consulate by telephone or fax for up-to-date information on security conditions. In addition, American citizens in need of emergency assistance should telephone the nearest U.S.

Embassy or Consulate before visiting the Embassy or Consulate.

Department of State travel information and publications are available at Internet address: www.travel.state.gov. U.S. travelers may hear recorded information by calling the Department of State in Washington, D.C. at 202-647-6226 from their touch-tone telephone, or receive information by automated telefax by dialing 202-647-3000 from their fax machine.

This Public Announcement supersedes the Public Announcement – Worldwide Caution of June 22, 2001 to inform U.S. citizens of unconfirmed threats against U.S. military facilities, personnel and establishments frequented by U.S. military personnel. This Public Announcement expires on December 22, 2001.

Posted by The Legacy Cycle at 2004-03-29T04:31:00-08:00

AN NYOUNG HA SAE YO SOUTH KOREA

Monday, March 29, 2004

Flight to South Korea & Details of Seoul City

The two-hour flight from Tokyo, Japan to Seoul, South Korea was pleasant and short as I had slept for most of it.

The Seoul-Incheon International Airport was modern, well designed, and complete with indoor gardens, a museum, a golf course, spa, and an ice-skating rink. But I had foolishly assumed that there would have been a metro line or train linking the airport to the city. A middle-aged Korean lady at the airport information desk explained to me in broken English that I had to take a bus. I walked to the bus terminal outside the airport, and with the aid of a young Korean gentleman who placed my bag in the storage compartment under the bus I was on my way to the South Korean capital.

The first aspect of South Korea that I noticed during the bus ride was that its topography was very different to that of Japan. It was a land of hills and distant mountains with a dry, chaparral-like terrain. To the left side of the bus I saw the low tide shore with fishing boats that had been beached on vast expanses of wet sand. I then saw a few—and then many—muddy rice fields. I believe that planting begins in the spring and so what I was looking at were rice fields that had been abandoned from the previous harvest in autumn. Some of the fields looked dreadful as they were full of scummy water and sludge. But I did see farmers burning a few fields to prepare them for planting. Of course, these are just observations and assumptions, I don't know too much about the process of planting, growing, and harvesting rice.

As the bus began to reach the outskirts of the city, I saw various vendors along the highway who had pulled their vans over to the shoulder of the road to set up shop and sell an assortment of goods. Some vendors were selling office chairs whereas others were cooking and selling food. And between the highway and the Hangang (han meaning south, and gang meaning river) there was a camping ground, but there was nothing of natural significance around it other than two or three empty Olympic size public pools that were a few kilometers away.

Once we entered the city I kept an eye on my subway map marking each stop that the bus had made that was near a subway station. I gathered that the bus was headed for Tapgol Park and decided to get off near Jongno 2-ga. The bus stopped, I stepped off, grabbed my bag, strapped it to my back, and went in search of a Yeogwan (cheap hotel). I tried to follow the map in my guidebook but could not find the Yeogwan I had made a reservation at so I booked myself into a motel for about US$24 a night.

After I took a shower in my run-down room and flicked through a few South Korean television channels I decided to explore the neighborhood. One of the first shops I came across was a small traditional Korean drum shop that was crammed with drums and cymbals of all sizes; I interpreted this as a good omen since I am a percussionist. I continued walking and realized that my motel was in a district of the city that was full of musical instrument shops. The street of shops selling wall-to-wall Korean drums, gongs, and china cymbals gave way to shops selling low-quality electric guitars.

I traversed narrow winding streets that were lined with grimy restaurants; a few of them displayed, at their front entrance, stacks of severed pig's heads that had been butchered open. I peeked into one restaurant from the street and saw that it was half full of people eating and drinking. I stepped back when a waitress began approaching me and then a short lady carrying a plate of pig snouts that had been piled up shouldered passed me to enter the restaurant. I quickly walked away.

Jongno (Bell Street) is a *ten-lane* street that runs east to west through the city. I was shocked to see such a wide street for I had never seen one in all my years in Tokyo. I was beginning to realize that I was interpreting South Korea through the cultural lens of Japan, which explained why I was also surprised to see so many people eating food and drinking soda in public (a Japanese taboo). But I was relieved to discover that it was socially acceptable to eat as you walked and talked. The sight of so many people enjoying a drink made my mouth water. I needed a vending machine (a convenience that is in abundance in Japan), but to my dismay I could not find a single one. Hungry, I passed the many food stalls on Jongno seeing stacks of pancakes, kimchi, and what looked like blood sausages filled with little balls of fat. It was getting dark and I desperately wanted to order something, but I was paralyzed by my inability to speak a single word of Korean. I then saw a vendor making and selling what looked like burritos. I built up the courage, entered the plastic tent that surrounded the vendor's food cart, and pointed my finger at a burrito. But I didn't know how much it cost. A teenaged girl eating next to me could see that I was searching for a price. She pointed to a hidden sign. I thanked her by bowing my head and paid the cook 2,000 won. The young lady then poured me a cup of Pepsi cola to show me that it was included in the price; there were three two-liter bottles of Pepsi on the food stall counter and a stack of paper cups.

The Korean style burrito was a hellish flame of spiced meat that charred my mouth and caused profuse sweating. After a few cups of Pepsi to wash the blazing inferno down into my abdomen, I continued my walk seeing in the distance the dark outline of the mountains that surrounded the city. I entered a district dedicated to the repair and sale of clocks and watches, which led to another commercial district that sold medical equipment. The streets were full of potholes so I needed to watch my step as I walked at night to avoid tripping on a loose stone or piece of concrete.

Although it was Monday night there was a district of Seoul that was illuminated by scores of neon and backlit rectangular signs advertising shops, restaurants, and services (the area reminded me of Shinjuku in Tokyo). Teenaged kids and young couples eating and talking populated the scene that was complete with street vendors selling pirated DVDs and food.

Still seeking something more to eat on the walk back to the motel I entered a Korean restaurant franchise that offered kimchi and bibimbap.

Annyeonghi gyeseyo.

Posted by The Legacy Cycle at 2004-03-29T04:31:00-08:00

Tuesday, March 30, 2004

I woke up to a warm, stuffy room; I tried to turn down the heat, but I was not able to figure out how to use the thermostat. After taking a shower and getting dressed I went down to the first floor of the motel to the room with a computer that I had used last night to update my travel blog. Upon entering the room, I saw three young North American women huddled around a table that offered slices of bread, jam, and eggs. I took a plate, three slices of toast, and a couple plastic packets of strawberry jam. As I ate I began talking to the three young women and learned that they were all taking a week vacation from their work on the Japan Exchange and Teaching (JET) program. Two of the women gave me some advice of where to go if I wanted to escape Seoul and see something different. I finished my breakfast, said goodbye, and left to continue exploring the city.

The Changdeokgung Palace was only two blocks from my motel. I arrived at 10:30 a.m., but the English tour was at 11:30; I had no desire to wait an hour so I joined a large group of tourists from Japan for a Japanese tour. Unfortunately, I was not able to understand much of what the tour guide explained (a sad reminder of my failed attempts to grasp the Japanese language after my years of living in Tokyo). But I read everything in my brochure. The palace was one of the Five Grand Palaces built by the monarchs of the Joseon dynasty (1392-1897).[1] The two-storey Injeongjeon Hall (National Treasure) served as the throne hall where the king received foreign dignitaries. It was originally built in 1405, but had been rebuilt in 1610 and 1804 as a result of being damaged by fire.

The arrangement of the palace grounds consisted of wide-open spaces between walls and halls. The architecture of the halls was similar to the more plain and dark temples and shrines I had seen in Tokyo, except the supporting structures beneath the curved roofs were colorfully painted in hues of pink, blue, yellow, light orange, and dark red against a light green background. These vibrant colors outlining flowery designs reminded me of the more elaborate shrines and temples in Nikko, Japan. As my tour group continued walking through the palace grounds I managed to make friends with a Japanese family. I mostly spoke to the older brother and sister in broken Japanese and they spoke in broken English. It was a humorous experience, which made me realize how comfortable I felt with people from Japan.

After the palace tour, I walked to Tapgol Park. Along the way I took pictures of a row of small restaurants that all had on display—outside their doors—piles of chopped-up pig's heads, snouts, and skins on basket plates. The stench produced by the butchered meat was brackish.

Tapgol Park was originally the site of the Wongaksa, a 15th century Buddhist temple. All that remained was a 10-storey stone pagoda housed and protected behind glass panels and a tortoise stele that dated back to 1471. The sidewalk that surrounded the park was lined with Korean palm readers and fortune-tellers who worked in small but tall tents—roofed by an umbrella—that were painted with lines of Hangul writing and pictures of palms divided into their metaphysical parts.

I continued walking west on Jongno to Sejong Boulevard where I immediately saw in the square that was between two five-lane streets the bronze statue of Korean national hero, Admiral Yi Sun-Shin (1545-1598); recognized for his victories against the Japanese navy during their invasion of Korea in the late 16th century.[2] Standing guard with sword in hand on a several meters high concrete pedestal the statue overlooked the wide boulevard that led directly to the Gyeongbokgung Palace two blocks away. I walked north on Sejongno toward the palace and passed the U.S. Embassy that was heavily guarded by South Korean police dressed in full riot gear. It was not a friendly site. I later discovered that the police had been on high alert in preparation for U.S. Vice President Dick Cheney's upcoming visit to South Korea.

The Gyeongbokgung Palace (the largest of the Five Grand Palaces that was destroyed by Imperial Japan in 1911, but had been slowly restored since 1989) was closed. Looking through one of the three closed entrances of the Gwanghwamun (the main gate) I could see the Heungnyemun or second inner gate that was rebuilt after the Japanese Governor General Building was torn down from 1995 to 1996.

I walked down Yulgongno and turned right on Insadong-gil, the main street of the Insa neighborhood that was dedicated to art galleries, quaint tea houses, Buddhist shops selling prayer beads, ornaments, and trinkets, and calligraphy shops that stocked a large variety of brushes of which many hung from the windows.

Somehow, I found my way to Deoksugung Palace, which was another of the Five Grand Palaces. There were royal guards dressed in traditional Korean uniforms before the main gate who performed a guard-changing ceremony three times a day. Inside the palace there were more halls designed and decorated in the same style as the Changdeokgung Palace. Walking through the gardens and forests of the palace I saw two newly married couples posing for photos. One couple was dressed in traditional Korean clothing dyed in vibrant hues of red, pink, and white while the other was dressed in the boring Western style of a black tuxedo and a white wedding gown.

I walked down Taepyeongno to see the restored 14th century Namdaemun (Sungnyemun), which is the most famed of the Eight Gates of the Fortress Wall of Seoul that now sits in the middle of a busy roundabout.

I continued to Seoul Station and then walked almost two kilometers to the War Memorial of Korea, a museum dedicated to the history of warfare in Korea. The walk proved extremely difficult for my asthmatic lungs. I inhaled from my inhaler several times trying to alleviate my wheezing and the tight pain I felt in my chest. I became very concerned that if my asthma persisted in the days and weeks ahead that I would need to cancel my trip through Asia.

I did not have asthma prior to moving to Japan, but as a result of the air pollution in Tokyo I began developing the disease. It was my hope that once I escaped Seoul for the tropical conditions of Southeast Asia that my asthma would no longer be a persistent problem.

Eventually, I arrived to the museum and spent most of my time in the halls dedicated to warfare in the first millennium and the first half of the second millennium. I took notes and drew pictures in my Moleskine notebook of the weaponry used and the communication systems employed in the span of that time as potential ideas and details that I could use for my second *Dark Legacy* book.

The hall dedicated to the Korean War provided many graphic images of the devastating conditions Korean refugees had to endure as they made and lived in makeshift homes composed of planks, cardboard, and cans while at times eating tree bark and pine needles to kill their unceasing hunger.

There were a few halls dedicated to the South Korean soldiers who fought alongside U.S. soldiers during the Vietnam War, and more recently in Somalia and in Afghanistan among a few other conflicts within the past 30 years.

I found the hall dedicated to all the UN soldiers that served during the Korean War particularly interesting, as I was not aware that Ethiopia had sent soldiers to fight in the conflict.

After the museum, I walked to Yongsan (Dragon Mountain) Station in search of the Yongsan Electronics Market where I was hoping to buy an outlet adapter for the battery charger of my digital camera. I entered a four or five-storey building that had been remodeled from a bus terminal to a shopping arcade that housed hundreds of independent electronic shops. I found a suitable adapter, bought it, and left–since it was getting late–to take a subway train to Jongno 3-ga Station.

It was night when I emerged from the station. I walked down Jongno toward Tapgol Park, but stopped for a bite to eat at a food stall where I pointed to what I wanted. A kind old lady served me a plate of sundae (blood sausage) and jeon (a kind of pancake). As I ate, four teenaged Korean girls approached the food stall to eat. I noticed that one of the girls had a bag full of drumsticks. I smiled and asked if she played the drums. The girl said no, but explained in broken English that she was holding the sticks for her friend. I introduced myself to the girls as a fellow musician. Each girl then introduced themselves and named the instrument they played: one was a guitarist, the other a bass player, another a drummer, and the other ... oops, I forgot. They told me that they were studying music in their university. To feed my ego I showed them pictures of my drum performances in Tokyo on the small screen of my digital camera. They were impressed and invited me to see their performance at the end of April. I explained that I was not going to be in South Korea at that time, but I gave them my business card (an old habit I picked up in Japan) and told them to email me if they ever came to the U.S. Meeting those girls and talking a bit about music made my day.

I am now in my motel. I should go, I'm taking up too much time on the only computer with Internet here.

Posted by The Legacy Cycle at 2004-03-30T03:50:00-08:00

Thursday, April 1, 2004

Wednesday, March 31, 2004

I went to the Korean Demilitarized Zone (DMZ) this morning to see the four-kilometer-wide and 248-kilometer-long militarized (despite the name) border that has separated North and South Korea since 1953. The entire zone was lined with two electrical fences that were separated by a road that was patrolled by soldiers riding in Humvees. No human being has ever set foot in the DMZ for the past half century and as a result it has ironically become an ecological paradise providing a home, for example, to a large flock of endangered red-crowned cranes. Some environmentalists are concerned that if the North and South unify human society will overrun the DMZ and destroy the natural habitat that has been a safe haven to many species of birds, plants, and animals.[3]

The ride north to the DMZ from Seoul took about an hour in a bus that traveled along the Han River before turning east along the Imjin River. It was along the Imjin River that I had my first glimpse of North Korea. The entire length of the river was lined with electrical fences and military personnel. Along the way I also saw anti-tank barricades and concrete gates; the gates were wired with explosives so that on detonation they would collapse over the road creating difficult terrain for invading military vehicles.

My first stop with the tour group was the Freedom Bridge (originally it was the Kyung-eu railway bridge); a pedestrian bridge that serves as the only route linking North and South Korea. It is on this bridge that the North has permitted prisoners of war to cross over to the South. If you saw the spy film *Die Another Day* there was a scene where James Bond had to walk across the Freedom Bridge after a prisoner exchange had been negotiated.

The second stop of the tour was the Third Tunnel of Aggression. The tunnel is one of four that had been discovered by the Republic of Korea Armed Forces over the past 30 years. It was uncovered in 1978 near the armistice village of Panmunjom, which is 44 kilometers north of Seoul. It is believed that the tunnels are being dug by North Korea in preparation for an invasion against the South. The fourth tunnel was uncovered in 1990 and it was wide enough for tanks to charge through.

To see the 1.635-kilometer long tunnel we had to travel 73 meters into the earth on a narrow rail car. The tunnel was wide enough for only two people to walk through shoulder to shoulder and was dug on an upward incline from North to South so that the ground water would flow from South to North. We walked for about seven minutes through the tunnel up to a point where we could see a series of barricades that prohibited entry to the area of the tunnel that was located below the Military Demarcation Line (MDL).

To be honest, I didn't understand how this tunnel would have achieved the intended effect of permitting enough soldiers to travel through and out of it to invade South Korea. Only two soldiers at a time could exit the tunnel and since the DMZ is so heavily guarded it would only be moments before South Korean armed forces detected an outpour of North Korean soldiers from a two-meter wide tunnel. Fire a rocket at the tunnel to collapse it and that would effectively end an ill-conceived invasion.

Supposedly, the North Koreans have their own tours of the tunnels in which they explain that the tunnels had been dug by the South as part of a planned invasion of the North. Who is telling the truth?

It is humorous to consider that Kim Il-sung's and Kim Jong-il's "tunnels of aggression" serve as tourist attractions for the South. But perhaps North Korea already uses that as an example of how a capitalist nation derives revenue wherever possible.

The next stop on the tour was the Dora Observatory that provided a panoramic view of the DMZ and North Korea. I could easily identify the North Korean village of Gijeongdong (referred to as "Peace Village" by the North Koreans and "Propaganda Village" by the South Koreans) by the 160-meter high flagpole (the world's third tallest) that towered above it. Just two kilometers south of Gijeongdong is the South Korean village of Daeseong-dong (referred to as "Freedom Village" by the South), which has its own rival flagpole waving the South Korean flag. The 500 South Korean residents of Daeseong-dong are exempt from taxes and conscription, which is mandatory for all South Korean citizens.

I also saw from the observatory the abandoned village of Panmunjom where the Joint Security Area (JSA) is located. The JSA is where North and South Korean officials meet to negotiate in two blue buildings that stand over the Military Demarcation Line.

The last stop of the tour was Dorasan Station (the northernmost railway station in South Korea). And although it was a railway station the building had no trains. What an easy job for the guys who worked there. Other than the tourist aspect of the station of having my passport stamped, the building was intended to stand as a symbol of hope that the South would one day be unified with the North. If and when that happened the Dorasan Station would open the Gyeongui Line to North Korea and to the rest of Asia and Europe via the Trans-Siberian Railway.

Now, if you talk to South Koreans you would be surprised to discover that most are not eager to unify the Korean peninsula. Why you ask? The main reason is that it would be a heavy blow to the already weakened (post 1997 Asian financial crisis) South Korean economy. Who would pay to develop North Korea's antiquated infrastructure so that it was up to speed with the modern economy? The South Koreans would have to foot the bill. There would also be a flood of North Koreans into the South trying to soak up whatever jobs they could get, which would drive blue-collar salaries down. The cost of rebuilding North Korea is probably somewhere in the hundreds of billions to trillions of dollars. South Korea is not ready to take on those costs. So, don't expect North and South to unify any time soon. It may happen in my lifetime, but not in the next 10 or 20 years.

After returning to Seoul, I decided to check out the Namdaemun Market, which is Korea's oldest (1414 AD) and largest traditional market. It is a half indoor and half open-air market of vendors by the hundreds selling neatly stacked or piled up mountains of shoes, pants, shirts, belts, boots, washcloths, and army gear from U.S. bases. And there was plenty of street food vendors offering chopped up pig's heads, pickled ginseng roots, and red peppers that had been pounded to dust. It was remarkable. The Namdaemun Market is a must see in Seoul.

All right, I'm off to bed; a cute Japanese girl is waiting for me to sign off from the Internet. I'm actually in a town called Gyeongju. I arrived this afternoon. I will write about it tomorrow since I'm a day behind in my journal.

Posted by The Legacy Cycle at 2004-04-01T03:05:00-08:00

Friday, April 2, 2004

Thursday, April 1, 2004

I took a four-and-a-half-hour bus ride from Seoul to Gyeongju, a coastal city in the southeastern corner of the peninsula facing the Sea of Japan—or the East Sea—as the Koreans prefer to call it.

Why Gyeongju? Gyeongju was the capital of the ancient Silla Kingdom (57 BC – 935 AD) and was ruled by the Gyeongju Kim clan for most of its almost 1,000-year history thus making it the world's longest continuous dynasty.

Although now close to nothing remains of the palaces and fortresses that had defined this area more than a millennium ago, large tumuli (burial mounds) of the monarchs of the Silla Kingdom are scattered throughout the city.

I arrived at around 3:00 p.m. and walked two blocks from the bus station to the Han Jin Hostel, which was owned by Master Kwon. What was he a master of, I had no idea, but that was how he introduced himself at check-in. He was short in stature, humble and gentle, and had operated the hostel for the past three or four decades. On a wall in the TV lounge there was a picture frame full of faded pictures from the 1970s of Master Kwon in his younger days alongside expatriates and travelers from all parts of the world. The other walls were decorated with Mr. Kwon's Korean calligraphies and poems that were all—as he pointed out—for sale.

I took a single room with no bath. I went up a flight of stairs with my backpack, passed the bathroom, turned left into a long corridor, saw my room number, and opened the door with my key. I entered and saw a mattress on the floor, a window, faded wallpaper, and a very high ceiling. Apart from me there was only one other person staying at the hostel: a sweet old woman (perhaps she was in her seventies) from Sweden.

Over the past few days I had been worried about how I was going to survive five months of solo travel. The answer to my concerns came from a casual talk I had with this Swedish lady in the TV lounge after settling in at the hostel. She explained that although she was from Sweden she had moved to the Costa del Sol in Spain nearly 12 years ago. And on December 9 of last year she left her Iberian home to begin her journey. She celebrated Christmas in Barcelona, flew to Madrid, and then to New York. From NYC, she traveled to Washington D.C. and then to Los Angeles. She then flew to Auckland, New Zealand and Fukuoka, Japan. And she was now here in South Korea. She had been traveling for the past four months and explained that she did not mind traveling on her own for such a long period of time. Those were words of encouragement for if she could do it, then I sure as hell could. Her independence and courage to take on such a journey at her age was an inspiration. She was also beautiful. I could easily see that in her younger days many, many boys must have gazed at her. She also told me that she did not like cities and that at all costs she tried to avoid them. Instead, she loved the countryside and thus she found the town of Gyeongju to be perfect.

Before the sun was to set I went out for a long stroll. Two or three blocks from my hostel I found a park with several burial mounds, notably the Geumgwanchong Tomb and Bonghwangdae. These Silla tombs were built between the 4th and 5th century AD and were excavated in 1921, and among the items discovered were two gold crowns.[4]

Across the street from these two tombs was Tumuli Park, which had over 20 Silla tombs. The Cheonmachong (the Heavenly Horse) tumulus dated to the 5th century AD and was 13 meters high and 47 meters in diameter.[5] It was excavated in 1973 and produced over 11,500 artifacts ranging from a gold crown, gold rings, gold bracelets, jade beads, pottery, and a sword, to a painted saddle flap depicting a white horse (from which the tomb derives its name), as well as the remains of a horse that had been buried with the unknown monarch of the tomb.[6,7]

Getting hungry I made my way to Wolseong Park and bought 14 Gyeongju bread pastries with red bean paste filling for about 5,000 won. I ate all of them and soon became ill from eating such a rich pastry as a substitute for a proper meal.

The evening became cloudy, cool, and grey, and as I walked through Wolseong Park I came across what remained of an ancient grove named the Gyerim Forest. The woodland is considered to be the birthplace of Kim Alji, the founder of the Gyeongju Kim clan (the clan to which 1.7 million South Koreans belong).

A plaque at the site explained the following:

According to Samgukyusa, during the reign of King Talhae, a man called Hogong heard a cock crying in the forest. He went into the woods and saw a golden casket dangling on a branch of a tree.

Hearing the report from Hogong the King went to the forest and pulled the casket down to find a male child. The child was given the surname Gim and the name of Al-ji.

Inspired by the legend and by the eerie mist that crept into the age-old forest I began composing a few lines:

The Sirim Forest

In the months after winter it is lifeless and cold.

The trees, ancient, twisted by centuries of disease, dig their crooked roots into a desolate land of sand and scattered patches of dried grass.

It is a sad place.

Long forgotten are the days of the Al-ji King for it was here in the Forest of Sirim that he was found by the monarch of Talhae.

The trees, devoid of leaves, are hunched over—bending down— pointing their wicked blame at the ground with bent and coiled branches.

In the night, a fog sets in turning the old woodland to death.
Owls do not stir.
Creatures dare not set foot within for it is a dark and haunted place.

North of the Sirim Forest rests the King Al-ji in the Tomb of Gyeongju.
It is a mound.
A mound.
And on its southern slope do the cherry trees bloom.

Posted by The Legacy Cycle at 2004-04-02T03:51:00-08:00

Friday, April 2, 2004

I woke up at about 7:40 a.m., but I didn't get up until just before 8:00. I took a shower, drank some tea in the TV lounge, and watched a bit of CNN with the Swedish woman I had met yesterday. Then I was off.

I decided to walk to Namsan Mountain instead of taking the local bus. Heading south I arrived to Orung (Five Tombs) after an hour to see where the burial mounds of King Pak Hyeokgeose–founder of the Silla Kingdom (57 BC – 935 AD)–and his Lady Aryeong as well as the burial mounds of "Kings Namhae, Yuri, and Pasa ... the second, third, and fifth kings" of the Silla dynasty.[8]

Another plaque explained the following:

> According to legend King Hyeokgeose ascended to heaven after ruling the country for 61 years. Seven days after his ascension his body was dropped from heaven in pieces and then buried in the tombs.

I continued south for a kilometer and arrived at Poseokjeong, which was once the site of a royal pavilion during the Unified Silla period where monarchs held banquets for their nobles. Although the pavilion is completely gone what still remains is an abalone-shaped water channel made of granite that at one end circles around the base of an old tree. It is six meters in length and was located in the royal pleasure grounds where the Silla kings and nobles floated their drinks and composed poetry. The terrain of the area is of dried packed earth dotted by barren trees providing no other significant sign that any type of royal structure had ever existed here.

Further along I found three standing, but heavily weathered, sandstone Buddha statues. The central figure was of Amitabha Buddha, the statue to its left represented Bodhisattva Avalokitesvara (compassion), and to my left the Bodhisattva Mahasthamaprapta (power). The three statues were roofed by a traditional Korean temple structure of red wooden pillars and a turquoise painted ceiling depicting ornate designs that highlighted pink lotus flowers. Two Korean women were seated before the statues. I approached the temple and noticed that the women's shoes were just outside the perimeter of the shrine and were pointed toward the statues, whereas in Japan shoes would have been placed to point away from a holy site. Directly before the central statue there was an old metallic desk. On the desk, there were two large candles and between the candles there were two incense urns. The candle to my left had a tiger design on it and the candle to my right had a dragon design. Within the desk–located at both ends where there should have been two drawers–there were several burning candles that over time had stained the desk black with soot. One of these candles was completely lined with Korean script.

As I took pictures two Korean women hikers stepped into the shrine area, clasped their hands before their chest, bowed deeply at the waist, and left. Suddenly one of the women who had been seated before the statues began giving full bows to the Bodhisattva of Compassion.

To perform a full bow, you must kneel and sit on your heels, bend forward at the waist so that your hands touch the ground, and then lower your forehead so that it touches the ground as well. Once your forehead touches the ground you must turn your palms up so that it looks like you are asking for something. What you are asking for, traditionally speaking, is knowledge (enlightenment). It is a symbolic posture of opening yourself up, and being humble before a greater force. When I used to live in the Shim Gwang Sa (a Korean Zen Buddhist temple in Boston) I had to give full bows to the central Buddha statue of the temple and to my Zen master, Chang Sik Kim. The woman at the shrine gave 20 to 30 or more full bows. After a while I could hear her begin to tire as her breath became heavy from the exercise; she then began to chant.

I walked a few paces to a smaller Buddhist temple. There was a ceremony in session and out of curiosity I walked closer for a better look. A Buddhist priest exited the temple and following behind him was a small procession of people. The people were wearing traditional monk garments making me think that they were students of the priest. I decided to film the ceremony with my digital camera but soon realized that I was filming a funeral. One of the people in the procession was holding a framed picture of a man. I felt ashamed for filming and stopped, and bowed my head in regret, sadness, and respect.

Compared to the Japanese, I have to say that Koreans are more religious. To be honest, I prefer the Japanese way in having traditional religion be nearly non-existent in your everyday life. The Japanese (from my understanding) are not religious. They are not Buddhists or faithful to the old national religion of Shinto. Koreans on the other hand are very religious. All over Seoul I saw churches and Buddhist temples, and Buddhist monks and nuns walking the streets.

I spent the next three hours hiking up Mount Namsan in search of as many Buddhist relics from the Silla period that I could find as they were scattered all over the western slope of the sacred mountain. I found Yukjonbul, which is a rock surface carving of six Buddhist images, and the Seated Yeorae image. In all, Mount Namsan possessed "122 temples, 53 stone statues, 64 pagodas, and sixteen stone lanterns".[9]

It took an hour and a half to reach one of the peaks of the mountain that provided a fantastic view of Gyeongju, a town nestled within a valley of modest mountains and surrounded by dry farmland awaiting spring rejuvenation.

Although in the morning it was extremely windy, by early afternoon I had the sun shining full down upon me. It was a peaceful experience to hike up the mountain as I rarely saw anyone during the ascent other than a few groups of women in their mid-forties, clothed and equipped in full hiking gear, who would stop and let me pass since they knew they were slowing my pace down.

To descend I took a path on the northern slope of the mountain where I came across several small stone pagodas, and a few other scattered Buddha images that had been carved into the mountainside.

Once I reached the base of the mountain I decided to walk all the way back to my hostel. And as I walked and neared the outskirts of town I looked into several mom-and-pop shops hoping to find a drink to quench my growing thirst. But I saw no one inside these shops, and being too self-conscious to simply enter in the hopes of being attended I continued to the next empty shop and the next empty shop until I had arrived back into the center of town. I finally bought—at a small grocery store—what had become my favorite drink in South Korea, a drink called "Rice Beverage," which looked like diluted milk, but tasted slightly sweet and had a texture between milk and soymilk.

Refreshed from the drink, I continued walking and bought a few snacks at a convenience store. I then returned to my hostel and ate in the TV lounge. At 6:00 p.m. Mr. Kim arrived, he was the nephew of Master Kwon. Mr. Kim sat down in the TV lounge with me and asked about my morning trip to the mountain. After I answered he explained that he was a high school art teacher, which prompted him to invite me to go to his school to see his artwork, and the artwork of his students. I was too tired to go, but he insisted, so I agreed.

We went in his car—a Hyundai—that had cigarette ash all around the gearshift; he apologized for the mess. During the drive, he explained that his high school was the only all-boys school in Gyeongju. After about a 10 to 15-minute drive we arrived to a large, new high school building that had been completed only a few months ago.

He parked the car, we got out, and he led me to a statue of the school's founder Sung-Ho (I believe that was his name). The school was founded in 1937. Right in front of the school there were three or four sports fields with one of the fields being used for baseball practice. Before entering the school, Mr. Kim took me around the back where I saw students playing a soccer match.

We entered the school through the main entrance and Mr. Kim took me up to his office where he unlocked his locker and pulled out a few of his finished artwork and *many* of his unfinished works. He explained that once summer began he would finally have the time to finish his unfinished projects. There was one portrait of a student within his collection that he completed 22 years ago. He explained that he liked her artwork and that she was "pure and innocent," but that he didn't know where she was now (a bit strange to hear such comments from a teacher). His style was faithful to Impressionism as there were elements that reminded me of Monet. There were a lot of landscape paintings, all different versions of the same theme of a beautiful tree (I thought it was a cherry tree, but it was a tree native to Korea) occupying the bottom half of the painting and a setting sun occupying the upper half. There was another painting he did about 25 years ago of a dark forest and the faint, haunting impression of a Korean temple in the background. As for his floral still life paintings, I did not care for them. They were technically very good–excellent–but I don't care for flowers in such detail. He explained that he loved flowers and gardening and that he did some of the garden work just in front of the school.

Afterward we went outside to look at a war memorial dedicated to the 133 students who gave their lives during the Korean War.

On the way back to the hostel, Mr. Kim asked me if I had eaten dinner. I said no and he offered to take me to a good restaurant. I was extremely hungry and accepted the offer.

We went to the Sun Restaurant, which was right next to the Intercity Bus Station. He spoke to the owner, who he knew well, ordered for me, and explained that he had to leave because his wife was waiting for him back home. I sat down and began reading to avoid the stares, uncomfortable smiles, and chuckles of the locals seated at the tables around me. The waitress–who was the wife of the owner–placed a platter that covered the entire surface area of the table! The platter had several dishes of kimchi, chopped vegetables, dried seaweed, a fried egg, and who knew what else. I ate and ate. I loved it. All this food for US$4 was a blessing, although my tongue and lips suffered from third-degree burns from the red peppers and minced garlic in the kimchi.

I returned to the hostel and here I am, but it is now time to go. A young lady from Germany would like to use the Internet.

Posted by The Legacy Cycle at 2004-04-02T04:44:00-08:00

Saturday, April 3, 2004

I am back at the motel I stayed at when I first arrived to Seoul. I woke up this morning and took it easy. I sat in the TV lounge talking with the young German lady that I had met late last night in the hostel. Then a Canadian joined us. He explained that he had been working in Seoul for the past three months and that he just arrived in Gyeongju to finally see something other than the capital.

I took the express bus from the Gyeongju Bus Station at 11:00 a.m. and arrived in Seoul at around 3:40 p.m. During the bus trip, I saw burial mounds in the distant hills and mountains. These mounds were much smaller than the royal mounds I saw in Gyeongju because they were for common Koreans. It is still a tradition in Korea to be buried in the mountains.

And well, here I am back in the motel. Tonight, I'm going to rest and prepare for my flight tomorrow to Singapore.

The following are some general observations of South Korea and its people compared to what I came to know in Japan.

In Japan, everything you buy is wrapped, bagged, and taped up. They take a lot of care into wrapping and packing every purchase. Gift-wrapping has a long and ancient tradition in Japan. Archaeologists have even found gifts wrapped in tree bark dating back to the prehistoric period in Japan. In Korea, you are lucky to even get a bag. I've bought a few things at the convenient store and seven times out of ten I didn't get a bag.

In Japan, when you walk into an establishment, you are saluted by nearly every employee with a loud and welcoming, "Irasshaimase!" And when you leave you are recognized and saluted. In Korea–nothing.

Just like in Japan, signs in English are fairly prevalent in Seoul. In all the train stations, restaurants, and bus stations information was provided in English.

Stores, restaurants, streets, and public transportation systems are much cleaner and better maintained in Japan than in South Korea. But streets and sidewalks in South Korea are much wider than in Japan, although in Seoul, cars rule and pedestrians do not because at nearly every major intersection–in order to cross the street–I had to go down into an underground crosswalk.

Life in a South Korean subway train is much like what you would find in Japan with people taking short naps, reading a book, magazine, or newspaper, and whispering to their neighbor. One difference is that trains in Japan scream with advertisements while there were few advertisements in the subway trains of Seoul.

Older South Korean women, they are loud! I witnessed a few cases of women in their sixties screaming and at times hitting a man. Even here in my motel there is a lady who is always screaming at the guy sitting at the front desk (I caught the guy this morning kicking a little dog around, perhaps the dog belongs to the lady).

In Seoul, there is a Starbucks on every block. Outback Steakhouse, McDonald's, and Burger King are in abundance, which is interesting because Burger King does not exist in Japan. Family Mart and 7-Eleven are the most widespread convenient store chains.

I should get off the Internet. I've been on the computer for too long again and motel guests are eager to use it.

All the best,

Domenico

P.S. I ran into the sweet, old Swedish woman that I met at my hostel in Gyeongju here in Seoul. Her name is Ingegärd and she lives in Arroyo de la Miel, Spain.

Posted by The Legacy Cycle at 2004-04-03T01:07:00-08:00

SINGAPORE

Sunday, April 4, 2004

During breakfast, at my motel in Seoul, I met two German musicians who had performed at a music festival in southern South Korea. We talked about jazz and I answered a few of their questions regarding the music scene in Tokyo before running back up to my room to finish packing.

I paid my bill at the motel and left to catch my bus to the airport. At the bus stop I met the German musicians again, they were also on their way to the airport. The bus arrived; we boarded it and shared stories of the curiosities that we had discovered in South Korea.

My flight departed Seoul at 1:05 p.m. About six hours into the flight I looked out the window and saw a glorious, deep blue ocean and bright white clouds that faded into the distant, dark grey of a brewing tropical storm. The plane then began to make its descent.

As we approached Singapore I became excited by the welcoming view of the lush tropical forests and palm trees of Malaysia! I felt that I had finally escaped the cityscapes of Tokyo, and its distant cousin Seoul, for paradise. My journey had now begun.

Singapore Changi Airport was modern and clean, which was to be expected considering that the airport is typically ranked as one of the best in the world. The ultra-modern feel immediately reminded me of Tokyo. On a sci-fi timeline, I would place Tokyo in the future, perhaps giving a glimpse of what life would be like in New York City in the year 2030 AD. Traveling from Japan to South Korea was like going from the future into the present year of 2004, and then flying to Singapore and arriving at their airport was like traveling forward in time again to 2020 AD.

I followed the airport signs to the Mass Rapid Transit (MRT) system. I bought my ticket, stepped into the nearly empty train, and sat down placing my backpack between my legs. The train was clean and devoid of advertisements. As I waited for the train to depart from the airport terminal I saw a sign that read:

No Smoking – Fine $1,000

No Eating or Drinking – Fine $1,500

No Flammable Liquids/Gas – Fine $5,000

I immediately understood that Singapore was strict. Prior reading informed me that any person caught distributing or in possession of any illegal drug or substance received a mandatory death sentence. In fact, Singapore had the second highest per-capita execution rate in the world from 1994 to 1999 after Turkmenistan.[1]

Gum, and obviously chewing it, is illegal here unless you can get a prescription from a doctor permitting consumption for therapeutic purposes. As you can expect of such draconian laws and penalties Singapore is an extremely safe country to live and travel in.

After reading the penalty warning I turned and saw a female middle school student eating a burger from Burger King and drinking a cold drink from Starbucks on the train. *Odd*, I thought. *She must not know or care about being fined $1,500 for eating and drinking on the MRT.*

After checking into The InnCrowd Hostel Singapore I took a stroll down Dunlop Street—and the surrounding areas—to quickly discover that my hostel was located in the heart of Little India. I saw Indian men by the hundreds talking, shopping, buying fresh produce in the open markets, and eating spicy meals from street vendors in all directions. But where were the women? Did these men not have female counterparts? I kept searching, but failed to see a single Indian woman. The scene reminded me very much of Morocco where the streets and cafés were the sole domain of men. I also saw Indian men holding hands or each other's arms, which again reminded me of Morocco where it was not uncommon to see men displaying their friendship by holding hands in public.

As I passed through the crowds I was relieved that no one tried to sell me some trinket or offer their unneeded services as a tour guide.

The experience of strolling through Little India at night was visually exotic, vibrant, and stunning. I am a U.S. citizen raised by South American parents whose ancestral roots trace back to Europe. I have friends from Israel and have experienced a bit of Islamic culture in Morocco. I have lived in Japan and know a bit about Asia, but India I do not know a thing about. My curiosity to learn more about India began to grow, but when I came across a Hindu temple my interest exploded. I had never seen a Hindu temple. I didn't understand the rituals I was seeing or what one was required to do within it.

The exterior of the temple above the main entrance was shaped like a tall trapezoid with four levels (each with a smaller and smaller temple entrance at the center) lined with hundreds of small statues of Indian gods and humans painted in pastel colors in what appeared to be different stages of a story—or series of stories. Scores of sandals and a few shoes littered the three walkways leading up to the temple's main entrance. I only saw men entering and exiting the temple and ringing one of the several bells that hung just beyond the entrance. I could see men inside carrying the statue of an Indian god and rocking it from side to side to the rhythm of the music that was being performed by a small group of musicians. The music would speed up at times and the men would quicken the rocking motion accordingly. At the center of the temple was a pillar. I saw several men bowing and then lying on the floor faced down before it.

After filming the temple and taking a few pictures I continued my walk through the colorful streets of Little India. I eventually sat down at an outdoor Indian restaurant for some chicken tikka masala and garlic naan bread. But I was not impressed by the food when compared to a hole in the wall Pakistani curry shop in Ikebukuro, Tokyo that I frequented after teaching English a few days a week at Berlitz Japan.

Later that night I crossed Serangoon Road and read the following from a historical marker:

Serangoon Road – built in 1905

A humble bird used to inhabit the muddy banks of the old Serangoon River. The Malay villagers called it Rangongi; the Europeans knew it as the Marabou Stork. From this feathered creature, the river and, later, Serangoon Road, got their names.

Serangoon Road is now one of the many main arterial roads that slice through Singapore, but when it was first built it stood as the only road that cut across the island. Early Indian immigrants gravitated here. Mostly milkmen and cattle traders, they were drawn by the natural pastures, fed by the waters of Rochler Canal.

Lime was also found here, giving rise to a brick-manufacturing industry. The Indians who worked here in the numerous brick kilns that used to line Serangoon Road called the area "Village of Lime." Over time, a thriving Indian community developed, which engaged in an array of different occupations, including gold-trading, astrology, tattoo artistry, tailoring and money-lending. Places of worship, like the Sri Veeramakaliamman and Sri Srinivasa Perumal Temples, and the Angullia and Abdul Gafoor Mosques were built. With the passage of time Serangon became known as Singapore's traditional Indian quarters – Little India.

Time to go.

Posted by The Legacy Cycle at 2004-04-04T18:18:00-07:00

Monday, April 5, 2004

I started my day by using the Mass Rapid Transit (MRT) metro to get to Raffles Place, which was located in the financial heart of Singapore. The exit of the metro station led directly to a central square composed of an elevated grass park framed by polished stone divided into four parts by two intersecting walkways; businessmen and women taking a break sat here and there along the polished stone. There was a large electronic screen advertising a live performance DVD of Red Hot Chili Peppers.

I walked to Marina Bay to see the famed Merlion statue, which has been promoted and used by the Singapore Tourism Promotion Board as a symbol representing the city-state since the 1960s.[2] I do not know the complete tale regarding the origins of the Merlion other than a story originating from the Malay Annals of a prince who arrived to an island where he saw a beast with the head of a lion and the body of a fish. The prince then named the island Singapura, which in Sanskrit meant "lion city".[3]

After viewing and taking pictures of the Merlion, I walked across Collyer Quay to the Marina Promenade where I bought a scoop of Häagen-Dazs ice cream. I then walked west along Raffles Avenue to the Civilian War Memorial; a monument composed of four towering white pillars.

A historical marker at the site provided the following information:

> The Civilian War Memorial is dedicated to all those who died during the Japanese Occupation of Singapore from 1942-1945. The memorial is composed of four towering pillars that stand at over seventy meters. The four pillars are symbolic of the four races (Chinese, Indians, Malays, and "other" races) that suffered during the occupation.

The remains of unknown war victims were buried beneath the monument.

> Among the civilians who lost their lives were numerous Chinese targeted under the Sook Ching (literally "to purge" or "to eliminate") operations.

> On February 18, 1942, large numbers of Chinese were driven from their homes and assembled at designated mass screening centers. Many were unjustly accused of involvement in anti-Japanese activities, or arbitrarily condemned.

Unofficial figures place the number of those killed by the Japanese between 25,000 and 50,000, while Japan has officially reported a death toll of only 6,000.[4]

I then walked to the City Hall building–architecturally defined by a Corinthian colonnade–and located in front of the Padang, a famed recreational field used for sporting and civic events, to see the site where former Prime Minister Lee Kuan Yew established the first Cabinet of Singapore as a self-governing state within the Commonwealth on June 5, 1959.[5] Four years later on September 16, 1963 Singapore was merged into the Federation of Malaya thus ending nearly a century and a half of British rule, but the union did not last as the city-state withdrew to become an independent nation on August 9, 1965.

The City Hall building was also the site where the British accepted the surrender of the Japanese on September 12, 1945.

The building was completed in 1929 and was used as the official office of the Municipal Council. During the period of self-governance and independence it became the home of the Prime Minister's Office, but since the late 1980s the Supreme Court, the Singapore Academy of Law, the Public Service Commission, and the Industrial Arbitration Court have occupied it.[6]

At the southern end of the Padang stood the upscale Singapore Cricket Club, which was known as "the jewel of the Padang" during the colonial period. The club was established in 1852 and was exclusive to British businessmen until 1861 when British women were finally admitted.[7] During the Battle of Singapore in February 1942 the club was turned into a temporary hospital, but after the British surrendered on February 15 it was transformed into a bar and restaurant to serve only Japanese officers. After World War II, all ethnic groups were allowed to gain membership to the club.

Located behind the cricket club was the Asian Civilizations Museum. I decided to escape the humidity and bought a ticket to enjoy the museum's air conditioning while learning more about Singapore's history and its geographic importance within the realm of international trade.

The following are the notes I took from the exhibits of the museum.

China-India-West Asia Trade

There has always been a constant flow of boat traffic between the South China Sea and the Indian Ocean for the past 2,000 years. It was through the Straits of Malacca that ships bound for either China or India would pass and as a result the tip of the Malay Peninsula was loaded with various stopping ports for ships that sought shelter from the monsoon rains and storms, or to trade with locals and other passing merchants.

Over time the Straits of Malacca became an incredibly important route for acquiring exotic commodities valued by the cosmopolitan elite of China, Arabia, and as far as the Mediterranean. Because of this, islands like Singapore became a meeting and settling point for scores of Chinese, Arabs, and Indians merchants and Malay traders.

Control of the trade routes led to the rise and fall of several successive maritime empires all the way up to the 16th century.

Malay became the lingua franca for all these sea-faring merchants sailing and trading through these routes.

Originally Singapore was called 'Temasek' which means 'Sea Town' in Old Javanese. In the 14th century Singapore fell under the control of a Malay kingdom and was then referred to as Singapura ("Lion City" in Sanskrit).

In 1511 the Portuguese conquered Singapore thus ending the maritime empires. And when they burned the Singapore settlement down in 1613 it fell into maritime obscurity until the famed British statesmen Sir Thomas

Stamford Raffles arrived in 1819 who then developed the island into a major seaport for the British Empire.

In the years after 1819 Chinese, Arabs, Indians, and Malays settled, traded, and worked together on the island. It was during this time that the demand for opium grew among all classes and races for it offered 'sweet relief' from the tiring workdays on the seaports.

It was estimated that a third of the Chinese 'adult' population was addicted to opium by the mid 19th century. Thus making the addictive drug a lucrative commodity for the British government, as Chinese workers would spend up to two-thirds of their wages to acquire it.

The drug was officially abolished in 1910.

I found the history of the Chinese Secret Societies in Singapore particularly interesting. The largest gangs were the Ghee Hin Kongsi and the Ghee Hoch. They were also known as "the triads". These gangs preyed on newly arrived Chinese migrant workers to Singapore by offering them "friendship, protection, and an identity".[8] Although these secret societies were outlawed in 1889 their presence was still felt, especially in the "brothels, gambling, houses, opium dens (which they effectively ran) ... and in the warehouses, from which they collected 'protection money' ".[9]

Members of the different gangs identified themselves through a membership token.[10]

After the museum, I took a quiet boat ride along the Singapore River. Although it was only three kilometers in length it experienced heavy traffic in the 19th and early 20th century during the colonial trade period.

Today the Singapore River was lined with a multitude of pubs and restaurants—painted in pastel colors of beige, yellow, blue, and purple—catering mostly to the expatriate community that worked within the towering corporate buildings of the nearby financial district.

Next was Chinatown, which I found to be unimpressive as it was littered with tourist shops selling cheap trinkets. There were traditional Chinese shops selling ginseng roots, tealeaves, and medicinal herbs, but other than seeing a Chinatown set within a neighborhood defined by its colonial architecture I did not find it to be visually unique or appealing.

I forgot to mention that in the early afternoon I went to Raffles Hotel–a five-star colonial-style hotel that was established by two Armenian brothers in 1887. Many famed politicians, artists, musicians, actors, and writers have stayed at the hotel.

The island is ideal for the rich. It is modern, safe, expensive, loaded with exotic restaurants and high-end boutique shops. It seemed to be a playground for couples who were well off and seeking a bit of paradise paired with convenience and luxury shopping. It would be a dream to be able to treat my parents to an all-expenses paid trip to the island city-state.

A must do in Singapore for couples seeking a distinct, exciting, charming, and romantic experience was the Night Safari; the world's first nocturnal zoo.[11] The park was located in the north of the island in the Upper Seletar Reservoir. It is open every day from 7:30 p.m. to midnight. The park can be explored through four walking trails or by tram. There were 2,500 animals "spanning more than 130 species" of which 37 percent were endangered.[12] I saw the endangered Indian rhino (only 2,000 left), the Asiatic lion (Panthera leo persica) of which there were only 250 remaining in the Gir Forest National Park of India. I also saw the clouded leopard (Neofelis nebulosa): "It is the only living saber-toothed cat. It has the longest canines in proportion to skull size. It is endangered due to poaching and habitat destruction."[13]

One section of the Leopard Trail that I followed led into an enclosed habitat where I came face to face with enormous Malayan flying foxes–the largest bats in the world! To be honest I was scared as a few of these fruit bats were hanging directly above me while others were right in front of me. These bats were probably half a meter long from head to toe with a wingspan of nearly two meters! One bat flew so close to me that I could feel a gust of wind caused by its flapping wings. If I had been in its flight path I would have screamed.

I highly recommend the Night Safari, and definitely go see the bats.

Posted by The Legacy Cycle at 2004-04-05T19:29:00-07:00

Tuesday, April 6, 2004

On Waterloo Street there was a Chinese Buddhist temple called Kwan Im Thong Hood Cho Temple. It was built in 1884 and dedicated to Guanyin, the goddess of mercy and a bodhisattva of compassion.[14]

Urban legend has it that about 60 years ago a thief broke into the temple and stole the temple's moneybox. But when he arrived home and opened the box he found oil instead of cash and coins. Fearing that the goddess of the temple had somehow tricked him he returned the box to the temple and soon became its caretaker. The story of the thief's foiled attempt to steal from the temple spread quickly among the Chinese practicing Buddhists of the island resulting in the temple gaining greater fame. The temple is also highly regarded because of the belief by its devotees that no prayer goes unanswered.

Outside the temple I saw vendors selling lotus flowers from their carts in front of the main temple gate. Devotees of the temple can buy—although they don't have to—one or more lotus flowers to be offered to the goddess of the temple.

I entered into a small courtyard from the main gate and observed the crowd of worshipers who were standing around a large, ornate brass cauldron on three legs that was filled with ash and burning joss sticks (bundles of joss sticks and stainless-steel portable propane gas torches to light the sticks were located near the cauldron). These devotees first kept their back to the temple while holding—before their foreheads—the burning joss sticks that sent faint lines of scented grey smoke into the air, and prayed to the Four Heavenly Kings. They then turned and faced the temple, prayed to the goddess of mercy, and placed their joss sticks into the ash of the cauldron before entering the temple.

I proceeded into the main hall of the temple and once my eyes adjusted to the darkness I was relieved to see that I did not have to take off my shoes. I then saw, at the other end of the hall, the shrine that housed the altar where stood two large golden statues: one statue representing Guanyin and elevated behind it the Sakyamuni Buddha statue. To each side of the Guanyin statue was a smaller statue: one representing "Bodhidharma (the founder of Zen Buddhism)" and the other representing "Hua Tuo, the Chinese patron saint of medicine and healing".[15]

There were offerings of flowers and plates of fruit arranged in rows at the foot of the shrine, and before these offerings a large, red square carpet that covered an open area where barefoot devotees prayed.

Suddenly, a middle-aged Chinese man approached me and offered to clarify what I was observing in regards to the fortune telling ritual (Kau Cim) these devotees were practicing. I accepted and bowed my head to him.

He explained that before a worshipper could step on the carpet he or she had to first go to a desk that was to the far right of the main hall and retrieve two items: a long, cylindrical bronze tube that was filled with 99 sticks that were each inscribed with a number, and two red painted crescent shaped wooden pieces (jiaobei blocks) that when fitted together looked like a red pepper. A devotee could then go to the red carpet after he had removed his shoes with these divination tools and ask the goddess a question or confess a problem. To receive an answer–or potential solution–the devotee had to shake the bronze tube at a 45-degree angle until one of the sticks fell out. The devotee then had to drop the red jiaobei blocks on the ground; these blocks had a curved side and a flat side–the curved side was read as "negative" and the flat side was read as "positive" thus the two blocks could provide the following combinations: positive and positive, negative and negative, or positive and negative or vice versa. If the two blocks provided a reading of negative and positive or vice versa then the Kau Cim stick that had fallen out of the tube was verified. If a devotee did not get a reading of negative and positive then he had to place the stick back into the tube, shake the tube again until another stick fell out, and try to verify it with the jiaobei blocks. With a verified stick the devotee had to then collect it, read its inscribed number, and bring all the divination items back to the desk informing the temple caretaker of the number. The caretaker would then pull a pink piece of paper from one of many shelf compartments that had stacks of paper for each number.

The paper would provide the devotee with a few lines of Chinese poetry, stories, and other information to be interpreted in the context of the original question, but if the devotee wanted a more detailed answer or explanation he could check his number in a red reference book.

Next to the Kwan Im Thong Hood Cho Temple there was a Hindu temple called the Sri Krishnan Temple. It was established in 1870 and was the only "South Indian Hindu temple in Singapore dedicated exclusively to Sri Krishna and his consort Rukmini."[16]

In the late afternoon, I took the MRT subway and a bus to Changi Village in the hopes of catching a ferry to a small rural island called Pulau Ubin (population: 38 as of 2012[17]), but when I arrived a group of ferrymen explained that they needed at least 12 people to fill the boat to make it financially feasible to travel to the island. There was only one other guy besides me so it was a no go unless I wanted to pay for the other 10 non-existent passengers, but I ain't rich so, no. Instead, I walked to a nearby beach, sat on a bench, and watched cargo ships and tugboats pass by with a distant first view of Malaysia on the other side of the Johor Strait.

Now I'm back at the hostel. I'm going to grab dinner in Little India and then call it a night because I have to wake up early to catch my bus to Kuala Lumpur.

Posted by The Legacy Cycle at 2004-04-06T04:54:00-07:00

Afterthoughts on Singapore (2019)

It is impressive to consider that Singapore, a small city-state that you can walk across in less than a day, and which has few natural resources, has been able to achieve a level of economic growth that places it as the top-ranking economy in Southeast Asia with a GDP per capita income of $57,714.30 (2017).[18] Now keep in mind that in 1965 (the year of its independence from the Federation of Malaya) Singapore's GDP per capita income was $561.30;[19] that is a 10,182.25% increase (essentially a hundredfold increase) in per capita income over a 52 year period! Also, keep in mind that the U.S. had a per capita income of $3,827.53 in 1965, which was almost seven times greater than that of

Singapore. But Singapore surpassed the U.S. per capita income in 2011! How was that possible? How does a tiny little island beat the U.S. per capita income in 46 years? How?

Did Singapore simply raise their minimum wage over time to $57,000? Obviously not. Instead, they invested heavily into the most important resource their country possessed ... their people, their human capital. And how does a nation invest in their people? Through education and health, essentially through economic policies that are referred to as interventionist supply-side. Government investments in education and health improve the quality and increase the productivity of their labor force, and thus, over time, these highly skilled and effective workers command a higher wage. Of course, these investments take time to make an impact on the macro economy—usually a generation. But the long run impacts of these investments are unmistakable and incredibly impressive, and Singapore is a great example of that.

Take a look at their education system today. According to the "influential Pisa rankings, run by the OECD", which is "based on tests taken by 15-year-olds in more than 70 countries" Singapore was "first place in all Pisa test subjects, ahead of school systems across Asia, Europe, Australasia and North and South America."[20] The United States ranked "an unimpressive 38th out of 71 countries in math and 24th in science."[21] The U.S.–the most powerful economy in the world–is falling behind. Former U.S. Secretary of Education John King Jr. stated: "We're losing ground – a troubling prospect when, in today's knowledge-based economy, the best jobs can go anywhere in the world."[22]

Pay attention politicians and members of society. Education is one of the most important keys to unlock incredible economic growth and increase per capita incomes, but simply pouring tax dollars into a public education system is not enough. Just as important is addressing the quality and effectiveness of that education system. According to "Prof Sing Kong Lee, vice-president of Nanyang Technological University, which houses Singapore's National Institute of Education," the "key factor" that has enabled Singapore to overtake "the wealthiest countries in Europe, North America and Asia to become the number one in education" has been "the standard of teaching."[23] He explained that "Singapore invested heavily in a quality teaching force – to raise up the prestige and status of teaching and to attract the best graduates."[24]

> The country recruits its teachers from the top 5% of graduates in a system that is highly centralized.
>
> All teachers are trained at the National Institute of Education, and Prof Lee said this single route ensured quality control and that all new teachers could "confidently go through to the classroom".
>
> This had to be a consistent, long-term approach, sustained over decades, said Prof Lee.[25]

This centralized system of training effective teachers and educating students in Singapore has definitely paid off; Singaporean taxpayers are thus getting a lot of bang for their buck. But a centralized system in the U.S. may be difficult to achieve when each of the 50 states set their own educational standards and funding system. Within the current fragmented U.S. education system "the US spent an average of $16,268 a year to educate a pupil from primary through tertiary education, according to the Organization for Economic Cooperation and Development's (OECD) annual report of education indicators," which is "well above the global average of $10,759."[26] But U.S. students continue to fall behind.

> According to the Washington thinktank the National Center on Education and the Economy (NCEE), the average student in Singapore is 3.5 years ahead of her US counterpart in maths, 1.5 years ahead in reading and 2.5 in science. Children in countries as diverse as Canada, China, Estonia, Germany, Finland, Netherlands, New Zealand and Singapore consistently outrank their US counterparts on the basics of education.[27]

It is apparent then that within the current system U.S. taxpayers are not getting a lot of bang for their buck, which may mean–in the long-run–that the U.S. may lose its competitive edge in the global market leading to falling per capita incomes. Marc Tucker, president of the NCEE, reiterates that the issues for the U.S. is "systemic … and getting worse."[28]

> The solution is clear … "We have to have more highly educated teachers and we need to pay them more …"

> But it doesn't seem like Washington is listening. "To some extent it is plain hubris. We were so dominant for so long that it's hard for us to accept that there are now so many countries pulling ahead of us," said Tucker.[29]

We can see that the U.S. has much to learn from the education systems of the following nations that have all outranked the U.S.: Canada, Singapore, Finland, Germany, and South Korea to name a few.[30]

Although Singapore has made great strides in its economic development it is far behind many other developed nations in terms of its human development, by which we mean the ability of a nation to enlarge social justice and protect human rights. Reporters Without Borders has described Singapore as having an intolerant government that practices self-censorship over "all forms of journalist content."[31] In fact, it was ranked 151 out of 180 nations in the Worldwide Press Freedom Index.[32] And according to the *Freedom in the World 2015* report Singapore scored a 4 out of 7 in the categories of freedom, civil liberties, and political rights (where 1 is the best, and 7 the worst).[33] An *Amnesty International Report 2009* stated that "Singapore failed to provide basic protection for foreign domestic workers, such as a standard number of working hours and rest days, minimum wage and access to employment benefits. The Employment of Foreign Workers Act continued to exclude domestic workers."[34]

It is concerning to consider that perhaps Milton Friedman's central thesis, as described in his book *Capitalism and Freedom*, that a free market is a prerequisite for political freedom is not necessarily true in Asia. Yes, it seems true when we look back over time at European and American nations that rising affluence leads to a populace that demands greater political and civil liberties, but this is the result of a shared history in which Enlightenment ideals are valued by those societies. This is not the case for Asia. John Locke (*Two Treatises of Government* published in 1689; his work inspired the founding fathers of the United States to include the natural rights of "life, liberty and property" [Thomas Jefferson changed property to "pursuit of happiness"] in the United States Declaration of Independence), Thomas Hobbes (*Leviathan* published in 1651), Jean-Jacques Rousseau (*The Social Contract* published in 1762), Adam Smith (*An Inquiry into the Nature and Causes of the Wealth of Nations* published in 1776), and other Enlightenment thinkers were all born in Europe, thus it is foolish to think that Western political and economic values and ideals are shared by nations in Asia. I bring this up because Western political and economic power and influence in the global arena is on the decline while Africa and Asia are on the rise.

> By the end of this century, the UN expects there to have been almost no change in the Americas and Europe but 3 billion more people in Africa and 1 billion more in Asia … More than 80 percent of the world's population will live in Africa and Asia.

> If the UN forecasts for population growth are correct, and if incomes in Asia and Africa keep growing as now, then the center of gravity of the world market will shift over the next 20 years from the Atlantic to the Indian Ocean. Today, the people living in rich countries around the North Atlantic, who represent 11 percent of the world population, make up 60 percent of the Level 4 consumer market. [Level 4 includes those making at least $32 per day; Level 3, at least $8 per day; Level 2, at least $2 a day; and Level 1, less than $2 a day[35]] Already by 2027, if incomes keep growing worldwide as they are doing now, then that figure will have shrunk to 50 percent. By 2040, 60 percent of Level 4 consumers will live outside the West. Yes, I think the Western domination of the world economy will soon be over.[36]

How will political, civil, and economic values change as Asian and African nations begin to dominate the world arena? Will greater economic development bring greater human development in Asia and Africa? Or will centralized planning and one-party rule become the norm? Beware of any encroachment and erosion of your civil liberties (especially from within your own country); protect freedom of the press and speech, freedom of conscience, freedom of religion, freedom of expression, freedom of assembly, and the right to life, liberty, property, privacy, and the right to a fair trial and equal treatment under the law, to name a few.

MALAYSIA

Wednesday, April 7, 2004

I took a six-hour, air-conditioned bus ride to Kuala Lumpur (KL).

The journey began with a short ride to the Singapore border where all passengers were required to get off the bus to go through passport controls. We then boarded the bus to cross the Johor Strait via the kilometer-long Johor-Singapore Causeway. Once on the Malaysian side the bus stopped again as we had to go through another passport and customs checkpoint.

The bus journey north revealed endless oil palm tree plantations on both sides of the expressway–it was a glimpse of the "14 million tons of palm oil" produced "from more than 38,000 square kilometers of land, making it [Malaysia] the largest exporter of palm oil in the world."[1] Although Malaysia has a tropical rainforest climate, I saw little evidence of any rainforests from the road because it had been cleared away by the palm oil industry–an industry that provided employment for nearly 500,000 people.[2] In recent years, the negative environmental impacts caused by the production of palm oil (reduced biodiversity, habitat destruction, displacement of indigenous people,[3] and increased greenhouse gas emissions due to exposed peat bogs that release CO_2 into the atmosphere[4]) have been criticized both domestically and internationally. But it is an industry that accounts for 5-6 percent of the nation's GDP and thus has led–over the past two decades–to the reduction of poverty through the narrowing of the income gap between rural and town populations and improved social infrastructure.[5] It is evident that a balance between sustainable palm oil production, employment, and the preservation of vital ecosystems must be found for a newly industrialized country (NIC) such as Malaysia.

It has been argued at times by the Malaysian government that the palm oil industry provides more positive than negative effects on the environment and society as biodiesel is one of the goods produced from sustainable palm oil, which could reduce greenhouse gas emissions[6] compared to its dirtier rival petroleum. But a study by Greenpeace argued that the net effect of the palm oil production process and the consumption of biodiesel did not collectively reduce the amount of CO_2 emitted into the atmosphere.[7] One of the main concerns expressed by Greenpeace is that the process of clearing rainforests, "draining the peat and burning it releases vast amounts of greenhouse gases into the atmosphere."[8] For example, "Indonesia's peatlands represent just 0.1 percent of the Earth's landmass, but contribute a staggering 4 percent of global emissions."[9] To address environmental issues such as deforestation the Malaysian government has passed legislation to preserve 50 percent of their natural rainforests while also limiting the expansion of oil palm tree plantations.[10]

But more must be done at the consumer, producer, and government levels to protect vulnerable ecosystems as the global demand for "biofuels for road transportation will grow from 32.4 billion gallons in 2013 to 51.1 billion by 2022."[11]

The expressway the bus traveled on was modern, perhaps of a standard to be found in any developed nation; a sign of the government's long run investment in what economists call physical capital. But I should have expected to see such investments in infrastructure as Malaysia is one of the strongest economies in Southeast Asia where 20 percent of the population spoke English[12]–the residual effect of a nearly two-century long colonization by the British that ended in 1957.

I arrived at the Puduraya Terminal at around 3:30 p.m. As soon as I got off the bus I was approached by an Indian man who sought to lure newly arrived backpackers into a hostel that most likely provided him with a commission. I had no hotel or hostel reservation and since he explained that the place was right next to the bus station I decided to follow him. We crossed a busy street and walked down a sidewalk that was lined with various low-end shops and restaurants that catered to budget travelers. He then led me through an open iron door gate and up a flight of stairs to the Anuja Backpackers Inn where I got my own air-conditioned room without bath; there was a communal unisex bathroom that I could use.

After getting settled, I left the hostel in search of food and relief from the head cold I had been battling since the early morning; the air-conditioned bus journey and the humidity of Kuala Lumpur was causing havoc to my body. I walked two blocks northwest of the heavily polluted Klang River before a few large drops of rain fell. Initially, it was nothing, but suddenly there was a huge down pour and I ran to take refuge under a covered bus stop. Five minutes later the rain let up just enough to allow me to run in spurts between buildings that provided shelter. I went north up Jalan Ampang, a street lined with stores selling dresses and shoes for Indian women. I soon saw the Petronas Twin Towers in the distance and headed east, but the rain was too much. In soaked clothing, I stopped under the entrance overhang of a glass-faced office building, rested, and read a book (I was in the habit of keeping a book in my bag) for about 45 minutes.

When it began to drizzle, I continued my walk to the impressive 1,483 feet tall Petronas Towers (as a native of Chicago I was pleased to know that the Sears Tower (Willis Tower) stood taller at its tip at 1,729 feet). But according to the Council on Tall Buildings and Urban Habitat (CTBUH), which did not count the antennas of the Sears Tower as integral parts of its architectural design, the Petronas Towers were the tallest buildings in the world from 1998 to 2004.[13]

As I wandered around the Petronas Towers, and within the Suria KLCC shopping mall at the base of the skyscraper, I found myself in the familiar Western surroundings of chain stores, cafés, and restaurants that I was accustomed to in the U.S. and in Japan: Starbucks, California Pizza Kitchen, KFC, Burger King, The Body Shop, and a Kinokuniya bookstore. It was disappointing because I naively did not want to see a country with so much rich history and culture to be eroded by the capitalist pursuits of Western modernization. Placing those thoughts aside to address my hunger and head cold I sat down at a DÔME Café and had wild mushroom soup, a pesto chicken sandwich, and some tea. After lunch, I went to Kinokuniya and was surprised to discover that about 80 percent of their books were in English. I bought the travel memoir *A Fortune-Teller Told Me: Earthbound Travels in the Far East* by Tiziano Terzani.

I should mention that I finished reading *The Aquariums of Pyongyang* by Kang Chol-hwan. It details the unimaginable hardships of Kang's 10-year ordeal within a North Korean concentration camp. It is an excellent autobiographical example of why North Korea and Kim Jong-il are a political sham and how the nightmare world depicted in George Orwell's *1984* is an unfortunate reality.

      As night approached, I decided to walk back to my hostel by crossing through the Golden Triangle, which was Kuala Lumpur's famed entertainment, business, and shopping district. But I was too tired to pay much attention to what I saw in this district. Eventually, I arrived to my hostel and went straight to bed.

I've been writing about what I've seen and done during this solo trip. But what has been going on in my head? Yes, there are moments when I feel lonely upon seeing couples traveling or backpackers traveling in groups, but then I think that I am free to go in any direction I please. And I have this feeling that this will be my last solitary journey, and that when I return to the U.S. I will be settling down and learning to be with others again. So, if that is to be, I should enjoy this last tour alone.

      My friend Thomas told me that we go through three stages in life: we come into the world *dependent* on the care of our parents, we then grow, graduate university, and become financially *independent*, and finally we find our counterpart and enter into the joys of marital union and *interdependence*. Interdependence is the next stage for me. It will be hard for me to learn to live with someone of the opposite sex, as my longest relationship lasted no more than three months. And it will be difficult for the person I spend the rest of my life with since she will have to deal with my need to be alone every once in a while; this has been the most difficult personal aspect that women I have dated have tried to get used to. They usually interpret this need as some kind of rejection and thus panic by demanding more intimacy, which only causes anger and frustration in me. I quickly break free of the relationship to embrace my solitude again and never look back.

      I can see this pattern now in my past relationships, but I don't feel like discussing this publicly. I don't plan for this journal to be too much of a personal account of my trip, but perhaps in the days and weeks ahead more of my affections and emotions will begin to pour into this travelogue. We shall see, right now my mind is at peace as it is on holiday from everything.

Posted by The Legacy Cycle at 2004-04-07T19:04:00-07:00

Thursday, April 8, 2004

I woke up and had a shower in a unisex bathroom that had fruit flies either buzzing about or clinging to the blue tiled walls; the bath area in the hostel ranked about five stars less than The InnCrowd Hostel in Singapore.

After I got dressed, I sat down at one of two computers in the lobby to check my email. But as I began to read through my messages I heard someone behind me with an East-Central European accent beginning to harass an American backpacker by showing him the local newspaper and telling him, "Don't you think it's funny that you—an *American*—are here in Malaysia, a *Muslim* country, when today on the front page there is news that the Americans in Iraq bombed a mosque!" The minutes passed and the badgering continued. I soon realized that I was more focused on listening to the stream of provocative comments—and getting upset—than reading my emails so I turned around and declared, "I'm American. Where the hell are you from?"

"Germany," he answered.

"Oh," I replied. "Where in Germany?"

"Hanover," he answered, and then he was silent. Perhaps he knew that if he pursued his verbal barrage against U.S. citizens traveling in Malaysia that I would probably begin talking to him about Germany during World War II.

I finished checking my emails, left the hostel, and crossed the street to the Puduraya Terminal to inquire about bus tickets to Pulau Penang, an island about five hours north of Kuala Lumpur and less than an hour away from the border of Thailand. After checking times and prices I decided to leave KL the morning of the 9th and bought my ticket. I then explored the poorly lit bus terminal finding more bus ticket vendors and small shops selling food, magazines, drinks, and trinkets. There were several staircases that led down to the ground floor where running passenger buses were parked and waiting to depart. The carbon fumes from these diesel-guzzling transport vehicles drifted up and through the open staircases to combine with the humid, enclosed air giving the station a dirty, dark atmosphere.

From the bus terminal, I took a five-minute walk to Chinatown and arrived at the Chinese gate that served as the entrance into Jalan Petaling or Petaling Street. A roof cover composed of framed rows of green-tinted plastic windows the length of the street (dubbed the "Green Dragon" by locals) provided shade to the pedestrians from the intensity of the tropical sun. The street was lined with Chinese restaurants, open-air markets, food stalls that had skinned ducks hanging from hooks, and stands selling pirated DVDs and counterfeit branded toys, clothing, handbags, and shoes.

One side street led me into a food market where I saw roosters locked in wooden cages, cut-up pieces of chicken, and plenty of fish, prawns, and fresh tofu.

After taking another turn or two I came across a Chinese temple. Upon entering the temple, I noticed several incense coils hanging above me, and to my right I saw devotees burning pieces of inscribed paper inside what looked like a large brick kiln; I assumed that the burning paper contained prayers that would rise up to the heavens as ash and smoke. Behind the devotees there was a central altar with a smaller altar to its left where I saw a man rubbing something along the lips of wild boar statue, *very odd*. I could not decipher what the hell was going on.

A few blocks away there was a Hindu temple, but I decided not to go in and continued walking south in search of the post office using the map in my guidebook. I crossed a bridge over the polluted Klang River and got my first glimpse of the unique "Neo-Moorish/Mughal/Indo-Saracenic/Neo-Saracenic"[14] architecture of the Kuala Lumpur Railway Station, which was completed in 1910. British architect Arthur Benison Hubback lived for a period in India and thus his experiences there influenced the Indo-Islamic design of the station. Many dome towers and minarets marked the station; supposedly the greatest number of dome towers on an architectural work in Malaysia.

North of the train station I walked passed the National Mosque of Malaysia (Masjid Negara), which had a very sleek, angular design, a towering white minaret of 245 steps, and could accommodate up to 15,000 worshippers! The former king, Tuanku Syed Harun Putra ibni Almarhum Syed Hassan Jamalullail, inaugurated the mosque on August 27, 1965 (eight years after Malaysia had formally gained independence from Great Britain).

Walking further north I found the National History Museum. Seeing that there was no entrance fee I went in and spent some time reading and learning about the Mesolithic (12,000–4,000 BCE) culture of Malaysia. The following are a few of my notes from the exhibits at the museum.

> Malaysians during the Mesolithic period were nomadic and typically lived in caves or under stone ledges. They used an assortment of stone and bone tools and buried their dead with pottery, stone tools, and a stone bangle or two. Red iron ore was used for their cave paintings and often depicted groups of winged human figures dancing or boats arranged in various ways.
>
> India and China began trading with Malaysia as early as the 1st century AD and it was at this time that Buddhism and its relics were brought to the region.
>
> According to written record Chinese and Middle Eastern pioneers were the first "Eurasian mainlanders" to document the geography and trading resources of the peninsula at around the 2nd century AD.
>
> The Kingdom of Malacca (named after the port city of Malacca located south of Kuala Lumpur) was founded in the late 14th century by Parameswara, a Malay prince from Palembang in Sumatera. He died in 1414 AD and was succeeded by eight kings or sultans who were all direct descendants of Parameswara.
>
> Foreigners in Malacca at that time included Arabs, Gujeratis, Indians, Siamese Chinese, Japanese, Cambodians, Persians, and Malay from throughout the Archipelago.
>
> Islam is thought to have arrived to Malaysia by way of Islamic Sufi's in the 14th century and it was believed that Sayyid Abdul Aziz converted the 2nd Sultan of Malacca to Islam.

In 1511 AD the Portuguese (the first European power to go to Malaysia) destroyed the Malacca kingdom. And just over two centuries later the British took control of Malaysia after the Anglo-Dutch Treaty of 1824.

Japanese occupation of Malaysia occurred from 1941 to 1945. The Japanese landed in Malaysia on December 8th, 1941 and on February 15th, 1942 the British finally surrendered to the Japanese.

When the Japanese surrendered to the British in 1945 they did so by symbolically giving up their samurai swords; approximately 1,500 swords were surrendered.

The former Prime Minister of Malaysia was Tun Dr. Mahathir Bin Mohammad; he was the 4th Prime Minister of Malaysia and held power from 1981 to 2003.

I also learned that Malaysia had a national automobile manufacturing company called PROTON, which has been producing cars since 1983 (an impressive economic achievement). After I left the museum I paid close attention to the vehicles that roamed the streets and realized that the Malaysian Proton car was everywhere–how foolish I was to have not seen this; I also saw plenty of cars by Hyundai and Toyota.

The Merdeka Square, a neatly manicured lawn located between the Royal Selangor Club and the Sultan Abdul Samad Building, looked essentially like the Padang in Singapore. In fact, it was originally referred to as the "Padang" and was used as a cricket field by members of the Royal Selangor Club during the colonial period.[15] One impressive feature of the square was a 95-meter tall flagpole that commemorated the site where the British flag was lowered and the Malayan flag raised to mark independence at midnight on August 31, 1957.[16]

I walked north, sat down for lunch, and continued reaching Chow Kit–Kuala Lumpur's infamous red-light district–where I grabbed a bus to the famed shrines within the Batu Caves that are dedicated to Lord Murugan (the Hindu god of war). The caves are located in a small limestone mountain on the northern outskirts of KL. The caves—a place of Hindu worship since the 1890s—is the site of the three-day Thaipusam festival that takes place at the end of January or the beginning of February. Over one million devotees partake in the event,[17] and thousands of tourists go to see worshippers perform acts of penance that include bringing offerings of milk within ornate brass or clay containers that are also carried in metal frames called kavadi that have long skewers that pierce the carrier's upper body.[18] It is not uncommon to see the cheeks and tongues of devotees pierced by sharp wires.

    I arrived at the base of the daunting 272 red and white painted and numbered steps that would take me up to the entrance of the caves. I began the ascent and although it was a painful climb for my calves I was constantly distracted and entertained by a small army of curious and hungry macaques that populated sections of the staircase. I saw one macaque breastfeeding its baby, so I slowly approached and began taking pictures until I felt a strong tug on my pinky finger. I looked down and saw an angry male macaque shining his canines at me. I instantly retreated from the breastfeeding monkey feeling my heart pounding against my chest. Luckily, I wasn't attacked.

    I reached the top of the staircase and entered the large, dark cave faintly seeing through the shadows colorful statues of Hindu gods depicted in various scenes from Indian mythology scattered along the angular limestone walls. Macaques chased one another while birds flew high above near the ceiling of the cave. Illuminated by a wide and penetrating beam of natural light at the far end of the cave I saw another set of stairs leading up to a Hindu shrine. I approached the shrine and saw above that there was a large opening in the earth that allowed the sunlight to shine through. I went up these last steps and observed the end of a ritual.

    On the way out, I saw more baby macaques hanging on to the torsos of their mothers who ran on all fours up and down sections of the 272 steps.

Posted by The Legacy Cycle at 2004-04-08T16:56:00-07:00

Friday, April 9, 2004

I woke up at around 7 a.m. and went to the shower where I found the leavings of someone that perhaps got a little too excited. I will not go into any details. Such is the—at times unpleasant—life of a backpacker going from one hostel to the next.

In any case, I took a shower, got dressed, and typed away about my previous day on the computer in the reception area. After I finished I still had time to kill before my bus departed for George Town, Penang so I sat in the reception area and watched a European fútbol (soccer) match while drinking canned tea that had bits of jelly; during my days in Malaysia I had been trying a variety of canned beverages ranging from sugarcane juice, sweetened soymilk, to coconut juice.

At 9:40 a.m. I made my way to the bus station across the street from the hostel. After looking up on the schedule what platform my bus was departing from I went down to the lower floor and stood far from the running buses to avoid inhaling their fumes. Once I saw people boarding my bus I took my bag, loaded it under the bus, got in, and sat down.

An Indian gentleman occupied the seat next to me. He was friendly and explained that he was on his way to Penang Island to escort a group of arriving laborers from Indonesia back down to Kuala Lumpur to work in the factories. We talked a bit about Malaysia and its Proton car of which he was very proud. At one point during the bus ride north he pointed out a Proton car factory to me.

During the journey, I saw more palm tree plantations and then mountains that had literally been blown in half to serve as quarries for stone or perhaps tin. Besides these scenes of extraction and production the natural vegetation along the way was beautifully lush, green, and tropical.

The bus made one stop. I followed everyone from the bus to a large, open-air eating area where there were sinks located to all sides. After washing up in the bathroom I lined up in front of what appeared to be the most popular place to get food. As I stood in line I noticed that the Malays who were already at the tables with their food were eating with their hands—thus the need for all the sinks! I began to worry that I would have to eat my meal with my hands too, but I saw a small plastic jar with a few forks and spoons. I took a fork and the lady behind the counter then gave me a plate of rice. With a ladle, I picked up some green something or other, chicken, and some curry. I then ate and enjoyed the spicy meal.

A half-hour later we were on the bus again, and after a couple of hours—and before crossing the Penang Bridge (the fifth longest in Southeast Asia[19])—everyone on the bus noticed a line of police cars driving in front of and behind a single luxury car. I asked the Indian fellow beside me what was going on and he explained that the police were escorting the mayor of Penang Island back to the island, which caused traffic along the toll bridge.

After crossing the 13.5-kilometer long bridge the bus finally arrived to George Town. As soon as I got off the bus an Indian rickshaw driver in his fifties wearing a purple patterned, short-sleeved casual button-down shirt approached and offered to take me to my hotel. I explained to him that I first needed to make a few phone calls to book a hotel. He shook his head and said that I did not have to make any calls because he could take me to the Cathay Hotel. I took this as a good omen as I was planning to stay at that hotel where a few scenes from the 1995 film *Beyond Rangoon* were shot. I then agreed to hire his services.

The rickshaw driver said his name was Richard. We talked a bit during the short ride and arrived. I paid and thanked Richard, entered the old but charming Cathay Hotel seeing a group of soft-spoken, elderly Chinese men seated around a table near the reception desk, and checked in getting a single room with en suite for US$15.

I walked up a flight of steps, located my room, entered, and rested for an hour before setting off to find a Citibank ATM.

I walked back to the bus station, found the ATM, and withdrew needed funds. I then spent a couple of hours walking along the northeastern coast of the island taking photos of abandoned properties for sale until I found a beautiful, but weathered, Victorian monument entangled in vines. The monument consisted of four statutes (one on each side) dedicated to the following virtues: wisdom, temperance, justice, and fortitude. A plaque on the monument's tablet had these words inscribed:

This monument is erected by the peoples of the Straits Settlements as a tribute of their respect and gratitude to James Richardson Logan.

Advocate, F.R.G.S._F.E.S.

Whose death in the prime of his manhood they regard in the public calamity.

He was always first, and sometimes stood alone, in every movement having the welfare of those settlements for its object and the whole colony, but most especially Penang owes much of its present welfare and success to his personal efforts and to his unflagging zeal and great ability.

He was an erudite and skillful lawyer, an eminent scientific ethnologist, and he has founded a literature for these settlements as the proprietor and editor of the *Journal of the Indian Archipelago*.

Above all he was an upright, true and honorable man, held in the highest respect and esteem by his fellow countrymen and loved and implicitly trusted by all the native races around him.

He was born at Hutton Hall in Berwickshire, Scotland, April the 10th 1819, arrived in the Straits Settlements in February 1839.

He died at Penang on the 20th Day of October 1869.

May we all be remembered in such a way.

I continued and walked along the coast passing through the Esplanade Padang Kota Lama seeing Chinese kids fishing while–in the distance–cargo ships came into and out of port. My travel guidebook explained that the Esplanade served as the gathering site where–on the 15th night of the Chinese New Year (Chap Goh Meh)–a procession of Chinese maidens from the strait throw mandarin oranges into the sea in the hope of finding a good match while young men watch and make note of which girls are available so that they could make enquiries through a matchmaker.[20]

Just beyond the Esplanade–at the center of a roundabout and near the Swettenham Pier Cruise Terminal–I saw the white painted Moorish-style Jubilee Clock Tower that commemorated Queen Victoria's Diamond Jubilee in 1897. The tower is "sixty feet tall, one foot for each year of Victoria's reign."[21]

I strolled south to the old but under construction streets of Penang near the coast seeing many shops owned by Indians. Although the streets were being ripped up so that they could be laid with new pavement it, only added to the exotic feel of the place; I felt as if I was in some ancient Southeast Asian town that had been traumatized by war or had yet to develop.

I should get some dinner ... it is getting late, and I have a lot to see and do tomorrow.

Posted by The Legacy Cycle at 2004-04-09T05:58:00-07:00

Saturday, April 10, 2004

Last night–after typing away on this blog at an Internet café–I went to a bar next to my hotel called 20th Leith Street. The bar was directly across the street from the late 19th century, indigo-blue painted Cheong Fatt Tze Mansion; a unique architectural work noted for the Chien Nien style of carved porcelain depicting colorful images of dragons and flowers, which adorns its outer walls and the ridges of its roof. The mansion has 38 restored rooms and was originally built by the Chinese merchant Cheong Fatt Tze who–although came from humble beginnings–built up his trading empire to become richer than rich.[22] The mansion stands today as a testament of what financial dreams may come true when you are strong in luck and will to pursue your entrepreneurial vision.

The 20th Leith Street Bar was spacious and had a few billiard tables and old arcade games. There were three long, narrow connected rooms that ran parallel to each other and a bar and bartender serving beer and hard liquor located in the room farthest from the main entrance. I walked toward the sound of live, contemporary music from a local band that played on a stage at the far end of the three rooms, and sat down at a round table just off center from the stage. Unfortunately, the band, with the exception of the overly enthusiastic Chinese male lead singer, looked like they were simply going through the motions.

As a result, I began to think about the work I did with The Hitmen (a famous gaijin corporate entertainment band in Japan) back in Tokyo and how difficult, and almost depressing, it was to play music in a bar like this one that was full of people who were apathetic of your performance.

The accompanying singer was a bored Chinese woman. To witness the comical dynamic between an energized lead and a lethargic supporting singer actually made up for the band's overall lifeless, robotic act. The woman was not into the gig, but at least she stepped from side to side in rhythm with the music. After a few songs, I could understand why she was bored to death; she was only singing, on average, about one out of every four songs. When she was not singing she simply had to stand and look attractive, which she clearly did not appreciate. The bass player would take turns singing a few tunes, which left about half of the songs for the male lead who sang with such excitement that I'm sure in his mind he was practicing to headline at a music festival in a Brazilian fútbol stadium for 500,000 people. It was amusing to see him really getting into the songs and his dance steps. Good for him. I hope his aspirations do come true.

After eating at my table and having a drink at the bar I walked to a nearby salsa dance club to see what was going on as I could hear the music from a distance. When I arrived, I saw through the window that the sex ratio was about ten men for every one woman and that the live music was more Latin pop than salsa. I decided not to go in. But I must confess that the band at this club was performing at a level way beyond the band that I saw in the 20th Leith Street bar. This band, from what I could see from the street window, had expensive, professional equipment, monitors, and smoke machines! I then decided to call it a night and walked back to my hotel.

This morning I had one main objective, to go to the train ticket agency near the ferry port and buy my ticket out of Pulau Penang and to Hat Yai in southern Thailand. And I succeeded, but the train's next day departure time is 6:10 a.m., which means that I need to wake up at 3:00 a.m. You ask, why so early? I have to take a ferry from Pulau to Butterworth, but the ferry doesn't depart very often in the morning so I have to depart from the port early enough so that I arrive on time to the train station. On the plus side, the train is direct to Hat Yai (a four-hour journey) and the ticket only cost me about US$3.

After I bought my ticket, I walked through Little India and Chinatown before entering—from Cannon Street—the Khoo Kongsi, a 100-year-old rebuilt Chinese clan complex[23] of 62-unit shop houses and terrace houses, an opera stage, and the clan house[24] for the Leong San Tong (Dragon Mountain Hall[25]) clan; a clan association that prided itself in being able to trace their ancestral lineage back 650 years.[26] It was in the stone courtyard of the complex, which separated the clan house from the opera stage, that a scene for the 1999 film *Anna and the King*, which starred Jodie Foster and Chow Yun-fat, was shot. The following were notes that I took from an information plaque describing the architectural styles of the clan house and opera stage:

> The Leong San Tong clan house and opera stage were designed in an exotic blend of Southern Fujian and Anglo-Indian architecture ... The columns and the roof of the clan house were done in the Southern Fujian design, and the staircase, the terrace, and the verandah were done in the Anglo-Indian style.

The main architectural attraction of the urban clan enclosure was the clan house. I stood in the courtyard and tried to visually absorb the numerous, intricate details of several colorful towers that dotted the curved roof and wing-shaped ridges of what looked like small blocks and other geometric shapes stacked vertically and horizontally on top of two angry, shirtless Chinese gods; I could also see carved, stylized images of cranes, snakes, dragons, and other Chinese mythical creatures along the ridges of the roof. The main entrance was guarded by two green lion statues (the male on my left and the female on my right) that stood on white stone pedestals, and between them stood a "green stone joss-stick urn" set on a circular stone pedestal.[27] Gilded wood carvings accented the truss of the curved roof of the Prayer Pavilion where just beyond the verandah I could see several large, red paper lanterns hanging from the truss of the roof of the main hall.[28]

I entered the clan house on the ground level through a door to my right of the Prayer Pavilion. I noticed as I took the tour through the offices and meeting hall of the building tiny mirrors (to ward off evil) set within the intricate details of the colorful, stylized painted wall panels. In summary, there was too much detail in this Southern Fujian style of architecture and interior design to absorb. An art historian could spend a decade studying and interpreting every minute design, carved figure, and story that existed throughout the clan house.

In terms of the architectural layout of the clan house there was a central or main hall and two annexes. Ancestral and deity worship was one of the most important practices of Chinese clan society,[29] thus the ancestral hall that was located in the annex to the right of the central hall was particularly significant to clan members and it was there that several ancient idols were enshrined: two of the idols (the patron saints of the Khoo clan) were of Tua Sai Yah (the Noble) and Ong Soon Yah (the Great Duke).[30] These two idols represented the famed Chinese generals Cheah Aun (Ong Soon Yah) and his nephew Cheah Hean (Tua Sai Yah) who in the 4th century AD–in the Battle of Fei River–miraculously defeated an army of one million with only 80,000 soldiers thus saving the Jin dynasty from being destroyed, or so goes the legend.[31]

I later stepped out onto the verandah from the main hall and descended the stone staircase to the Prayer Pavilion and saw at the base of the staircase two turbaned, armed watchmen statues carved from green stone, and seated on stone pedestals (at the base of each stone handrail) two stone monks: one depicted in a state of laughter and the other crying, which represented the "interplay of the joy and sorrow of human existence."[32]

In the rear corridor, behind the main hall of the clan house, there were three large and four small murals. I took pictures of the large murals and was particularly attracted to one entitled "Nine Old Men" where five old men stood around a scroll depicting the "Twin Fish Chart," which represented the yin and yang of Chinese philosophy, while the remaining four old men played "a game of chess reflecting the strategies of the past and the present."[33] Another mural entitled the "Fisherman, Woodsman, Farmer and Scholar" emphasized ancient Chinese values as explained on another informative plaque:

> Traditional agricultural societies in China preached that it was the duty of the peasant to work hard and to be self-sustained while cultivating good morality and improving his temperament through reading.

Another mural entitled the "Eight Immortals" depicting eight men sitting or standing while enjoying leisure activities that included playing the flute and scratching one's back with a stick was flanked by couplets that read in Chinese "loyal officials and dutiful sons are first-class human beings" and "farming and studying are the two things that matter most for peasants."[34] The former emphasized the Confucian values of loyalty and filial piety while the later repeated the meaning of the "Fisherman, Woodsman, Farmer and Scholar" mural.[35]

After checking out these murals, I went down to the souvenir shop and bought a drink. The kind lady at the counter who served my drink asked me to pick up and open a box that was sitting on a shelf to my right. I fumbled a bit as I put down my drink and picked up the box. Suspicious, I opened the box slowly and saw something, but I could not tell what it was exactly, so I opened it completely and a spider jumped out and grabbed my finger. I screamed and threw the box on the floor while the lady laughed and tried to apologize with a wide grin. When I was able to catch my breath again I took another look at the box and saw that it was rigged so that a black rubber spider jumped out when opened. It was a good trick, and I told the lady behind the counter (who was still laughing) that she had succeeded in fooling me.

I exited the Khoo Kongsi complex and walked to the Menara KOMTAR Complex (Penang's tallest building) to seek relief from the intense sun, heat, and humidity since its interior was air conditioned. My initial impression of the first few floors of the KOMTAR was that it was like any other shopping mall in the U.S. I was upset by this, especially after seeing a Starbucks on the ground floor facing the street. Malaysia had some of the most delicious exotic fruit and coffee drinks. Why would anyone, Malaysian or tourist, want to go to Starbucks? It angered me to see Western franchises like Burger King, A&W Root Beer restaurant (I didn't know this existed), and a Kenny Rogers Roasters (first time I saw one) here in Pulau Penang. What was economically unique about Malaysia from my Occidental perspective were all the run-down mom-and-pop shops that had been selling, buying, serving, bartering, negotiating, and repairing for what appeared to be decades or generations; that to me was the charm of a place like George Town for in the U.S. these types of small, family-owned businesses have been in decline due to the more rapid growth of competing franchise small businesses and chain stores. And giant shopping centers like KOMTAR seemed to pose a threat to the future livelihood of the mom-and-pop shops of Penang Island. Of course, economists would argue that franchise small businesses and chain stores—due to economies of scale factors such as bulk buying—are able to lower their long run average total costs, which translates to lower prices for consumers. Thus, price sensitive consumers in both developed and developing countries benefit when being able to access low-priced goods. In addition, there is the argument that franchises and chains create more employment due to the increased demand by consumers for these cheap goods and services, but the counterargument is that typically low-paid, low-skilled employment is created. There is also the argument that local, family-owned businesses (mom-and-pop shops) prior to the entry of franchises were not productively efficient since they did not face strong competition, thus, in the long run, they provided higher priced goods and/or slower services to their customers. Increased competition created by incoming franchises and chains is then a beneficial factor to society since these mom-and-pop shops must improve, adapt, and implement creative measures to maintain their market share. But it seems that in the long run, most mom-and-pop shops are not able to compete against the aggressive tactics of multinationals that seek to break into new and emerging markets via low-priced, low-quality goods and services.

But my criticisms were quickly dashed as I continued to the higher floors of the KOMTAR shopping mall because I found store after store selling pirated DVDs for less than US$1; an opportunity cost in the form of revenue diversion hitting Western firms in the film industry as a result of an increasingly global, digital economy. I traveled further up the escalators to the floor that had a movie theater to see what was playing, but found that there was nothing that I wanted to see. Instead, as I continued walking around, I discovered one pirated DVD shop with two massive television screens complete with plastic lawn chairs placed in rows for anyone who wanted to sit down and watch a free movie. So, I sat down and watched Tim Burton's *Big Fish* for free. What a wonderful story; I nearly cried, but since I was in a public and well-lit place I tried desperately to hold back my tears.

In the end, the KOMTAR was not a shopping center in the Western sense of a complex of buildings lined with legitimate retail chains and franchises, instead it was a center for illicit goods. Although Malaysia is typically ranked as the third wealthiest Southeast Asian nation after Thailand and Indonesia, the average Malaysian (GDP per capita in 2004 was $4,924.59^{36}$) is still not able to afford most genuine Western goods ranging from brand name clothing to electronics, but the demand for them is high as Western pop culture is so prevalent as a result of films, television, music videos, and the Internet.

After the KOMTAR, I had some Chinese food and then went to the Penang State Museum. The following are notes that I took from the museum's exhibits concerning the multi-ethnic diversity of Penang:

Siamese: They are from Southern Thailand.

Eurasians: They were so named by the British administration in Penang to denote the mixed ancestries of Portuguese, Dutch, English, Irish, Scottish, French, Italian, and German on the one hand and Malay, Chinese, Indian, Siamese, and Burmese on the other.

Traits of the Eurasians: Roman Catholic religion, and a unique English dialect that had elements of Portuguese, Siamese, and Malay.

Acehnese: They immigrated to Penang from Aceh in northern Sumatra.

The Arabs: Today most of the Arabs in Penang have been absorbed into local Malay communities, but a couple of centuries ago they were among the wealthiest inhabitants of Penang …

Today in Penang the Malay, Chinese, and Indians compose about 90 percent of the population.

Indians: The Indians of Penang came from all over the Indian sub-continent, but the dominant group is the Tamil from southern India. The other groups include

Sikhs, Gujaratis, Bengalis, and Sinhalese ...

Europeans: Compared to Singapore the European enclave in Penang was much smaller ... The British were stationed in Penang to senior administration and military positions. Many early European settlers owned large spice plantations ...

The Japanese: The Japanese settlements were obscure and limited to individual traders, artisans, and adventurers! After WWI (1914-1918) the development of mining, agriculture, etc. attracted more Japanese entrepreneurs and workers. Entering the financial and commercial spheres they played an important role in handling the country's vital commodities of tin and rubber.

The early Japanese settlements tended to be self-contained; they operated their own schools and maintained religious and other socio-cultural organizations.

Armenians: The first Armenians to Penang came around 1800 from their homeland in the Caucasus Mountains. They came as traders and were small in number. The most prominent Armenians were the Sarkies Brothers, Tigran and Martin. They were major hoteliers and established, among others, the Eastern and Oriental Hotel in George Town (Palau Penang) and the famed Raffles in Singapore.

Most were Christian Armenians, but there were also a significant number of Armenian Jews who came to Penang.

Burmese: Many came as well to Penang as a natural result of its close proximity to the Malaysian island.

> The Chinese secret societies in Penang: The Hue (secret society) emerged in China during the 13th century as a brotherhood with a mission to engineer the downfall of the ruling Mongol Yuan Dynasty.
>
> Revived again in the 17th to the 19th century ... they were formed to bring an end to the foreign Manchu Qing dynasty ...
>
> The secret societies were established in the British Straits Settlements and Western Malay States for self-help and self-protection in an alien environment ... In 1867 there was a major ten-day clash between two main Chinese secret societies.

Also of note:

> Thaipusam is a religious festival that is celebrated in January mostly by the Tamil community in Penang honoring Subramnya (Murugan) the Hindu god of war. Devotees (both Indian and Chinese) bring offerings of coconuts, cow's milk, and honey in brass pots to the Nattukkottai Chettiar Temple on Waterfall Road. There they receive sacred ash, holy water, and kumkum (vermilion powder).
>
> In Hinduism, the smashing of a coconut symbolically represents the smashing of one's ego. As a result, Waterfall Road is covered in smashed coconuts during the festival thus purifying and paving the road for the gods.
>
> In reverence for the deity (Subramnya) many devotees carry the kavadi, a gaily-decorated wooden or steel frame composed of hundreds of hooked spikes that penetrate the flesh.

> Some penitents pierce their tongue and cheeks with a silver vel skewer ... And at the sacred altar in the Subramnya Temple priests remove the skewers and the barbed hooks from the flesh of devotees and rub holy ash on their wounds.

Final Thoughts on Malaysia

The thing that has made the biggest impact on me thus far has been the prevalence of religion; and as I type I can hear the Islamic call to prayer from the mosque across the street from this Internet café. Japan—in my opinion—is a country nearly devoid of religion. The Japanese do not practice any sort of religious faith to the degree that can be found in most Western countries that adhere to an Abrahamic religion. After living in Japan for three-and-a-half years I had nearly forgotten about how important faith was to so many people around the world.

In fact, in my last year in Japan, I had forgotten about most Roman Catholic holidays. And this weekend was an example of that for if I had not received emails from relatives yesterday wishing me a "Happy Easter," I would not have known or remembered, or cared. I'm afraid to say that after living in Japan for so long I have changed in that respect. I am no longer a religious person by Western standards, or even by Chinese Buddhist, Taoist, Confucius, or Hindu standards, although I do consider myself to be very spiritual. I no longer possess the need to discuss with friends and family my beliefs. My faith—my multicultural, spiritual way—has evolved from what I had learned, and experienced, through my education and travels, of the world's many unique cultures, countries, peoples, faiths, and religious texts. I do believe in reincarnation; it is a belief that I adopted many, many years ago, and one that crept into the story for *Dark Legacy*. Zen Buddhism was another influence that found its way into my writing for *Dark Legacy: Book I – Trinity*. But I no longer actively practice Zen Buddhism, although a few years ago I had lived for nine months in a Zen Buddhist temple.

I don't preach anymore. I have found my truth and do not have the need to discuss it or defend it (defending my perspective came often when I studied at Indiana University as I encountered many Christians who challenged any faith that was not their own). One of many reasons as to why I transferred from IU to BU was to be in a more open-minded environment where people of alternative perspectives, faiths, and religions were respected. And Pulau Penang provided a beautiful example of that as Indian Hindus, Chinese Buddhists, Taoists, Confucians, and Malay Muslims all lived on the same island and respected each other's culture, faith, and religious practices.

In being aware that India and China possess a third of the world's population I was grateful that I had the opportunity in Malaysia to taste a bit of both Indian and Chinese culture.

When I return to the U.S. I may have to face many diehard Christians who believe that it is their duty to save those who worship false gods and idols. All I have to say to them is ... ☺.

Posted by The Legacy Cycle at 2004-04-10T03:11:00-07:00

ENTERING
THE LAND OF HUNGER

THAILAND

Sunday, April 11, 2004

I'm in Hat Yai, Thailand and I really don't care for this place—especially after experiencing the beauty of Malaysia's cultural diversity. Hat Yai seems to be a way station. I'm going to Krabi tomorrow; a beach resort town on the Andaman coast about four to five hours north of here by car.

Since I don't feel like "reporting" on this place I thought that I'd let my imagination go and type a story inspired by what I have seen and felt in Hat Yai.

Hat Yai Avi

My name is Avi Lukason. I live here in Hat Yai, Thailand. It's in the south, the way south of the country. On the tip of its tail you could say. It's the biggest city in the south of Thailand, which really is sort of a joke for a guy like me—I'm from New York City for Christ's sake. So, what the hell am I doing here? I knew you probably were thinking that. And it's going to surprise you when I tell you that I've been here for God knows how long—What? Two years now? No, more than that. Let's say two years and a bit—*"and a bit"*? Who the hell says that? The Aussies say that, Oz for Australia that is.

I came to Southeast Asia to take a break—a deep breath you could say. Simply wanted to get away. "Why?" you ask. Well, to cut to the chase. My wife cheated on me and I wanted to forget her and all that stupid shit in the States. I used to work on Wall Street. I used to make *big* bucks thinking that it would get me everything: a beautiful wife, a lovely apartment on 5th Avenue, and a Porsche. And it did. I had a beautiful wife, a lovely apartment on 5th Avenue, and a Porsche—a 911 to be exact. And now here I am with nothing.

Actually, I shouldn't really say that. I have tons of cash back home sitting in a few banks. But, I haven't touched that dough for over a year and a half. I live like a pauper here in Hat Yai—this dump of a place. I guess I'm seeking to be like some kind of urban monk hermit. I'm in Southeast Asia for Christ's sake—so I might as well do the old Buddhist thing. That is the problem though for a guy like me and for most backpacking Americans I come across here. We Americans are so fascinated with the exotic. We think practicing the next hip exotic faith or discipline like Buddhism or yoga or tai chi—or whatever—has all the spiritual answers that we have been looking for. That is the problem with us; we go from one exotic fad to the next. And what is up with our obsession with dieting? How many freaking different kinds of diets are advertised in the U.S.? For Christ's sake it's insane, it's a joke! The "Atkins Diet" ... didn't Atkins die of heart failure due to being obese? Some say yes, and some say no—who really knows? Now it seems, from what I've read on the Net, that Americans are into fasting? They are catching on to the Muslim tradition of fasting believing that it will bring them health, and clean out their system, or what have you. It's a joke. Next year it will be something else. Muslims fast for a month every year for Ramadan, but Americans just try it on for a couple of weeks until some other amusement is trending on TV.

Well, I think it's obvious from all this venting that I ain't ready to go back to the States ... I guess I'm still trying to get over the fact that my wife cheated on me and never really loved me. She just married me for the money—and boy did she get a bunch of it when I filed for divorce.

I live at the Cathay Guest House here in Hat Yai. And let me tell you this. It's never overbooked. All the touts at the train and bus stations will tell any-and-all tourists that it's booked, in fact they'll tell you it's booked "straight on for three days". They're all liars—never pay any attention to them. The Cathay Guest House sits on the corner of Thanon Niphat Uthit 2 and Thanon Thamnoovithi. It's only a three-block walk from the train station. I'm in room 356. It's all the way in the back down a dark, old staircase. The guest house is all right. I was a bit disgusted with it when I first arrived though. But I've been living here for so long it's simply home now. The dark corridor where the majority of the rooms are located is wide and seems almost like an old high school hallway. But everything is falling apart. I guess it most looks like the way I'd expect a Cuban prison to be. My room is away from all the noise that the other "guests" can be caught making–if you *know* what I mean. My room is appropriate. Not big or small. The bathroom is descent by Thai below-the-poverty-line standards. There is a squat toilet that I have mastered and no button to flush it. There is a bucket instead. Simply fill it up and dump it into the toilet and *ta-da*, a flush toilet. My bed is a very firm mattress on an old bed frame and boy is it full of bed bugs. There ain't a morning that goes by where I don't end up scratching all the bites that I got during the night.

As for the shower, I got cold water and cold water, and with this tropical humidity that is all you need. I usually shower in the dark. The broken window in my bathroom has no curtain–never bothered to put up one–and some of my Thai friends have a thing for peeping into other people's hotel rooms like it's a hobby, which makes me paranoid. So, I shower in the dark.

When I first came here I used to take two to three showers a day. Now only one. You get used to the heat after a while. You'll soon find that you don't mind to wake up anymore with a sweaty, greasy, sticky face.

I got an old table, a mirror, and a few posters put up on the walls. I like to buy *Guitar* magazines because it's the only thing of interest that I can find in English here. The magazines are expensive though by Thai standards. About 350 baht, which pretty much covers two nights at my guesthouse. I tape up the pictures that I like from my growing collection of magazines on the walls. When I have guests come over to my room they usually ask if I'm a guitarist. I tell them no, which leaves them a bit confused. I used to play keyboard, but there is no keyboard magazine in English here so *Guitar* magazine is simply the next best thing.

As for food, I'm a regular at a place called The Ballad, a quaint little place. A waitress there used to be my girlfriend. She is actually Vietnamese. Cute girl, but a little insecure, and in serious want of a husband ... no thank you. In any case, I usually get the green curry and a Thai iced coffee; I always order three Thai iced coffees. The green curry is a serious lip kicker–I'd say ass-kicker, but it ain't kicking my ass, it's kicking my lips. It's seriously spicy, but it will cure any stuffy nose.

So, what the hell do I do in Hat Yai? To be honest this place is really nothing special. Everything you need to know about this place you can learn in an afternoon. Hat Yai seems to be, for tourists anyway, a "passing through" kind of place. No foreigner ever really stays here–except for me. They are either coming from Malaysia or on their way to it. Malaysia–from what I've seen–is fantastic. I've only been to Pulau Penang. And on that island, I was shocked to see Indian Hindus, Chinese Buddhists and Taoists, and Malay Muslims living in such close proximity and getting along so well. The buildings there, kind of like here, were falling apart. Most were a century old or more and probably infested with termites. All the buildings were in serious need of a fresh coat of paint. But that was the charm of the place I guess, old colonial, two-storey buildings with mom-and-pop shops on the ground floor.

I was intrigued to see, hanging dead center over the street entrance of every Chinese commercial establishment or home I passed, an octagon–I think that was the shape–kind of mirror thing used to ward off evil spirits. And on the back wall of every Chinese mom-and-pop shop I passed there was a small ancestral shrine surrounded by lit candles and joss sticks. Some of these shops were a sight. I came across one shop literally littered with massive piles of electric fans; some of the piles were caked in dust and grime.

Well, back here in Hat Yai, we get quite a few Malay Muslims on the weekends. Most are men. Can you guess what they do here? They partake in the Thai flesh trade. When I arrived, I was initially disgusted with the travel agencies offering sex tours around the country. It's a big hit with the Japanese, although they'll never admit it. What hypocrisy for these sex consuming Malay Muslims. In Malaysia, they are obedient to their faith, but when they take that train and cross the border suddenly the moral code of their faith no longer applies–like it's in suspended animation until they return.

I mentioned that I haven't touched my dough back in the U.S. for a year and a half. Can you guess what I do here? I prey on these fresh off the train sex tourists and take them to the sex agencies here in Hat Yai. I make a good commission, and I now have a great eye for those Malay Muslims, Japanese, European, and American midlife crisis tourists, and anyone else looking for a good time. Yes, I'm a part of this sinful trade. I don't care anymore. My wife cheated on me and I couldn't care less now of encouraging love at any level. To me, it's all a lie so I scout the streets looking for men, who are probably married, and help them find their one-night stand. I don't expect you to like me after learning this. I don't like me either. I guess I'm in purgatory. Every day giving myself more reason not to like my life.

So, if you come across a fifty-year-old, beer belly New Yorker on the streets of Hat Yai you have been warned.

That is what Hat Yai can do to you. Throw you down a filthy, pitiful spiral of self-loathing. No Buddhist enlightenment have I found. But I never really made it out of here. I'm sure if I went further north I would have turned out different.

Posted by The Legacy Cycle 2004-04-11T05:57:00-07:00

Monday, April 12, 2004

It's 10:48 a.m. and I'm still in Hat Yai killing time until my bus to Krabi leaves at 1 p.m. I want to buy another bottle of soymilk at the nearest 7-Eleven; I've become a soymilk junkie while traveling in Southeast Asia. From Singapore, to Malaysia, to Thailand, I can't get enough of the sweetened stuff–it tastes better than whole milk.

After I finished typing my story about Avi last night I went back to my guesthouse and watched a fútbol match in the lounge room. Tired, I later left the lounge, walked down the long, dark hall that led to my room and saw a Thai man step out of his room. I smiled and said hello, but he pointed to his room and asked with a whisper, "Sex? Sex?"

"What?" I asked not believing what I'd heard.

"Sex?" he asked again.

I was so angry at that point. I wanted to punch him in the face and tell him to go @$!# himself! What the hell is up with these people? Keep your dicks in your pants and get a life or a real job. That experience is only adding to my already strong dislike for Hat Yai.

I woke up periodically during the night to street noise–revved up scooter engines–and the discomfort from feeling sticky from the tropical heat. There was no air conditioner in my room. Instead, there was a fan at the top of a high ceiling that did nothing to relieve me of the heat.

Well, I'm going to buy that soymilk and wait for my bus. Let's hope that Krabi is a much better place than Hat Yai.

Posted by The Legacy Cycle at 2004-04-12T20:47:00-07:00

Tuesday, April 13, 2004

I'm on the Ton Sai beach facing the Andaman Sea about an hour west–by boat–along the coast from Krabi Town, Thailand. Yesterday I fled Hat Yai by minibus. The bus was shoulder to shoulder packed at fifteen people. I chose–very unwisely–to sit in the back so that when the driver stopped to pick up another person, and opened the rear door, I could keep an obsessive eye on my bag that was crushed between the rear door and my seat. The car ride was over four hours; a hellishly long ride. The guy next to me–almost on top of me because it was so packed–had strong body odor. Luckily there was a little fan pointed at my head, which helped to keep some of that odor away.

The driver was fairly sane–by Thai standards–in his road warrior quest for Krabi. We didn't hit anything or go flying off a cliff, but he slammed on the gas every time he tried to pass the car in front of us. And at those excessive speeds the bumps and potholes in the road launched us all up from our seats causing me to giggle like a kid on a ride in an amusement park. But most of the Thai passengers did not approve of the repeating jolts to light speed.

Arriving at a pier in Krabi Town at 6 p.m. I got out of the minibus and was approached by a young Thai man named Shat who wanted to know if I needed accommodations. The sun was beginning to set and I had no desire to stay in the resort town; I wanted to take a boat to one of the secluded beaches along the Krabi coast. Shat explained that it was too late to catch a boat since most of boats had already left in the morning and afternoon. So, we made a deal. Probably a great deal for Shat. I hired him to take me on his boat to Ton Sai. The ride was about an hour. I had the entire boat to myself. I enjoyed feeling the warm wind on my face and sea spray on my lips while I gazed at a setting sun and distant, Stonehenge-shaped scattered islands.

As we approached Ton Sai at dusk I saw several bars and lax outdoor restaurants along the beach. Shat revved the engine, accelerated, and temporarily beached his boat. I grabbed my bag, paid and thanked Shat, climbed over the port side of the boat, and walked across the beach to the Ton Sai Hut check-in counter where I got the keys to a basic bamboo stilt bungalow for the night. I then walked up a path that led to the bungalows, but in the dark of night I had a difficult time trying to find bungalow number 406. After walking up and down the path to check the number of several bungalows I found mine, walked up a few steps, inserted the key, and opened the door. I searched the wooden walls with my hands for the light switch, soon found it, turned it on, and saw the vegetation of the ground below the stilt bungalow between the cracks of the wooden planks that served as a floor. The room had just enough space for a bed that had a mosquito net hanging over it (I had never before slept in a bed with a mosquito net). I opened the door that led to the back and found the bathroom. There was a Western toilet with no seat and next to it a white bucket that I would have to fill with water and dump into the toilet if I were to use it. The bathroom walls were concrete, but there was no ceiling, just a view of the canopy of the tropical forest and the night sky. The shower simply had a shower head that when turned on would spray cold water in all directions.

After organizing a few things in my bag, I walked back to the beach where I walked up and down the length of it to see what was available for dinner at the outdoor bars and restaurants. I chose a restaurant that seemed to be popular with backpackers, sat at a table on the beach, and had green curry and a coconut milk shake.

After dinner, I walked back to my bungalow and took a quick cold shower. I crawled into bed and fell asleep listening to Dream Theater's *Awake* album on my MiniDisc player. But I woke up when the album finished and saw that my room's useless, little electric fan had stopped. I tried to turn it back on, but had no luck. I then tried to turn on the lights, but the lights didn't work either. I was in complete darkness. Although I was a little scared, I realized after looking out my window screen that the other bungalows also had no electricity. I could hear people in the distance inquiring loudly as to what the hell was going on. I then saw two Thai men with flashlights walking up the path to the bungalows repeating the words: "Sorry, accident." Fifteen minutes later the power was back on, and my fan began rotating again.

I woke up at 6 a.m., took another shower, and went for a walk through a forest that led to Rai Leh Beach. As I neared the beach I walked past a couple of rock-climbing shops and schools, and several signs advertising rock climbing tours and adventures.

I reached Rai Leh, took a few photos of the beach at low tide, and walked back to Ton Sai for breakfast. I sat at a table, under a tree, on the beach again listening to the buzzing, metallic sound of cicadas. I then felt droplets of water on my face and looked up trying to see the source. The waiter came and I ordered banana pancakes, toast, and another coconut milk shake. While I waited for my food I kept looking up into the tree trying to see what continued to spray droplets on me. I stood up, looked closely at the tree branches, and then saw a cicada shoot liquid from its rear. I then sat down and debated whether I should move to another table, but I saw that most backpackers at the tables around me simply ignored the droplets and ate their food. So I had my breakfast under a light shower of cicada urine.

After breakfast, I went to the Ton Sai Hut counter to check-out and to book a bus to Bangkok for the following day. I then went to the Dream Valley check-in counter next door and upgraded my stay to a concrete bungalow. Although the bungalow did not have air conditioning it did have a nice bathroom with a flushing toilet that had a seat.

After I changed bungalows I spent more time at the beach walking, taking photos, and watching rock climbers scale limestone rock faces. In the afternoon, I read a few chapters from the novel *Girl with a Pearl Earring* on the porch of my bungalow. And here I am now at an Internet café. I'm now going to grab some dinner. Tomorrow I leave for Bangkok by overnight bus.

Posted by The Legacy Cycle at 2004-04-13T04:22:00-07:00

Friday, April 16, 2004

I'm at the Bangkok International Airport about to take my flight to Yangon (Rangoon), Myanmar (Burma). I'm excited because I expect to find a country that has not been heavily impacted by the 1990s rise of global trade and capitalism. Instead, I expect to find a nation nearly devoid of the elements of a rising consumerist society that I had seen in my travels thus far in Southeast Asia; elements such as Western franchises, shopping malls, and fast food. For example, in my 24 hours in Bangkok I had seen more 7-Eleven convenience stores than I had ever seen in my entire life; there was one on nearly every city block. I even saw two 7-Elevens directly across the street from each other; comedian Lewis Black in his rant about Starbucks would have argued that I had found the end of the universe! My taxi-driver, who went by the name F, told me that about six years ago there were no 7-Elevens in Bangkok, but now they are everywhere.

Western pop culture—music, clothing, fast food—and individualism have penetrated the mainstream culture of the Asian countries I have visited thus far. As a result, I want to see an Asian nation that has not been significantly changed by Western capitalist ideals. I believe that Myanmar is the closest I will come to experiencing some preserved essence of Southeast Asian culture.

I'm behind in keeping this travelogue current, but as soon as I return to Thailand from Myanmar I will I bring it up to date.

Before I sign off and take my flight to Myanmar—where I will not have Internet access—I would like to briefly explain what I had done the past couple of days.

I took a 14-hour overnight bus ride from Krabi Town to Bangkok, which was in the midst of the Songkran festival (the Thai New Year's festival) where for three days people crowd into the streets of Bangkok and throw buckets of water and talcum powder at each other in what seemed to be a citywide party. After a full day walking around the Thai capital and taking photos I returned to my guesthouse in soaking wet clothing and my face and hair caked in talcum powder. Luckily, I was able to protect my digital camera from the spray of water guns and the bombardment of water balloons. Songkran was an entertaining way to purify your inner and outer being for the New Year.

I have to run. I will return to Bangkok on April 27.

Posted by The Legacy Cycle at 2004-04-16T16:42:00-07:00

MYANMAR (BURMA) & BANGKOK, THAILAND

Wednesday, April 28, 2004

I'm in a Thai shopping mall. It is an evil place. I'm smiling as I say that because I believe it, and then I don't. My heart is split between being an American who is comfortable with the familiar Western surroundings of this shopping center (a hallmark of a consumerist society), and feeling sad, disgusted, and angered by the rising tide of an interconnected global economy that is turning Southeast Asia into a twisted image of the U.S. As I look at the scene before me from this Internet café I see Thai teenagers desperately trying to be part of the Thai pop culture mainstream through the type of clothing, music, and food that they consume. A part of me hopes that Myanmar does not fall prey to the same social, cultural, and economic long run fate as Thailand, Malaysia, and Singapore. I selfishly hope that Myanmar can continue to maintain the innocence that I saw in a people who have not fallen into the trap of a greedy, capitalist society that encourages the populace to seek self-gratification through consumerism.

I returned to Bangkok yesterday from my twelve-day journey through the central part of Myanmar. My thoughts and emotions are still raw, so I will do my best to accurately convey what I experienced.

Where shall I begin? I will begin by confessing that yes, indeed, I fell in love with Myanmar. The people, the culture, the Buddhist traditions, the temples, the ox-drawn carts, the old, beaten roads, the red-stained, betel nut chewing teeth of the Burmese, the beautiful Burmese women and children wearing thanaka on their faces and arms, and the colorful longyi (sarong) worn by everyone.

And although I had a severe stomach bacterial infection from something I ate soon into the trip, I can tell you that if afforded the opportunity to return, I would do so in a heartbeat.

Yangon
April 16, 2004

The Thai Airways commercial airliner began its descent toward Yangon International Airport. I looked from my aisle seat across the row of seats to my left and saw through the airplane cabin window the dense canopy of a tropical forest that stretched to the horizon. The only signs of civilization were the occasional golden pagoda spires that broke through the lush greenery marking the locations of Burmese Buddhist temples. I did not see buildings or a grid street plan typical of urban areas near most capital cities. I only saw distant golden spires and the vast expanse of tropical vegetation as the plane continued its descent. I then thought of what Joseph Campbell once said in his 1988 *The Power of Myth* television miniseries: "If you want to see what a society really believes in, look at what the biggest buildings on the horizon are dedicated to." He explained how during the Middle Ages Roman Catholic cathedrals defined the skylines of most, if not all, European cities. In the decades after the American and French Revolutions government buildings were constructed to compete with the tall spires of Protestant and Catholic churches. Today, corporate skyscrapers are the architectural apex of developed cities. These towering feats of the First World reflect Western civilization's cumulative, excessive, and corrupting adoration of money. But in Myanmar, you find only Buddhist temples that reach for the skies, and that–according to Joseph Campbell–is a clear sign as to what is respected and practiced among the Burmese.

The plane approached the runway and landed. As we neared the main terminal building I realized that the Thai airliner was the only commercial aircraft in the entire airport; an indication of Myanmar's political and economic isolation. The plane stopped, the fasten seat belt sign turned off, I unbuckled myself from my seat, stood up, and began to gather my bag and belongings. Passengers began to line up in the aisles, the airplane cabin doors were opened, and we exited the plane by walking down a passenger boarding staircase where we were immediately hit by the thick, humid air. Parked at the base of the staircase was a decades-old Japanese public bus. I boarded the bus, and when it was partially full the driver turned the ignition key and drove it to the terminal building. I tried to read bits and pieces of the Japanese script on the bus while thinking that it was odd that the Osaka bus route map and safety instructions were still in the language of the Land of the Rising Sun. It felt as if the bus had been snatched from Japan two decades ago and dropped magically into Myanmar to continue working a new route without any need to provide information in Burmese. Later in my trip I would see public buses that still had the painted logos for JR (Japan Railways), Keio (a train and bus line in Tokyo), and Seibu Bus.

  Going through customs at the airport was quick and easy. I didn't see any armed security guards or military men–in fact I did not see a single firearm during my time in Myanmar. But what did catch my attention as I passed through customs was the face of one of the customs officials who had applied–in a circular motion–a yellow cream to her cheeks. I later learned that most, if not all, Burmese women applied thanaka (a cosmetic paste made from ground bark) to their face and arms;[1] a tradition that has continued for over 2,000 years.[2]

  I exited the Yangon International Airport and was instantly approached by a Burmese taxi driver in his early thirties wearing a blue plaid shirt with rolled up sleeves and a dark blue longyi. He took off his sunglasses and offered to drive me to the city center. I asked him how much for the ride. He gave me his price, which I calculated into US dollars and agreed. But he insisted that I look for another tourist to share the ride to cut down the cost. I was pleasantly shocked by his recommendation. In Thailand taxi drivers did their best to cheat me out of my cash. But in Yangon this Burmese taxi driver was trying to help me save money! I told him it was no trouble for me to pay his fare, but he pointed out a young, lone female backpacker with dark brown, shoulder length hair that was walking out of the airport. He said he would wait for me to ask her. Deciding to give it a shot, I ran to catch up with the backpacker who appeared to be in her late twenties, and asked if she wanted to split a cab with me. She agreed and away we went to Yangon.

I formally introduced myself in the taxi. She reciprocated by telling me that her name was Daisy, that she was from the Netherlands, and that she had been traveling for nine months, which made me a backpacking novice compared to her.

The taxi neared the outskirts of the Yangon, and along the sides of the street we saw thirty or more people standing on covered platforms elevated by scaffolds spraying water from garden hoses down at the passing cars, pedestrians, and traffic police; they were celebrating the last day of Thingyan (the Burmese New Year festival), which was similar to the Songkran festival in Thailand with the exception that no one used talcum powder or water guns. The taxi continued slowly as we watched to our right people seated in the back of a blue pick-up truck get heavily doused. Then in an instant a Burmese teenager armed with a garden hose ran up to our taxi and sprayed directly into the driver's open window. Daisy and I could only giggle like children in the attack that left us soaked. The taxi continued further into the capital, and we saw more and more people spraying water from scaffolds while others jumped out of their cars to dump, launch, throw, and catapult buckets of water at other cars and pedestrians.

Everyone was so happy, but to put it in the words of a Frenchmen I met later that day: "Judging by how happy these people are today you would never guess that they are under a military dictatorship."

The taxi driver took me to the May Shan Hotel, which was located just in front of the supposedly 2,500-year-old Sule Pagoda (a 44-meter-high Burmese stupa at the center of Yangon) that served as a rallying point during the 8888 Nationwide Popular Pro-Democracy Protests. Daisy chose to stay at a hostel, but we decided to meet at her hostel in an hour. After I checked into my hotel, dropped my bag in my room, and washed my face I began walking in the direction of Daisy's hostel.

The walk was wonderful. Everyone was smiling at me. I was the only foreigner within several city blocks and everyone looked at me with great curiosity. It was delightful to see so many friendly, curious faces. And beautiful teeth! The Burmese had perfect white teeth, whereas in Japan I regularly saw people who had teeth that looked as if a small explosive device had gone off in their mouths. And then I saw a few Burmese men who had teeth stained red. I later discovered that men, as well as women, in Myanmar often chewed paan, which was a "stimulating, psychoactive preparation of betel leaf combined with areca nut and/or cured tobacco,"[3] which had "adverse health effects."[4]

    I arrived to the hostel and saw Daisy waiting on the porch wearing a blue, short sleeved shirt, beige cargo shorts, and flip-flops. We quickly decided to explore the Burmese capital. The first thing we went to see was Yangon City Hall, which was blocked off to ensure that uninvited pedestrians did not obstruct or gather before a large stage with an already active show. In front of the stage there were many rows of perhaps four to five hundred white or red plastic chairs; and there were already approximately two hundred VIP guests seated and enjoying the live spectacle while vertical blue pipes sprayed water all over them. A few of the seated guests held umbrellas. As Daisy and I watched we soon realized that the crowd around us was staring at us; we felt like aliens. Everyone looked at us as if they had never seen a foreigner before, and I'm sure that for a few of them that may have been the case. We were then initiated into the celebration as one Burmese after the other approached us to pour water–and sometimes ice water–down our backs and on our heads. I held my camera at arm's length so that it would not be damaged. After a few moments, my shirt was so soaked that it looked like I had taken a shower in it. Daisy and I decided to politely walk away so that we could see more of the city.

    Upon my first impressions, I would say that Yangon was a very poor city: it was dirty, and characterized by dilapidated, neglected colonial buildings; the streets were lined with decades-old cars and buses, and–as I would discover at night–it was a city plagued by constant power outages. But for some reason, during my first day–and for the duration of my time in the country–the poverty I witnessed did not cause me to feel the type of discomfort and culture shock I had felt when I traveled through developing countries such as Peru, Mexico, Morocco, and Chile (back in the 1980s). I felt right at home in Myanmar. It was strange to feel such a thing because for all the countries I had been fortunate to travel to in South America, North Africa, and Asia, I had felt some degree of discomfort, shock, and/or sadness as a result of the visible poverty, but in Myanmar that was never the case. A Buddhist monk might say that I had lived a past life in Myanmar, but the real reason as to why I felt so at home in Burma was because the people there made me feel at home.

Soon enough, while walking along the streets of Yangon, locals from the black market approached Daisy and I to exchange money. We agreed to a rate of 810 kyats to the dollar. We were then led to a teashop that had a satellite TV showing some Hollywood action film (Myanmar's military junta seemed to be relaxed about broadcast censorship—in my hotel room I saw programs from China, Thailand, MTV from Indonesia, and movie channels from the U.S.). We exchanged our money and left with huge wads of Myanmar kyats.

We began our 30-minute walk to the famed Shwedagon Pagoda, and along the way we were doused, yet again, in water by locals before running into a group of fun-loving Burmese punks who sported dyed blue hair. I asked to take a picture with them, and they quickly posed with me for a photo. But after Daisy took a few clicks with my camera they sprayed my hair and shirt blue with cans of spray paint. I *then* looked like them!

We continued walking and stopped at the Maha Wizaya Pagoda where we saw a row of makeshift restaurants near its main entrance. We chose a restaurant that appealed to our senses, sat down, and ordered traditional Burmese food and drinks while gazing at the towering golden pagoda.

After lunch, we went to the main entrance, took off our shoes as required, and entered. But quickly realizing that the intense midday sun had baked the smooth stone flooring around the pagoda, Daisy and I quickly walked on the white marble tiles, as opposed to the scorching black tiles, to reach the entrance into the pagoda.

The interior of the pagoda was cool and quiet. We saw, lined along the wall, several bodhisattva statues that had concentric rings of colorful, small light bulbs that flashed intermittently to display animated geometric patterns behind their heads. The walls had colorful painted murals of scenes depicting Burmese men and women kneeling and praying to an illuminated Buddha; in one particular scene, a demon could be seen raising its hand before striking down a fearful disciple. The walls of the arched passageways that led to the main stupa chamber had painted landscape scenes of forests, which transitioned into three-dimensional tree trunks and branches made of plaster with plastic green leaves to add to the effect. At the center of the chamber was a white and gold stupa perhaps three meters high with seven or eight seated bodhisattva statues surrounding it; all around the stupa were offerings of flowers and burning joss sticks. The domed, blue tiled ceiling of the chamber depicted the Buddhist cosmos composed of constellations outlining the shapes of animals and objects: a horse, a crane, an elephant, an alligator, a cat, a seated Buddha, an arrow, a Burmese house on stilts, etc.

After snapping a few photos, Daisy and I decided to continue our walk to the Shwedagon Pagoda. Upon arriving we saw two massive, white and golden leogryph statues guarding the southern entrance (there were four main entrances: one for each of the four cardinal directions). We approached the entrance gates, took off our shoes (as required), and walked through the wooden, roofed step walkway that led up Singuttara Hill. It was a pleasant experience to ascend the hill in the cool darkness of the walkway that was lined with shops that sold drinks, flowers, books, Buddhist charms, joss sticks, and other items. We reached the exit and saw the Shwedagon Pagoda directly in front of us.

The Shwedagon Pagoda is the most sacred Buddhist temple in Myanmar, and in my opinion, one of the most beautiful temples I had ever seen. It is 99-meters-tall and is clearly visible to any aircraft that arrives or departs from Yangon; the current stupa dates to the 18th century, but archaeological evidence dates the pagoda back to the 6th century.[5] The base of the stupa is covered with 8,000 golden plates; the crown is encrusted with 5,448 diamonds and 2,317 rubies; and the diamond bud at the very top of the pagoda has a 72-carat diamond.[6]

For a country with a GDP per capita of $256.66 (2006),[7] I was surprised to see so much wealth invested into the Shwedagon Pagoda. In addition to the diamonds and precious stones there were glass containers filled with cash donations throughout the holy complex. It was apparent that the Burmese believed in the spiritual power of their temples and gave willingly and gladly to support them.

The Burmese are devoted to the practice of Theravada Buddhism (about 87.9 percent of the population practice the religion).[8] The majority of Burmese men live in a Buddhist monastery at least twice during the course of their life: the first time when they are young (between the ages of 7 and 13)[9] and the second when they are much older. All the men I had spoken to during my time in Myanmar described their experience in the monastery as wonderful. Burmese women can also live in a monastery as nuns (they are required to shave their heads; and wear light pink robes, and a light orange cloth across their chests or on their heads to protect against the sun). Many men and women I met—husbands, wives, taxi drivers, and hotel managers—practiced meditation and prayed on a daily basis. This religious dedication was perhaps a significant factor as to why it felt like 99 percent of the people I encountered in Myanmar were so genuine, loving, innocent, giving, simple, kind, and honest. They truly practiced their Buddhist beliefs. I could not say the same about Thailand since in cities and towns that attracted tourists there were many touts that tried to cheat the *farang* (foreigner).

I should mention that during my last night in my guesthouse in Bangkok (the night before I left for Myanmar) the lady who washed and ironed my clothes came to my room to deliver them and explained that she was tired and that she was going to go sleep in my bed! I couldn't believe it. I thanked her for the clean laundry and asked her to leave, which she did. Bangkok, unfortunately, did live up to its infamous reputation of easily available prostitution. In contrast, my hotel in Yangon displayed signs in nearly all directions that read: "NO PROSTITUTION, please!"

It became readily apparent to me within the first day in Myanmar that the country was at the top of my list of Asian nations that I would like to return to. I had yet to see Laos, Cambodia, Vietnam, and China, but I had a strong feeling that none of those countries would be able to hold a light to what I was experiencing at a spiritual level in Myanmar.

Well, getting back to the Shwedagon Pagoda. I wish I could keep writing about it, but I should stop for today. I will write more about it tomorrow, and the taxi journey I took through the central part of the country. I should mention that while walking around the grounds of the Swedagon Pagoda I had another idea for a book (tentatively entitled *Thieves of Burma*). The story (a heist story) would entail a team of American or European thieves who plan to steal the 72-carat diamond at the top of the Shwedagon Pagoda; events in the story would lead to each team member's spiritual transformation. A tremendous amount of research would be required for the story as I would want it to detail Burmese Buddhist and nat superstitions, the history of the country, the current military regime, while working in a love story between one of the thieves and a Burmese native. Please note, although this is a public blog, my idea for this story has already been registered with the Writers Guild of America, West.

Posted by The Legacy Cycle at 2004-04-28T04:55:00-07:00

Thursday, April 29, 2004

I'm back again, so let us begin.

Yangon
April 17, 2004

While I had breakfast in the hotel dining area I asked the Chinese lady who owned the establishment the best means of traveling to Mandalay. She said that a good way to go would be to hire a taxi who could not only take me to Mandalay, but provide stops at towns and cities along the way. She explained that it would cost me about US$250 for about ten days of travel. I thought about it, and told her that it would be a great way to see more of the country. She explained that she would make a couple of phone calls so that a private driver could come to talk to me about planning my travel itinerary and negotiating a price, but she added that since it was the New Year holidays it might be difficult to get a hold of a driver since most Burmese people would be praying at the pagodas. "No worries," I told her. "I'll go out for a walk and return by 12:30 to see if you've been able to find a driver."

I left the hotel, walked around Yangon City Hall, and met an old Indian woman on the street whose shoulders and upper back were severely hunched forward. She spoke perfect English and asked, "Hello, do you remember me?" I entertained her and answered, "yes." She went on, "There you see. I saw you yesterday, and I tried to talk to you, but you disappeared. Do you want to have a coffee with me?"

She seemed harmless. I agreed to her request. She then led me down the streets of Yangon telling me how she "knew all," and how she had taken various foreigners around the city and the country and that she had even been in a magazine. We soon sat down in a yoghurt shop. She had some buttered bread and a drink while I ate strawberry yoghurt.

"Yes, there you see. I know all," she began as we started eating. "My father was British. Long ago, you see, long ago. Here–have a look at this," she began shuffling through her ragged purse and pulled out a decades-old identification card with a black and white photo of her when she was young and beautiful. "That is me, you see. That is me."

I took and looked at the frayed photo, and smiled.

"I was beautiful then, you see. Now, no more. I am falling apart. You see this?" she asked holding a plastic bag full of pills and plastic prescription bottles. "This is my medicine, you see. I was riding these old buses a month ago. Sitting in the back, I was. And then there was a bump, and I flew off my seat and landed hard back down. A terrible pain I felt in my back after that. Terrible pain. Now I have to take these medicines, you see. Where do you stay?"

"At the May Shan Hotel," I replied.

"The Chinese. The Chinese own that hotel, and a restaurant too. Rich, they are. Why do you give your money to them? How much are you paying for you room?"

"Ten dollars," I lied.

"Too much," she said shaking her head. "Too much. I know all. I can show you everything. Where to stay and eat for nothing–nothing for you. I can help you. I don't need much. If you are happy you can give me a little something. Pay for my food or a bit of money so that I can buy my medicines."

"Yes, that sounds nice," I said trying to assure her that there was a likely (unlikely) possibility that we could forge a relationship of her as travel guide and I as patron.

"You see. I know all. All! We can go around the country if you want–by bus if you like and stay at cheap hotels. I don't need much. You will save much money with me. And at the end you can give me what you like. I was in a magazine, you see. I wish I had that article with me. I will bring it tomorrow so that you can read it. It's in English. You can read it. In an Australian magazine."

"You're famous," I complimented her.

"Then," she lowered her voice, "when we are away from the streets, and the listening ears of others, I can tell you all you want about the military, the British, the Japanese. Everything. I know all."

I barely said more than a few words during our conversation, which is usually the way I like it as I prefer to listen and observe than talk; people love to talk … so I let them. As the conversation went on and on I solidified my decision to not hire her to show me around. She talked too much! Too much for my tastes, which says a lot–she rambled continuously without really saying anything. If someone loves to talk, and I am learning something, then great, but I wasn't learning much from her. But, she did entertain me. She was a character. Her way of speaking, her strong-willed personality, and constant use of the phrase "I know all," painted a portrait of a personality in my mind that I would never forget; a personality that will find its way into defining a character in one of my stories.

When I returned to the hotel the Chinese owner approached me and explained that a taxi driver would soon arrive to negotiate the cost of hiring his services for a nine-day journey around the country. I waited in the lobby, and soon enough I saw the same man who had driven me from the airport to my hotel the previous day accompanied by another man by the name of Aung who was dressed in a cream-colored, button-up shirt and dark brown, tiny-squared plaid longyi. We sat down and decided that for nine days I could travel to the following places: Bago, Kyaikto, Taungoo, Nyaungshwe (Inle Lake), Bagan, and Pyay (during our negotiations they explained that nine days would not be enough to go to Mandalay). We agreed upon a price of $350, which included all travel expenses (gas, repairs if needed, etc.), and my driver's accommodations and food expenses. Cheap. Very cheap. So, we shook hands and decided that Aung and I would leave the next morning at 8 a.m.

Afterwards I walked to Daisy's hostel and was informed by the receptionist that she had left for lunch. I decided to wait, and sat down on the veranda of the hostel to read a book. She returned about 30 minutes later, and before making our way to Kandawgyi Lake we went in search of a camera shop where she could transfer the photos from her digital camera to a CD.

We eventually found a camera shop, but the shop assistant didn't know how to operate the store computer. Nervous that she might lose a sale the assistant allowed me to try to work the computer to download the photos from Daisy's camera, but Daisy grew impatient and we left.

Our next stop was the train station, where Daisy got the train schedule to Mandalay. We continued our search for the lake—I led the small expedition because it was my idea—but as we walked and walked I could feel Daisy growing impatient with me. She then told me that she didn't think I knew where I was going. The comment angered me, but I kept quiet until I found the lake. It looked pleasant, but there was a high fence all around it preventing us from gaining access. We chose a direction and walked along the fence hoping to find a way in until we met a petite, young German traveler with short, wavy brown hair and thin metal frame eyeglasses by the name of Manuela. After brief introductions, she said that she had been backpacking in Myanmar for the past month. She offered Daisy and I some travel advice with a sweet German accent before we parted ways.

Daisy and I decided that our quest to find a way in to see the lake was not worth the additional time we would need, so we decided to see the Chaukhtatgyi Buddha Temple. We took a taxi, entered the temple, and saw the massive 66-meter-long reclining Buddha statue that was enclosed in what appeared to be an airplane hangar. After marveling at the statue, I participated in a game of kick the plastic bottle cap in random directions with a wonderful group of Burmese children. It should be noted that the temples in Myanmar are leisurely in nature; a place where one can come to seek shelter from the intense sun, pray, relax, and socialize. The children in the temple found an unlimited number of ways to play games because, as any child knows, to sit and listen with the adults who were talking and gossiping is flat out boring. So, there I was, barefoot, playing with these wonderful children. Daisy watched and took a photo.

We left and returned to Yangon, where Daisy, skilled in bargaining, finally had her digital photos copied onto CDs. We had our last meal together at a Thai restaurant, said goodbye, and I went back to my hotel to pack my bags and sleep.

Yangon to Bago to Kyaikto
April 18, 2004

Aung and I set off bright and early in his decade-old, white Toyota sedan. We first had to stop to see his wife and young son; he had to give them some money. But before we arrived to meet them, Aung pointed out, as we passed it, a nat (spirit) shrine dedicated to those on long journeys; he explained that he had already paid homage to it this morning.

As I was to discover the nats (spirits worshipped in Burma) are everywhere; there are 37 Great Nats, and many other nats who hold dominion over trees, animals, places (both natural and artificial), and other elements. The Burmese are very careful to never offend the nats. They always pay their respects to them, and as I experienced with Aung he paid homage to them not only for himself, but for me as well.

Aung shared a story with me about a group of German tourists that he had driven around the country. He explained that one of the German men in his car had to empty his bladder. He pulled the car over and the man walked up to a tree and urinated on it. Aung immediately begin chanting. When the German was done, he asked Aung what he was saying. Aung explained that it was rude for him to urinate on the spirit (nat) of the tree, so he chanted on his behalf to apologize to the nat. The German felt guilty and together they prayed and offered their apologies and respects to the tree spirit.

We stopped at Aung's village, got out of the car, and approached the open-air market and shop that his wife operated. Aung's three-year-old son was standing in front of the shop wearing clothes that had a patterned design that was the same to the clothes his wife was wearing. I said hello to his wife, who was beautiful! Aung said goodbye stoically—no hug or kiss—and we left.

Bago is about 70-kilometers northeast of Yangon. We arrived in an hour and a half, but only stopped at one temple because I was not interested in seeing a temple that was so similar in design to the temples I had already seen in Yangon. So, we stopped briefly at Kyaik Pun Pagoda (built in the 7th century AD, although it did not look that old due to its renovation), which was a temple of four back-to-back 27-meter-tall seated Buddha statues. I was approached by a little Burmese girl selling postcards when I got out of the car. I told her that I did not need any postcards. She then took me all around the temple and we exchanged a few words. I decided that I wanted to take a picture of her so I offered her some money for her photo. She refused to take my money and said that I could go ahead and take a picture of her. I then forced some money into her hand and she posed taking a very proud stance. The picture came out great: she had a wide smile and stood with such terrific pride.

Aung and I returned to the car and drove to Kyaikto.

The great thing about traveling by car in Myanmar was that I could see what life was like for many of the people outside of the cities. *That's obvious*, you may say, but it was interesting to see, for example, the horrible state of the road system that were, at times, composed of only one lane for traffic moving in both directions. Not too many people can afford a car in Myanmar (four cars per 1,000 people in 2004)[10] so it was not a problem to travel on these one lane roads between towns and cities because we rarely came across another car or bus. The means of transportation that I did see on a regular basis were ox-driven carts that moved at a snail's pace. At times these carts were piled high with harvested bundles of long, dried grass or bundles of bamboo sticks. I also saw two-wheeled, horse-drawn carts and trishaws. But the vehicles that continually caught my attention were tractors that had been converted to serve as open-air passenger vehicles. I took a photo of one of these vehicles and saw many different improvised versions of them. As for the buses, there were many, and packed well beyond capacity; the roofs of the buses were covered with seated Burmese men, monks, teenage boys, and women. And hanging for dear life during long, arduous journeys on the rear bumpers of these buses were more Burmese men wearing poorly made sandals that provided very little grip. Another means of transportation were old pickup trucks that had rows of wooden benches (essentially planks) bolted down in the cargo bed where people sat and crammed together. These pickup trucks were the most common way people traveled in Myanmar, and after seeing all of these examples of travel in the country I was very thankful for having the foresight to rent a taxi during my nine-day journey. I don't think I could have survived three days traveling by these local means of transportation simply because those buses and pickup trucks were packed beyond comprehension.

In the afternoon, we arrived to the Golden Smiles Hotel in Kyaikto. The hotel was rustic, and my room unnecessarily spacious; at the end of my journey I met the owner of the hotel in Yangon (she was from Belgium and had been doing business in Myanmar for the past six years). After I got settled into my room and ate lunch, Aung took me to an informal, open-air station where I jumped into the cargo bed of one of those pickup trucks and traveled up the Eastern Yoma mountains on a pilgrimage to Golden Rock.

Golden Rock (a picture of it is on the cover of the *Lonely Planet Myanmar (Burma)* 2004 edition) is a "massive, gold-leafed boulder delicately balanced on the edge of a cliff at the top of Mt Kyaiktiyo."[11] Golden Rock, like Shwedagon Pagoda, is one of the most sacred Buddhist sites in Myanmar because, according to legend, the rock sits on top of a strand of the Buddha's hair.

The pickup truck stopped, and all passengers (many devout Buddhists) had to get off and ascend the rest of the mountain by foot. The hike up the mountain was painful; I was completely out of shape. I sweated, trekked, and sweated more until I finally made it to the top of this beast of a mountain. Along the way I walked through a row of shacks selling religious trinkets, medicinal roots, herbs, monkey skulls, severed goat heads; and toy guns made from bamboo that were painted red, white, and blue with the letters "USA" inscribed on them. I wasn't proud. Myanmar, in my mind, was a land of smiles and dedicated Buddhists who spoke honestly and acted honorably. But the people of Myanmar saw the U.S. not as a land of liberty and democracy, but one of oppression; a society that lived by the gun to settle their international disputes or to forcefully take what was not theirs. With the ongoing war in Iraq, I think the Burmese were accurate in their view of the United States.

Once I arrived to the top of Mt. Kyaiktiyo I found a large, flat expanse of marble tiled floors, shrines, and the Golden Rock itself, which I could have touched if I chose to but did not because I found it unjustified that Burmese women (devoted practitioners of their faith who prayed before the rock) or any women for that matter were prohibited from approaching and touching the rock.

I was surprised to find that there was a town just beyond where the Golden Rock was located. I spent some time walking through the town until I decided to call it a day. I descended the mountain by foot and pickup truck, and returned to the hotel with Aung where I collapsed on my bed with a throbbing headache.

I later woke up that night to find that the electrical power had gone out (a daily occurrence in Myanmar), and to the most horrible case of diarrhea. I will not say more.

Posted by The Legacy Cycle at 2004-04-29T04:42:00-07:00

Sunday, May 2, 2004

I can't believe it's already May 2. I will depart Bangkok tomorrow and continue my journey home. I just read an email from my friend Aaron Deupree who had traveled through Southeast Asia in 2002, and is currently living and working in Switzerland. He offered some very insightful comments that I would like to share.

> I've heard recently that Cambodia and Vietnam have changed a lot. Backpackers wearing dumb shirts saying, 'Beware of Landmines: Cambodia', as if that's cool. Well, I think you'll enjoy those places anyway.

> I felt the same way as you at times. Why does everything have to be homogenized, globalized, and Americanized? Well, for better or for worse, people want prosperity and security, so right now that means skyscrapers and McDs. Nevertheless, the cosmetic changes that happen in a society are often only skin deep. Thais will always be Thais and do Thai things, even in big shopping malls with Gap and Kmart. Just like Japan—a very Americanized country, but it's still very Japanese—the Japanese psyche remains strongly in place, even when little Japanese boys and girls want American stuff, they will be Japanese, and their parents have enjoyed the postwar prosperity—and when Yankees like us step off at Narita, the familiar signs of 7-Eleven are not really enough to make us feel at home.

What Aaron said was true, and now that I have been in Bangkok for nearly a week I do not deplore it as much as when I had first arrived here from Myanmar.

I'm reading a book entitled *Night Market: Sexual Cultures and the Thai Economic Miracle* by Ryan Bishop and Lillian S. Robinson. The book takes a very critical look at the sex industry in Thailand and its impact on the Thai economy and people. It is impossible to walk through this city and not see *farang* (foreign) men in their thirties, forties, fifties, and sixties with a Thai prostitute attached to their arm. What is the motivation for these men to travel halfway around the world to fulfill their pathetic, sexual fantasies? The authors of the book cite one study that estimated that about half of all child Thai prostitutes are HIV positive.[12] If that is true, along with increasing infection rates among Thai men and women due to prostitution and injecting drug use (30 percent to 50 percent prevalence among IDUs),[13] then how much of the virus is being transmitted to the West by these American and European sex consumers? How many of these foreign sex tourists from developed nations, which include Japan and Malaysia, partake in this $4.3 billion per year Thai sex industry (3 percent of their GDP in 2003)[14] and transmit STDs to their unknowing spouses or partners? Will HIV/AIDS prevalence continue to increase in Thailand (1.4 percent of the population from 2003 to 2005)[15] to that of South Africa (the highest prevalence with just under 12 percent of the population infected).[16] What is worse is the impact the HIV/AIDS epidemic is having on the increasing demand for young, virgin girls from the Thai countryside (in part due to the "high HIV prevalence among female sex workers" in urban settings such as Bangkok where rates are as high as 20 percent).[17]

Children and young adults are "lured under false pretenses"[18] or sold off to brokers by family members in the rural, poorer areas of Thailand to become commodities within the Thai sex trade. The younger the girl, the more likely she is a virgin, and the higher her value to a sex consumer or tourist. Burmese girls are sought and smuggled into Thailand through the Golden Triangle (the northern border that Thailand, Burma, and Laos share) or through other "various waterways" along the "porous borders",[19] because HIV has a slightly lower prevalence in the Burmese population (1.3 percent in 2005 according to UNAIDS)[20] in part due to its political and economic isolation. Conservative estimates place the number of men, women, and children, "but particularly women and young girls—engaged in prostitution as part of Thailand's illegal sex tourism industry" between 200,000 and 300,000 (the "figure does not include foreign migrants").[21] Of that number 30,000 to 40,000 prostitutes are under the age of 18.[22] It is sickening to consider these figures, and disturbing to contemplate why there is even a demand for such an exploitative industry.

In the end, it is apparent that HIV/AIDS will become an increasingly larger health problem that will erode a prospering Thai economy that in part has been built on a sex tourist industry.

> The ESCAP study points out that the expense of caring for an AIDS patient can be devastating. In Thailand's Chiang Mai province, families report spending an average US$1,000 a year in direct medical care costs – the equivalent of half the average annual household income in the region. In the Chiang Mai study, a third of AIDS-hit households reported that their incomes fell by 48 percent. By the time the AIDS patients had died, 60 percent of families had used up their savings, 44 percent had sold land, 42 percent had cut down their food consumption, 28 percent had sold a vehicle, and 11 percent had borrowed an average of US$1,700 each.[23]

In speaking with Thais in Bangkok most have explained to me that they despise the sex industry in their country. They say that if they could have it their way they would shut it down for it does not reflect proper Thai thought and behavior. The Thai government would be wise to confront the sex industry and diminish it, and with it the increasing prevalence of HIV/AIDS, but attempts by the Ministry of Public Health "to publicize the dangers of AIDS for both Thai sex workers and tourists" have been challenged and met with protests by the Tourist Authority of Thailand[24] that seeks to preserve a multibillion dollar industry that generates employment (legal and illegal), spending, and tax revenue. So as long as the big bucks flow into the country from the pockets of Occidental sex tourists—as well as from Thai, Southeast Asian, and East Asian consumers—the sex trade and industry in Thailand, and other nations, will continue to thrive.

But even if a nation's government takes a strong stand to limit the sex industry's supply chain, typically, and unfairly, through legislation criminalizing (in the case of Thailand's 1960 Prostitution Suppression Act) "the provider of sexual services" while leaving the "consumer of sex … immune to prosecution,"[25] it will mean little if there is persistent demand. The people of all nations will need to address the sex trade and industry within, and beyond their borders, by bringing to light those who drive the demand for a global sex industry that has enslaved 22 percent of modern slaves (current estimates of the total number of forced laborers in the world is 20.9 million).[26]

The tentacles of Thailand's sex industry supply chain stretch far beyond the borders of Southeast Asian nations:

> Organized trafficking groups such as the yakuza in Japan and Russian gangs have slowly emerged in the country. What is certain is that sex trafficking in Thailand is no longer limited to its East Asian neighbors. Russian and Eastern European victims have become more common in the country.[27]

I remember when I went to renew my visa in Japan in the summer of 2003 at the Immigration Bureau office in Tokyo that I saw many young women (perhaps just under a hundred in total) from Thailand, Russia, China, the Philippines, and Eastern Europe escorted–guarded–by Japanese men who I assumed were part of the yakuza red-light district network. These women, in plain sight, were brought to the Immigration Bureau to submit and renew their visa working papers.

> Louise Brown explains in her book *Sex Slaves: The Trafficking of Women in Asia* that "because Japan is a collection of islands, the only way to enter the country are by boat or by air, and potential entry points are limited and closely monitored. Prostituted women have therefore usually entered on legitimate visas – either as tourists or entertainers. These allow them to stay for three months, and they can be extended to a maximum of six months. A few of the women vanish when their visas expire and

will stay on illegally. Others return home. Another group enter the country on expensive, false passports that have been produced by the criminal underworld's lucrative forgery department. This is especially true in the case of Thai women and is one of the main reasons why they incur such high debts."[28]

Taungoo to Inle Lake
April 20, 2004

The ride from Taungoo to Inle Lake was a rough and long one–eight hours if I recall–on a one-lane road that was in desperate need of repair. During the journey, I saw the landscape change drastically from a dry, tropical savanna climate and environment to a vast desert. Cactuses, shrubs, and scattered trees dotted the terrain with the occasional pond and bathing wild water buffalos.

Along the journey I saw small communities of Indians whose women wore traditional, brightly colored sari garments in shades of purple, red, and orange, which was a striking contrast to the plain blue, brown, and grey colors that defined Burmese patterned longyi.

One thing that I have noticed on my travels is that countries with strong, developed economies tend to favor styles of clothing that utilize more mundane colors. Go to New York City or Tokyo (the financial capitals of the two most powerful economies in the world) and the majority of working professionals wear black, grey, or dark blue business suits. Travel to a developing country like Myanmar or Thailand and you will see more people wearing bright and vibrant colored clothing. Why is that? Why have we Westerners repressed the vibrant colors from our wardrobes? The paintings on ancient Greek vases reveal that the Greeks wore brightly colored dress "decorated with elaborate designs".[29] Yellow was one of the most common colors in the ancient world (the source of the dye derived from a "number of plants"); along with blue, which was derived from indigo (a plant native to India and southeast Asia);[30] while Tyrian purple ("a dye extracted from the murex shellfish, which was first produced by the Phoenician city of Tyre in the Bronze Age") was desired due to its striking color and "resistance to fading," but expensive as a result of the difficulty in manufacturing the dye,[31] thus the color became a status symbol often associated with aristocrats and emperors from the time of the Roman Empire to European monarchs in the 18th and 19th century. It is strange that now we Westerners with our increasing per capita incomes and ability to import whatever dyes we seek through international trade do not increase our demand for interesting and vibrant colored outfits. Instead we settle for dark blue, black, grey, and white.

At one point during the journey Aung pulled the car over to the shoulder of the road so that I could try toddy (palm wine) from a roadside stall. Burmese farmers produce the alcoholic drink by extracting it from the sap of palm trees to then leave the collected liquid out to ferment. After a couple of hours or a day (depending on the percent level of alcohol desired) the alcoholic beverage is ready to be consumed.[32] I had three glasses and felt a slight buzz, which caused me to smile for a portion of the journey north to Inle Lake.

Inle Lake is located in the central eastern mountains (Shan Hills) of Myanmar. As we ascended the mountains Aung drove cautiously around the many curves of the battered road. Suddenly we began having car trouble; the car kept stalling. I wasn't worried for some reason; part of me was curious to discover how we would solve the problem of being stranded in the middle of nowhere. But we didn't get stranded. Aung pulled the car over on two separate occasions to work on the engine. We continued to have car trouble, but luckily, we came across a nat shrine dedicated to cars and safe travel. Aung pulled the car up to the shrine and advanced and retreated from it as he chanted. We then heard the caretaker of the shrine begin to howl her chants behind our car. After, she approached us—Aung gave her a donation—and explained that there was a Buddhist monk that needed a ride. Aung and I agreed that we would be more than happy to have the monk join us; we were both selfishly thinking that a Buddhist monk in our car would bring us not only good luck, but also the good favor of the nats to provide a temporary end to our car troubles for the day.

The monk was in his late seventies. His skin was dark brown and he only had a few teeth left, which he revealed when he smiled. Who knew what he thought of me. I must have been as curiously interesting to look at as he was to me.

The monk got into the back seat of the car. We said goodbye to the shrine caretaker, reversed the car onto the road, and continued (we did not have any more car trouble for the rest of the day). About 30 to 40 minutes later the monk told us to stop and we dropped him off. Aung and I then decided that it was best to soon stop and park the car in the shade of a tree to keep the engine from overheating. We drove another 10 to 15 minutes and stopped in a small village. All the children of the village quickly gathered around me when I got out of the car. I pulled out my digital camera and began filming them and then showed them the images that I had recorded. They were absolutely astonished by my camera, and all they could do when they saw themselves in the camera's small monitor was laugh hysterically. I then decided to begin making them paper airplanes. Before Aung and I left I gave the children the pad of paper I had been using to make the paper planes, and a few pens and breath mints.

Aung and I arrived in Inle Lake before nightfall. We checked into our hotel and later had local Burmese food.

I will be departing Bangkok tomorrow so I will continue to discuss the journey in Myanmar over the next few days. For now, I must go.

Posted by The Legacy Cycle at 2004-05-02T21:40:00-07:00

Tuesday, May 4, 2004

I am now in Ayutthaya, Thailand, which is about an hour north of Bangkok by car. Before I came here I was in Bangkok for six days—much longer than I expected as a result of recovering from a severe stomach infection that I had developed in Myanmar.

I must share with you an incredible chance meeting I had while in Bangkok. If you remember, on my second day in Myanmar, I met a petite German woman by the name of Manuela; I later learned that she was from Hamburg. We had exchanged emails on that day in the hope of meeting up in Thailand. As soon as I returned to Bangkok we emailed each other, met up, and spent several enjoyable days together.

On Saturday, April 1, Manuela wanted to go to the Chatuchak Weekend Market, the largest market in Thailand.[33] Manuela was on a mission to find and buy fake Swatch watches in the hope of selling them for a profit on eBay back in Germany. When we arrived at the market we saw thousands of Thais and foreigners shopping for copycat brands ranging from knock off Levi's jeans to The North Face backpacks and European fútbol club jerseys. We searched high and low for the Swatch watches with no luck, but funny enough I ran into Angela Nichols (a talented artist and good friend who I had known during my three-and-a-half years in Tokyo; I own three of her paintings: two paintings are in my parent's house and the other hangs over the fireplace of my sister's house). Angela's paintings are colorfully vibrant and uplifting, just like her. We were both pleasantly shocked to have run into each other in the most unlikely of places as she had left Tokyo at the end of January, whereas I had left at the end of March. Both of us had thought, as we said our goodbyes in January, that it would be a few years before we ever saw each other again, but there we were, standing before each other, in this massive market in Bangkok. What a small world!

    Angela explained that she was spending time with her friend Laura, and so she gave me Laura's cell number so that I could contact her to meet up with them in the evening. After leaving the Chatuchak Weekend Market with Manuela, and having lunch, I called Laura and met up with Angela and her, and their other expatriate friends, at Nana Station, which was near the infamous Nana Entertainment Plaza (a three-floor, red-light district building). We actually had drinks at a bar on the ground floor entrance of the Nana Plaza (the bar was full of foreign men with Angela and Laura being the only foreign women in the sleazy establishment). We then walked to Little Arabia to have dinner (where I learned that none of the restaurants in the Arabic district served alcoholic beverages thus explaining why we had gone to Nana Plaza first for drinks). After eating kebabs, couscous, falafel, and lamb tagine we sat outside and smoked from hookahs in an Arabic-style café. I got a buzz from the scented tobacco and beamed with a wide grin for most of the night.

    Well, here I am in Ayutthaya at an Internet café killing time because I have to wait to take my overnight train to Chiang Mai. Ayutthaya makes for a great day trip or overnight stay from Bangkok. It was originally the "second Siamese capital after Sukhotai" until 1767 when the Burmese invaded and destroyed it.[34] The former capital is located on an island that is surrounded by three rivers giving it access to the sea,[35] which enabled trade with merchants throughout Southeast Asia, East Asia, and Central Asia, and as far as Europe (Portugal, Spain, the Netherlands, and France) in the 16th and 17th centuries. It is a

UNESCO World Heritage Site and was the world's largest city in 1700 AD with over a million citizens.[36] The archaeological ruins of the city are "characterized by the remains" of Buddhist monasteries and "tall *prang* (reliquary towers)"[37] whose architecture reminded me of the temples that I had seen in Bagan, Myanmar; but I also saw several temples that looked like temples that I was expecting to see in Angkor Wat, Cambodia.

> The Ayutthaya school of art showcases the ingenuity and the creativity of the Ayutthaya civilization as well as its ability to assimilate a multitude of foreign influences. The large palaces and the Buddhist monasteries constructed in the capital, for example at Wat Mahathat and Wat Phra Si Sanphet, are testimony to both the economic vitality and technological prowess of their builders, as well as to the appeal of the intellectual tradition they embodied. All buildings were elegantly decorated with the highest quality of crafts and mural paintings, which consisted of an eclectic mixtures of traditional styles surviving from Sukhothai, inherited from Angkor, and borrowed from the 17th and 18th century styles of art of Japan, China, India, Persia, and Europe, creating a rich and unique expression of cosmopolitan culture and laying the foundation for the fusion of styles of art and architecture popular throughout the succeeding Rattanakosin Era and onwards.[38]

A famous landmark at the Wat Phra Mahathat temple in Ayutthaya is the severed sandstone head of the Buddha entwined in the vein-like roots of a banyan tree.[39]

Let's see if I can finish up my Myanmar thoughts.

Inle Lake
April 21, 2004

The most pleasant aspect of Inle Lake was its location in the mountains, which provided a cooler climate. I stayed at a quiet and charming hotel in Nyaungshwe that Aung had recommended over another hotel that he insisted was haunted.

After eating breakfast at the hotel on the morning of the 21st Aung drove me to a river that fed into Inle Lake where I met a man who was to be my guide. My guide (whose name I cannot recall) and I boarded a long, thin wooden boat, and our pilot maneuvered the boat out of the pier and south into the lake.

Our first stop was Kaung Daing, the site of a five-day market (every five-days villagers from around the lake converged on the site to bargain, buy, or sell). We stepped off the boat and walked toward the market, but on the way, we saw several men, women, and monks gambling. My guide quickly explained that I should not take any pictures since it was illegal to gamble in Myanmar. There were two games that I saw people playing. The first consisted of three very large dice (perhaps the size of one's head) with each side depicting the colored image of a particular fish or animal. The dice were held up against a short wooden vertical board, and after people had placed their bets the dice were released so that whoever had bet on the three sides of the dice that faced up won. The other game consisted of another type of dice that was spun and then covered by a large bowl so that no one could see which side of the dice faced up when it stopped. After people placed their bets the bowl was lifted to reveal who had won.

In the market, I saw vendors selling fresh fish, skinned chickens and pigs, grounded red peppers, mounds of a very salty paste, dried fish for snacking on, tofu, and anything else the Burmese considered appropriate for an outdoor rural market. There were also hygienic items such as soap and organized piles of thanaka wood used to make the cosmetic cream that I had seen applied to the cheeks and faces of many women and children in Myanmar. Weighing scales and measures were always used in the transaction process.

After the market, my guide and I boarded the boat again and traveled to a collection (or village) of simple houses that were built on stilts over the lake. In the village, I met two blacksmiths that were working with their young apprentices in fashioning metallic items that would be sold to the villagers, fishermen, and farmers all around the lake. I watched as they cut scrap metal, heated and molded it, and hammered it down into shape. They produced knives, fishing spears, teakettles, gongs, hoes, and farming tools.

We boarded our boat again and headed south to the floating village of Inbawkon. On the way, I saw tomato fields that rested on thick marshes being attended to by farmers who appeared to glide on their boats as they moved from one row of crops to another. I also saw farmers in the middle of the lake raking up marine vegetation and piling them onto their boats; this collected vegetation was to be used as natural fertilizer for their crops. The technique employed by these farmers to maneuver their boats consisted of wrapping one of their legs around the oar and moving it in such a way that it not only moved the boat forward but also steered it.

In Inbawkon I went into a silk weaving factory. Everything was made by hand and I spent a significant amount of time watching the women operate their foot-treadle looming machines trying to understand how they created the patterns in the cloth they were weaving. I also saw a girl cutting open lotus flower stems and extracting thin fibers, which she moistened by sprinkling water from a bowl. I was absolutely amazed by this and later saw a scarf made from these lotus stem fibers.

> Creating the lotus fabric itself is a handmade artisanal process that requires time ... as it takes approximately 32,000 lotus stems to make just 1.09 yards of fabric; approximately 120,000 for a costume.[40]

After Inbawkon we traveled slowly by boat through another lake village built on stilts to observe the daily life of the people. I smiled at the villagers with fascination as they smiled at me with perhaps the same kind of wonder while I took photos. I am particularly fond of a photo I took of a young girl sitting on her boat with a beautiful, and slightly chubby, smile.

We had lunch before we continued to Nampan village where I saw the traditional process by which paper was produced, as well as umbrellas that were waterproofed by coating it with juices from a wild berry.

We then went to Hpaung Daw U Pagoda to see its famed five gilded and small Buddha statues. But inside I did not see the golden

Buddha statues. Instead, I saw centered within the shrine of the main hall five golden, ball-like (snowman shaped) objects elevated on a stepped hexagon pedestal that could only be approached by men who displayed their devotion through the act of gently placing thin square sheets of gold—no bigger than a large coin—onto the Buddha images. Over decades of devotees continuing this gilded practice the five images have been so caked in layers of gold leaf that today they simply appear as golden balls.

My guide led me up the few steps of the shrine to get a closer look at the five golden images, but he then stepped back and kindly complied to the request of three women to take their gold leaf offerings and place them onto the images.

Upon exiting the pagoda, I saw a boy wearing what appeared to be make-up, a crown, and dressed in shiny, silk, pink embroidered garments; he was surrounded by proud family members and an emotional mother. I first thought that he was a boy, but then assumed from the make-up and pink dress that he was a girl. But my guide informed me that he was indeed a boy and that I was witnessing the Theravada Buddhist shinbyu (novitiation) ceremony, which symbolized the most important obligation of parents to release their son to become a monk and embrace the life and teachings of the Buddha. He said that the boy was dressed in traditional royal attire to represent the same path taken by Prince Siddhartha 2,500 years ago who rejected the luxury of his material, royal upbringing to set forth in search of the Four Noble Truths through a monastic lifestyle.[41] I later saw the boy seated on a throne and shielded from the sun by two golden Burmese umbrellas in a private, long-tail boat that had large arrangements of flowers at its center while traditional Burmese music blasted from a bullhorn located near the bow. My guide further explained that the boy was most likely being taken to the monastery to complete the ceremony by exchanging his fine silk garments for white robes before Buddhist monks shaved his head. After, the boy would be given his saffron-colored robe and alms bowl.

After resting at a monastery where I was able to pass some time by playing fútbol with monks who were half my age we went to Nga Phe Kyaung (also known as "jumping cat monastery"), our last stop. A satisfying and consistent breeze flowed through the dark wooden temple built on stilts as men and women sat or lay lazily all around the floor of the monastery while children played outside. A monk threw dried fish crumbs to a group of temple cats and held out a metal ring that the cats eagerly jumped through.

Later that night Aung–dressed up, which was unusual, and full of joy–picked me up from the hotel so that we could eat dinner at his friend's house. I later learned that he had been in the markets shopping and cooking for me for most of the day. It was a very kind gesture. We arrived at his friend's house and I saw outside in the fenced backyard of the home a table with candles. He poured me a glass of Mandalay Rum and the feast began. This, unfortunately, was the beginning of the end for my stomach (as I'll explain in a moment). The Burmese family was very hospitable; it was actually the family of the guide who took me around Inle Lake. Over dinner I learned from my guide that he had lived and worked in Malaysia and in Bangkok, Thailand, but when his father passed away he returned to Myanmar to take care of his mother. He confessed that he missed working in the factories in Malaysia and Thailand and that he wanted to return because he did not like working as a guide around Inle Lake. He also confessed that his brother had died five years ago from a heroin addiction, and that heroin consumption was a big problem in the Shan State ("the average level of [opium] addiction [in 2004 as reported by village headmen] was 2.2%" in Shan State villages that cultivated opium versus 0.2 percent in non-opium producing villages).[42]

Portions of the Shan State, mostly the areas east of the Salween River, are not controlled by the Myanmar military junta. Instead several ethnic armies, including the Shan State Army and the United Wa State Army, operate independently of the Myanmar central government, essentially creating a state within a state, and are heavily involved in the heroin trade. These ethnic armies defend their territories and provide only enough in social services to sustain farmers through the revenue generated from opium production and the export of heroin[43] to Thailand and China. (A 2012 UN report stated that Burma produced 25 percent of the world's opium, ranking second after Afghanistan.[44] The report also highlighted the increased production reaching a record 690 metric tons valued at $359 million.[45]) Unfortunately, Thai and Burmese sex slave trade agents also operate in the Shan State to lure impoverished girls and young women (ranging in age from 12 to 22)[46] with false promises of lucrative jobs in Thailand; once recruited they are quickly sold "into brothels in Thailand".[47]

There are nine dominant ethnic groups in the Shan State: Shan, Intha, Pa-O, Danu, Lahu, Lisu, Taungyo, Ta-ang, Ahka, and Jinghpaw (Kachin),[48] as well as other ethnic groups such as the Wa headhunters. I saw a few Pa-O women in Inle Lake wearing traditional black garments (blouse, jacket, longyi) while wearing orange, red, or yellow turbans.

Getting back to dinner. The Burmese family displayed their generosity by continually filling my plate with fish, rice, and other traditionally cooked foods. In my want to be polite and not waste the food that I had been served I desperately tried to finish everything on my plate while complimenting them on the taste. What a mistake. They mistook my false appetite as a sign to keep feeding me, and by the time I had my last spoonful of fish I began to feel sick. Finally, dinner was over and Aung dropped me off at my hotel. I then went into my room and tried to rest, but my upset stomach turned for the worse. To make a long story short I spent most of the night either on the toilet or vomiting into the sink. Thank God no one was there to see or smell the horror in my bathroom that night.

Inle Lake to Bagan
April 22, 2004

This was a long eight-hour journey by car. It was on this trip that I came across beggars for the first time in Myanmar. Aung and I had lunch in a town on the way to Bagan (I couldn't eat much) and when we returned to our car a very old woman approached me and held out her hand. Then a boy dressed in rags came up to us. I thought the woman and the boy were together so I gave some money to the boy, but he ran off. The woman kept holding out her hand. I told her that I had nothing left to give her, and the boy, now across the street, called out to us and began to make fun of the old lady and her inability to get any money from me. I then got into the car and we left.

When we arrived to our hotel in Bagan I simply went straight to my room and rested. I was very sick and suffering from severe diarrhea.

Bagan
April 23 to 24, 2004

During my stay in the semi-arid landscape of Bagan, I explored as many temples as I could handle. There were over 2,000 temples and chedis (remnants of the 10,000 plus temples built during the height of the Pagan Empire) dotting the region in all directions. Many of these temples were built nearly 1,000 to 700 years ago. The construction of these temples started with King Anawrahta (founder of the Pagan Empire) who in 1057 AD–after his conquest of Thaton–brought back to Bagan tens of thousands of artisan and craftsmen captives who were used to build the religious monuments.[49]

Bagan was a magical place, especially at sunset. I climbed one of the numerous temples with a small group of tourists on my last evening in Bagan, sat and relaxed with bare feet, and looked out into the horizon to see the silhouettes of temples peppered throughout the area. Bagan was a ghost of its former imperial self, and it was often said by locals that many of the temples were haunted. In fact, I saw a ghost! Well, not personally, but funny enough I was shown a photo that a Frenchman took at the Dhammayazika Pagoda a couple of years ago, and right there in the photo was an image of a man that should not have been there … it was a *real* photo of a ghost. And it was a bit frightful to see.

All right, I am caught up on Myanmar. After Bagan, Aung and I traveled south to Pyay for a night and then back to Yangon.

Stay tuned for my travels into Northern Thailand and Laos.

Posted by The Legacy Cycle at 2004-05-04T00:57:00-07:00

Free-Rider Problem: Thank God for Public Health Care (2019)

I mentioned in my April 28, 2004 entry that I had suffered from a severe stomach bacterial infection while in Myanmar caused most likely from something I had eaten. The infection got to a point where during my last few days in the country my abdominal cramps worsened, I was getting weaker as a result of not eating much, and there was blood in my stool! I spent my last two days in bed at my hotel in Yangon counting the hours until I could take my return flight to Bangkok where I planned to go directly to the hospital. I was very hesitant at the thought of going to a hospital in Myanmar because after traveling for a couple of weeks around the country I could see that it was an isolated and impoverished nation. Since I had spent time in Bangkok and saw that Thailand was a rising, developing nation I believed that the hospitals in Bangkok would be more capable in treating me than the public health facilities in Myanmar.

I flew back to Bangkok on Tuesday, April 27, withdrew a significant amount of cash from an airport ATM to pay for the upcoming medical expenses, took a taxi into the capital, checked into the same hotel I had stayed in before flying to Myanmar, and then got ready to go to the hospital. I left the hotel, hailed a tuk-tuk, and went directly to the emergency room of a public hospital. The ER was modern and very clean, which eased my anxiety of being treated in a developing nation. I went to the front desk, explained my symptoms and condition to a nurse, and waited in the waiting room. After waiting for nearly an hour my name was called and I was led by another nurse into a consulting room where I waited to see a doctor. Ten minutes later the doctor came in to see me and I explained to him that I had been traveling in Myanmar and while there I developed stomach cramps, had diarrhea, vomited on two occasions, and that I had blood in my stool. He then asked me to provide a stool sample in a plastic cup. I went to the washroom and returned with a sample. The doctor then asked me to wait in the waiting room again until he had the results of the stool sample culture test.

I went back into the waiting room and prayed that the money I had withdrawn from the airport ATM would be enough to pay for the medical visit and treatment. About an hour later the doctor came to speak to me in the waiting room and explained that I had shigella gastroenteritis and that I needed to take antibiotics, he then gave me a small medical plastic bottle with the pills. He said that I should be fine, but if my condition worsened to come back. I then asked him how much I owed the hospital for the visit and the pills. He answered with the following words that I will never forget: "Nothing, we are a socialist country, health care is free for the people."

My jawed dropped. I was amazed by his answer. As a U.S. citizen accustomed to paying for every medical visit and pharmaceutical drug I was absolutely amazed that a developing nation like Thailand could offer free public health care whereas my country, which was much wealthier, could not. This experience had absolutely opened my eyes to the incredible benefits of universal health care.

According to a 2012 World Bank report: "Under Thailand's health schemes, 99.5% of the population have health protection coverage."[50] In comparison, the percentage of people in the United States "with health insurance coverage for all or part of 2016 was 91.2 percent, higher than the rate in 2015 (90.9 percent)."[51] But keep in mind that these percentages are–in part–a result of the Patient Protection and Affordable Care Act (Obamacare), which was passed in 2010. Prior to the passing of Obamacare, the Census Bureau's 2006 data revealed that "the percentage of people without health insurance for the entire year was 15.8%, an increase from 15.3% in 2005."[52]

- During 2006, 47.0 million people were without health insurance for the entire year, a 2.2 million increase from 44.8 million people in 2005.

- The uninsured are disproportionately between the ages of 18 and 24, and have family incomes below $25,000. In 2006, 29.3% of 18 to 24 year olds are uninsured, the highest uninsured rate of any age group.

- While the majority of the uninsured are low-income, almost 38% of the uninsured have family income above $50,000.

- Employer-sponsored insurance continues to be the largest source of health insurance coverage in 2006, covering 59.7% of the population, a decline from 60.2% in 2005.

- The percentage of children under 18 without health insurance rose from 10.9% in 2005 to 11.7% in 2006.[53]

It is perplexing to think that the world's most powerful economy is unable to achieve Thailand's level of universal health care. In addition, it should be noted again that Thailand has successfully achieved universal health care for **99.5%** of its people by allocating 3.15% to 4.1% of its GDP (2000 to 2018) toward health expenditure.[54,55,56] Thai government expenditure on health as a percentage of total government spending ran anywhere between 12% to just under 18% from 2000 to 2015,[57] and was 15.6% in 2017,[58] and 15.3% in 2018.[59]

The U.S., on the other hand, allocates between 16.4% to 17.1% of its GDP (2010 to 2017)[60] to provide health care coverage for only 90% of its total population. U.S. government expenditure on "Medicare, Medicaid, the Children's Health Insurance Program (CHIP), and Affordable Care Act (ACA) marketplace subsidies" accounted for "26 percent of the budget in 2017, or $1 trillion."[61]

> As would be expected, wealthy countries like the U.S., tend to spend more per person on health care and related expenses than lower income countries. However, even as a high income country, the U.S. spends more per person on health than comparable countries. Health spending per person in the U.S. was $10,224 in 2017, which was 28% higher than Switzerland, the next highest per capita spender.[62]

In a data analysis report published on the Peterson-Kaiser Health System Tracker website it is stated that "on average, other wealthy countries spend about half as much per person on health than the U.S. spends."[63] More specifically, "the average amount spent on health per person in comparable countries [similar OECD countries] ($5,280) is roughly half that of the U.S. ($10,224)."[64]

Why does the U.S. spend such a "disproportionate amount on health care"?[65] The answer lies within the size of its private health care system; "its private sector spending is triple that of comparable countries."[66]

While the U.S. has much higher total spending as a share of its economy, its public expenditures alone are in line with other countries. In 2016, the US spent about 8.5% of its GDP on health out of public funds—essentially equivalent to the average of the other comparable countries. However, private spending in the U.S. is much higher than any comparable country; 8.8% of GDP in the U.S., compared to 2.7% on average for other nations.[67]

Free market economists often argue that there is improved productive efficiency as a result of the competitive nature of a market that is not influenced by government intervention. In theory, and in reality, there is a high degree of truth to that statement as long as there is the competitive element in the market that results from low barriers to entry, which provides the opportunity for hundreds, to thousands, to tens of thousands, or more, firms to enter the market and compete. The competition between firms fulfilling a similar consumer need provides a market equilibrium price to be established; a firm that charges too high a price loses since consumers gravitate toward the firms offering a substitute good or service at a lower price; and a firm that charges too low a price sees the opportunity to raise price to the market equilibrium. Competition is key to any well-functioning free market. The U.S. propagates itself as a high functioning capitalist nation. U.S. citizens, buying into the propaganda, often confuse socialism with communism and support further capitalist legislation that erodes their own federal government social benefits. But U.S. government financial bailouts (like the $700 billion U.S. financial-sector rescue plan of 2008) are rarely categorized as a socialist, interventionist policy by right wing politicians.

This all aside, how productively efficient is the U.S. (predominately private) health care system? According to the World Health Organization, the overall efficiency of the health system in the U.S. ranks 37 out of 191 nations (Costa Rica is 36, and Slovenia 38).[68] The top ten ranking countries are as follows:

1. France
2. Italy
3. San Marino
4. Andorra
5. Malta
6. Singapore
7. Spain
8. Oman
9. Austria
10. Japan[69]

The European nations in this list would typically be categorized by U.S. conservative politicians and supporters as socialist. When your health is on the line would you rather be living in a full-fledged capitalist or socialist nation?

But getting back to the question, why is it that health care in the U.S. is so damn expensive? From an economic standpoint, part of the answer is the lack of competition within the sector–thus that central element to any free market capitalist system is missing within the U.S. health industry. According to the "Centers for Medicare and Medicaid Services (CMS) … 91.1 percent of the U.S. population had medical insurance" in 2016.[70] To break that percentage down, "according to the 2017 U.S. census, 67.2 percent of people have private insurance while 37.7 percent [66.6 million people enrolled in Medicaid and 56 million enrolled in Medicare[71]] have government health coverage."[72,73] The U.S. population in 2017 was 325.7 million, thus 218.8 million Americans have private health insurance as their only option as they do not qualify for either Medicare or Medicaid. Private health care providers and pharmaceutical companies know that the majority of the U.S. population has no access to a cheaper alternative (namely public health care), this places them in the unique position to raise price as much as they would like (remember, as stated previously, on average the U.S. spends about $10,224 on health per person whereas similar OECD countries spend about $5,280[74]).

In addition, private health care providers and pharmaceutical companies also know that the elasticity of the drugs and health services (necessities) they provide are inelastic, which is an economic term describing the phenomenon in which a company is able to raise price by a percentage that is greater than the percentage decrease in the quantity demanded. A horrifying example of this was when former hedge fund manager, founder, and former CEO of Turing Pharmaceuticals, and convicted felon, Martin Shkreli increased the price of the "lifesaving drug Daraprim [a drug that costs "around $1 to make" and "used to treat AIDS, malaria and cancer patients"] by more than 5,000 percent ["$13.50 per pill to $750 per pill"] in September 2015."[75] If no cheaper alternative is provided to consumers in desperate need of a lifesaving drug such as Daraprim, then consumers simply pay the hiked up price.

 Another example is the high price of insulin for those suffering from type 1 diabetes ("the average U.S. list price (WAC) of the four insulin categories increased by 15% to 17% per year from 2012 to 2016"[76]). This price gauging (the price for one vial in 1996 was $25, but in 2019 it retails "around the $300 range"[77]) is typical behavior of oligopolistic firms, in this case, the three biggest manufactures are "Sanofi, Novo Nordisk, and Eli Lilly, who account for more than 80% of the insulin supply globally."[78] Economists often warn that when a few firms dominate the market there is the danger that they may collude and become, collectively, a monopoly. Thus, this market for the provision of insulin has failed absolutely for T1 diabetics such as Ms. Marston who has to spend "$2,880 a month just to keep" herself "alive," which is more than she was making "even working 50 hours a week."[79]

 How do U.S. citizens solve all of this? It is an extremely daunting question, but I feel that I found part of the answer in that Thai public hospital that treated me (a foreigner) for free.

CHIANG MAI, THAILAND

Thursday, May 6, 2004

I arrived to Chiang Mai, Thailand yesterday morning by overnight train from Ayutthaya; the journey was 12 hours.

I bought my train ticket in Ayutthaya for the sleeper car and made sure that I was assigned a lower sleeper because I knew it had a window and was more spacious than the upper one. As soon as I boarded the train I jumped into my bed, which had already been prepared by a train attendant, and sat with my legs crossed staring out into the night as the train began the journey to northern Thailand. The sleeper car was very quiet because most of the passengers had boarded the train in Bangkok and were already fast asleep or keeping to themselves behind the curtains that provided some privacy.

After watching the passing night view beyond my window and listening to a selection of progressive rock songs on my MiniDisc player I decided to lie in bed and try to fall asleep, which was difficult because the train continually rocked my body from side to side; it also didn't help to hear the door at my end of the sleeper car bang repeatedly against its own door frame. Regardless of the train rocking and the door banging I eventually fell asleep.

The light of the rising sun woke me up because there were no window curtains to block it. Lying in bed I looked out seeing the tops of tropical trees pass by. Eventually I sat up and watched my "window vision," which was permanently stuck on The Moving Landscape Channel. I saw villages of thatched homes built on stilts–much like the homes that I had seen in the rural areas of Myanmar–and Thai men working along the tracks clearing land or burning dried grass.

About an hour before arriving to Chiang Mai a Thai train attendant converted my sleeper into formal train seats. When he was done, I sat down and continued to look out the window. And as we arrived into Chiang Mai the same train attendant sat on the arm of my seat and rested his hand on my leg as if it was completely normal to touch a stranger. I'm sure it was normal for him, but I was not comfortable at all with him touching my leg. Luckily, he stood up and began assisting the other passengers unload their belongings.

As expected there were Thai male and female touts running up to all the backpackers (there were quite a few of us) exiting the train to persuade us to go to *their* particular hotel. I wanted to find a guesthouse on my own, but I finally gave in to a Thai lady who was relentless. She guaranteed a nice hotel room complete with air conditioning and television for 400 baht a night. I agreed and she whisked me away to her driver where I met two other victims, a backpacker from Finland and another from France, and we were then driven to our respective guesthouses.

When I arrived to the Winner Inn Hotel, which was located just outside the southeastern corner of the Old City wall, I first inspected my room before agreeing to stay; I was pleased to discover that the room was clean, and had an air conditioner and television as promised. After signing my check-in documents, I began unpacking a few things from my bag in my room until I received a phone call. *Odd?* I thought. I picked up the receiver and heard a male Thai voice that said, "Hello, sir. I want to give you a map. Can you come down?"

"Sure," I answered without really thinking whether this was some type of money scheme. After locking up all my important belongings again into my bag I went downstairs to the lobby.

The Thai man asked me to sit down at one of the hotel's restaurant tables. Then began the barrage of sales pitches for trekking tours and elephant rides just outside Chiang Mai. I quickly rejected the tour guides offers and returned to my room.

After taking a shower I left my hotel in search of breakfast and was soon approached by a young, twenty-something, scruffy-looking Mexican traveler named Juan. After speaking a bit with him in Spanish about places we had traveled to in Southeast Asia he decided to join me on my search for a morning meal.

We soon found a place and as I ate he told me about the work his father did in Mexico as well as some aspects of PRI's (Partido Revolucionario Institucional) 71-year hold on the nation's political system that finally came to an end in 2000. As he spoke I recalled from the news that I had seen or read, bits and pieces of the political events that he was referring to such as the assassination of PRI presidential candidate Luis Donaldo Colosio Murrieta in 1994. I spent most of the day with him, and we talked about everything from yoga to his travels in India, to my travels in Myanmar, to our families, to the importance of respect and loyalty in all relationships.

This morning (May 6) I walked in the area southeast of Tha Phae Gate and was disappointed to see what looked like streets in Niagara Falls or Wisconsin Dells where tacky tourist shops and fast food restaurants reigned. On one particular four-way intersection–just a block or two from the tourist information center–there was a McDonald's, Starbucks, and Häagen-Dazs. And further down the street I saw a Pizza Hut and Baskin-Robbins. There was also a strip along the infamously sleazy Loi Kroh Road that had several German restaurants complete with German flags, German beer, and Thai staff wearing either Bavarian lederhosen outfits or dirndl dresses!

I saw tourists along these streets in all directions buying Thai shirts and pants that had been altered from their traditional design to satisfy the apparel needs of foreigners. Most of the restaurants that I saw accepted Visa and MasterCard and offered Italian, Mexican, and Japanese cuisine, as well as other types of ethnic food. It was obvious that the city thrived on tourism. And at night there was no shortage of bars that catered almost exclusively to foreign men by providing billiard tables, beer, and Thai women ready and waiting to be picked up.

I felt–to a degree–that this part of Chiang Mai, along with many other towns and cities throughout the country, had lost itself in its quest to gain the $, € or ¥ from tourists (travel and tourism made up 17.2 percent of Thailand's GDP in 2004 and increased to 20.8 percent in 2015).[1] There were many travel agencies in Chiang Mai that provided one, two or three-day trips through the northern regions of the kingdom. And because tourists continue to come by the train, bus, and airplane load (11.6 million visitors in 2004, which increased 29.8 million in 2015)[2] the exotic essence, which was perhaps the initial reason why tourists began coming here, is being lost to the increasing number of Western franchise businesses. As a result, tourists, in the years ahead, will go to other Southeast Asian nations in search of the exoticness that is being eroded by the tourism boom in Thailand. Perhaps Laos and Myanmar will become the next hot tourist travel destinations (I already heard predictions from backpackers I had met in Thailand that Laos would soon lose the unique (as perceived by Westerners) essence that had made it so special). At this rate, Myanmar will be the last of the Southeast Asian nations to fall to the armies of marching tourists and the capitalist demands of a globalized free market economy.

While living in Japan I came across the website for a DJ who went by the name Yukalicious, and on her site, there was a link to a Japanese not-for-profit organization called Ban Rom Sai based in Chiang Mai. Ban Rom Sai (www.banromsai.org) is an orphanage for Thai children who were born with HIV. I contacted Ban Rom Sai a few months ago informing them that I would be traveling to Chiang Mai and that I would be able to help them create an English version of their website—which I later completed with the aid of my incredibly talented friend Janusz Migasiuk—so that they could begin soliciting and getting donations from individuals and organizations from English speaking nations. This afternoon I was able to contact a volunteer at Ban Rom Sai by the name of Nanako, and we arranged to meet at Tha Phae Gate.

Posted by The Legacy Cycle at 2004-05-06T22:04:00-07:00

Friday, May 7, 2004

Chiang Mai is a popular destination for tourists because it is a starting point to visit the northern hill tribes of Thailand and to trek through the surrounding mountains. Travel agencies abound offering package tours of all the overexploited sights and sounds of northern Thailand, as well as package journeys to Luang Prabang, Laos. On the exterior, Chiang Mai appeared to cater solely to tourists (particularly the following roads: Loi Kroh, Chang Klan, and Tha Phae), and because of that I quickly lost interest in the place. Prostitution and sex tourism were apparent; rare was the moment when I didn't see a lone Western man on the prowl for a young Thai girl. At night, I saw Western men of all ages with a Thai girl or two.

The only thing that I really enjoyed in Chiang Mai was Gekko Books because they had the largest collection of English secondhand books that I had seen thus far in my travels in Southeast Asia. And here on the table before me, in this Internet café, are a few purchases that I had made at that bookstore; I'm sure I will go back tomorrow to buy another book or two.

If you want to come to Chiang Mai and do something that is not so typical I recommend volunteering at one of the many surrounding orphanages. Yesterday and today I spent some time at Ban Rom Sai.

During the Vietnam War Bangkok gained a reputation as an R&R sex capital for GIs.[3] Today, sex tourists from the U.S., Canada, Europe, Japan, Malaysia, and other Asian and Western countries continue to flock to Thailand to indulge in its thriving $4.3 billion sex tourism industry,[4] which–in part–has resulted in a 1.4 percent HIV/AIDS prevalence in the population from 2003 to 2005.[5] As I mentioned in the previous chapter the Tourist Authority of Thailand has blocked attempts by the Ministry of Public Health "to publicize the dangers of AIDS for both Thai sex workers and tourists" to protect a multibillion dollar industry[6] that composes three percent of the nation's GDP.[7] Effectively, the Tourist Authority of Thailand does not want to scare away the sex tourists that come to their country to fulfill their sexual fantasies with Thai men, women, and sadly, girls and boys. It is impossible to travel through Thailand and not see or be confronted by this vibrant sex industry. The fear among sex tourists of contracting HIV due to the high (at times 20 percent) "prevalence [of the virus] among female sex workers" in urban settings like Bangkok[8] has increased the demand for very young women and girls. They are typically lured or sold off by family members in the rural, poorer regions of Thailand, and bordering Southeast Asian nations, to become commodities within the sex trade. The younger the woman, the more likely she is a virgin, and the higher her value for a night's pleasure to a middle-class Westerner. As I stated in the previous chapter:

> Conservative estimates place the number of men, women, and children, "but particularly women and young girls–engaged in prostitution as part of Thailand's illegal sex tourism industry" between 200,000 and 300,000 (the

"figure does not include foreign migrants").[9] Of that number 30,000 to 40,000 prostitutes are under the age of 18.[10]

And who is to pay for this? Children. A September 2000 UNAIDS report estimated that each year "15,000-20,000 HIV-infected women" give birth, and based on a "transmission rate of HIV from pregnant Thai women to their infants is between 19 to 25 per cent, about 3,000-5,000 HIV-infected Thai children would be born annually if no interventions were implemented."[11] A 2002 report by UNAIDS, USAID, and UNICEF "estimated [for 2005] that the number of orphans due to AIDS was 34.8% of total orphans [in Thailand]"[12] and that there were to be 84,000 who would be maternal orphans, 320,000 who would be paternal, and 30,000 who would be double orphans.[13]

I have spent the past two days at Ban Rom Sai learning from the Japanese volunteers about how they support and nurture 27 HIV-positive, orphaned Thai children: there are five infants between the ages of two and three, 11 children between the ages of four and seven, and 11 children between the ages of nine and ten.

The children live in a small, secure tropical paradise built and maintained by the Ban Rom Sai staff. There are three dormitory buildings with rooms for three to four children. Each child has their own bed, closet, and clothes, but they do not have many toys; although they have plenty of outdoor space to play and run around, and they have a beautiful pool. Nanako (the twenty-something Japanese volunteer who picked me up at the Tha Phae Gate, and who has been working at the orphanage for the past three years as an art teacher) explained to me that the children used to go to a public pool. But when it was discovered by the pool staff that the children were HIV-positive they were banned. In response Giorgio Armani Japan Co., Ltd. donated funds to Ban Rom Sai so that a private pool could be built within the grounds of the orphanage to allow the children enjoyment of a pool free from any negative comments or acts of discrimination. Nanako went on to explain that the Ban Rom Sai staff try to keep knowledge of the fact that the children are HIV-positive from the administrators of the schools they are attending because they fear that if discovered the children may be discriminated against or asked to leave; already some of the children are no longer admitted into a local school. As a result, the

Ban Rom Sai staff must drive these children to a school that is farther away.

There is a Ban Rom Sai office in Tokyo, Japan that organizes events to raise awareness, funds, and increase membership. The majority of Ban Rom Sai's financial donors are from Japan. This is in part due to the fact that their website is only in Japanese. To solve that issue I will work with web designing friends back in the U.S. to build an English website for them (I have already bought the domain name www.banromsai.org).

The children at Ban Rom Sai were wonderful and so well loved and cared for by the Japanese and Thai staff. It was a fulfilling experience to play with these children and enjoy their laughter, smiles, and hugs.

I returned to my hotel exhausted after a day at Ban Rom Sai. I don't know how the staff at Ban Rom Sai maintained the energy and strength needed to keep up with so many energetic children. The staff are making a wonderful difference to these children by giving them a home, a sense of family, and a sense of possibility and wonder. Please have a look at the Ban Rom Sai website (www.banromsai.jp). Although you may not be able to read the Japanese text you can search and look through the pictures of the staff and children.

Posted by The Legacy Cycle at 2004-05-07T07:56:00-07:00

Saturday, May 8, 2004

After having pancakes, toast, and tea for breakfast, and buying my bus ticket to Chiang Khong, I returned to Ban Rom Sai for my third and final visit.

I spent most of the day with the three oldest boys at Ban Rom Sai: 10-year-old Surachai and Pond, and 11-year-old Nat. In the afternoon, we drew and painted with Nanako in her open-air art room that was on the second floor of a wooden building; the ground floor was where workers dyed handmade Thai style clothing to be sold online to raise funds for the orphanage. The art room had several shelves full of art supplies, a sink, and short tables.

I watched the boys mold paper clay into the shapes of various animals and objects. But when I saw Surachai, the only boy of the three who wore steel rimmed spectacles, creating a paper clay airplane it sparked my creativity, and I set to work to making an aircraft carrier for the plane. With the help of the boys we began cutting up and folding cardboard into boxes that we put together and painted to make the aircraft carrier. Pond, the shortest and funniest of the three, made a few more paper clay airplanes to complete the carrier. After we finished Surachai grabbed a few paint markers and began tattooing a colorful design of an anchor on my right forearm. When he was done, I painted his bicep with a smiley face and a skull. I painted a few other designs on his forearm, but Surachai soon washed it off out of fear that the Thai staff would scold him.

Gen, a six-year-old, also came up to do some art with Nanako. He was the weakest child at Ban Rom Sai. He had skinny arms and legs and coughed from time to time. But Nanako told me that he had been getting stronger. She explained that he had been having difficulty adjusting to the medicine he was taking and that he needed to change his prescription soon. They had no records of the medication he took before he came into the care of Ban Rom Sai and so it was feared that the medication he was taking was possibly the same medication that he took before he came to the orphanage. Ban Rom Sai receives their medication from the Thai government for free, but this comes with bureaucratic problems. The paperwork needed to change prescriptions for the children takes several months. As a result, a child, such as Gen, must suffer as all the administrative steps are followed. This procedural situation is frustrating for the Ban Rom Sai staff for they are at the mercy of the civil servants who process the paperwork. They feel helpless in their ability to alleviate the children from suffering since they can only wait for the government to approve the change in prescription and to provide the new medication.

After the arts and crafts session, I went to the pool and watched Nat, the eldest and most responsible of the boys, and Pond swim with the Japanese staff who were helping them practice several different swimming strokes.

In the afternoon, I played "super kung-fu fighter" with the younger boys. They had various weapons (toys) and attacked me–the Evil Giant. My secret fighting technique was the paralyzing tickle finger attack to the armpit. It was fun to grab the boys and tickle them until they were laughing so hard that they nearly lost the ability to breathe; it reminded me of when my father used to do the same thing to me when I was young.

It was dinnertime at 5:30 p.m. and I sat down with the infants and youngest children at the low dinner tables to encourage them to eat. I spoiled a few of the kids by spoon feeding them and making dog chomping noises as they bit down on their spoon and chewed their food. I was most impressed with the youngest child at Ban Rom Sai. He was maybe two-and-a-half years old and there kneeling at the table with his spoon in hand feeding himself rice and bits of chicken. I thought that someone would help him eat but no, he was completely independent, determined, and able to eat by himself. I took several pictures of him. He was a little champion.

After a couple of children finished their meal I took their bowls to the kitchen and saw seven-year-old Muu at the kitchen island busy peeling cucumbers; I later learned from Nanako that Muu loved cooking elaborate meals (although his favorite snack was dry ramen noodles) and that he helped the kitchen staff every day.

I had some fruit with the boys for dessert and then sat out on a porch with Asama and a few of the girls. Asama, an orphan with a beautiful smile, was 20-years-old and did not have HIV. Technically she was part of the Thai staff at Ban Rom Sai. Because Thai law requires children to leave their orphanage at the age of 18 Asama was able to find a new home at Ban Rom Sai by helping in the care of the children while also serving as an older sister/role model to the younger girls. The girls gossiped with Asama while complimenting each other on their new haircuts. When I pulled my camera out the girls quickly posed and pointed to their hair.

The sun began to set. It was near bedtime for the children. Members of the staff escorted the children to the bathroom where they took a shower and then dressed in their pajamas. Surachai, Nat, and Pond asked me to wait near their rooms as they began their night routine of meditation, breathing, and stretching exercises.

On a side note, I would like to mention that Nat really looked out for all the other boys (serving them as an older brother), and if needed, he disciplined them. On one occasion, the younger boys played a game of throwing sticks into the air and catching them, but during the course of the game a stick fell on the head of one of the boys. The boy instantly began crying. I ran up to the boy to check on him, but Nat told me not to help so that the boy could learn from his mistake and not repeat it.

When the boys finished their exercises, we went to the art room and I tattooed their arms again with black markers. Nat wanted me to write "I Love You" on his right arm and to draw a flower on his left arm, which I did. I also painted the yin-yang symbol on both his ankles. On Surachai's left arm I painted another skull, and on Pond's arm I painted a skull and the head of Spider-Man. The boys then led me to the television room to watch *Treasure Island* with all the other children.

After only watching the movie for about 10 minutes, one of the Japanese staff members invited me to a birthday dinner celebration back in town for two of the Ban Rom Sai staff. I accepted, and said my goodbyes to the children. I then went to the parking area and joined a group of Thai and Japanese Ban Rom Sai volunteers as they boarded two vans.

We had dinner at a large, open air Thai restaurant, and sat at a long table to eat, drink, talk, and laugh. After dinner, the Ban Rom Sai staff decided to go to a karaoke bar. I told them that I had to get up early the next morning to take a bus to Chiang Khong, and so we said our goodbyes.

Posted by The Legacy Cycle at 2004-05-09T02:13:00-07:00

Sunday, May 9, 2004

I woke up today at 6 a.m., left my hotel at seven, and boarded a bus for Chiang Khong at eight. Six hours later I arrived to my destination.

Chiang Khong is a sleepy little town right on the Mekong River, and right across the river is Laos. After checking into my guesthouse, dropping my bag in my room that had a view of the river, and washing my face, I walked up and down the only road that cut through town and found a few more guesthouses and outdoor Thai and Mexican restaurants that offered evening and night showings of movies on their widescreen televisions.

There is not much to do so I will go to one of these restaurants tonight and watch a movie before going to bed.

Posted by The Legacy Cycle at 2004-05-09T03:15:00-07:00

LAOS

Wednesday, May 12, 2004

When I was in primary school, my teachers explained—on a couple of occasions—that if extraterrestrials were to come to our planet, then logically, they would be a peaceful species for only a "higher intelligence" would be able to travel across galaxies.

Why would anyone believe such reasoning?

If extraterrestrials had achieved a level of technology to travel to Earth they would immediately define the human species as primitive and in desperate need of being brought up to their own civilized standards. Alien colonizers, scientists, adventurers, conquistadors, and missionaries would come and take possession of our lands and resources while killing, enslaving, raping, pillaging, and destroying any human who did not go along with their "higher" and more "civilized" plan.

Western developed nations have a higher material standard of living and produce more sophisticated technology than developing nations. Does the ability of these developed nations to design and produce cutting edge technology mean that they possess higher intelligence? Are developed countries today any different from the empires of the past? After being educated on the "evils" of warfare by our parents and teachers how many of us really take a stand against the unjust social, political, and/or economic conflicts and wars waged abroad by the nation to whom we are a citizen? It seems that in many cases, the majority of the voting population of many Western developed nations such as the United States, simply go along with the decisions of the political party in power. Yes, there may be protests and discontent expressed by those who do not support the war effort, but have these efforts ever really stopped prolonged acts of attrition against weaker nations? Those that speak up against the political and economic decisions of the majority can and will be marginalized.

When the United States and its "coalition of the willing" invaded Iraq in 2003, it was claimed in an effort to gain support at home that the Iraqi people would be freed from the repressive regime of Saddam Hussein. The media filled our newspapers and television sets with images of the torture chambers used by Saddam Hussein's security police to brutalize the Iraqi people.[1] Now from Abu Ghraib (a U.S. military prison) we see images of Iraqi men and women being tortured by U.S. military personnel and contractors.[2]

This is one of many shameful moments in U.S. history. Can Americans really parade the belief that their developed country is devoted to defending the values of equality, peace, freedom, human rights, and democracy? Although there are many Americans that are ashamed of these images from Abu Ghraib prison we must also remember that in the U.S. no one is above the law. Not even the U.S. president. And that *is* something that Americans should be proud of *if* they back it up with action by holding those responsible–up to the highest command–for these crimes in Abu Ghraib to be accountable for their actions. We shall see if that is the case.

Chiang Khong, Thailand to Huay Xai & Luang Prabang, Laos
Monday, May 10, 2004

I left my guesthouse at 8 a.m. after eating breakfast on an old wooden terrace that overlooked the Mekong River and the Lao border. I took an auto rickshaw (tuk-tuk) to the Chiang Khong pier and handed my passport to the Thai authorities so that I could exit the country. Once the exit procedures were done I, along with Sarah and Katie (two British women in their early twenties who I had just met), walked down to the river, hopped onto a very narrow boat and crossed over to Laos. On the other side, I walked up to the border patrol, filled out some paperwork to obtain a Laos visa, paid US$30, and in five minutes I had my visa. Next to the border patrol office there was a money exchange office where I handed over 1,500 Thai baht and received a high stack of cash worth over 360,000 Lao Kip (my first experience in seeing the effects of hyperinflation; the result–in this case–in the wake of the 1997 Asian financial crisis–of dramatically reduced regional demand for Lao exports and thus their currency in the foreign exchange markets[3]). It was an unusual experience to hand over a small quantity of Thai currency and receive such an obscene number of central bank notes (due to hyperinflation there are no coins in circulation in Laos).

After the other backpackers received their visas we all walked a block into Huay Xai–the Lao town across the river from Chiang Khong, Thailand, and the capital of the Lao province of Bokèo. The difference between Thailand and Laos was immediate. Huay Xai was small and quiet with only a few locals walking along the streets. There was no road between Huay Xai and Luang Prabang (my destination). As a result, we had to travel on the Mekong by either "slow boat" (a two-day journey) or speedboat (seven hours). I chose the speedboat.

Katie, Sarah, and I, along with a tanned Japanese man with slightly long hair (he later explained to me that he had worked as a volunteer for an NGO in Iraq before and after the 2003 invasion) and two other American men (who had just finished college) got onto a jeep in Huay Xai to reach the speedboat pier. When we arrived, and began making our way toward the pier, I could see that the speedboats were very narrow and could only seat six passengers, the pilot, and all our baggage. When we boarded the speedboat, we began to comment to each other about how little space there was for each of us; we had to sit with our knees tucked right up to our chests. Before we knew it, we were off accelerating at unbelievable speeds on the Mekong River. Every boat that approached us generated waves that would cause our speedboat to fly off the crests of the waves and back down onto the river with a hard punch to our bottoms. When the river was devoid of ripples, our speedboat would easily glide across the river's surface; and if the boat had wings I'm sure we could have flown for several meters at a time. But when the river was full of ripples and waves the ride was very unpleasant.

About two to three hours into the journey we stopped at another pier to go to the bathroom and have something to drink and eat while locals gambled. At around 2:00 p.m. we switched to a smaller speedboat and continued our journey to Luang Prabang.

An hour later we stopped again at another pier–which was essentially the home of a local–to get gas. This pier was located in the middle of nowhere, but there, in this little thatched home on the Mekong, was a fine selection of soft drinks ranging from Pepsi to Coke to Fanta. It seemed that no matter where you go in the world–no matter how remote the location–you will find someone ready to sell you either a can of Coke or Pepsi (kudos to the extensive distribution network of these two competing soft drink duopolies).

Laos is nearly the same size as the England,[4] but has only 9.5 percent of the population (calculated using 2004 demographic data from the World Bank); and the country has a population density of about 24 people per square kilometer.[5] The population can then be divided between those who live and survive along the Mekong River and those who live in the highlands and hills. As we journeyed along the river I would see a small village here or there or simply an isolated single thatched home.

Laos is also the poorest nation in Southeast Asia (GDP per capita income in 2001 was US$300),[6] which seems to be just enough to cover basic necessities; I have seen more extreme poverty in South America than I have in any part of Southeast Asia thus far.

The speedboat finally arrived to a short bamboo pier that was surrounded by nude children swimming. After we grabbed our bags and ascended the steps of a wooden staircase that led up a steep hill, touts immediately approached and solicited us to stay at one of several guesthouses. After agreeing to take a look at one of the guesthouses we boarded a small truck and bargained the driver down from 600 Thai baht for all six of us to 300 baht; we knew we were still being cheated, but what difference does it make to a traveling foreigner when the overcharged amounts are nothing to lose sleep over. The truck drove away from the pier and after a few minutes we began to drive through the outskirts of Luang Prabang until we crossed an old, iron bridge that took us right into the center of town.

Luang Prabang is small, and feels more like a town on a tiny island in the Caribbean complete with scores of coconut trees and old French colonial buildings. It is a quiet, safe, and pleasant place. Unfortunately, Luang Prabang is being overrun by tourists. At night, it seemed like the locals retired to their homes while foreigners paraded about in search of a restaurant or bar that catered specifically to their dietary needs. One backpacker that I met in town said that he was a bit baffled because at night it seemed like the "tourists outnumbered the locals two to one."

It is upsetting to find that the "isolated" (according to other backpackers I met in Southeast Asia) and landlocked nation of Laos is really not so isolated. It appeared to me that provincial Southeast Asian towns like Luang Prabang were becoming overly dependent on the injections of foreign financial capital from tourists, which is not economically speaking a bad thing. As I learned from Estelle (a young and beautiful French woman with Laotian and Vietnamese roots) the number of Americans who traveled to Laos has decreased dramatically after September 11 causing the economy of the country to decline to a degree. It is dangerous for any nation to be so heavily dependent on a single industry such as tourism, thus the need to diversify the economy, but developing nations do not have the capital resources to do so.

All right, I must go ... I will write more soon.

Posted by The Legacy Cycle at 2004-05-12T21:44:00-07:00

Thursday, May 13, 2004

Luang Prabang
Tuesday, May 11, 2004

I had breakfast at the Joma Bakery Café. The interior and atmosphere of the café seemed to have been inspired by Starbucks. After battling severe diarrhea in Myanmar, I decided to play it safe and stick to foods that reminded me of home; I am done with trying the local dishes in food stalls along the streets. As a result, I deemed the Joma Bakery Café a safe and familiar place for my stomach. The clientele of the café was composed mostly of foreigners who could afford (by local standards) the expensive prices. I had a bagel with eggs and cheese, and a coffee. After reading through a few more pages of the sociology book *Night Market: Sexual Cultures and the Thai Economic Miracle* by Lillian Robinson and Ryan Bishop I decided not to waste more of the morning and left to explore Luang Prabang.

Travelers in Luang Prabang can easily be found on Thanon Phothisalat because it is a street lined on both sides with hotels, restaurants, and travel agencies. The Royal Palace (constructed in 1904 with an architectural mix between Lao and French Beaux Arts styles[7]) is also located on Thanon Phothisalat, and is now a museum. In 1975 the Lao royal family was forced into re-education camps in the north of the country and from what I understand were all killed. I believe that a few extended members of the family are still alive, but they are living lives no different than that of the lowland people of Laos.

I entered the grounds of the Royal Palace through the main entrance that was lined with tall palm trees and had a nice walk around its gardens while taking pictures of a beautiful temple because the palace-turned-museum was closed.

Just in front of the Royal Palace was a path that led up Mount Phou Si, which was a 100-meter high hill that the town of Luang Prabang was located around. I ascended the hill, and at the summit, I found a few small Buddhist shrines and a panoramic view where I could see Luang Prabang stretch out in all directions until it faded into the surrounding tropical forests and mountains to the south and east; and the sky was filled with clouds so large that they looked like mountains. I had never seen a sky so magical as the one that I saw from the top of Mount Phou Si.

After I descended the hill I returned to Thanon Phothisalat and continued walking east toward the end of the peninsula where the Nam Khan River joins with the Mekong River. All along Thanon Phothisalat there were wats (Buddhist temples) that were smaller and more ordinary, architecturally speaking, in comparison to the ones I saw in Thailand; and in the monasteries surrounding the wats I saw many young male monks living and working. Towards the end of the road I came across an elementary school that had just ended for the day. Fathers sitting on their scooters waited for their children who ran toward them with tremendous joy; some children would hop on the back of their father's scooter and be whisked away. Most of the other fathers treated their children to drinks and treats that they had bought from local vendors before heading home.

Life in Luang Prabang is peaceful. I have not heard or seen people arguing in public, and since there are few cars (I have yet to see traffic lights) the sounds of large combustible engines, and the honks of car horns, are absent. Instead, Laotian men and women ride bikes or scooters (and in the case of the women, they steer with one hand while the other holds an umbrella to block the afternoon sun).

The air in Luang Prabang is dry, but the sun is intense. In the afternoon, most locals stay home and lay down on mats on the ground floor of their homes to nap or to look out onto the street. Middle-class homes in Luang Prabang are usually two floors with the ground floor used as either the living area or a combination of a living area and commercial space. People here leave their large front doors open making it easy for any passerby to look in to see them lounging, eating, or napping. Initially, I felt like I was intruding on their privacy as I looked into each open home, but after a while I got the sense that they simply could care less of who looked in. I also noticed that the common hobby at home in the early evening among men and boys was playing checkers with bottle caps.

Once I arrived to the end of Thanon Phothisalat, which actually became Thanon Xieng Thong, I walked down the steep side of a hill to where the Nam Khan River converges with the Mekong. There I saw fishermen on their long and thin boats and children—usually naked—playing in the river. I then traveled north along Thanon Khaem Khong and came across Wat Xieng Thong. I approached the Buddhist temple entrance and noticed an attractive Laotian woman in her early to mid-twenties looking through a *Lonely Planet* book, which sparked my curiosity as I had initially assumed that she was a native. I paid my entrance ticket and proceeded into the grounds of the wat. The Laotian woman also entered and from the corner of my eye I watched her as she ascended the white steps of the main temple, kneeled before the temple shrine, and prayed. I ascended the steps of the main temple as well, and pretended to be interested in the intricate golden designs on the interior walls, but once she stood up I approached her and asked where she was from. She explained that she was from France, but that her parents were from Laos and Vietnam. We began to talk, and soon enough we agreed to have lunch together. Her name was Estelle, and for the duration of the day she was my unofficial guide to understanding aspects of Laotian culture. For example, at lunch she ordered a typical Laotian salad with sticky rice for me, and instructed me on how to eat the dish in the traditional way. I should mention that on my plate there were three or four red peppers. I popped one of the peppers into my mouth thinking I could brave the spicy pain, but I immediately regretted my gamble and found that the pepper was so strong that I began to tear and turn red. I will never do that again.

After the restaurant, we walked along Thanon Phothisalat until she decided to go to her hotel and rest. We said our goodbyes, but before we departed she informed me that at 4:00 p.m. all the monks would begin playing drum music in their wats to mark the phases of the moon.

I continued walking until I sat down in the shade of the trees along Thanon Lim Khong, which is a road that runs parallel to the Mekong. The winds gradually grew stronger, and the sky turned dark. A storm was approaching. Then a branch from a palm tree fell on me as a result of the increasingly strong winds. I left trying to avoid the palm trees and walked south along Thanon Kitsalat, which then turned into Thanon Sethathirat. I traveled east and then north and found the old, iron bridge that I had crossed my first day here from the pier. The threat of a storm subsided and I decided to walk across the bridge to take a few pictures.

After the bridge, I went to Wat Wisunalat (the oldest temple in Luang Prabang; founded in 1515 AD[8]) and watched a boy monk who sat at the top of a very tall palm tree cut something down from it. Drums were then struck—it was 4:00. I went toward the source of the music and found a monk striking a large drum that was enclosed within a temple. I then saw Estelle walking into the wat to see the percussive performance. I followed. She saw me and we greeted each other, and after the performance we continued our explorations of the town until we took a break at the Joma Bakery Café where I was able to learn more about her life in Paris.

We parted again, and at 7:00 I met up with Sarah, Katie, and two Americans that I had briefly met back at Huay Xai. We found a restaurant to eat dinner at and spent the rest of the night talking, laughing, sharing backpacker stories, eating, and drinking. I enjoyed their company; I hadn't laughed so much in so long.

Later that night the two Americans and I met a couple from Wales, and we all decided to sit down in an outdoor bar to drink and share more stories from our travels.

Posted by The Legacy Cycle at 2004-05-13T22:10:00-07:00

Thursday, May 13, 2004

Luang Prabang & Kuang Si Falls
Wednesday, May 12, 2004

I had breakfast and read more pages from *Night Market* for about an hour at the Joma Bakery Café. At 11:00 a.m. I went to a cybercafé to bring this blog up to date. At 12:30 I met up with Katie and Sarah again, and their English friends Paul and Tom (two muscular guys who reminded me, at times, of obnoxiously funny frat boys). The five of us hopped onto a truck headed south of Luang Prabang to the Kuang Si Falls.

The truck dropped us off at a designated area and from there we followed a path that led to the falls. Along the path we saw a small zoo of monkeys, bears and cubs, and a Bengal tiger! We continued and arrived to the beautiful, multi-tiered Kuang Si Falls. We each jumped into one of the pools before the falls and although the water was cold it was a relief from the intensity of the tropical sun.

The ride back into town provided more magnificent views of the surrounding mountains and colossal cloud formations that seemed as if they were the gates to the kingdom of heaven.

That night Katie, Sarah, Tom, Paul and I met up for dinner. I really enjoyed their company and British humor. Katie and Sarah had been friends since the age of 11, and they met Tom and Paul when they were living in Sydney, Australia. Tom seemed to tease Katie and Sarah like an older brother. I enjoyed listening to the jokes they made to and of each other. It was a very pleasant night.

I should mention that Tom and Paul warned me that they had been giving off bad luck to the travelers they had come across during their travels. They provided several stories of travelers who–after meeting them–experienced some horrible or near-death situation.

This leads to my adventure on May 13.

Posted by The Legacy Cycle at 2004-05-13T23:03:00-07:00

Thursday, May 13, 2004

Luang Prabang to Vientiane

Did you know that Laos is the most "heavily bombed nation in history"?[9] During the Vietnam War the U.S. military "flew 580,344 bombing missions over Laos ... dropping 260 million bombs – equating to two million tons of ordnance" targeting the Hồ Chí Minh Trail that crisscrossed between Vietnam and Laos (this worked out to "eight bombs a minute" being "dropped on average ... between 1964 and 1973 – more than the amount used during the whole of World War Two").[10] And it is estimated that "30% of these munitions did not detonate" meaning that there are approximately "288 million cluster munitions and 75 million unexploded bombs" still "left across Laos."[11]

Now with the war in Afghanistan and Iraq it looks like we–as Americans–can really pride ourselves at being exceptionally good at bombing the poorest, least developed nations in the world. What is wrong with us? If the U.S. is so tough, then we should go to war with China or North Korea–isn't North Korea aggressively seeking to develop a nuclear weapons program[12]–shouldn't we launch, in accordance to the ridiculousness of the Bush Doctrine, a "pre-emptive strike" against North Korea? In the eloquent words of George W. Bush's National Security Advisor, Dr. Condoleezza Rice, do we really "want the smoking gun to be a mushroom cloud"[13] delivered from a legitimate villain such as Kim Jong-il? But no, such a confrontation between two nuclear powers would lead (according to the strategic interdependent decision-making rationale of game theory, which can be illustrated in a prisoner's dilemma payoff matrix) to mutual assured destruction of both participating nations.[14] As a result, the dominant strategy (or Nash equilibrium) is deterrence (a draw in which neither nation makes an initial move in this deadly nuclear game).[15] Thus, for a nuclear-armed state such as the U.S., the only aggressive military moves that can be made are against nations that *do not* possess a nuclear arsenal, which explains, to a degree, why the U.S. can get away with invading and/or going to war with poor nations such as Vietnam, Afghanistan, and Iraq.

The eastern portion of Laos continues to be littered with tens of millions of unexploded ordnance (UXO).[16] As a result, "20,000 people have been killed or injured by unexploded ordnance in Laos since the Vietnam War-era bombings ended."[17] It is tragic and sad to know that the world's wealthiest country that is responsible for this destructive mess does not do more to help the people of Laos rid their landscape of these hazardous, life-threatening unexploded weapons. The pages of our history for the 20th and 21st centuries reveal that the U.S., and other powerful Western nations, like to make a mess in poorer nations and leave it there? What wicked things will come to the nations of the First World when, in the immortal words of W.H. Auden, "those to whom evil is done, do evil in return"?

I bought a $16 ticket for an air-conditioned minibus (it was really a van) to take me from Luang Prabang to Vientiane. The staff at the travel agency in Luang Prabang explained to me that the journey would take about seven hours. Now that I've lived to tell the tale, I can tell you that the journey took nearly 12 hours! And I didn't arrive to the capital of Laos in a minibus. Instead I arrived on the top of a truck during a tropical rainstorm that soaked me to the skin.

This is what happened …

Two Israeli women (in their early twenties) and I waited outside our guesthouse from 8:50 to 9:20 a.m. for the minivan to pick us up. When it arrived, we tied our bags to the top of the vehicle as instructed by the driver, and found that inside there were seven passengers headed to Vang Vieng; I was the only one headed to Vientiane, but the driver explained to me through a Thai woman who served as a translator that I would switch to another minibus headed to the capital.

The ride to Vang Vieng was one of constant twists and turns as we ascended and descended the limestone mountains and hills of northern Laos. I nearly became carsick. The views of the mountains with ring cloud formations surrounding their peaks reminded me of the Andes Mountains in Cuzco, Peru. A couple of hours later we saw dark storm clouds rolling towards us, and in the minutes before the rain struck our road we could see a wave of heavy rain shooting down into the valley we were descending into; it was absolutely breathtaking.

In the seat behind me was an American from San Francisco. He had recently turned fifty, and had been traveling through Southeast Asia for the past three months. And he wasn't alone. He picked up a Thai woman—a prostitute—in Chiang Mai to accompany him for the duration of his travels. He was a very nice fellow, much like any professional you would meet in any city in the U.S. (now I had come face-to-face with one of the hundreds of thousands or perhaps millions of men that compose the demand side of the sex tourism industry in Southeast Asia).

The majority of the men I had seen in Thailand with Thai prostitutes were between the ages of 40 and 60. And most of these men were either single or recently divorced from their first or second wife. It seemed that they had come to Thailand in search of some sense of companionship to fill the void and loneliness that they felt in their older years.[18]

This man from San Francisco—I'll call him Mark—was very nice. He could have been my uncle or neighbor or bar buddy. He was a businessman, well educated, professional, and well informed of current events (I was happy to discover that he was anti-George W. Bush). We spent most of our time talking about U.S. politics and the state of things in California. The Thai woman he was with was perhaps my age or a bit older—late twenties. She was also very nice, and she would translate for me when our Laotian driver—who spoke Thai—needed to tell me something. But it was clear by the way she dressed (faded and ripped clothing) and by her chipped, multicolored nail polished nails that she was poor. I tried to be as friendly as I could to her because I felt sorry for her. Here she was traveling with Mark, and perhaps traveling with him was a preferable escape from her life as a prostitute in Chiang Mai ... or not. Mark seemed to treat her well, but in a month or two he would be returning to the U.S. and she would be returning to Chiang Mai to look for her next customer; someone who may not be as nice, someone who could potentially abuse her, beat her, or give her a sexually transmitted disease if she was not already infected. I should mention that the majority of the men who employ the services of Thai prostitutes in Thailand are Thai men and not farangs—foreign men. In fact, it is estimated that about 75 percent of Thai men have paid for sex at least once in their lifetimes.[19,20]

Five hours later we arrived to Vang Vieng, which didn't look like a town at all because the dozen or so two and three-storey buildings housing guesthouses, travel agencies, restaurants, bars, and Internet cafés catered almost exclusively to young backpackers. I soon discovered that Vang Vieng was a popular backpacker destination because it offered white water rafting, kayaking, and inner tubing on the Nam Song River.

As soon as we arrived to the town, the driver looked a little worried, but he continued driving and dropping the remaining passengers at their guesthouses. I was the last one in the minibus. The driver then explained to me in limited English that I needed to get out, and so I exited the vehicle, pulled my wet bag off the roof of the vehicle, and walked around looking for my next ride to the capital of Laos. Surprisingly, I saw Paul, Tom, Sara, and Katie. We spoke briefly until my driver approached and led me to the bus station. He told me to have a seat, but I knew that something was wrong.

On the way to Vang Vieng our minibus got a flat tire. We had to stop in a very remote local village for about 25 minutes to change the tire. As we waited around the minibus, the children in the village ran around naked or in filthy clothing, at times approaching or retreating from us. One girl in particular (she must have been seven years of age with an infant sibling hanging from her back) ran to stand behind one of the stilts that held up a thatched home and stared at us. We must have looked like aliens to the people and children of the village with our bags, portable music players, sunglasses, and relatively clean, lightweight backpacker clothing. I noticed that some of the village girls would hit each other on occasion. And then we saw an old man approach one of the girls and hit her after scolding her, which shocked all of us. We looked at each other wondering what we should do. Unfortunately, we did nothing.

As a result of getting a flat tire and arriving late to Vang Vieng, I learned from the driver that the minibus that I had bought an advance ticket to take me to Vientiane from Vang Vieng had left without me. The driver arranged for a local pickup truck to take me to the capital. I jumped into the back of the enclosed pickup truck with four other locals: there was a middle-aged Laotian man, and a Laotian couple with their three-year-old son who was dressed in dirty clothing, but he carried on with little care as his parents fed him slices of mango and lychee from a plastic bag. I sat opposite the family on one of the two wooden benches that ran along the enclosed cargo area of the pickup truck. A couple of hours into the journey the mother of the boy became carsick and began vomiting into the plastic bag. I offered her my bottled water, but she did not want it. And for the duration of the ride she would continue to vomit from time to time into the bag.

Over the next few hours we picked up more locals who were also headed to the capital, and as we began to cram into the back of the pickup truck I noticed that they preferred to sit away from me. Was there something wrong with me? Did I smell? Soon enough the back of the truck was crammed with travelers, but that did not stop the driver from picking up more people who stood on a short, steel platform that protruded from below the rear bumper while holding on to the roof rack.

About two to three hours later we arrived to Muang Phôn-Hông. We were instructed by the driver to get out of the truck because that was the final destination. As we exited the truck one of the women began talking to me in Laotian. I had no idea what she was saying or asking of me, but after she repeated the word "Vientiane" several times I reasoned that she wanted to know if I was going there. I quickly figured out that she was going to the capital as well. So as soon as we got out of the truck we waited for another pickup truck that was headed to Vientiane. Within 15 to 20 minutes we found another ride. I threw my bag on the roof rack of the enclosed pickup truck while the woman crammed into the back. The only space available for me was to stand on the short, steel platform that extended out from below the rear bumper with several other locals, and hold on for dear life! And off we went.

I thought that at this point it would be impossible for more people to get on and fit in the truck, but we continued picking up more and more people until there were eight men–including me–standing on the steel platform at the back of the truck. I was worried that if the truck made a sharp turn or hit a bump or hole in the road that I would lose my grip and fall straight into the pavement. Luckily, hanging on to the back of the truck was no big deal. The men on the platform chatted away as we drove toward our destination. But that all changed once we saw tropical storm clouds ahead of us, but again the men laughed it off giving me the sense that we were in for a fun and soon to be very wet ride. I quickly pulled some plastic bags from a pocket in my backpack and covered the pouch that had my digital camera. The storm clouds were then upon us. I held on and prayed, but I must confess that I did enjoy the challenge and the adventure of this road trip.

After we stopped for gas we picked up more people! One individual was physically challenged and used a tricycle type of contraption to be mobile. As a result, several Laotian men exited from the packed and enclosed cargo area to provide space for the handicapped man, and climbed onto the roof to help lift the tricycle onto the roof rack. These Laotian men then motioned for me to get onto the roof with them to make more room for the people who were now getting into the truck. From that point on I traveled to Vientiane on the roof knowing that if this overcrowded truck flipped over I was either going to crack my head open and lose a limb or die. I held on to a roof rack side rail and watched the electrical storm fill the dark horizon.

We drove straight through the storm and arrived to the outskirts of the capital without incident. We were instructed by the driver to get out and from there I took a three-wheeled taxi into town with three Laotian women—one of them kept touching my leg—and another Laotian man.

Once we arrived to the center of the capital I got out and took another three-wheeled taxi to Nam Phou Fountain. I then walked until I found a guesthouse to stay in for the night.

And here I am, alive and well after my adventure to Vientiane.

Posted by The Legacy Cycle at 2004-05-13T23:27:00-07:00

Sunday, May 16, 2004

Friday, May 14, 2004

Just as in Luang Prabang, all I needed was one day to explore the small city of Vientiane. The capital sits right along a huge curve in the Mekong River with Thailand on the other side, perhaps not the best strategic location. But, why would Thailand ever invade Laos and ransack its capital? Laos is landlocked, considered to be one of the most corrupt countries in the world,[21] in 2002, 33.5 percent of the population lived below the national poverty line,[22] and it is the most "heavily bombed nation in history"?[23]

I decided to change hotels Friday morning since the one I had slept in was dingy and unpleasant, and I had to use a shared bathroom in the hallway. I found a brand-new guesthouse on Thanon Setthathirath. The owners of the establishment were very friendly. They did not have a single room available so I took a double with a fan for US$6. The room was very clean (it was only a week old) and I had my own private bathroom.

At the front desk of the guesthouse I met a Laotian man who had been helping out with the opening of the guesthouse. He explained that he had lived in California and that he came back to Laos to help his wife's sister with the hotel because she owned it.

During my first morning walk through Vientiane I noticed a few city blocks that had restaurants and shops that catered to tourists. In addition, along the streets there were plenty of three-wheeled taxis, which puzzled me as to how much business these drivers could get since most of what a foreigner would want to see was easily within walking distance. Perhaps that explained why most of the taxi drivers I passed (for the sake of diversification) offered pot.

"No thank you," was my constant reply.

I had breakfast at another Joma Bakery Café; it was a chain with only two locations. The café in Vientiane was essentially the same as the one in Luang Prabang. As soon as I sat down with my "Egger Bagel" and apple juice I noticed a Caucasian man walk in. He was kind with the staff and after getting his cinnamon roll and coffee he sat at the table next to me. He then introduced himself by asking the question I never fail to hear now, "How long have you been traveling?" I answered his question and explained that I had been living in Japan prior to my travels. He then told me that he had been living in Laos for about 10 years with his family. He was an English teacher and was originally from Miami, Florida. He explained that he was also a pastor of a Baptist congregation. He was very talkative, but it was nice to listen to him and how dedicated he was to his faith, his relationship with God, his work, and his family; he had seven children (the oldest and the youngest were boys and the rest were girls). By 10:30 a.m. he had to run to work, but he invited me to have lunch with him. We agreed to meet at 12:30, but I wasn't completely sure if I could make it or not since I had just arrived and I wanted to explore the capital first before sitting down with anyone for a chat.

As soon as I was finished eating breakfast I decided to check my email. After that I walked to the Nam Phou Fountain and continued north for a block and then east and then north again until I came across That Dam, a weathered brick stupa that looked abused by both natural and human elements (I discovered later that it was originally covered in gold, but that during the Lao Rebellion of 1826-1828 the Siamese pillaged the precious metal[24]). Just next to the stupa was the U.S. Embassy where I saw the old red, white, and blue waving from a towering flagpole behind a tall, white wall. I walked toward the flagpole and realized that the embassy actually occupied both sides of the street with Laotian security officers and policemen sitting lazily along it. As for the embassy, I couldn't see much of it because the walls were too high.

I continued northeast and walked past the Talat Sao morning market, but because it was afternoon the market was lifeless. I soon came across Patuxai, which appeared to be the Laotian version of the Arc de Triomphe in Paris; a reminder that Laos was a colony of France. When I walked under the "Victory Gate" I saw a plaque that read as follows:

> At the northeastern end of the Lane Xang Avenue arises a huge structure resembling the Arc de Triomphe. It is the Patuxai or Victory Gate of Vientiane, built in 1962, but never completed due to the country's turbulent history. From a closer distance, it appears even less impressive, like a monster of concrete. Nowadays this is a place used as leisure ground for the people of Vientiane and the 7th floor on top of the building serves an excellent view point over the city.

I thought it strange that the plaque described the arc as a "monster of concrete." I guess you could say that. It wasn't particularly attractive, but I wouldn't have described it as a monster. There was a park behind the arc where I saw groups of locals (families, teenagers, and children) using the grass areas to lounge about or to play games such as fútbol.

I continued walking northeast and saw something up in the clouds that I could not explain—it appeared as a black dot in the sky—and just below it I saw in the distance the large, gold-covered stupa Pha That Luang. Although the stupa was far and the sun was beginning to set, I decided to walk toward it, and the black dot in the sky. It took about 25 minutes to reach the stupa and along the way I saw several embassies and Vientiane College, which was simply a four-storey building.

Arriving to Pha That Luang I saw a large car parking area with no cars, a gate that led to the stupa, and, in all directions, I saw many women and a few men jogging while scooters sped past me. I walked through the gate and discovered that the black dot in the sky was actually a sizeable kite that three foreigners were flying. I took some photos of the stupa and decided to make my way back before sunset. Upon exiting the car parking area, I saw a public aerobics area complete with a stage and an aerobics instructor going through the motions as locals of all ages moved their bodies to the thumping beats of house music. And as I walked back I saw more locals jogging; it seemed like the whole city was exercising.

When I arrived back to the center I sat down at an Indian restaurant to read a book, eat, and listen to the loud conversations that a group of young travelers were having about sex and other related topics.

I left as soon as I finished my meal, went to an Internet café to send a few emails, and retired for the night.

Posted by The Legacy Cycle at 2004-05-16T04:45:00-07:00

Sunday, May 16, 2004

Vientiane
Saturday, May 15, 2004

Since I felt that I had seen most of the city I bought an overnight bus ticket back to Bangkok that would depart at 5:00 p.m. I then spent the rest of the morning walking west on Thanon Setthathirath where I came across more temples that were on both sides of the street. I took a few photos of the temples against a backdrop of the most amazing cloud formations.

The skies and massive cloud formations that I had seen in Laos should be considered a tourist attraction. I am typing here in Bangkok in longing to see again the glorious Laotian sky after having only seen dull skies today.

After Thanon Setthathirath I had lunch and spent some time reading a book detailing the evils of the sex trade in South and Southeast Asia.

Five o'clock came and so did my bus, which picked me up near my hotel. I boarded the bus and it continued through the streets of Vientiane picking up more backpackers. Twenty minutes after picking up the last backpacker we arrived to the Thai-Lao Friendship Bridge, which was where we would cross the border. We had to exit the bus and line up before a customs office to have our passports reviewed and stamped. As I waited in line I was able to glimpse the passports of the Laotian women before me as they were being stamped and it appeared from the dates that these women crossed the border nearly every night. Based on their passports, their clothes, and tattoos it was my guess that they were Laotian prostitutes crossing over to the Thai side for work. The Thai baht is stronger than the Laotian Kip so there is an economic incentive to work across the border and bring back the stronger currency.

The bus ride back to Bangkok was pleasant, although it was cold because I was sitting in the back right next to the air conditioner.

Posted by The Legacy Cycle at 2004-05-16T05:36:00-07:00

BACK IN BANGKOK

Sunday, May 16, 2004

The bus arrived in Bangkok at five in the morning—an hour ahead of schedule—and stopped at Khaosan Road; an infamous, ghetto-like street lined with cheap hostels, guesthouses, food stalls, restaurants, bars, persistent touts, pirated and assorted goods, and crap catering to the needs and wants of backpackers. I didn't like the atmosphere so I took a metered taxi to Siam Square to stay at any of the guesthouses along the street of where I had stayed the last time I was in the city. When I arrived, it was 5:20 a.m., I paid the taxi driver and walked up and down the street, but all the night security men and women of the guesthouses explained that they were full and that I had to come back at noon to see if there were any vacancies. I walked to the end of the street, to the guesthouse I had stayed in before, sat on an outdoor chair, and read. By 7:00 a.m. the owner of the guesthouse arrived and told me that she had a room. I quickly realized that the security man of the guesthouse (including all the other security men and women I had spoken to earlier) had told me to come back at noon because it was not his responsibility to check me into the establishment. Regardless, I was pleased to get a room. I went to bed and woke up at about 10:30 a.m.

After taking a shower, getting dressed, and eating breakfast I decided to visit and photograph the three notorious streets that catered to sex tourists in Bangkok. I took the BTS train to Ploenchit Station and walked to Sukhumvit Soi 4, which is also known as Nana Tai. The other two infamous roads in Bangkok are Patpong and Soi Cowboy. As I walked to Soi 4 I saw an increasing number of foreign men either speaking to a young Thai woman or walking with a Thai woman or two. And when I arrived to the intersection of Sukhumvit and Soi 4 I saw a man in his forties with a Bangkok guidebook to sex tucked into the back pocket of his khaki pants.

    Soi 4 was lined with several bars that had open-air seating facing the street. The patrons were all foreign men ranging in age from twenty to sixty, and wrapped around them were young Thai women. I continued walking and saw more bars with Thai prostitutes standing outside trying to attract men into their establishments to drink and play billiards. And then to my left I saw an entrance gate with a large unlit neon sign that read Nana Plaza. I walked through the gate, passing bars on each side of the entrance, and stopped in the courtyard of Nana Entertainment Plaza and found the three-storey, U-shaped red-light district building complex—that had short-time hotels that rented rooms by the hour on the second and third floors—to be a hole. In the light of day, it looked beaten up, filthy, and caked in grime. It was here that men attempted to fulfill their sexual fantasies since the early 1980s.

    Right across the street from the plaza was the two-star Nana Hotel. There was a world of difference between the ultra-clean, modern hotel and the decrepit Nana Entertainment Plaza. But it was symbolically fitting from a *Dorian Gray* point of view. To one side of the street you had the Nana Hotel, which was posh, beautiful, well groomed, and catered to middle-class to upper-class foreign professional men. And then across the street you had the filthy, abused, battered, and impoverished Nana Entertainment Plaza. This was literally a visual representation of a demand and supply diagram. The demand was composed of foreign men from developed nations who had come to Bangkok to buy sex from the supply of poor, uneducated Thai women who typically came from the northern countryside (Chiang Rai, Phayao, and Nong Khai)[1] as a result of having been lured, coerced, and/or sold into the sex trade by members of their own family to pay down parental debts or as a means to increase familial wealth.[2] Here on the grounds around me Western men continued to exploit poor Southeast Asian women.

> Sex tourism makes tangible a small part of a global relationship, where the rich depend to an increasing degree for their comfort and advantage on the labour of the poor.[3]

I exited the plaza and continued walking down Soi 4 where I saw more hotels with "massage parlors" located between them. I also saw a modeling agency, which appeared to be a front to fool naïve, young Thai women into believing that they could work as a model in Bangkok when instead they would actually be working in the sex industry. Soi 4 stopped at a dead end where the Thailand Tobacco Monopoly compound was located.

The following will provide a short history and explanation of how the sex industry operates in Southeast Asia, particularly in Thailand. The first written accounts by Europeans concerning prostitution in Siam (Thailand) was by Dutch traders in 1604. One of these accounts from the 17th century explained that a "Thai official was given a government license … to establish a prostitution monopoly" and that it was "staffed with six hundred women whom he purchased for this purpose."[4] Ryan Bishop and Lillian S. Robinson explain in their book *Night Market: Sexual Cultures and the Thai Economic Miracle* that "much of the early prostitution in the Kingdom, in fact, was an extension of concubinage or slavery (often debt based, as it is in the present)" and that "in the patriarchal, feudal society of Siam the number of concubines a man possessed provided a measure of his power."[5] Donald Wilson in his 1994 article "Prostitution in Thailand: Blaming Uncle Sam" stated that as a result of the Bowring Treaty of 1855 that liberalized foreign trade in Siam (and admitted foreign laborers into the country) that thousands of southern Chinese workers emigrated to the country to work in the tin mines followed by thousands of prostitutes.[6] Wilson goes on to explain that in the 1940s there were approximately 85 cabarets on Nares Road, "with one block sporting about two thousand hostesses, and that Yaowarat Road reputedly housed in a nine-story building the largest brothel in the world."[7]

> Bangkok also enjoyed the dubious reputation of being a major producer of pornographic movies during the 1940s. From 1902 until 1960, prostitution was legal in the Kingdom. It being made illegal opened the door for the corruption and victimization that so characterizes the industry today.[8]

It should also be noted that although slavery (the buying and selling of adults and children) was abolished in 1908 as part of the enactment of the Criminal Code that "a child could still be offered as a gift to a debtor, by way of cancellation; a girl could be offered as debt payment and she would become the mistress of the creditor, since this was not expressly forbidden."[9]

> Later, even when the Civil and Commercial Code was enacted and the trading in persons was outlawed, ways around the commerce in children given as labour on the land of others, ensured that traditions were perpetuated …
>
> The rights and duties of children remained under parental control until 1934 …[10]

Although prostitution was declared illegal in Thailand in 1960 under the Prostitution Suppression Act, the Entertainment Places Act in 1966, which provided legislation for the regulation of "nightclubs, dance halls, bars, massage parlours, baths and places 'which have women to attend male customers'" signaled that prostitution would be tolerated to an extent.[11] Soon after, in 1967, during the Vietnam War, the U.S. government contracted Thailand to "provide 'Rest and Recreation' (R&R) services to the troops."[12] Charles Keyes goes on to explain in his book *Thailand: Buddhist Kingdom as Modern Nation-State* that the presence of U.S. troops during the war "helped create a new wealthy class in Thailand from among those people who held contracts for construction or service to the United States or the Thai military. It also contributed markedly to corruption in the military and police, as well as to a dramatic rise in prostitution, alcoholism, and drug use."[13] Thus by 1970, US military personnel (numbering up to 70,000 men[14]) were spending in excess of $20 million.[15]

In 1971, Robert McNamara (U.S. Secretary of Defense under John F. Kennedy and Lyndon Johnson during the Vietnam War) visited Bangkok in his role as president of the World Bank and "arranged to send the bank's tourism experts to plan the development of Thailand's tourist industry."[16] In 1975 the bank's Tourism Projects Department issued a report that "assessed the growth potential of tourism ... irrespective of R&R."[17,18] This "growth potential" of Thailand's tourism industry was more the result of the envisioned and targeted increase in the "single traveler with disposable income (which, in the first instance, means an unaccompanied male)"[19] to Thailand who would continue to provide–in peace time–the demand for the R&R services established during the war. As a result, Robert McNamara (who oversaw the 1967 R&R contracts in his role as U.S. Secretary of Defense) negotiated the World Bank's agreement with Thailand[20] confident in the country's ability to repay the loan in part due to its thriving sex industry and growing sex tourism industry.

The head of the Tourist Authority of Thailand acknowledged in 1976 "the truth of the accusation that tourism encourages prostitution but added, 'prostitution exists mainly because of the state of our economy because everyone needs to earn their income. If we can create jobs, we can provide per capita income and do away with prostitution' (qtd. in Truong 1990, 179)."[21,22] But the authors of *Night Market: Sexual Cultures and the Thai Economic Miracle* argued that "it is hard to see how economic growth arising from prostitution-based tourism could do away with prostitution. On the contrary, since the market set up a permanent demand for sex- and age-specific labor force which, as it happens, ages very rapidly, the way to assure the constant availability of fresh supplies from the rural areas is precisely to pursue national planning policies that systematically deemphasize agriculture and displace fishing and to withhold resources from the regions where they historically constituted the economic base."[23,24]

Jeremy Seabrook supports this perspective by highlighting the following demographic trends in his book *Travels in the Skin Trade*: "Thirty years ago, 1.7 million children were working, mainly in agriculture. There are now 5 million children working, half of them in manufacturing, the rest in the commercial and service sector, including the sex and entertainment industries. In 1960, there were six million working women; this had risen to 12 million by 1995, with up to five million in the sex and entertainment industries. There are an estimated 200,000 prostitutes in the country. There are now half a million drug addicts and more than half a million who are HIV positive."[25]

Many, if not most, developed and developing nations during and after the 1973 oil crisis experienced a dramatic increase in the price of needed inputs such as oil; OPEC (Organization of Petroleum Exporting Countries) increased the price of oil by 70 percent[26] (OPEC oil is priced and traded in US dollars), which made it incredibly difficult for nations to purchase these imported inputs (in the modern industrial and post-industrial economy inputs and outputs are directly or indirectly tied to the price of oil) as they either used more and more of their reserve currency (typically the US dollar)–or more and more of their domestic currency to buy US dollars–to buy a unit of oil. Those nations that quickly ran out of foreign-exchange reserves, which then led to balance of payment problems, resorted to international financial institutions such as the International Monetary Fund (IMF) for short-term loans (injections) of the needed reserve currency. As part of the loan, fiscal and monetary policy conditions were imposed by the international bank on the borrowing nation to ensure that the loan could be repaid. But there have been numerous examples of developing nations being unable to pay back loans set in US dollars due to their domestic currency depreciating over time or due to forced devaluations. The documentary film by Stephanie Black entitled *Life and Debt* illustrates this being the case for Jamaica.

> At present (2001) Jamaica owes over $4.5 billion to the IMF, the World Bank, and the Inter-American Development Bank (IADB) among other international lending agencies yet the meaningful development that these loans have 'promised' has yet to manifest. In actuality, the amount of foreign exchange that must be generated to meet interest payments and the structural adjustment policies which have been imposed with the loans have had a negative impact on the lives of the vast majority. The country is paying out increasingly more than it receives in total financial resources, and if benchmark conditionalities are not met, the structural adjustments program is made more stringent with each re negotiation. To improve balance of payments, devaluation (which raises the cost of foreign exchange), high interest rates (which raise the cost of credit), and wage guidelines (which effectively reduce the price of local labor) are prescribed. The IMF assumes that the combination of increased interest rates and cutbacks in government

spending will shift resources from domestic consumption to private investment. It is further assumed that keeping the price of labor down will be an incentive for increasing employment and production. Increased unemployment, sweeping corruption, higher illiteracy, increased violence, prohibitive food costs, dilapidated hospitals, increased disparity between rich and poor characterize only part of the present day economic crisis.[27]

But Thailand has not met the same fate as Jamaica—and so many other developing nations—that have been economically crushed by the increasing weight of foreign debt. Although Thailand's "rate of borrowing is very high—yielding a deficit in yen, as well as in dollars—Thailand has not been reduced to the debt peonage characteristic of so many other oil-importing nations that have no stable source of foreign exchange. Thailand has been able to meet the interest if not the principal on its deficit, so that economic growth has not been slowed, even as the proportion of foreign debt to GNP (Gross National Product) has more than trebled".[28,29,30] This effectively means that Thailand is able to achieve both economic growth and debt repayment in large part due to the high number of North American, European, and Japanese sex tourists providing a constant supply of foreign reserves (as of the late 1990s, six million tourists visit Thailand annually).[31]

The entertainment sector made a significant contribution to the rapid industrialization of the country in the 1970s. And even though a majority of the clients of prostitution are Thai men, vested interests of the ruling elites made successive governments promote the expansion of tourism while integrating the sex industry with it. Between 1985 and 1990, earnings from tourism increased by 50 per cent; and it remains one of the country's major earners of foreign exchange. A *Bangkok Post* survey in 1987 found that almost 70 per cent of foreign tourists were single men.[32]

Thailand is—to an extent—a central "hub" for the sex industry in Southeast Asia.[33] The majority of the girls and women recruited or sold into the Thai sex industry are from the rural, northern villages and towns of the country. In and around Chiang Mai (Chiang Rai, Phayao, and Nong Khai[34]) procurers from Bangkok recruit and buy women and girls as young as twelve-years-old.[35] Women are also "illegally trafficked from Burma and South China, as much as Thai women are taken to Japan and Europe, revealing an infinite regress in which one nation exploits the female bodies of another, 'less developed' country."[36,37,38]

The northern rural areas of Thailand are extremely poor "where the per capita income can be less than $250 a year"[39] and as a result it is not uncommon for rural families ("85 per cent of the population"[40]) to sell their girls into prostitution to recruiters who provide a payment "representing several months' advance salary, with the rest to be remitted after a ten-month or one-year term."[41] The initial "lump-sum payments" from recruiters provides "subsistence for a family with few other resources and may even finance a new home, cultivation of the family's land, or schooling for younger siblings."[42] But "this form of contract, stipulating interest that can be as high as 100 percent, binds the sex workers to her job, [and] her sense of family obligation."[43]

> As part of brothel recruitment strategies, procurers who prey upon impoverished rural people offer a sum of money up front to a young woman's family for services to be rendered later. The lump sum carries a very high interest rate, however. Women who work in brothels to pay off these debts incurred by their families participate in a unique blend of traditional bonded labor and contemporary capitalism. This is often the only means by which families forced off subsistence farms can acquire the money needed to survive in the cash-based developing economy.[44]

It may be argued that a number of poor families may not be aware or are in denial that they are effectively selling their daughters into prostitution, but from what I have read, I would have to say that these families are not totally blind to the indentured and sexually exploitative servitude these women will be chained to in the end. Thai agents (some of whom were raised by mothers who were prostitutes themselves[45]) approach Thai families and explain to them that they will take their daughters into the city to work as a maid for a rich family, and with the money she makes she can send it back to support them. These poverty-stricken farming families that are desperate for cash, and in some cases, they are not [a study in 1990 "found that 60% of families sending daughters to the brothels were not forced to do so because of acute poverty. Instead they were motivated by the desire to own consumer goods ..."[46,47]], sell their girls off relieved that they have one less mouth to feed.

In an article published in the 1980s by the *Bangkok Post* entitled "I Didn't Sell My Daughter" and part of Sanitsuda Ekachai's collection of newspaper articles in her book *Behind the Smile: Voices of Thailand* the story of Moon Wonglah is provided to illustrate the denial and reasoning of a parent who had sold their child into the sex trade.

> As part of the Lua hill-tribe minority, Moon, and the others in her village are routinely subjected to racial prejudice and exploitation by corrupt officials. Because they are often unable to make their rice farms pay enough to ensure subsistence, many of the men engage in illegal logging (mostly for influential officials who profit from this enterprise), and young women are encouraged to "go south"–a euphemism for entering prostitution–to help their families out of crushing poverty. Across the North "it takes a girl or two to break the rigid cultural taboo," but "when everyone sees the immediate improvement in living standards that the girls bring to their families, all hell breaks loose, and everyone wants to go."[48,49]

> When Moon's husband was arrested and tossed into prison for illegal woodcutting, the mother-in-law of a brothel owner living in the village suggested that Moon send her daughter south. Moon breaks down as she tells Sanitsuda [the author of the article] of her plight. Operating out of denial, she claims not to have sold her

daughter, but only to have accepted a loan, and declares her daughter is washing dishes at a resort. This is why, she claims, she borrowed only 2,000 baht ($80) despite being offered 10,000 baht for the girl. She says the smaller amount was all she needed to buy rice for her other children, and she did not want her daughter to have to work a long time to pay off the money. With the interest charged on such loans, however, 2,000 baht is just as unpayable as 10,000, so the brothel owners always win in these arrangements.[50]

Sociologist Pasuk Phongpaichit estimated in her "1982 study for the International Labor Organization (ILO)" that "the income of sex workers" to be "at twenty-five times that available in other occupations," and that there are "entire families in the countryside" that "are supported on the earnings of one daughter in Bangkok, and entire rural villages are made up of such families."[51]

Northern communities face increasing debt problems because of decreased self-sufficiency, medical bills, consumerism, and investment in modernized agriculture ... These debts can only be paid off by sending youth to work in the cities, the youngest men as hired laborers or construction workers, the women as household servants or prostitutes.[52]

In another article published by the *Bangkok Post* entitled " 'Go South' Young Girl" and part of Ekachai's book *Behind the Smile* the author explained that prostitution "provides virtually the only viable means for rural women to keep their families from starving and to purchase some of the amenities that urban dwellers take for granted."[53] Thus it is indirectly argued that "hunger, poverty," and "greed" are the factors that drive families to sell their young women into the sex trade while also demonstrating to villagers their daughter's virtue through the material possession they obtain from her indentured labor.[54]

The houses, paid for by the girls' remittances, are evidence of a daughter's virtue: her readiness to sacrifice herself, her gratitude to her parents, and, more importantly, her success.[55]

Not only are rural families becoming dependent on the remittances of the women they have sold into the sex trade, but on a macroeconomic level the government of Thailand is also becoming dependent on the continued export of sex tourism services to foreigners thus converting their indentured women into "*the* commodity necessary for the survival of the nation's economy as a whole."[56] According to a study at Chulalongkorn University, "the 1993 income from the export of women ... totaled $20-23 billion, some two-thirds of the Thai national budget (*Bangkok Post*, 15 April 1996). And as the single largest source of foreign currency, tourism provides the nation the means to procure the much-needed fuel resources that keep the engine of industrialization humming."[57]

Another technique a Thai agent may use to acquire a girl for the sex trade is raping her. In rural areas, a girl's virginity is a prerequisite for marriage. As a result, an agent or one of his associates will rape a girl to render her unable to marry, and thus a liability to her family. Thus, the family would be eager to get rid of her since she cannot be used to forge a relationship with another family for economic, social, or political gain.

Louise Brown explains in her book *Sex Slaves: The Trafficking of Women in Asia* that "a girl who has lost her virginity is irredeemably altered. Within marriage, defloration is a symbol of a husband's possession of his wife. It is a travesty for a woman to lose her virginity outside marriage. In the context of the moral codes of large parts of Asian societies a woman is thereby considered to be 'damaged goods'."[58]

The author of *Sex Slaves* further explains that "in the most sexually and gender repressive societies in Asia rape is an initiation into prostitution. A raped girl is unable to marry because she is no longer a virgin. Such women resort to sex work because it is the only form of work available to them and because they cannot survive as single women. Ironically the trauma of the rape and the devastating consequences that flow from it can sometimes bind the girl to her rapist. The perpetrator of the crime then becomes her trafficker and her pimp.[59] In other words, he creates the prostitute and then he profits from her."[60]

There are variations of rape being the instrument to initiate a girl into prostitution ranging from a father raping his own daughter and selling her off, to a brother, to an uncle. There are accounts of husbands selling off their wives. In *Sex Slaves* a Bangladeshi woman explained the following:

> After we had been married for a few days my husband said that we had to go to India to look for work … we travelled by bus to many different towns and villages. My husband knew lots of peoples in these places and we stayed in small hotels. My husband let his friends use me and they gave him money. At first, I refused, but then he would beat me. He was pleased with me when I earned money for him. After a few weeks, we came to Calcutta and he sold me to a brothel. The work here [the brothel] is not much different than when I was married.[61]

In one case a Thai agent fooled a Burmese girl into marrying him. He then took her to Bangkok after having his way with her and sold her off to a brothel.

> Burmese women imported to work in Thai brothels tell Asia Watch's interviewers (1993) stories in which rape is the dominant motif: as a means of recruitment and a form of labor control, as well as a description of the initiatory and subsequent transactions.[62,63]

What is difficult to fathom is how these women accept the idea that someone is able to possess them as property with the right to sell them off to a brothel. But since the vast majority of these women are uneducated and highly dependent on their families or husbands they do not have the skills to survive on their own and simply see themselves as the property of their families, or husbands, or brothel owners.

The fear of contracting HIV (estimates place the percentage of child prostitutes in Thailand that are HIV positive to be 50 percent[64]) has resulted in a growing demand for very young girls; the logic being that the younger the girls, "even if no longer virgins," the higher the probability that she is devoid of a sexually transmitted disease.[65] The author of *Sex Slaves* explains that "the premium age for prostitutes in Asia is between thirteen and sixteen. Virgin girls are in greatest demand and the price that the customers are willing to pay for them is very, very high."[66]

> In South Asia ... A major selling point for virgin girls is that they are not infected with HIV and other sexually transmitted diseases. The health-conscious consumers of virgin prostitutes therefore pay a premium not only to deflower the girls but also to enjoy them without nagging doubts about unpleasant diseases. Condoms are therefore disposed with ... [leaving] girls ... highly vulnerable to infection because they are having unprotected sex on a critical occasion with a man who is likely to have had multiple partners.[67]

Local men, who can afford to do so, will pay up to "sixty times the usual" to "deflower" a young girl who has "not yet menstruated."[68]

The brothel owner also has an incentive to buy or forcibly bring in young girls because the span of their attractive years—and thus work years—will be longer and more profitable than an older adolescent or younger woman. Bernard Trink, writer for the *Bangkok Post*, stated in Seabrook's book *Travels in the Skin Trade* that prostitutes "are finished by the age of 29-31."[69]

A 1992 survey by the Thai Health Ministry indicated that 76,863 prostitutes were working nationwide at 5,622 establishments (20,366 in Bangkok alone). The numbers suggest precision, but the figures are generally considered absurdly low. Political scientist Linda Richter [in her book *The Politics of Tourism in Asia*] (1989) reports estimates of a million prostitutes, which she translates into 4 percent of the female population and a considerably higher proportion of those in the prime years of fifteen to thirty-four.[70]

When girls and women are procured by a brothel owner they are made to believe that they have accumulated, and will continue to accumulate, debt as a result of the investment made to purchase her along with the cost of maintaining her by providing food, ragged clothing, deplorable living quarters, while also paying for her medical bills (periodic health checks, abortions, and medical treatment for sexually transmitted diseases, but it should also be noted that in many cases "should they become pregnant or infected with the AIDS virus [the number of HIV positive female workers as of 1995 was about 700,000[71]], they are tossed into the street with no money"[72]). After having been sold by a family member, violated by a procurer, and bought by a brothel owner these girls accept their indentured servitude and work in the hopes of paying off their fraudulently imposed debt to regain their freedom and dignity.

In regards to prostitutes being diagnosed as HIV-positive and losing their job (after being constantly screened because they work in "areas of high-profile international sex tourism") it is common for them to gravitate down to the "cheaper brothels, karaoke lounges or restaurants" that are less regulated and more "frequented by Thai people – especially migrant labourers, construction and factory workers."[73] These male customers native to Thailand will then contract HIV, return to their villages, and "infect their wives and ultimately, their unborn children ... the number of HIV-positive pregnant women has reached 7 per cent."[74]

The conditions these girls and women work in ranges as a result of the financial spectrum of those who demand these services. Local men from Southeast Asia make up a far greater portion of the demand for paid sex in the region than Western sex tourists who are the minority. As a foreign traveler to Thailand you may not agree because you will see a Western man with a Thai girl half his age hanging off his arm on nearly every corner. But if you dig deeper within the cities and towns of Southeast Asia you will find streets lined with brothels for local men.

> Male privilege in traditional Thai society means, according to the Public Health Ministry of Thailand, that 75 percent of all Thai males regularly visit prostitutes and 47 percent of teenage boys have their first sexual encounter with a prostitute.[75]

Men from North America, Europe, and Japan represent the high end of the industry. The girls they solicit sex from may work in comparably decent conditions. But for Thai men who do not have the purchasing power of a Westerner the women they solicit will be found to be working in horrendous conditions.

> Many are essentially imprisoned in the brothels where they work, some even chained to their beds in concrete-walled rooms without windows. Forced to accommodate five to fifteen clients a day, the women receive breaks only during menstruation. They are often denied any contact with their families and are threatened with prison or beaten if they refuse to meet every demand made of them by the brothel owner ... These women live in constant fear of arrest because when the police raid a brothel, they are always the ones imprisoned; pimps, clients, and brothel owners usually go free.[76]

According to Jeremy Seabrook, women working in brothels in Thailand "work between 10 and 18 hours a day, 25 days a month, with between 5 and 15 clients a day ... they are frequently moved around from brothel to brothel to satisfy the 'need' for new faces."[77]

These brothels could never exist without the protection of local organized crime groups, crooked police officers, and politicians that may even profit from or be clients of the prostitution operation. The sex industry is woven into the very fabric of Southeast Asian society where villagers, city dwellers, procurers, crime syndicates, property owners (someone owns the buildings where these brothels are located within), sex tourists from the region and beyond, and corrupted police officers and politicians continue to play some part in either the supply or demand side of this dark economy.

Dr. Voravidh Charoenloet of the Department of Economics at Chulalongkorn University stated in his interview with the author of *Travels in the Skin Trade* that "trafficking is in the hands of the mafia, in collusion with police and politicians. You cannot touch them. Much of the speculative building boom in Bangkok [which ultimately led to the 1997 Asian financial crisis] has been a means of laundering black money, whether from prostitution, drugs or illegal logging, which are three of the most lucrative trades in the enterprise culture of Thailand."[78]

> In places where the democratic process is weak, high-ranking military and government officials are involved in running the sex industry. In Cambodia, Burma and Pakistan, for instance, there is no real clear line of demarcation between the criminal underworld and the respectable world supposedly above it. They merge into one.[79]

Surveys and reports conducted by NGOs that work with illegal migrant prostitutes highlight reasons why women "forced into prostitution … feel unable to approach the police for help."[80,81] These reasons include the fear of deportation, "difficulty communicating in a foreign language," lack of knowledge about their legal rights, "no access to legal assistance and no confidence in either the legal system or the law enforcers."[82,83] The lack of confidence in "law enforcers" by these women is the result of their knowledge of the collusion between brothel owners and police officers.

> Police forces give their blessing to prostitution. Some participate directly in the trade as clients and as the recipients of bribes and protection money. Some officers

even own parts of the business. In northern Thailand police officers own brothels and they trade in girls. They do not take action against traffickers because they themselves form the largest single group of traffickers. In Cambodia, a survey by the International Organization for Migration revealed that many female brothel owners were married to policemen, and to military or border officials, or that they had very close contacts with them.[84,85]

In the case of southern Thailand there are accounts of Thai officers competing to "land jobs in the Hat Yai police station so that they can take a cut in the lucrative sex trade generated by Malaysian men's sex trips to southern Thai brothels."[86]

Even more frightening "an Asia Watch Report in 1991 stated that over 70% of women in police custody in Pakistan were subject to sexual or physical abuse."[87,88]

Who are these men that compose the demand side of this sex tourism industry? They are every sort of man you can think of from the CEO to the college professor; from your business partner to your neighbor; from your drinking buddy to your friend at church; from your brother to your father; from your uncle to your son to even your grandfather.

Why do Western men fly halfway around the world for sex? Most of the men who partake in the sex tourism industry are in their thirties, forties, fifties, sixties, or seventies. They are single men, divorced men, twice divorced men, and men who never had the courage to ask a woman out on a date. They are lonely in their old age and seek affection and companionship. Many of these Western men will hire a woman for a few days, a week, or more and travel with them around a Southeast Asian country as if they were on their honeymoon. At times, you may encounter a Western man who is convinced that his "hired wife" loves him. But most of these women simply pretend that they care when all they really want and need is the money.

Many male tourists establish a relationship with a particular prostitute that extends far beyond simply satisfying carnal demands. In such situations, the women aid the men in negotiating the vagaries of being in a different country and culture. They shop and bargain in the local markets for the men, help them make intracountry travel arrangements, accompany them on trips, cook for them, and take them to doctors and help them procure medicines if needed. Such an arrangement combines comforting nanny/nurse with naughty night partner and untroublesome travel companion, and it does so without any real commitment from either party. Under the false consciousness of economic reciprocity ... these temporary relationships provide a late twentieth-century postcolonial replication of eighteenth- and nineteenth-century postcolonial hierarchical relations, themselves likewise justified at the time under the ruse of reciprocity ... [But] what must remain absent from tales of reciprocal interaction, however, is the asymmetrical power relations involved, because reciprocity assumes equality. When equality is assumed and remains unsaid, then inequalities are either elided from accounts of interactions or dismissed as not having existed in the first place. Either way, the 'mystique of reciprocity,' integral to the international sex industry, perpetuates exploitative policies and enactments of them under a general misconception that if each person works for his or her own personal profit in all social and economic relations, the community as a whole will advance. The false consciousness that results from this misconception does a great deal to unburden the subjectivities of those who do profit and benefit from the assumptions upon which reciprocity functions.[89]

The demand that drives sex tourism in Southeast Asia also stems from Japanese men. Although the Japanese in the public sphere are non-confrontational, conservative, formal, and courteous. Interviews that have been conducted with prostitutes from the Philippines revealed that Japanese men go "crazy" behind closed doors and are physically brutal, at times forcing them to act out degrading sexual situations.[90]

> The Japanese treat us really badly – and so do the Arabs. I am always a bit frightened to go with a Japanese customer because some of them are really crazy. They seem OK and then something happens and they go crazy. My friend was burned by cigarettes on her nipples by two Japanese men. They treat us like animals.[91]

It can be easily argued that Japanese men are racist toward other Asians. The darker the skin of the girl the lower they will look at her to the point that she may not even be considered human.

> Racism complicates and deepens the domination theme in sex purchase by Japanese men. The Japanese consider themselves to be the 'whites' of Asia ... Japanese customers treat prostitutes differently according to the colour of their skin. Japanese and Caucasian women are treated far better than dark-skinned Asian women.[92]

In Japan, Japanese prostitutes are extremely expensive and never treated as harshly as Thai and Filipino women are treated.[93]

If you go to Japan, I suggest that you walk into any manga (comic book) store and see with your own eyes the type of horrendous sexual fantasies that are played out in their comic porn. They are disturbing to say the least, and reflect the twisted desire that some Japanese men have to brutally dominate a woman or women.

> An element of sadism runs as an unpleasant undercurrent through Japanese society. *Manga* are like giant comics principally produced for Japanese men and boys. Torture, mutilation and rape of young women and girls are a regular feature of the storylines.[94,95]

It has been argued from a psychological perspective that Japanese boys are too smothered by their mothers. And I have seen this while living in Japan. Since married women in Japan may not receive the affection and love that they want from their overworked and nearly absent husbands they seek it out in their sons by excessively caring for them. As a result, over dependent Japanese men in their thirties and forties prefer to live alone or at home with their mothers who continue to cook, wash and iron their clothes, and baby them. If and when these Japanese men marry they may find that their wives fulfill the roles that their mothers had once occupied and thus psychologically are unable to relate to them sexually. Japan has one of the lowest sex rates between husbands and wives in Asia.[96] This may be a major factor as to why Japanese men may seek out "dirty" sex with a prostitute–a woman who is outside the boundaries of accepted societal behavior. It is with a prostitute that a Japanese man will unleash all his pent up and confused anger, frustration, and distorted sexual fantasies.

> A mother who pushes her son to achieve high levels of academic performance and who combines this pressure with a smothering lover will produce a sexually and emotionally inadequate man who cannot relate to sexually mature women.[97] A significant proportion of Japanese marriages are sexually sterile after a few years.[98] This is because Japanese husbands are unable to perform sexually with their wives after a period of time, as their wives have substituted for their mothers.[99] In order for men to separate their sexual partners from their mothers they need to feel a sense of power and independence they did not feel when in their mother's presence. They need to feel dominant. In the initial years of a marriage a man might feel in control of his bride but very quickly the power dynamics of the relationship change. The wife gathers power as she establishes and extends her influence over the household. Within the home the husband is no longer master. And if he is no longer master he becomes, at least psychologically, his own wife's son.[100]

Prostitution exists in all villages, towns, cities, and states regardless of the taboos against it. And in regards to religion the stricter and more repressive it is toward sex the higher the likelihood that there is a very strong and very hidden sex industry serving as an outlet; examples of this may be found in extreme forms of Islam and Catholicism. But although Buddhism may be tolerant of sexual behavior we also find a very strong and not-so-hidden sex industry in Asia.

If you would like to understand more about the long term causes and consequences of the sex industry in Thailand I recommend these three books:

- *Night Market: Sexual Cultures and the Thai Economic Miracle* by Ryan Bishop and Lillian S. Robinson. This is an excellent book that is very well researched and documented. It rarely puts forth its own interpretations and opinions, and addresses the economics causes and consequences of the sex industry in Thailand.

- *Travels in the Skin Trade: Tourism and the Sex Industry* by Jeremy Seabrook is composed of interviews conducted between 1995 and 1996 with several "sexpatriates" and sex tourists that compose the demand side of the industry. The interviews provide "some insight into the motives, responses and attitudes of foreign [Western] men in Bangkok."[101]

- *Sex Slaves: The Trafficking of Women in Asia* by T. Louise Brown. This is a good book, but it is full of the author's own opinions and perspectives, thus making it not a very objective read. But it paints a wider and more interesting picture of the sex industry in South Asia and Southeast Asia. It discusses the type of men who purchase sex and why they do so, the pimps, the brothel owners, the politicians, the organized crime groups, the Japanese yakuza, and all those who play a part in the industry. The book also emphasizes that the number of Western men who purchase sex in Asia are far lower than the number of Asian men who purchase sex in the region.

This journal entry is an attempt to explain the history, and the causes and effects of the sex industry in Asia, particularly in Thailand.

There is so much more that I haven't been able to touch on or discuss. I recommend that you read more about this topic to gain a better understanding of this industry and the awful, illegal situation these women who are often forced into prostitution must work and survive in. The more aware we are of the sex industry the more likely we are to educate ourselves and discuss the problem with friends and family to find ways to put a dent against it by protesting, electing politicians who will fight against it, and by supporting and donating to organizations (such as End Child Prostitution in Asian Tourism (ECPAT), Education Means Protection Of Women Engaged in Recreation (EMPOWER), the Thai Red Cross Aids Research Centre, and the Center for the Protection of Children's Rights Foundation (CPCR)) that combat the sex slavery industry and care for the women and children who are victims of it.

Posted by The Legacy Cycle at 2004-05-16T05:50:00-07:00

Wednesday, May 19, 2004

Monday, May 17, 2004

On May 16, I took it easy by going to the movie theater, which I love to do, especially if I can go alone. I have found that after traveling for two months on my own that I really enjoy the freedom of traveling in any direction I please, doing whatever I want, without compromising to anyone. Close friends could tell you that I am a "nomad," a "loner" or at least not afraid to do something by myself.

I went to see *Troy*. This was the third movie I had seen in Bangkok. Before I went up to Ayutthaya and Chiang Mai I saw the *The Passion of the Christ* and *Starsky and Hutch*. *Starsky and Hutch* was exactly what I expected, a stupid, fun comedy. *The Passion of the Christ* was excellent as a fine work of movie making mastery. As for *Troy*, well, to be honest I didn't like it at all. It was a Hollywood blockbuster filled with attractive young actors and actresses that really added nothing to the film in terms of their talent. Brad Pitt gave a poor performance. I respect him as an actor—I loved his portrayal of his characters in *12 Monkeys* and *Fight Club*—but in *Troy* I felt like I wasn't watching Achilles, but

Brad Pitt being Brad Pitt in a Hollywood epic piece of crap.

And I didn't understand Briseis's relationship with Achilles. Achilles took her hostage with the intent to rape her, but did not. After he killed the priests and destroyed the temple that she was devoted to, she, in a matter of days, falls in love with him? And she continued to love him after he had choked her when he discovered that his cousin had been killed? Out of vengeance Achilles killed Hector (her cousin) and she still loves him? Then Achilles set her free and she still loves him? What the hell does this say about women? Women love men that conquer them by forcibly taking them hostage, mounting them within a day or two, choking them, and killing members of their family? And Hector's wife ... all she does is cry, and she was so skinny in the film that I wanted to jump into the story and give her some of my popcorn. I don't think she said more than two words in the movie. I haven't read the *Iliad* so I don't know how close the film is to the epic poem, but as a film I thought the dialogue and believability of the characters was very weak.

In any case, the funny thing (or annoying thing depending on how you want to look at it) about going to the movie theater in Thailand is that after the trailers the audience must stand for a two-minute salute to the projected image of the king of Thailand. For me, personally, I hated it. I think it was ridiculous that I (or anyone) was required to stand up before a movie screen to pay homage to someone I have never (nor will ever) meet personally. I don't know anything about this monarch, but unless he has special powers to heal the sick, feed the poor, and rid his country of corruption and the sex trade I find no reason at all as to why I–or anyone–should stand up and salute this person. Is he higher than me? Is he Jesus, the Buddha himself, God? No. He is a human being just like the rest of us.

Speaking so harshly about the royal family in Thailand is taboo. No one in public can say anything derogatory about the monarchy. This also upsets me. It is dangerous when no one can speak their mind about individuals in their government or royal family for that matter. It's a form of control and a breeding ground that allows these individuals that are beyond public criticism to, at times, get away with murder. I'm sure that if any Thai official comes across this rant that I will be prohibited from re-entering the country.

On May 17, I was to meet Dan Remon of Fitcorp Asia at a hotel near the Nana train station. I met Dan before in Bangkok through a friend who introduced me to him via the Internet. Dan is originally from Australia, but he has been living in Bangkok for about five years. He started Fitcorp Asia in 2002, which caters to expatriate executives that want a personal trainer. Dan (as I later found out) was unable to make it to meet me, but as I waited for him I noticed a Toyota Land Cruiser about to leave the hotel. The interesting aspect about the Land Cruiser was that it had a variety of stickers on its rear window from all the countries that it had traveled through. The sticker that caught my eye was one from Iran. I saw the driver who he looked Spanish, but then they took off.

Posted by The Legacy Cycle at 2004-05-19T22:44:00-07:00

CAMBODIA

Wednesday, May 19, 2004

Tuesday, May 18, 2004

On May 18, I took a bus from Bangkok to the Thai/Cambodia border town of Aranyaprathet. On the bus, I met a man from the Philippines by the name of Ricardo who was traveling with his wife and a friend on a visa run. He spoke fluent Thai and imported clothes from the Philippines into Bangkok.

On our journey, Ricardo explained to me that when he was a teenager he made a living by shining the shoes of the U.S. soldiers based in Manila during the Vietnam War. He then told me the story of one U.S. soldier (we'll call him Dave) who asked him while he was shining his boots, "What is the capital of Missouri?" Ricardo didn't know the answer, but Dave challenged him by offering him a dollar if he could tell him the capital of that state the next day. Ricardo ran back home asking friends and family the name of the capital of Missouri. He eventually found a book that provided the answer, and the next day he told Dave and made a dollar. Over time Dave continued to quiz Ricardo on the state capitals; today (three decades later) Ricardo can still recite all the U.S. capitals. They soon became friends, and to help Ricardo make more money Dave would sneak him into the U.S. base so that he could expand his client base.

"I charged ten cents a shine," Ricardo told me with a proud grin, "and some of the soldiers ran a tab so that after some time I would have to approach those soldiers and say: 'Hey, Charlie. Time to pay. I shined your shoes eight times. That will be 80 cents.'"

As time passed, Dave did what he could to help Ricardo achieve his dream of becoming an electrical engineer. He bought books for him on the topic and even offered to help him come to the U.S. to study. Ricardo's mom could not contemplate his absence and so he had to stay in the Philippines. A decision I could see that Ricardo still regretted as he now imports clothes from his country into Thailand. Sadly, Ricardo told me that Dave died of cancer at the age of 37.

When we arrived to the bus station in Aranyaprathet, Ricardo told me that I could join him, his wife, and his friend on a tuk-tuk (auto rickshaw) ride to the border. We found a tuk-tuk, but the driver wanted to charge more because I was a foreigner. Ricardo bargained the price down and we rode to the border. But when we arrived, Ricardo did not allow me to pay my portion of the fare (a sign of his deep gratitude to Dave the U.S. soldier for having made such a positive and lasting impression on him during the Vietnam War). I thanked him.

As I walked to the border between the towns of Aranyaprathet, Thailand and Poipet, Cambodia I saw a large market on the Thai side with hundreds, maybe thousands, of Cambodians who were traveling to or from the border. The majority of them were pulling or pushing large wooden carts that were either filled with goods (if they were going to the Thai market) or empty (if they had just come from the market); the strong incentive for these Cambodians traders to sell their wares in Thailand was to earn the stronger Thai baht. All of these Cambodians were extremely poor; some appeared to be wearing the only clothing that they possessed. Children begging for money were quick upon me. With the exception of Ricardo and his wife, I was the only foreigner crossing the border. I saw several large, luxurious three or four-storey casino buildings on the Cambodian side. It didn't make sense to see so many poor Cambodians hauling their carts into Thailand to make a survival living to then see casinos that exuded wealth. Ricardo explained to me before we parted ways that since gambling was illegal in Thailand many Thais crossed the border here to indulge in games of chance.

I saw an old man who was sitting on the ground of the bridge that we had to cross. He had no forearms and his face had been shredded and scarred from the shrapnel of an exploded landmine, a quick reminder of the five million unexploded ordnance in the country.[1] I continued on through the visa checkpoints. Along the way a teenaged Cambodian tout leeched on to me and kept asking where I was going. I relented and told him that I was going to Battambang. He explained that I could share a ride with two other Japanese travelers that were waiting in a taxi to go to the same destination while another tout was getting their visas. I knew immediately that the tout was lying because it was not possible for a traveler to get a Cambodian visa at this border crossing. But the tout went on to explain that a friend of a friend was a Cambodian police officer who could obtain a visa (illegally) for me if I needed one. I interrupted and told him that I had already obtained my visa in Bangkok; I'm sure there were a few naïve travelers who paid the touts their fee to gain a visa and end up never seeing the tout, their money, or their passports again. In an attempt to legitimize his claims, he showed me two pieces of paper that were *supposedly* being used to process the visas for the Japanese travelers. I started to fall for it. I told him that if these two Japanese travelers were going to Battambang that I would go with them. He then led me to a tuk-tuk, and off we went to meet up with these Japanese travelers.

After riding through the streets (if you could call them that) of Poipet we arrived to a row of run-down, white Toyota Camry taxis. The tout then said, "Oh, it looks like the Japanese are gone." He had been lying the entire time. There had never been any Japanese travelers. It was just a story to gain my trust and get me to the taxis. Now the exhaustive process of bargaining began. The tout translated that the taxi driver wanted $20 for the journey. I was shocked. "You go— you go in front, sitting alone," the tout began trying to sway me, "other people sit in back. It has air-con. Very good for you."

"For twenty dollars, I can go from Bangkok to Laos—a seven-hour journey," I replied. "It is only two-and-a-half hours from here to Battambang. Ten dollars. That's it."

"No, you pay twenty," the tout insisted. "You sit in front."

"I don't need to sit in front," I answered. "I'll sit in the back. Ten dollars."

This debate went on and on while a small crowd of men began to form around us. The tout continued to tell me that I would be traveling with other people. He opened the trunk of the taxi and showed me all the boxes and bags of the people who would be traveling with me. I then asked, "How many people are going with me?"

"Three in the back, and you in the front," he answered.

"Look, I don't need to sit in the front. And where the hell are these people that are traveling with me?"

The tout pointed to some random lady buying fruit in the market.

This tout continued to lie. In the end, I decided to take the taxi for US$15, which was a rip-off, but, whatever. The taxi driver then said in English, "We go."

I put my bag in the trunk, entered the back seat of the car, and turned around so that I could keep an eye on my bag, but my view was blocked because three large plastic bags that were filled with smaller bags of potato chips covered the rear window. I was afraid that the rear window was intentionally stacked with these bags to block my ability to see if someone would try to take my bag out of the trunk and run off with it. I quickly removed the bags of potato chips and kept an eye on the trunk for a few minutes, but I then decided to exit the car since it became apparent that the driver was not ready to leave. The tout then said to me, "You wait inside."

"No!" I shouted. I waited outside watching the closed trunk in the midday sun for about 10 minutes. I then asked the tout, "Where the hell are these people that are traveling with me? Where did that lady go? The one buying fruit!"

"She left, but you go to pick her up," the tout lied again.

Finally, the taxi driver was ready to go. I asked him to open the trunk so that I could see my bag. He complied and the bag was there. But before we left the tout had the audacity to ask me for his tip. I reluctantly gave him more than he deserved, twenty baht (US$0.50). He was upset with the amount, but for all his lies he didn't deserve a thing. I simply turned my back on him, entered the taxi, and we took off leaving trails of dust.

The taxi drove through and out of Poipet, and we did not pick up a single person. I had essentially hired a private taxi for $15 to Battambang (a 114-kilometer journey), which was not a bad price, but from the Cambodian point of view I had clearly been ripped-off. On the plus side, the taxi did have air conditioning. Surprisingly, about 20 minutes into the trip I saw the very same Toyota Land Cruiser that I had seen the previous day in Bangkok when I went to meet Dan

Remon of Fitcorp Asia. I waved as we passed them.

The roads and the scenery on this trip reminded me of Myanmar; a single lane coated in dust and littered with potholes that the taxi driver had to continually swerve and maneuver around. Occasionally, along the road, I saw a row of thatched stalls selling packs of cigarettes, canned soda drinks, and racks of used one and two-liter plastic soda bottles filled with gasoline.

Outside the town of Sisophon, I saw two long lines of cars that had pulled over to the sides of the road. I had no idea what was going on, but it was apparent that we could go no further. We pulled over and behind us the Land Cruiser we had passed also stopped. I got out of the car and introduced myself to the drivers. They were an Argentinean couple, but they had been living in Spain for the past few years. Their names were Marcelo and Luisa. I explained to them–in my rusty Spanish–that I had seen their car the previous day in Bangkok. They then told me about their journey as I told them about mine. They had been traveling by car for the past eight months. They had driven through Iran, Pakistan, India, and then went to Singapore, Malaysia, and Thailand. They were on their way to Saigon where they were going to ship their car to Argentina and continue the journey north to Mexico and the U.S. To chronicle their adventures around the world they maintained a website at http://www.galeon.com/madridsingapur.

My taxi driver called me into the taxi. Once I got in he tried to start the car but it stalled. *Great*, I thought. The taxi driver called for help from some locals who pushed the car from behind as the driver revved the engine and put the car into gear. The engine started up. The taxi driver then turned the car around and drove right into a dirt path. The engine did not sound like it was doing well and I was afraid that the car was going to stall again. As we drove on the dirt path to avoid the backup of cars on the road we had to pay a toll to the locals who had created the path. I then could see from a distance that the traffic jam had been caused by the failed efforts of drivers from cars on both sides of a single lane bridge to coordinate a system to allow drivers to take turns to cross it.

At around two in the afternoon we arrived to Battambang, which is the second largest city in Cambodia; but to my Chicago and Tokyo eyes it was a tiny town. Once I settled into my hotel and had some lunch I hired a moto taxi (a motor scooter taxi driver) to take me to the killing caves of Phnom Sampeau.

Phnom Sampeau is a limestone mountain, and at its summit there is a complex of temples. After we arrived, I hired a local boy who spoke English to guide me to the infamous killing caves. We followed a path the led up and around the mountain. As we made our ascent the heat, and the climb, caused me to perspire tremendously, which attracted legions of mosquitoes.

The boy was very intelligent. He asked me how much an English teacher made in the U.S. In reference to my experiences teaching English in Japan I said, "About twenty dollars an hour." He was shocked by the amount. He explained that he had taken English classes after school for three dollars a month, but that it had been too expensive and he had to stop. Although my moto-taxi driver told me to tip the boy only about one thousand riel (US$0.25), I decided that I would give him three dollars to help him continue his studies.

We arrived to a few small, old temples. The boy led me down into a cave pit, which served as the entrance to one of two locations on the mountain that was a killing site during Pol Pot's Khmer Rouge reign from 1975 to 1979. The boy showed me an area of the cave that was used by the Khmer regime to execute Chinese families. He then pointed up, and above us from where the evening sun shined through a large opening I saw the cliff from where the Khmer Rouge (in an effort to save bullets) bludgeoned thousands of Cambodians before throwing them down to their deaths. The dark scene before us was once piled high with the bodies of men, women, and children. And further into the cave, to our left from this horrific site, there was an opening that led to a smaller cave. In there the boy showed me a cage that was filled with the skulls and bones of the victims. He told me that previously these bones were not in a cage, but simply placed on a rock altar. But because tourists began to take these bones as souvenirs the locals decided to make the cage so that no one could take and disturb these remains. I kneeled before the bones in awe and sadness. The boy informed me that there was another cave. He led me back, around, and down a staircase to the other site. He said that before there had been a statue of the Buddha in the cave, but that the Khmer Rouge had it destroyed. Years after the fall of the Khmer Rouge locals and foreigners who had traveled through the area donated enough money to make another statue of the Buddha, but of a lower quality and craftsmanship.

Before having a look at the statue, he showed me another cage filled with human skeletal remains, but I noticed that there were a few bones on the floor just before the cage. The boy informed me that the monks who came to the cave on a regular basis to pray had placed the bones there; a sign that still, after more than two decades since the mass killings, monks continued to find human remains around the site and mountain. I then saw the golden reclining Buddha statue before we hiked further up to another cliff that the Khmer Rouge had used to throw their victims to their deaths. I did not want to imagine what this site must have been like when these atrocities took place.

Pol Pot (who died in 1998) led the Khmer Rouge with the support of the People's Republic of China[2] to overthrow Cambodia's Khmer Republic (effectively a military dictatorship that supported U.S. interests in the region) in 1975. In four years, the Khmer Rouge killed an estimated 1.5 to 3 million Cambodians,[3] which was about 25 percent of the population.[4] Many were mass executed, tortured, or starved to death in forced agricultural labor camps; "famine claimed somewhere between 500,00 and 1.5 million lives through a combination of starvation and disease ... making it one of the deadliest famines in modern history."[5] And although rice production was a priority for the regime as a means to feed their enslaved population there exists evidence that the "CPK [Communist Party of Kampuchea] exported large quantities of rice throughout the Khmer Rouge period"[6] to China in "exchange for munitions, further escalating the food deficit."[7] As a result, Cambodians resorted to eating insects, rats, and even large spiders to survive.[8]

Essentially, every Cambodian I met that was my age or older (I was born in 1977) witnessed, survived, and suffered through the genocide of the "Red Khmers"; haunting memories of this horrific period plague about 40 percent of the population: "According to research conducted after the Khmer Rouge period, two out of five Cambodians have [suffered] mental problems and psychosocial crisis ... studies ... also found that some 14 percent of Cambodians aged 18 and older have suffered post-traumatic stress disorder (PTSD)."[9] This combined with the fact that Pol Pot killed off nearly all academics, high-skilled workers, and technocrats has left Cambodia, in the decades after the fall of the Khmer Rouge, as one of the most corrupted, uneducated, and poorest nations in Southeast Asia.[10,11] As I traveled through Cambodia I saw an incredibly wide income gap between the political, military, and entrepreneurial elite and everyone else.[12] Government and military officials all drove Toyota Land Cruisers (it was the same in Myanmar) while everyone else traveled by scooter or by riding on the back of a pickup truck with forty other impoverished people on poorly maintained dirt roads.

> By the World Bank's reckoning, 21 per cent of the population lives on or below the poverty line ($1.25 a day), 56 per cent live in 'vulnerable poverty' (below $2.60 a day), 20 per cent live in the so-called middle class and just 3 per cent are considered prosperous.[13]

As for democratic elections, they are anything but. Although the United Nations Transitional Authority in Cambodia (UNTAC) oversaw a general election in 1993 the Cambodian People's Party (CPP) have controlled both the upper and lower chambers of parliament since 1979 (the CPP was originally named the Kampuchean People's Revolutionary Party or KPRP) thus establishing it as one of the longest-ruling parties in the world.[14]

It should be noted that UN peacekeeping troops stationed during the 1993 general election period were reported to have raped and abused women, increased the demand for prostitution, and increased the proliferation of AIDS. The number of "sex workers [women and children] in Phnom Penh in 1991 was estimated to be about 6,000 ... After the arrival of UNTAC, prostitution grew dramatically ... [and] By the end of 1992, sex workers in Phnom Penh alone was estimated to number more than 20,000."[15,16] This has resulted in 50,000 to 90,000 Cambodians being HIV positive in 1995.[17]

According to Cambodia's 1993 constitution the country is a constitutional monarchy, but Hun Sen, the prime minister, has held power since 1985 (thus making him at the time of writing (2017) one of the longest serving political leaders in the world) and was a former Khmer Rouge battalion commander who later became a rebel army and government leader.[18] He has maintained his iron grip through violence and oppression; in 1987, Amnesty International accused him and his government of using "electric shocks, hot irons and near suffocation with plastic bags" to torture thousands of political prisoners.[19]

The Cambodian people have no real political power or voice; and that coupled with their passive Buddhist beliefs (to an extent they believe that they are living out the bad karma of a previous life) adds to their acceptance of the corrupt political climate of their nation. I still find it unfathomable that Pol Pot died in 1998 supposedly of heart failure having never to face a war tribunal.[20] But perhaps we can take solace in the story that Pol Pot had died from "the shock of him hearing" on a Voice of America broadcast that "Khmer Rouge leaders—desperate for food, medicine and international support—had decided to turn him over to an international tribunal to face crimes against humanity."[21]

Today you can still find former members of the Khmer Rouge living out peaceful lives in remote towns and villages. They committed some of the most atrocious crimes against their own people, but now they live without having to face any form of justice. They—by all means—got away with the murder of nearly two million people. I'm sure the average Cambodian will simply shrug his or her shoulders and say, "Well, their next life will be a bad one." And that is that. They leave justice in the hands of divine, mystic forces.

After the caves, the boy took me behind the Buddha statue and showed me the remains of the original statue that had been destroyed by Pol Pot's soldiers. We then walked into another cave and stood quietly. It was eerily silent; I had never heard such silence. The movements of bats that were hanging high above us broke the quiet.

When we returned to the base of the mountain, I tipped the boy, and hopped onto the back of the scooter with my driver, and away we went down the dirt road that soon layered my glasses, shirt, and shorts with dust. Twenty minutes later we were driving through town, and at a traffic light my driver asked me if I wanted to see a crocodile farm that was on the outskirts of Battambang. I said yes.

We arrived to the crocodile farm, which was composed of a series of pool pits and high walls. I walked along the tops of the high walls that was about half a meter thick looking down into the pits and saw that all the crocodiles were so inanimate that I considered asking the scooter driver and farm owner if they were statues. But then I saw one of the crocodiles move. I soon learned from the farm owner that part of the crocodile's hunting strategy was in their ability to lie completely motionless with their mouths open for hours until a significant prey comes near or into their mouth and then SNAP! It's all over.

After the crocodile farm, the driver took me to his home. His family was kind and their two-storey brick home humble. Within the unlit house there was a concrete floor, brick walls that divided the first floor into a couple of rooms, a bookshelf, a bamboo bed, and plenty of pictures of his oldest daughter's engagement ceremony. His engaged daughter was only 17 years old! But she was not engaged to a local man. She was engaged to a 37-year-old American! My driver, the father, really didn't like the American, and he hinted that his daughter didn't like him either, but he was a financial answer–a hopeful escape from poverty. The father explained that the scooter he had, the main source of his income, had been given to him by the American. The American had the money to buy things that his fiancé's family needed. And I'm sure once she turned eighteen the American would take his soon-to-be bride to the U.S. But this was another example of the developed world (a wealthy American) exploiting the resources of the developing world (a girl) with the full blessing of the girl's father. How many other Southeast Asian families were offering their children to North American and European men in exchange for material possessions?

The driver had two other boys (one about nine years old and the other in his early teens) and another girl who was about 15 years old; the three of them were very shy. In front of their home, in the porch like area where we sat and spoke, there was another bamboo bed and a hammock. There were also six massive ceramic pots to the side of their house where they poured the water purchased from the local market into to be boiled for purification purposes. In the end, it was apparent from their home and their faded clothing that they were poor.

After, I returned to my hotel, took a shower to wash off all the dust and grime that clung to my skin from traveling on the scooter, and had dinner. I then walked around town a bit, but became nervous and returned to my hotel to inquire about traveling by boat to Siem Reap. The owner of the hotel explained that the journey would take about seven hours and that I would need to leave at seven in order to catch the boat that departed at 7:20. I then went to my room to watch the news, and went to bed.

Posted by The Legacy Cycle at 2004-05-19T22:44:00-07:00

Saturday, May 22, 2004

13-Hour Boat Journey from Battambang to Siem Reap
Wednesday, May 19, 2004

I woke up at five, but while I was taking a shower there was a knock on the door. I thought that there was a fire in the hotel because why would anyone be knocking at my door at 5:15 in the morning? I put on a towel, opened the door, and found a hotel staff member that could hardly speak English. I did not know what he wanted. I was worried that perhaps I had woken up too late; maybe I had the wrong time on my alarm clock. I looked at the hotel staff's watch and saw that it was 5:15 in the morning. I didn't really understand what he wanted, but he left and I returned to my shower and got ready. I went down to the lobby of the hotel at 6:10 and asked the owner why one of his staff had knocked on my door. He told me that they wanted to make sure I had woken up early enough so that I had time for breakfast. I decided to pass on breakfast since I didn't think there was enough time for them to prepare it. Instead I took a brief morning stroll through Battambang.

I returned to the hotel and saw a few other backpackers in the lobby waiting to be picked up for their bus journey to the Cambodian/Thai border. I sat down and began speaking with a Swiss girl who spoke English with an American accent. We ended up talking about music and the education system in Switzerland. Just before seven I was asked to get into a van that would take me to the Sangkae River boat pier. After a brief ride the van stopped, I got out and walked to the pier. It was hardly that. It was a metallic ladder/staircase that led down to the muddy banks of the river. I descended the ladder and saw my wooden boat; it was filled with locals and bags of vegetables, bread rolls, and other goods that were to be transported for sale to the local markets around Tonlé Sap Lake. I boarded the narrow boat and made it to the rear where I sat in front of a Cambodian family (a mother, father, their three-year-old daughter, and their two-year-old son). In total, there were about 15 locals, plus myself, in this thin and long river boat filled with bags and goods. The boat crew was busy trying to fix the engine. While we waited three boys in dirty, ragged clothing were fishing in the river with fishing rods they had made. Most of us in the boat, including myself, kept ourselves entertained by watching the boys as they fished. It appeared that the boys were brothers. The oldest was about 11 years of age, the second oldest was about eight, and the youngest was five. At one point the middle brother yanked out his fishing line from the river and the fishing hook nearly hit his younger brother in the face. Everyone in my boat then began yelling at the middle brother to be more careful for the hook could have ripped out his younger brother's eye. I then saw another foreigner, a stocky man in his early forties with short, brown hair, descending the metallic ladder to the pier. He approached our boat, boarded it, and we all had to make a little more room for him so that he could sit down.

An hour after we were supposed to have left the boat crew finally got the engine to work; it was 8:30 a.m. About 20 minutes after we left we docked at an impoverished village of several thatched homes on stilts where a woman was taking a bath in the swirling, brown river (most locals urinate and defecate on the shore of this river). The woman kept a thin robe around her body to not expose herself to the traffic of boats.

The boat crew disembarked and began negotiating on the dock with another lady about all the goods that she wanted to have shipped to Siem Reap. As the negotiations went on I watched the woman who was bathing in the river brush her teeth. I managed to take a quick shot of her with my camera. Once the negotiations were settled the boat crew began loading all the bags and baskets of food and berries that the lady wanted shipped. There was not enough room at the front of the boat so the crew put the goods on a smaller boat from the village and rowed it toward the back of the boat. There they began loading the goods, but then one of the handles of a large basket filled with berries snapped and about 20 percent of the contents poured directly into the river. The woman who wanted these goods shipped gave a quick look of saddened shock and then began screaming at the boat crew. She immediately boarded the boat and confronted the crew to ensure that they did not accidentally pour more of her hard-earned agricultural work into the river. A few minutes later the crew finished loading the goods; it was nearly 10 o'clock. We set off again and traveled for the next few hours. The scenery beyond the river was tropical grasslands dotted with the occasional village of a few thatched homes on high stilts and children playing and waving in the river.

The two-year-old boy of the family that was sitting across from me was sick unfortunately. He urinated all over his father's legs. The father removed his son's shorts, wetted them in the river, and began cleaning his son and wiping his pants. But as soon as he finished cleaning his seat his son defecated all over his leg and seat. The father patiently wetted his son's shorts again and began wiping the feces from his pants and seat. He then held his son over the boat and splashed river water up to clean his legs and buttocks. The boy just looked around smiling as if nothing had happened. He then began defecating into the river. Twenty minutes later the boy's older sister had to go to the bathroom and so her mother and father held her arms and helped her to squat over the side of the boat so that she could urinate into the river. An hour after that, when the boy's shorts had dried in the sun, the father put the shorts back onto the boy. And as soon as the shorts were on him he defecated again. I could only laugh. His feces went all over his father and onto the seats again.

At 1:30 p.m. we arrived at a rest and transfer point. I disembarked along with the other passengers onto a wooden pier and walked into a large wooden shack with an open view of the river that stood on stilts. In the shack, there were other backpackers who had arrived earlier on a smaller boat from Siem Reap and a bar counter. I bought a bottle of Sprite and began speaking with the stocky foreigner that had boarded the boat before we left Battambang. His name was Robert and he was from Australia. He told me that he had been to Poipet, which according to him was a "Wild West" town near the Cambodian/Thai border that was rumored to be a hideout for former Khmer Rouge soldiers. He pulled out his video camera to show me the footage he had taken of the mines in the town. As I watched Robert explained to me that the methods used to mine sapphire and other gems were very crude; Robert, as I was to discover, was a miner. In the footage, I saw Cambodian men and boys hosing down large piles of rocks. Robert highlighted that the runoff from these mines was contaminated by the toxic chemicals used in the mining process and as a result would most likely seep into their ground water. Who knew what kind of health problems this was causing among the people in this town. I then saw footage of a man grinding down the gems from the mines, and right next to him, on a table, was a very large handgun. Robert explained to me that in the rural towns it was very common for nearly every male to have and carry a gun.

> It is estimated "that the total pool of Cambodia conflict weapons was between 320,000 and 463,000, and that a total of 285,000–366,000 weapons have been brought under government control since the singing of the Paris Agreements in 1991. Of these, some 155,000–236,000 were brought into the government stockpile through the creation of the RCAF [Royal Cambodian Armed Forces] and the police and the defection of the Khmer Rouge. Weapons collection programmes removed 130,000 weapons from outside of government control. Destruction of 180,000 of the surplus of government stockpile has substantially reduced the potential for leakage of unused arms into the general population. Combining all of these figures, it is estimated that some 22,000–85,000 weapons continue to circulate illegally in Cambodia."[22]

Next, I saw in the footage a bare-chested man with tattoos on his chest and arms that marked him as a former Khmer Rouge soldier. He was an unpleasant looking fellow. Who knew what atrocities he had committed against his people during Pol Pot's evil reign. And here he was living in this "Wild West" town never having had to stand trial for his crimes.

Robert noted, as I continued watching the footage, that the metallic plates that the cutters had used to place the gems on were made from the shell casings of unexploded bombs dropped over Cambodia by the B-52 heavy bombers during the Vietnam War.

After resting for about 30 minutes in the shade of the wooden shack the boat crew called to us to begin boarding. They signaled to Richard and I to get on the smaller, more uncomfortable boat (our bags had already been transferred to it) that the backpackers from Siem Reap had traveled on. The Siem Reap backpackers were then directed to get on our boat from Battambang, but before they did they explained to Robert and I that it would take about three hours to reach Siem Reap; by their estimates we would be arriving at five in the afternoon.

I boarded the boat and sat down to find that—yet again—the family with the urinating and defecating boy was seated across from me. I prayed silently that the boy would cease his soiling offensive against his father. Luckily, about 20 minutes after we had departed, the father took his son and sat all the way at the front of the boat. As you can imagine, I was relieved.

As the hours passed we dropped off more and more passengers from our boat at various villages along the way. Robert and I were the only passengers left in the boat, which was terrific because we now had plenty of space to stretch and move around. We finally entered Tonlé Sap Lake. The lake was massive, but as we began crossing it the crew began to worry for they could see that the lake was becoming shallower. I too began to worry as soon as I saw the boat propellers flinging mud up into the air instead of a spray of water. Then we were stuck. The boat simply refused to move. One of the crew jumped into the lake; it was apparent that the water was just too shallow for us to move through for the water line came up to the knee of the crewmember! Another crewmember jumped into the lake, and for about two hours the two tried to push the boat or get back onto the boat to work on the engine that would occasionally die. The sun was beginning to set. Robert and I were worried that we were going to be stuck in the middle of this lake until the next morning. Little by little we moved forward. In the distance, we saw other boats with the same problem. Then, just as the sun was to set and night to settle in, I decided to jump into the lake and help push the boat. Robert stayed on the boat. The mud came up to my shins and the water up to my knees. The mud was filled with grass stems that would scratch up against my foot and leg as the crew and I pushed the boat across the muddy lake. After about 20 minutes the boat began to move easily and we all hopped back into the boat.

I was exhausted. My legs were covered in mud and I just sat in my seat drinking an entire liter of water. The boat moved gradually toward a few lights in the distance. Night was soon upon us. I looked back and saw that the boat's propellers were still kicking up mud. At around seven in the evening we neared a lake port village, but since it was dark I was unable to see much of the village except for the lights and sounds that emanated from television sets. The boat docked along a wooden pier and Robert and I disembarked with our bags and walked toward the only light we saw.

We then heard, "Hey mister. You buy drink. One dollar for drink—you buy. You buy."

Robert and I walked toward the young voice and found several girls around a large cooler ready to sell us anything. Robert bought me a large bottle of water while he treated himself to a beer. From what I saw there appeared to be no way that we could get into the town of Siem Reap from our location. We sat drinking while getting harassed by more kids that tried to sell us anything until a taxi pulled up. The taxi driver wanted US$20 to take us into town.

I told him, "No way! For twenty I can go from Bangkok to China! Five for the both of us. Final deal."

The taxi driver did not accept my offer. We bargained more and only got him down to 15, which was still a ridiculous price. We then told him to go home for we weren't interested in being ripped off.

So there Robert and I were in the middle of nowhere after just having sent off a taxi that was probably our last chance of getting into Siem Reap. We took it easy. Funny enough I was highly entertained by the whole experience. Then one of the crew from our boat approached and explained that we could stay in his home until morning when there would be plenty of scooters, cars, and buses to take us to Siem Reap for a cheaper price. I was seriously considering the offer when Robert had the idea of calling the hotel in Siem Reap that I had planned to stay in for he figured that the owner of the hotel could cover a portion of the cost of our ride to his hotel.

Originally, there was supposed to be someone from the hotel waiting for us at the pier to take us to the hotel, but because we arrived nearly four hours late the person had left.

I asked if there was a phone, and one of the locals offered his cell phone. I called the Millennium Hotel and spoke with the owner, but the line cut. I tried again. The hotel owner answered, but I could barely understand what he was saying as a result of the language barrier. And the line cut again. The third time I called I quickly gave the phone to one of the locals who spoke descent English and could translate for me. The local said a few things to the owner, listened, kept nodding his head, and then gave me the phone. The hotel owner said something through the line about 10 dollars and five dollars. I had no idea what he was trying to tell me. After I hung up Robert advised that we should have two of the locals take us to Siem Reap for whatever price and have the hotel owner sort out the cost of the ride.

We found two scooter drivers and nodded our heads when they wanted 14 dollars to take us into town. Somehow my driver managed to place and balance my heavy bag on the bike between his legs, and off we went driving through a sandy path and then onto a dirt road. In the distance, we saw a bush fire, and after we passed it we heard a fire truck in the distance on its way to put it out. About a kilometer away from Siem Reap my driver's scooter died. Robert's driver stopped and waited. I pulled out my flashlight so that my driver could repair the engine. After working on the engine for a few minutes my driver explained that he would come back. He then started pushing the scooter toward Siem Reap. As we watched my driver soon disappear into the night, Robert and I joked about our day on a boat that had a broken engine in the morning, getting stuck in the middle of a muddy lake just after sunset, and my scooter stalling out in the middle of the night.

Ten minutes later my driver returned having fixed the scooter. I jumped on the back of the vehicle and Robert jumped onto the back of his ride and we continued until we reached the Millennium Hotel. We pulled into the hotel parking area, and the owner took us in to show us a twin room that Robert and I would share. We then had to sort out the cash for the scooter drivers.

What happened next was an argument between the hotel owner and the drivers. The hotel owner said that he had made an agreement with one of the drivers over the phone to transport Robert and I to Siem Reap in a car for 10 dollars (but neither of these drivers were the individual he had spoken to). The hotel owner emphasized that we had not been taken in a car and that he would not pay 14. As the argument went on and on I just thought to myself: *All I want to do is go to my room and take a shower.* Finally, somehow, an agreement was made and we were rid of the drivers.

I took a shower washing off all the dried mud from my legs and discovered scratches all over my feet and shins from sloshing in the lake while pushing that boat.

I later walked into town alone to get a bite to eat and noticed a bar called Zanzibar, which was full of foreign men and Cambodian working girls. I found a spot to eat, ate a tuna sandwich, returned to my hotel, and went to sleep.

Posted by The Legacy Cycle at 2004-05-22T02:36:00-07:00

Saturday, May 22, 2004

Sun Set Temples
Thursday, May 20, 2004

Robert and I woke up, got ready, and walked down to the reception area of the hotel where we hired two moto-taxi drivers to pick us up at half past four in the afternoon to begin our tour of Angkor Wat. We then made our way to Zanzibar to have breakfast. After breakfast, we decided to go our separate ways until we were to meet again after four.

I walked to a bank and was badgered along the way by one moto-taxi driver after the other who either offered to take me anywhere in Siem Reap or to be my guide through the temples of Angkor. I politely refused all offers and kept walking. At the bank, I exchanged some money and then walked past the Psah Chas ("Old Market"), which was lined on the outside with small vendor shops that sold souvenirs to tourists. I decided to walk across a bridge and explore the area just outside of town. As I walked I saw many thatched homes built on stilts while also seeing the occasional affluent home. I also found a small library that had been founded by a Japanese woman.

I backtracked and decided to walk east out of town on a main road, and along the way I saw several two and three-storey massage parlors with tinted windows and large parking lots. What was curious about them was that the signs that advertised their services were in katakana (the Japanese writing system used for words of foreign origin), which meant that a significant portion of their clientele were Japanese.

I continued walking and saw a hotel named the Get Lucky Hotel. I then knew that the massage parlors that I had seen were a front for prostitution.

The afternoon sun was intense. I was sweating profusely and after walking for another 30 minutes I turned back.

Once in town I found a section of Siem Reap that seemed to be the local brothel area. There was a line of four two-storey buildings that had on the ground floor rows of plastic lawn chairs and tables facing the interior of the building. I saw Cambodian men lounging and smoking inside while watching one of the two to three television sets that were broadcasting a boxing match or some other sporting event. And right next door there were several massage parlors with tinted windows; thus, these businesses complemented each other by providing Cambodian men a place to watch a game, socialize, gamble, and then walk next door to buy sex.

I was back at the hotel by 4:30 to meet with Robert and our two moto-taxi drivers; my driver's name was Leonardo, a nickname he had given himself as a result of his insistent belief that he resembled Leonardo DiCaprio. Although the resemblance to DiCaprio was stretching it, Leonardo had short, well-trimmed hair that was slicked back with hair gel and a wide smile that revealed self-confidence. He wore sun glasses, a dark-blue, long-sleeved shirt, a nice knockoff watch, and blue jeans.

Leonardo and the other driver took us to Prasat Trapeang Ropou. Many tourists and backpackers were gathered at this site to hike and climb Phnom Bakheng, a Hindu and Buddhist temple built in the 9th century, to view the sunset from its peak. We followed the crowd to a ruined stone staircase to ascend a hill covered in thick tropical vegetation. At the top of the staircase and across a flat open plain stood the impressive walled pyramid temple ruin of Phnom Bakheng, which was composed of five levels. We walked across the plain that was peppered with stone ruins to the nearly vertical sandstone staircase that led up the eastern side of the temple. Once we had climbed the staircase Robert and I took in the beauty of the thick, green canopy of tropical trees that expanded in all directions to the grey horizon. Hidden within this verdure were the monuments of the long and once lost civilization of Angkor.

We waited for the sun to set knowing that the cloudy evening would prevent the best experience. Regardless, it was interesting to wait at the top of this temple that was crowned by five towers with so many other people from all over the world.

After the sun had set, Robert and I climbed down the ruined staircase, and walked back to our drivers. I arrived first to the hotel;

Robert arrived about a half hour later. I asked him what had taken him so long and he explained that his driver had taken him to visit two brothels. I was shocked by his answer. He quickly added that he had only gone to look, but that if I was interested he could take me so that I could see with my own eyes what they were like. I grew very nervous by the prospect of this visit. But he assured me, as did the moto-taxi drivers, that it was no problem for me to simply look. And so, with strong hesitation, I agreed to go and see for myself what these exploitative brothels that I had read so much about were like.

We first pulled into a two-storey brothel called Hollywood Massage. It had a large parking area and the building had tinted black windows. We got off the scooters and entered. I saw a Chinese shrine at the far end of a long room that had a row of three couches that were positioned to face a window wall that nearly took up the entire length of the room. We sat down and one of the men that worked there sat next to us with a pad of paper in his hand. Suddenly, girls between the ages of 16 and 23 began filing into the room on the other side of the window wall. Robert explained to me that the girls could not see through their side of the window although we could see them. The girls began sitting down on three elevated rows of benches and watched a television set in complete boredom as they waited to be picked by one of us. All the girls had colored numbers pinned to their shirts that were either yellow or white; the yellow color signified that the girl was Cambodian, and the white color signified that the girl was Vietnamese. The man with the pad of paper was there ready to write down the number of the girls we wanted. I sat there feeling very uncomfortable. When most of the girls had filed in and sat down I estimated that there were about 30 to 40 of them.

In this brothel, 16 to 23 was the working life span for these girls and young women. Once they turned 24 their brothel career in this establishment was over. What would happen to them after that? They are not educated because they have spent their formative years servicing men, which has forced them to see their sexuality as a commodity that can be bought and sold and used and abused. They know nothing else and as a result they will go on to earn a living as a working girl, a brothel owner, or a recruiter. But for the working women older than 23 it is a sad economic fact that the demand for their services drops significantly causing them to command a lower value. Cambodian men and sex tourists alike want young girls.

At one point the man with the pad of paper stood up and left. I pulled out my digital camera and began filming for about eight seconds. I had had enough. We stood to leave. And just as we walked out a 40-year-old European man walked in.

The moto-taxi drivers drove Robert and I to one more brothel. It was called Madonna. It was set up in the same fashion as the last brothel, but this one did not have a one-way mirror for us to view the girls and young women. Instead, they were in an open room watching television. After we arrived more and more girls began filing into the room; they all had numbers pinned to their shirts. They could see us and we could see them. Then the "mama-san" (the brothel manager and in some cases the owner) approached us. She was an extremely attractive and well-dressed Cambodian woman who was in her late twenties. She was very professional in how she managed her operation and explained to us that 10 minutes with a girl was around $10 whereas an overnight stay with the girl ranged from $25 to $35. I then explained to my driver that I wanted to see what the rooms looked like. He communicated the request to the "mama-san" who assured me that the rooms were clean and descent. I asked my driver again to tell her that I wanted to see the rooms. My driver then explained to the "mama-san" that if she showed me the room there was a higher probability that I would buy a girl for the night, which, of course, was not true. She then agreed and led Robert and I into a labyrinth of dark hallways that were painted pink and littered with closed doors. We arrived to a door and she opened it for me. I walked in and saw a clean bed with towels on it and a very clean bathroom with a urinal, sink, and shower. I then walked out and said thank you and left.

I had seen enough, and we all returned to the Millennium Hotel.

Robert and I decided to have dinner, and on our way to the restaurant we ran into a friend he had met a week before during his travels. He joined us and I spent the rest of the night listening to Robert and his friend talk about all the brothels they had been to in Vietnam, Thailand, Cambodia, and Russia. Robert boasted that from all the brothels he had experienced he had never seen one like the two we had seen today in which the girls were behind a glass window with numbers pinned to their shirts. I listened to Robert and his friend and realized that the men who frequent brothels are simply any type of man, and at times women (lesbians do hire prostitutes), from your business partner, your college professor, your neighbor, to your best friend, brother, or maybe even your own husband or father; the men that frequent brothels come from all backgrounds and social classes of society.

Prostitution, as I am beginning to realize, is everywhere. It is interwoven into the fabric of all societies and cultures to the point that the police, organized crime groups, politicians, business professionals, et cetera are all, in some way or another, a part of the industry. As long as there are men there will be brothels. It does not matter if a man is happily married, has children that he adores, lives a successful life or not, any type of man can, may, and does visit a brothel. The percentage of men that go to brothels may vary from culture to culture and from country to country, but regardless, the industry is there operating within the shadow economy. Which then brings one to ask, why do men go to these brothels? As I have mentioned in earlier journal entries some men visit brothels to experiment, to dominate, to abuse, to seek affection, a fantasy, and to enjoy the illusion of love. And they do it because they simply can. All that keeps them from being with a prostitute is money, and that is it.

Posted by The Legacy Cycle at 2004-05-22T03:21:00-07:00

Monday, May 24, 2004

The Temples of Angkor Wat
Friday, May 21, 2004

Robert and I woke up at five in the morning, and about a half hour later we left our hotel with our moto-taxi drivers so that we could catch the sunrise over the sandstone towers of the temple complex of Angkor Wat, which is the largest religious structure in the world.[23]

We rode through Siem Reap watching the sky turn from the black of night into the light blue of an early morning. We arrived to the massive Hindu turned Buddhist temple and saw other backpackers converging upon the site for the sunrise as well. Vendors approached us and tried to sell anything from T-shirts to flutes to breakfast at an outdoor café.

We walked on a stone bridge that led to Angkor Wat and were immediately impressed by the size and scale of the square moat that surrounded the complex.

Hmmm … for this blog entry I will not go into extreme detail about all the temples that I saw today. Instead I will provide my impressions and observations of them. To learn more about this enormous religious site, I suggest reading *The Civilizations of Angkor* by Charles Higham. There is simply too much history and archaeology to cover in a single journal entry so I will not attempt to do so.

Impressions: I have never come across another archaeological marvel such as the Khmer Empire capital city of Angkor. The size and scale of this urban complex is considered to be the largest in the preindustrial world with a "settlement landscape integrated by an elaborate water management network covering >1,000 km^2."[24] There are perhaps over 1,000 temples in varying states that were built between the 9th and 15th centuries. I was most surprised to discover (due to my ignorance prior to visiting the site) that these temples had Hindu motifs and relief carvings. The successive kings of Angkor either followed a Hindu inspired religion or a Buddhist one until the 14th century when Theravada Buddhism became the state religion.[25]

Upon the walls of Angkor Wat, and many other temples, I saw stone reliefs of dancing, bare breasted Khmer women wearing elaborate headdresses and dresses while holding a flower near the lower part of their stomachs, which was most likely a fertility symbol. It was rare to find a stone relief of men in the temples of Angkor. But in the Bayon temple I found a series of bas-reliefs all around it that provided a glimpse into the history of the Khmer Empire for I saw carvings of the kings and all the tribute paid to them by lords, merchants, and farmers. I also saw carvings of men fishing and hunting, and the defeat and destruction of enemies in far off lands by Khmer kings and their soldiers.

A common motif for the entrance gates to certain temples was a short or long path lined on both sides with a series of statues depicting Khmer men gripping the tail and body of a five-headed serpent.

The majority of the temples were in great condition, which was amazing considering that there were a few temples such as Ta Prohm (a scene from the film *Tomb Raider* (2001) was filmed at the temple) that have centuries old roots from towering trees growing over and into their stone walls and roofs nearly breaking them down; this provided me with the sensation that the jungle sought to reclaim the land altered by the monuments of man.

An archaeological buff could spend years, decades, or more carefully investigating the architectural details of all the temples throughout the vast Angkor complex.

As I traveled with my driver from temple to temple I began to enjoy the verses and techniques used by the Cambodian children who tried to sell me anything from a drink to a T-shirt to a flute or some other trinket. Over and over the voices of Cambodian boys and girls chanted: "Hello. Where are you from? Oh, Chicago. Your country's capital is Washington D.C. There are 285 million people in your country. You buy, sir. You see–you buy. I have Cambodian T-shirt for you–very good! You buy–you buy."

I would respond: "I'm sorry, but I'm not interested."

They would then answer: " 'I'm sorry,' doesn't get me anything. You buy. I sell this T-shirt for three dollars. Two T-shirts for five."

"No, thank you."

" 'No'? It's not expensive. Please, sir. You buy. If you buy I pray good luck for you every day. If you don't buy, I pray bad luck for you every day. You buy–you buy."

"No."

" 'No'! You are a bad man."

These children could say all this not only English but in Spanish, Japanese, Thai, and even Chinese. They were very bright and clever, and had a great sense of humor and a strong determination to sell their goods. They were excellent little sales people. In most cases I caved in and bought drinks for my driver and myself.

At times, I came across children who were selling scarves and pirated books in the temples, but they quickly ran away when the tourist police approached. Most of the children and adults that sold souvenirs did so just beyond the entrance to the temples, which the tourist police tolerated. It was amusing to see touts swarm around a tourist using every line they knew to sell an item, but then stop as soon as the tourist crossed over an invisible line into the temple that the vendors could not pass.

Later in the day I ran into two Americans that I had met in Luang Prabang, Laos. Since we were at the Ta Prohm temple we decided to search for the stone doorway that served as the cover for their edition of *Lonely Planet: Cambodia*. We scoured the location and, in the process, met a group of Canadians that joined us. Finally, one of us asked a guide about the famed doorway and he led us directly to it. We then took out our digital cameras and began taking a barrage of photos. And before we went our separate ways to further explore Angkor we decided to meet up for dinner at the Dead Fish Café.

Posted by The Legacy Cycle at 2004-05-24T22:11:00-07:00

Meeting *Her* at the Summit of Ta Keo

Nicholas held his digital camera steady, looked at the image on the camera screen, tilted it slightly, and took a photo of a short, bald Cambodian man dressed in a light green, long sleeved buttoned shirt, grey fisherman pants, white flip flops, and a light red, patterned krama scarf that was draped over his left shoulder. He took a moment to look at the frozen image of the man framed within the Ta Prohm stone doorway that was overgrown with strangler fig plant roots suffocating a towering tropical tree. He liked the contrast of the image; the organic, thick, descending white veins of the plant roots intertwining themselves over the tanned, smooth bark of a tall tree whose branches reached upwards, but whose base had enmeshed itself into the linear sandstone corners and cracks of millennia old temple architecture. Scattered along the floor before the doorway were broken, weathered stone blocks. Yet again, he saw that no monuments of man last against the persistent, reclaiming strength of nature. Civilizations, such as the one before him, all sadly come and go.

He took another two photos of the man, and continued walking through the Khmer ruins in the tropical heat. He felt as if he was living a childhood desire to discover and explore some unknown jungle city. He tried to imagine what the ancient temple had been like in the time of the Khmer King Jayavarman VII. *What role and rituals were played out on this land by the king, his court, and his servants?* He wondered if the Khmer people of that time had ever thought that centuries later people from half a world away would be walking over these hallowed grounds. *Did they ever think that the impressive, imperial power of the Khmer would ultimately come to a devastating end and be forgotten for a time?* He then wondered the same of his own civilization: *Could it come to an end?* But he knew the answer, and then asked himself: *When would it end? What will people think of us in a thousand years' time? Will the human race even survive another thousand years?*

He took a few photos of the intricate bas-relief patterns on the columns and walls of the temple and decided that it was time to visit the next site. He began walking east through the ruins along a beaten, dirt path that served as the tourist entrance to the temple toward the road where Leo, his hired Cambodian moto-taxi driver, would be waiting for him. He saw at a short distance away Leo talking with three moto-taxi colleagues on the road ahead. He kept walking.

Leo turned his head, looked at the path, recognized Nicholas, smiled, checked his watch, and explained to his working friends that his patron for the day was arriving. He adjusted his imitation Ray-Ban Wayfarer sunglasses, checked his short, slick back, black hair in the rear-view mirror of his scooter, got on the vehicle, and started the engine.

"How was it?" Leo asked when Nicholas arrived.

"Amazing," he replied.

"They filmed *Tomb Raider* here."

"Yes, I know. You told me."

"Did you see the movie?"

"No, not yet," he answered knowing that he had little desire to see the film as he did not play video games and cared very little for the character of Lara Croft, which he considered to be a modern take on Indiana Jones mixed with the wealth of Bruce Wayne.

Nicholas got on the back portion of the motorcycle's seat looking forward to the breeze he would feel from the ride to the next temple. Leo revved the engine, and they sped down a poorly paved road that was lined with a few makeshift shops offering food, drinks, and Cambodian trinkets. They rode north for a few minutes, and at a T-intersection, Leo turned left, sped the motorcycle up from first to second gear, and then slowed down to a stop at the south gate of a sandstone, five-tier step pyramid built a thousand years ago to represent Mount Meru; a sacred mountain of five peaks in the Hindu, Jain, and Buddhist faiths.

"This is Ta Keo," Leo announced.

Nicholas looked at the southern side of the temple-mountain and noticed that there were no carvings or bas-relief patterns along its walls, but at the summit he saw three impressive stone block towers.

"It's unfinished," Leo added. "They say it was struck by lightning—bad luck, my friend, bad luck," he said with a smile. "So—they stopped building it."

Perhaps it looks better this way, Nicholas thought as a result of seeing so many stone temples in Europe and Asia littered with so many symbolic details that it was nearly impossible for an observer to take it all in.

"I'll wait for you here," Leo informed Nicholas.

Nicholas got off the scooter, drank some water from the water bottle he had in his small back pack, and made his way up the short, dirt path to the south gate. He walked looking at the two towering trees at opposite sides of the path wondering if they were mere saplings when worshippers came to pay homage to Shiva, but it was unlikely since the temple was a thousand years old. He noticed as well that near the summit of the temple there were three Cambodian monks traditionally dressed in orange garments.

He reached the base of the temple, ascended eight stone steps, and walked through a gopura (an entrance building). He ascended more steps to the second-tier walking through a second gopura, and continued his ascent up the many steep steps of the pyramid until he reached the final tier that provided impressive views of the surrounding jungle landscape. At each corner of the summit there was a stone sanctuary tower, and elevated by a four-meter stone base was a central sanctuary tower, thus collectively the five towers represented the five peaks of the sacred Mount Meru.

He took out his water bottle and drank some more while feeling the intensity of the sun beat down on his forehead causing more perspiration. He finished drinking, returned the bottle to his backpack, and wiped his brow with his right forearm. He looked around and saw the three monks he had seen before now entering the dark of one of the protruding vestibules that the central sanctuary tower had on each of its four sides.

    He decided to sit down on a stone block and rest for a moment. He looked back up the remaining steps to the central tower, but he did not have the interest to walk up and explore it nor the other four sanctuary towers. He felt that after seeing so many temples all morning and early afternoon he would most likely see the same patterns of architecture that he had already seen—a symptom that temple fatigue was beginning to set in. He wanted to just rest, listen, and watch the landscape and the tourists on the temple. He heard the voices of two North American English speakers. He looked toward the voices and saw a young twenty-something woman wearing an orange T-shirt with an image of the famed eyes and eyebrows of Buddha painted on the sides of the Swayambhu stupa in Kathmandu, Nepal, green cargo pants that had been rolled up to just below her knees, and grey hiking shoes. She was climbing up the steps of the temple and speaking with a young man who wore a blue baseball cap, a blue T-shirt, black shorts, and brown hiking shoes. They soon reached the summit, caught their breath from the climb, and took in the glorious tropical view.

    Nicholas asked where they were from, and they explained that they were from Toronto, Canada. He then told them that he was from Chicago, and they began to talk of the countries that they had traveled to in Southeast Asia. The conversation soon gravitated toward the U.S. presidential election and whether or not President George W. Bush would win re-election, the 2003 invasion of Iraq, and health care in which they commented that their publicly funded health care system was essentially free; something that was very difficult for Nicholas to imagine as he had to pay a portion of the costs for the health care services he used in the U.S. and Japan. The two Canadians then saw a commercial bus pull up to the temple site below, and after a few moments a line of South Korean tourists beginning to exit the bus with cameras in hand ready to take photos. The Canadians quickly said goodbye to Nicholas and began to descend the steep stone temple steps in the hopes of avoiding the approaching crowd of South Korean tourists.

"Vamos! Que vienen los Charlies!" a young woman in her early twenties shouted jokingly to her friend who was trying take a photo of the three Cambodian monks that were now located on the tier below.

Nicholas looked to the woman–she had short, brown curly hair, wore a black tang top, turquoise colored Thai fisherman styled pants, and white gym shoes–and said with a smile, "Hola."

The young woman turned and asked with the hope that after a couple of months of traveling she and her friend had finally come across another Spanish backpacker, "Hola, español?"

"No, I'm from Chicago," he answered in English.

The young woman's hopes were dashed as she wondered why anyone would initially speak in Spanish to then speak in English. She continued her descent to reach her friend who was dressed in a white tang top, a black skirt, and dark grey gym shoes.

Nicholas began to step down as well.

The woman realized that she had been rude to cut the conversation so short, but she had had enough of interacting with so many overconfident, and at times arrogant, American backpackers. She stopped, looked back to Nicholas noticing that he was tall, skinny, almost bald from shaving his head down to the skin a week before, and that he wore a dark blue T-shirt, green cargo pants with pant legs rolled up to just below his knees, and black Adidas Samba indoor soccer shoes. "I'm sorry, I thought you were Spanish," she explained.

"Oh, but my parents are from Chile," he answered.

The young woman's eyes widened by the response. *Did he not hear that I had thought he was Spanish? What does it matter if his parents are Chilean?* "So, you speak Spanish?"

"No," he replied laughing at his inability to speak the native language of his parents.

What the hell, she thought, but pleased that he could laugh at himself. *His parents speak Spanish, but he doesn't other than saying, "hola".* She wanted to shake her head at him.

"You're traveling?"

Obviously. "Yes, I'm traveling with my friend," she answered and pointed to her companion who was still trying to take a photo of the Cambodian monks.

"I'm traveling by myself," he said thinking that she would be impressed.

Okay! Congratulations. Qué le pasa a este flipado? Her friend then called her to hurry up. "Enjoy, goodbye," she said.

"Goodbye," he replied as he watched her move down to the next tier to help her friend take a few more photos of the Cambodian monks. He then descended to the next level of the pyramid, passing the two Spanish women, and continued down to the base of the temple. He then walked down the path to the street seeing his driver Leo finish a bottled drink. He then stopped, turned, and took a photo of the pyramid capturing the two Spanish women at a distance making their way down the path toward the street. He packed his camera into the soft camera case that he had attached to the black, nylon strap of a waist pack that ran across his chest and kept walking until he reached Leo who had started the motorcycle. Nicholas got on the back seat, Leo revved the engine, and they rode away turning right with the street that wrapped around the southeastern corner of the temple.

"Wait, wait a moment," Nicholas asked Leo thinking of the Spanish woman he had met. "Stop the moto, I want to take one more photo of the temple."

Leo slowed the motodop, and stopped.

Nicholas got off the motorcycle-taxi, took two more photos, and turned seeing the two Spanish women riding up the road on motorbike taxis and passing and leaving him behind.

"We go?" Leo asked.

"Yes, we go," he answered.

*   *   *

Nicholas walked up Sivatha Boulevard in Siem Reap just after sunset; he was headed toward the Dead Fish Café to meet a few American, Canadian, and British backpackers for dinner at 7 pm. He saw the blue lighted sign that advertised the café, reached it, and entered the establishment for the first time to discover that it was essentially a bistro bar and guesthouse that catered mostly to backpackers. He was amazed as he looked up to see that the short leg dining tables of the restaurant were raised on a second-floor platform that was connected to the bar through a rope and pulley system that elevated drinks not only to the tables, but also to the windows of the guesthouse rooms located on the third and fourth floors. In addition, next to the first-floor bathroom there was a small pool filled with hungry baby crocodiles that patrons could feed by buying bits of raw chicken from the bar. There was also a baby monkey on a leash that customers could pet. Live lounge music emanated from a blind Thai pianist who took requests and wore Ray Charles-like sunglasses.

Nicholas did not see any sign of the travelers he was to meet on the second floor. He took out his watch from the waist pack that he had strapped across his chest and saw that he was about twenty minutes early. He walked toward the end of the bistro bar where he saw free Internet advertised. But as he neared the computer cubicles where several backpackers were reading or typing emails, he saw the young Spanish woman he had met earlier that day at the summit of the Ta Keo temple; she was drinking a milk shake while sitting on an elevated platform with one foot planted on the ground and the other hanging down and swinging slightly back and forth. He looked up to the second floor trying to appear as if he had not seen her, but he heard her say to him: "Hola."

He looked at her, smiled, and said, "Hi! Great to see you again." He approached her and asked if he could sit with her while he waited for the backpackers he was to have dinner with.

"Yes, of course."

He sat down and asked why she was at the Dead Fish. She explained that they were lured in by the free Internet that was advertised, but there were only two computers free for her, her friend Zaira, and another friend from France by the name of Veronique. Since she was not particularly eager to read and write emails she volunteered to sit and wait while Zaira and Veronique used the computers. She then introduced herself to him as Carmen, and he introduced himself to her.

He asked her what other countries they had been to on their backpacking trip. She explained that they had been to Thailand, but that they had been living prior to the trip in Sydney, Australia. He told her that he had never been to Australia, but that he had always wanted to go, especially after he learned that *Star Wars: Episode II* was filmed at Fox Studios Australia in Sydney. She thought that that was a poor reason to visit Australia as there were so many wonderful things to witness and experience in its capital, national parks, to its wildlife such as the adorable, short-legged, furry wombat. He had no idea what a wombat was and thus had difficulty imagining what the mammal looked like.

      She asked him about his travels and he listed the countries he had been to after leaving Japan, where he had lived for over three years. She felt that he was trying to impress her again, but she also saw that he was genuinely interested in her life in Australia and the life she had left behind in Barcelona, Spain. He told her that he had been to Barcelona in the summer of 1997 for two to three days and that there was something unique about her city that called to him to return to explore it more. She then extended an invitation to him as she reached out and touched his right arm: "Please, if you ever are in my city, let me know."

      "Thank you, I will," he then saw a few of the backpackers he was to have dinner with arrive. "They're here, I have to go, but let me give you my card." He unzipped his waist pack and searched for a plastic box that had his meshi (business) cards from Japan. "I have a travel blog so if you're interested to know where I am or you want to read about where I've been to you can check it out."

      She didn't like that attempt at self-promotion, but she was pleased that they could stay in touch.

      "Let me give you my email, and my address in Spain if you ever come to Barcelona."

      "Yes, that's great," he said. He found the plastic box, opened it, and gave her one of his Japanese business cards. She then wrote down her contact details on a piece of paper he had taken out from his waist pack.

      They then said their goodbyes not really expecting to ever see each other again, but excited by the unlikely possibility.

* * *

Nicholas joined the American, British, and Canadian backpackers for dinner. And after eating a warm meal, he sat with a banana milk shake listening and sharing hilarious, and at times dangerous travel stories. One of the most shocking stories came from the two Americans and their friend Sarah from England who explained that when they had returned to their hotel in Siem Reap the previous night they found two hotel staff members having sex on one of their beds.

And after a long day, and enjoyable night, Nicholas went to bed at midnight.

* * *

The next morning, Monday, May 24, Nicholas woke up sweaty from another tropical night. He took a shower, got dressed, and left the Millennium Hotel wanting to take it easy and get caught up on his travel blog. He walked down Psa Kroum Road ignoring several offers from moto-taxi drivers, and turned left onto Sivatha Boulevard looking for a good place to eat breakfast. He saw a café with open air seating, but he did not want to eat in the light of the morning sun, so he entered the café and sat down at a table facing the window. He ordered fried eggs, toasted bread, grilled tomatoes and mushrooms, and a cup of café au lait. As he typically did while waiting for his food he pulled out the secondhand book he was currently reading entitled *The Damage Done: Twelve Years of Hell in a Bangkok Prison* by Warren Fellows. After reading a few pages his food arrived and he began eating.

Outside he saw a young backpacking couple looking at the café's blackboard street sign that listed the food and prices from their breakfast menu. The couple nodded to each other and walked toward the interior of the café. They took a seat at a table across from Nicholas, placed their The North Face day backpacks on the empty seat near the wall, looked through the menu, made their order, and began looking through their guidebook deciding what they were to see that day. Nicholas noticed from the way they spoke and dressed by wearing stylish Nike running shoes that they were most likely from the U.S.

"Where are you from?" Nicholas asked the young couple.

"From California," the young man answered; he had blond, short hair and looked physically fit. "How about you?"

"I'm from Chicago," he answered.

"My name's Kent, and this is my wife, Tawnya."

Tawnya, although American, looked either of Japanese or South Korean descent to Nicholas. Nicholas then shared his name with them and they began asking each other the usual backpacker questions of how long they had been traveling and where they had traveled to. The conversation then led to the couple explaining that they were on their honeymoon, which later led to Kent explaining that he was a software engineer with aspirations to work in the video game industry, and Tawnya explained that she was a medical student.

The young couple finished their morning meal and began to leave, but stopped to ask Nicholas what he had planned that morning. He explained that he was going to an Internet café to write a few entries in his travel blog, and they decided to join him, but they first needed to find a bank to exchange some money.

At the Internet café, Nicholas first checked his emails and wrote a few friends and family members informing them of where he was in Cambodia and that he was alright. He then decided to write Carmen, the Spanish woman he had met last night, to say hello to her in the hopes that they at least could stay in touch via email, and to also inform her that he would next be traveling to Saigon, Vietnam in case she and her friend were headed in the same direction. He then worked on updating his travel blog for the next two hours.

After the Internet café, Kent, Tawnya, and Nicholas decided to grab lunch at the Dead Fish Café. As they ordered and ate Kent and Tawnya continued talking about their travels, life in California, how they met in college, and their plans to move from San Francisco to Los Angeles.

Nicholas enjoyed listening to their every word, and watching a young couple in love and traveling through so many exotic places together. He hoped for something like what they had. He began to hope for love again.

Posted by The Legacy Cycle at 2004-05-24T22:11:00-07:00

Monday, May 24, 2004

The Beatocello Concert
Saturday, May 22, 2004

In the evening, I went to a free concert at the Jayavarman VII Children's Hospital. Dr. Beat Richner, a Swiss pediatrician who founded and runs the Kantha Bopha Foundation (http://www.beat-richner.ch), plays his cello every Saturday night in Siem Reap, and between his performances of several classical pieces he educates the audience on the chronic illnesses in the country as a means to raise awareness and donations.

This is what I learned from Dr. Beat Richner. Last year (2003), there was not a single tourist that came to his hospital in Siem Reap to give blood or donate cash. The reason for this was the SARS (severe acute respiratory syndrome) outbreak. Dr. Richner explained that since SARS was affecting Asian financial capitals such as Hong Kong and Singapore it became a major concern for developed nations. As a result, Western media heavily covered the SARS outbreak. And although there was not a single reported case of SARS in Cambodia, the number of tourists traveling through the country dropped significantly. Dr. Richner argued that Cambodia was perhaps the safest place to be in Southeast Asia during the outbreak, but the exaggerated media attention had scared foreign travelers away from the region. At the same time, there was a massive dengue fever outbreak in Cambodia resulting in 9,000 children's cases, but yet CNN and the BBC did little to bring public light to this health crisis. Instead, they focused on SARS because it was affecting the moneymaking cities of developed nations in Southeast Asia.

Developing nations such as Cambodia have very little political influence or power over developed nations and their institutions such as UNICEF and the World Health Organization (WHO).

Last year there were 67,000 children who were admitted to the Kantha Bopha Children's Hospitals in Cambodia, which works out to about 122-240 severely sick children per day. Eighty percent of these children would not have survived if it were not for these three Kantha

Bopha hospitals (as of 2017 there are five Kantha Bopha hospitals).

According to Dr. Richner, the number one killer in Cambodia is tuberculosis, which is the result of three factors: Pol Pot's regime, the attitude of developed nations in regards to how to handle health care in developing nations, and the 2003 dengue fever outbreak. A child suffering from dengue fever needs a blood transfusion, but international health organizations such as the WHO and UNICEF have argued that it is too expensive for developing nations to receive the necessary funds to check their blood supply properly for sexually transmitted diseases such as the HIV virus. As a result, for every 100 blood transfusions seven children will contract the HIV virus.

In 1970 the Nixon/Kissinger administration launched a "secret war" in Cambodia, which resulted in the bombing of 40 percent of the country. Five hundred thousand Cambodian civilians were killed and two million refugees flocked to Phnom Penh to seek shelter and safety from the US air raids. These refugee camps became a breeding ground for tuberculosis. And during the Pol Pot regime tuberculosis spread rapidly among the population as a result of the unsanitary conditions of the concentration and work camps.

Today, 45 percent of the children hospitalized in Cambodia have tuberculosis. Tuberculosis weakens the child and although it is a common virus it can prove fatal for children. Tuberculosis can remain dormant within an individual, which has resulted in the transmission of the virus from unknowing mothers to infants through breastfeeding.

Eighty-five percent of the families that take their children to one of the Kantha Bopha hospitals in Phnom Penh are too poor to afford the hospital fees. In Siem Reap, 95 percent are unable to afford the hospitals. The Kantha Bopha Foundation receives $50 million a year and 90 percent is derived from private donations. Because of these donations no family or child is ever turned away from the Kantha Bopha hospitals. All patients are treated and given prescription drugs for free. With these private donations Dr. Beat Richner maintains a very high and modern standard for his hospitals. The hospitals are state-of-the-art and all the hospital's 1,400 staff are paid. Thirty-five percent of the donations are used to pay the hospital's staff and 45 percent is spent on modern medicine and technology that is imported from developed nations. The hospitals have the ability to detect tuberculosis in children by using computed tomography (CT) scans of the brain; but Dr. Richner highlighted that the WHO and UNICEF have made the case that a poor nation such as Cambodia should not have such a device!

Over and over Dr. Richner said, "Every child has the right for the correct drug, the correct procedure, the correct treatment." He is perplexed as to why international organizations such as the WHO and UNICEF try to prohibit developing nations from receiving the exact same medical treatment that people in developed nations receive. Dr. Richner also explained that the WHO and UNICEF recommended that developing nations use medicinal drugs that are prohibited in developed nations because of their unwanted side effects!

After the concert, I donated cash to the hospital. Although Dr. Richner at the beginning of the concert asked for the young members of the audience to give blood instead of money I was more than happy to give money for I had never given blood before. I left the hospital relieved that no one after the concert who worked for the hospital approached any of the travelers to request that they give blood. But when I met up with Leo, my driver, I expressed how unusual I thought it was that no one asked the members of the audience to give blood. Leo misunderstood me and thought that I had said I wanted to give blood. The next thing I knew he was leading me back to the hospital gate where a security guard then led me through the hospital to the blood bank. I was very nervous. I filled out all the paperwork and found myself lying down about to be poked with a syringe to begin the blood donation process. I was uncomfortable, but five minutes later it was over and I walked out of the hospital with a bag full of cookies and a T-shirt.

After the hospital, Leo drove me to a restaurant where I sat at a table outside for a bite to eat. While I waited for my meal a poor Cambodian girl came up to me asking for money. I didn't want to give her any cash because I knew that she would give it to her parents who I could see were watching from a distance. Instead, I gave her the bag of cookies from the hospital and ordered a sandwich for her. I told her to wait. The girl then sat on the ground before me like a dog waiting for its meal. I pointed to the chair across the table from me and she stood up and sat down; she was my date for the evening. I was served the Pepsi soft drink that I had ordered, but the girl pointed to it. I gave it to her and with a smile she drank it. Our sandwiches were served and together we ate until Tawnya saw me and sat down with us. When the girl had finished her meal, she left. Kent soon joined us along with other people I had met in Siem Reap.

After eating and talking I went back to my hotel.

Posted by The Legacy Cycle at 2004-05-24T23:15:00-07:00

Wednesday, May 26, 2004

Siem Reap to Phnom Penh
Sunday, May 23, 2004

On the bus from Siem Reap to Phnom Penh I met several travelers in their twenties: Jacky from South Africa, and James, Shane, and Tina from the United Kingdom. We spent the first half of the bus journey talking and joking about our experiences in Cambodia and in other Southeast Asian nations. About two hours from Phnom Penh we stopped for about a half hour in a town called Skuon. It was here that we saw women selling breaded, deep fried tarantulas piled high on basket serving trays. The locals in Skuon are famed for eating these large spiders for breakfast, lunch, and dinner. It is said that this unique taste started out of necessity due to the famine of the 1970s caused by the disastrous communist economic policies of the Pol Pot regime. It is also said that Cambodians ate insects and rats as a source of protein to survive during this period.

We crossed the Tonlé Sap River via the Chroy Changva Bridge and arrived in Phnom Penh at two in the afternoon. Our bus stopped at a point along the river, and as soon as we began to step off the bus we were immediately approached by touts that sought to take any and all of us to one of several guesthouses. Jacky, James, Tina, Shane, a young French woman named Annie, and I teamed up to take separate moto taxis to search for a guesthouse overlooking the Boeung Kak Lake. This was the second time that Jacky, James, Tina, and Shane had been to Phnom Penh and so Annie and I simply followed their lead to a dirt road just west of Monivong Boulevard that was lined with a few travel agencies, Happy Pizza restaurants, Internet cafés, and several guesthouses with views overlooking the lake; it was the "Khaosan

Road" of Phnom Penh. Jacky, James, Tina, and Shane then led us from one lakeside guesthouse to the next until they finally recognized the one that they had stayed at.

We checked in, dropped our bags in our rooms, washed up, and ate lunch on the deck as we took in the scenic view of the lake. Annie, Jacky, and I then decided to explore the city.

Annie wanted to buy a pair pants so we walked to the Central Market (constructed in 1937), which was a massive, X-shaped concrete structure with a dome at its center that was filled with an endless number of small shops that sold anything from clothing to toys to shoes to food. The food section offered chopped pieces of pigs, cows or chickens that hung in the humid air from hooks while flies fluttered around them.

Annie—dressed in black short shorts and a white tube top—spent an hour looking at, trying on, and bargaining for pants—Jacky and I were slowly losing our patience. In the end, she did not find a pair of pants to her liking and she decided to leave. Jacky and I were relieved. We traveled further south seeing a few "massage parlors," plenty of food vendors, shops, and scores of people traveling this way and that in a city that seemed nearly devoid of traffic signals. We then came across a small Chinese temple and an outdoor farmers' market where locals could buy live or dead chickens, butchered meat that hung from hooks, and fresh fish.

We arrived to Sisowath Quay and took a stroll south along the Tonlé Sap River walking parallel to Sisowath Boulevard (a street that was lined with hotels, restaurants, cafés, bars such as the Foreign Correspondents' Club, and shops). It was along this walk that I fell in love with Phnom Penh, a hidden gem in Southeast Asia. The city had tremendous potential to develop and become a very romantic destination. The views of the Boeung Kak Lake from my guesthouse combined with the quaintness of Sisowath Quay and the flowing calm of the Tonlé Sap River made Phnom Penh a pleasant city; I felt safe, curious, and at peace. But there was poverty. It was everywhere.

As Annie, Jacky, and I strolled along Sisowath Quay we saw a very skinny and weak 17-year-old Cambodian sprawled on the grass beside the sidewalk. Annie covered her mouth and pointed to the exposed left side of his abdomen. I looked and saw something I had never seen before; the area just beneath his left rib cage had a massive hole—there was no skin or flesh. There—literally—was a hole the size of my hand from fingertips to the base of my palm on his left side. I could actually see into his body. I could see his lungs! Flies were hovering above him and nesting within his hole. Jacky, Annie, and I panicked. We did not know what to do although we wanted to help him. We decided to run to a hotel across the street and call for an ambulance or a hospital for help. As a result of attending Dr. Richner's concert and lecture I knew that at least the hospitals that he ran were free so I looked up two in the phone book that were located in Phnom Penh and called, but no one answered; it was Sunday. Jacky and I then looked through our *Lonely Planet* guide and decided that the Calmette Hospital was our best bet. I called the number in the guide and spoke to a doctor who thought that I was sick. I tried to explain that I was going to bring someone to his hospital. But he did not understand. I then asked him how much it would cost to treat the Cambodian adolescent, but the doctor did not know since he had not seen the patient. I told him I was on my way.

Jacky, Annie, and I left the hotel and I hailed a cycle rickshaw taxi driver. We told him to cross the street and on the other side I called another cycle rickshaw taxi. The homeless young man with the hole in his side was lifted and held up by a few of his homeless friends. They then placed him on the seat of one of the cycle rickshaws. I sat in the other rickshaw and away we went to the hospital leaving Jacky and Annie behind.

The ride took about 15 minutes. Once we arrived I got out of my rickshaw and then led the other rickshaw driver into the emergency area where two male nurses exited the hospital with a stretcher. We all lifted the adolescent, placed him on the stretcher, and took him inside. I gave the rickshaw driver $4 and told him that $2 was for him and the other $2 was for the other driver who was waiting outside. I repeated those instructions to him several times. He just smiled and peddled away.

I went into the emergency room and saw four other poverty-stricken patients that had been brought in. Most of them were with their families. The adolescent that I brought in had no one to comfort him. I waited to speak to the doctor and when he was free I took him over to the adolescent. He looked at the hole in the young man's left side and asked him a few questions. The doctor then turned to me and thanked me for bringing him in and that I could go. I asked what was going to happen to the young man. The doctor explained that he would undergo surgery to have his left lung removed and that he would spend several nights in the hospital free of charge. I asked if there was anything else that I could do. The doctor said that I could give the young man some money so that he could eat when he left the hospital. I then walked to the young Cambodian and gave him $10. He thanked me, and I stepped back, away, and left.

When I walked out of the hospital I saw the rickshaw taxi driver who had taken me to the hospital. I asked him if he received the $2 from the other rickshaw driver. He did not seem to understand what I was talking about but when another local stepped in to translate I discovered that the other rickshaw driver had run off with $3 and had only given this driver $1. I was extremely upset that this rickshaw driver had been cheated by one of his own people. I gave him an additional dollar.

From the hospital, I walked back to my guesthouse. And later that night Jacky, Annie, James, Tina, Shane, and another Shane from Australia, and I decided to go for dinner back on Sisowath Quay. We got along wonderfully. It was a pleasant way to end an unusual day.

Posted by The Legacy Cycle at 2004-05-26T05:58:00-07:00

Thursday, May 27, 2004

The Shooting Range, The Killing Fields, S-21, & Happy Pizza
Monday, May 24, 2004

Monday morning Annie (wearing yet again short shorts and a tube top), Aussie Shane (who wore a white empty top hat, a burgundy T-shirt, and dark brown cargo shorts), and I hired three moto-taxi drivers to take us to a shooting range on the outskirts of Phnom Penh; I had first heard about this shooting range while I was living in Japan. After we rode passed the Phnom Penh International Airport we veered off the highway and entered an open field that in the distance had a large, single-storey thatched building. We entered the building and saw racked on the bamboo wall to our left a variety of rifles and machine guns along with two Cambodian flags and framed pictures of soldiers parachuting from a military aircraft or posing with their platoon. We sat down at a table on red, plastic lawn chairs and were given a menu of firearms that we could rent from one of the Cambodian men who ran the establishment.

Menu of Firearms
RIFLES

AK-47 – 30 bullets – $20 U.S.

M16 – 30 bullets – $30 U.S.

UZI – 30 bullets – $30 U.S.

K-50M – 30 bullets – $30 U.S.

Shotgun – 5 bullets – $20 U.S.

HANDGUNS

CZ 75 – 13 bullets – $26 U.S.

K59 – 8 bullets – $16 U.S.

K54 – 8 bullets – $10 U.S.

.45 ACP – 7 bullets – $10 U.S.

Revolver .38 – 6 bullets – $12 U.S.

Ruger .22 – 10 bullets – $12 U.S.

Hand grenade – 1 grenade – $20 U.S.

MACHINE GUNS

M60 – 100 bullets – $100.00

RPD (Russian) – 150 bullets – $100.00

Rocket launcher – 1 missile – $200.00

I had heard from backpackers in my guesthouse that for an additional $100 on top of the $200 for the rocket launcher you could attempt to blow up a cow. I asked one of the men working at the firing range if I could target a cow if I rented the rocket launcher. He nodded. A man from the Netherlands at another table who overhead my question then asked, "Can we keep the meat?" The Cambodian said no, but that they would grill whatever was left of the animal, which we could eat.

I could not believe it! But the next day I heard from other backpackers that they had witnessed other travelers shooting ducks and chickens at the same firing range. So as a perk to traveling to Phnom Penh foreigners can rent guns and rocket launchers and kill animals? I did not want to kill any animals, but I did want to experience firing an automatic weapon. I rented the AK-47 loaded with thirty rounds for $20 and Shane rented the Revolver .38; Annie chose not to participate.

Shane and I were escorted into an enclosed brick building with a long and dark passage. At the end of the passage was a paper target that was clipped to an upright wooden board with rubble and debris piled up behind it. One of the Cambodian men that worked at the firing range prepared my gun, and after I put on my shooting earmuffs I shot my first round. I immediately turned to Shane in a state of shock; firing this weapon was one of the scariest experiences of my young life. The gun had kicked back with such extreme force, and the bullet that I shot off was invisible to my eyes. I could not begin to fathom what it must be like to be shot at and feel a bullet rip through your skin and blow apart organs. I then looked through the gun sight, aimed, and fired again and again trying to hit the paper target. My aim was no good. I missed repeatedly. I then adjusted my aim based on where I had seen the bullets hit the pile of dirt and rubble behind the target. A few shots later the Cambodian changed my AK-47 setting to automatic and from then on it was chaos. I held down the trigger feeling the weapon spit out the rest of my rounds in less than a few seconds.

It was Shane's turn to shoot the revolver. We exited the building and walked to an outdoor shooting range. Shane took up his weapon and aimed, but I did not have my shooting earmuffs on when he fired his first shot–I instantly went deaf in my right ear hearing a constant ringing sound that lasted for most of the day.

Guns are incredibly loud. And after firing the AK-47 and seeing Shane fire his six-shooter I finally knew from experience that the glorified gun fighting scenes from any Hollywood film that I had grown up watching was all a load of crap. In real life, after you fired off one or two shots without ear protection, you would be deaf and shouting instead of speaking dialogue. Just imagine sitting in a foxhole during combat with three other soldiers all firing their weapons. You would be completely deaf within the first minute of it and from that point on you would need to scream at the top of your lungs to communicate with the man just next to you. The film industry rarely shows that reality of war or gun violence.

Shane and I both found that the sights on our guns were useless. We learned that we were eventually able to hit our targets by adjusting our aims based on seeing where the bullets had hit.

It was an interesting experience to fire a weapon, but something that I hope to never do again.

After the shooting range Annie, Shane, and I headed to the Choeung Ek mass grave, which is one of the Cambodian Killing Fields sites. In 1980, a year after the fall of the Khmer Rouge regime, 86 communal graves were identified with 8,895 bodies exhumed around the Choeung Ek site; 43 of the 129 mass graves at the site have yet to be excavated.[26] Analysis of more than 19,000 grave sites by the Documentation Center of Cambodia (DC-Cam) Mapping Project, which was established by the Cambodian Genocide Program at Yale University, has indicated that there are more than 1.3 million executed bodies in the Killing Fields.[27,28,29] The forensic evidence at Choeung Ek revealed that the victims had been blindfolded, beheaded, bound, and/or beaten to death as a means for Khmer Rouge soldiers to save bullets. The majority of those that had been executed at Choeung Ek were transported from the S-21 prison.

Upon entering Choeung Ek, we saw a Buddhist stupa with acrylic glass protecting its four sides, and as we approached the stupa we saw that it had been filled with thousands of human skulls that were organized and separated by age and sex. Upon closer examination, I noticed that many of skulls had a sizable hole located at the frontal or parietal bone that had been caused (according to analysis by forensic anthropologists) by the strike of a hammer or other farming implement such as a hoe.[30] As I was to learn, Cambodian prisoners were blindfolded and forced to sit on their knees waiting for a Khmer Rouge soldier to execute them by striking their skull with a hammer or hoe, cutting their throat, or striking the base of their neck with an iron bar[31] before throwing them into a mass grave pit four to six meters deep. Other prisoners had been beheaded not with a machete or other sharp implement, but had their heads sawed off with the sharp edges of palm tree branches.

At the site, there was a tree where many prisoners had been hung to death. There was another tree where soldiers murdered babies and children by grabbing them by the legs and slamming their heads against the tree's trunk to then throw their limp bodies into a nearby pit.

As we walked among these mass graves we could see scattered on the ground in all directions the fragments of bones, teeth, and the faded, torn clothing of the victims who had been exterminated nearly 25 years ago. We were walking over the remains of the dead. So many people were killed here that only 86 of the 129 mass graves had been excavated. As we walked, we gained a very real sense of the horrific scene: the cries of mothers who saw their children smashed against a tree, the screams of husbands being slowly beheaded, daughters gang raped, grandfathers poisoned, and grandmothers electrocuted to death. It is a tortured place. And in the night locals say that they hear the lamentations of the ghosts that haunt this wicked land.

Beginning in 1969, U.S. President Richard Nixon (based on the recommendation made by Earle Wheeler, Chairman of the Joint Chiefs) ordered his National Security Advisor, Henry A. Kissinger, to launch a "secret war" (codenamed Operation *Breakfast* with the following bombing missions codenamed: *Lunch, Snack, Dinner, Supper,* and *Desert* thus all missions were referred to as Operation *Menu*) that entailed the carpet-bombing of Cambodia, Laos, and Vietnam by the United States Strategic Air Command (SAC). In all, SAC dropped 108,823 tons of ordnance from 3,800 B-52 sorties.[32] They were targeting the "sanctuaries and Base Areas of the People's Army of Vietnam (PAVN) and forces of the Viet Cong, which utilized them for resupply, training, and resting between campaigns across the border in the Republic of Vietnam (South Vietnam)."[33] It is estimated that two-fifths of Cambodia was heavily bombed, which left unexploded ordinances (UXO) and cluster munitions all over the country.

> In addition, "landmines became prevalent in Cambodia following the ousting of the Khmer Rouge in 1979. After driving the Khmer Rouge into Thailand, the Vietnamese military forced civilians to create a defensive minefield along the Thai-Cambodian border. In subsequent years, the new state, Khmer Rouge remnants and monarchist opposition forces laid more landmines as battlefronts shifted."[34]

Since 1979, there have been 64,000 landmine casualties of which approximately 30 percent resulted in death.[35] Cambodia, today, "has one of the world's worst land-mine problems and the highest number of amputees per capita of any country – over 25,000 Cambodians have lost limbs due to mines and other military explosives."[36]

Two million Cambodian refugees fled to Phnom Penh (as well as to Thailand and Vietnam) between 1969 and 1975 as a result of the U.S. carpet-bombings and civil war between "the American-backed Lon Nol government and the North Vietnamese soldiers and their Cambodian communist allies, the Khmer Rouge."[37] Many, in their attempt to reach the capital, fell victim to these unexploded ordinances and were either killed or lost a limb(s). These refugees then went on to live in the unsanitary conditions of the refugee and border camps, which became a breeding ground for tuberculosis.

> U.S. bombing continued at a high level after the withdrawal of U.S. forces from Cambodia. By late 1971, an investigating team of the General Accounting Office concluded that U.S. and Saigon army bombing is "a very significant cause of refugees and civilian casualties," estimating that almost a third of the seven-million population may be refugees. U.S. intelligence reported that "what villagers feared most was the possibility of indiscriminate artillery and air strikes," and refugee reports and other sources confirm that these were the major cause of civilian casualties and the flight of refugees.[38]

In 1970, U.S.-backed Lon Nol (a rightist) led a coup d'état against Cambodian Prince Norodom Sihanouk (a leftist) due in part to his tolerance of Viet Cong and People's Army of Vietnam (PAVN) operations within Cambodia.[39] In an effort to reclaim his "kingdom" during the Cambodian Civil War, Prince Sihanouk supported the Khmer Rouge (backed by Communist China) and the North Vietnamese (the ranks of the Khmer Rouge increased dramatically from 6,000 to 50,000 as peasants sought to restore their king; they did not support the ideology of communism).[40] The Khmer Rouge thus were able to gain control of most of rural Cambodia and ultimately sacked the capital in 1975, which began a four-year horrific period of mass executions and famine that resulted in the deaths of 1.4 million to 2.2 million people.[41] In 1979, the Vietnamese invaded Cambodia and freed millions of Cambodians, who had been working in forced labor camps at near starvation levels, from the brutality of the Khmer Rouge.

Annie, Shane, and I traveled by hired moto taxi to the Tuol Sleng Genocide Museum (the former Khmer Rouge Security Prison 21 (S-21)) after visiting the Killing Fields of Choeung Ek. The prison (one of approximately 150 execution centers)[42] was originally a high school. It was here that Cambodian intellectuals were brought after the fall of Phnom Penh to be interrogated, tortured, imprisoned, and executed. From 1977 to 1978 it was estimated that the prison held on average about 1,200 to 1,500 prisoners at any one time. Prisoners were kept at the location anywhere from two to four months. Some political prisoners were kept at the location from six to seven months. According to historian Ben Kiernan, "all but seven of the twenty thousand Tuol Sleng prisoners" were executed.[43]

Tuol Sleng Genocide Museum Notes

The prisoners were kept in their respective cells and shackled with chains fixed to walls or the concrete floors. Prisoners held in large mass cells had one or both of their legs shackled to short or long pieces of iron bar. The short bar was designed for four prisoners and the longer bar was designed for 20 to 30 prisoners. Prisoners were fixed to the iron bar on altering sides, so they had to sleep with their heads in opposite directions.

Before the prisoners were placed in the cells they were photographed, and detailed biographies of their childhood up to the dates of their arrests were recorded. Then they were stripped to their underwear. Everything was taken away from them. The prisoners slept directly on the floors without any mats, mosquito nets or blankets.

Every morning at 4:30 a.m., all prisoners were told to remove their shorts, down to their ankles, for inspection by prison staff. Then they were told to do some physical exercise just by moving their hands and legs up and down for half an hour, even though their legs remained restrained by iron bars.

The prisoners had to defecate into small iron buckets and urinate into small plastic buckets kept in their cells. They were required to ask for permission from the prison guards in advance of relieving themselves; otherwise, they were beaten or they received 20 to 60 strokes with a whip as punishment.

Unhygienic living conditions caused the prisoners to become infected with diseases like skin rashes and various other diseases. There was no medicine for treatment.

The number of workers in [the] S-21 complex totaled 1,720 ... within each unit, there were several sub-units composed of male and female children ranging from 10 to 15 years of age. These young children were trained and selected by the Khmer Rouge regime to work as guards at S-21. Most of them started out as normal before growing increasingly evil. They were exceptionally cruel and disrespectful toward prisoners and their elders.

Although the vast majority of prisoners at S-21 were Cambodians there were foreigners that had been imprisoned and later executed at the prison or at one of the Killing Fields. These foreigners came from the following nations: Vietnam, Laos, Thailand, India, Pakistan, the U.K., the U.S, Canada, New Zealand, and Australia.

If you would like to learn more a good place to start is the Documentation Center of Cambodia (DC-Cam), a Cambodian NGO.

The day ended among a group of backpacker friends at a "Happy Pizza" restaurant; a restaurant that served pizza topped with cannabis. While we waited for our pizzas the waiters gave us two rolled cannabis cigarettes to share. And when the pizzas arrived, we ate and watched a couple of pirated DVDs on the restaurant's TV screen.

Posted by The Legacy Cycle at 2004-05-27T20:45:00-07:00

Thursday, May 27, 2004

"Happy Pizza" Relaxing Day
Tuesday, May 25, 2004

Today was uneventful. The "happy pizza" I ate last night made me extremely sluggish. I was in no mood to do anything. I just wanted to rest and catch up on this blog.

After breakfast at the guesthouse of a Canadian young woman by the name of Tara that I had met in Siem Reap, I went to an Internet café. I typed and typed, but found my ability to focus a bit off and slow. After that I returned to Tara's guesthouse and took a nap on a hammock on a terrace that overlooked the Boeung Kak Lake.

I should mention that Tara's guesthouse was at the end of a street that was in a severe state of disrepair. On my walks to and from her guesthouse there was a Cambodian teenager who badgered me to buy marijuana or cocaine. I didn't buy anything.

Domenico

P.S. I will never have another "happy pizza" again.

Posted by The Legacy Cycle at 2004-05-27T22:04:00-07:00

VIETNAM

Thursday, May 27, 2004

Journey from Phnom Penh to Saigon
Wednesday, May 26, 2004

The bus journey went without incident; no bandits attacked our bus to steal backpacks full of wrinkled, dirty clothing, and no flat tire. On the bus, I met a young twenty-something couple from England (the woman was of Indian descent and wore a red tang top with a white floral pattern and dark green pants, and the man had blond hair and wore a white T-shirt and khaki shorts) and an American (who wore a white T-shirt, beige cargo pants, and a red bandana around his neck) who I had previously met at my guesthouse in Phnom Penh.

The border crossing at Mộc Bài was nothing more than a few scattered shacks and muddy, unpaved roads. We exited the bus, grabbed our bags, and had our passports stamped as we exited Cambodia. We then walked toward the Vietnamese border gate to get our passports stamped for entry. But the process took nearly two hours; and the intense afternoon sun and humidity did not add to our enthusiasm as we went through this tiring immigration process.

In Laos and Cambodia, I had heard several stories from backpackers of foreigners being cheated in Vietnam. As a result, the four of us (the English couple and the American had also heard similar stories) assumed that the lengthy immigration process was some corrupt ploy to extract excessive amounts of money from us and all the other backpackers in line. But that was not the case. We eventually received our passports with the required entry stamps.

Although we had not been cheated by the Vietnamese immigration officers, I was swindled by the money exchange lady at the border who had shortchanged me by about US$5.

We–along with everyone else from our bus–hopped back onto the bus to continue the journey to Ho Chi Minh City (formally called Saigon).

As we entered the city limits of Saigon and drove into its congested interior we looked out from the bus windows shocked by the infinite number of scooters that crisscrossed the roads with little regard for the traffic light signals. I was in awe of the city's size for as we drove further into the urban labyrinth the streets and buildings seemed to stretch in all direction forever. But there were no skyscrapers; most of the buildings were no taller than six or seven-storeys.

The bus dropped us off on Bùi Viện Road, which appeared to be a Vietnamese version of Khaosan Road. The street was lined with guesthouses for backpackers, travel agencies, and restaurants. No touts swarmed us when we stepped off the bus. And as we each went on our independent search for a guesthouse I found the Vietnamese that I interacted with to be very pleasant, but apathetic in trying to sell me anything. I instantly like Saigon. Throughout my travels in Thailand and Cambodia I had been continually harassed to hire a tuk-tuk or buy some pirated book or T-shirt, but in Saigon there seemed to be far less of that.

The guesthouse room I took was on the top floor of a four-storey family home that was immaculate and had its own shower, sink, and toilet. I unpacked a few items, took a shower, and went for a walk.

On the streets of Saigon I saw hundreds to thousands of speeding scooters, beautiful Vietnamese school girls and young women dressed in uniforms of either a white shirt, red scarf, and checkered skirt or the more traditional áo dài (a white, tight-fitting silk tunic worn over white or dark colored pants), and walking food vendors wearing Vietnamese style conical hats and carrying large steel woks or baskets that hung from opposite ends of a long bamboo stick they had balanced over their shoulders. I also saw two buildings that I believe were brothels; these buildings had extremely dark–almost uninviting–

interiors, but neon signs on the exterior advertised ice cream? As I stood watching the activity around these two buildings I realized that for its size (four-storeys), layout, and the men and women working outside of it that it had to be an upscale brothel for locals.

    I walked more and ended up in a French café where I ate a baguette sandwich and drank ice tea. After my meal, I returned to my room and retired for the night.

Posted by The Legacy Cycle at 2004-05-27T22:11:00-07:00

Monday, May 31, 2004

Saigon Notes
Wednesday, May 26 to Sunday, May 30, 2004

I am behind on this blog. To get caught up I will combine all of my thoughts and observations of Saigon into one entry.

The "Same, same, but different"
Economic Philosophy of Saigon

Bùi Viện Road is colorful; the narrow six to seven-storey guesthouses that line the street are painted in tropical green, pink, or blue. Commercial shops are located on the ground floor, the majority of which are mom-and-pop shops that also double as the entrance into the homes of the families that run these shops. The Vietnamese are opposite to the Japanese in this sense. The Japanese are very private as their businesses, shops, restaurants, bars, hostess clubs, and homes are all hidden behind walls, tinted windows, and closed doorways. The Japanese take the necessary precautions to ensure that no "outsider" can see within their home or place of work. The Vietnamese on the other hand could care less if some passersby looked into their place of work or living space.

    My guesthouse was located in an alley filled with multistorey buildings that served as urban homes for two to three generations of

Vietnamese families. The ground floor of these homes had a metallic gate that was typically left open throughout the day. Looking in and beyond the gate I usually saw the living room, which–for some–doubled as a shop that sold drinks, food, or some other perishable or nonperishable goods. Every morning, to exit my guesthouse, I had to walk through the family living area, and once outside I would sit down on the doorstep to put on my shoes while observing the activity in the alley or looking into the living room of the home across from me where I saw children watching television or teenagers playing pirated video games. Every home I looked into had a small familial shrine for ancestor worship.

The Vietnamese were not embarrassed to blow or pick their noses within the comforts of their homes that was faced to the public. In essence, they were apathetic to what others thought of them, and for that I loved them more.

There were travel agencies all along Bùi Viện Road that catered to backpackers as well as Italian restaurants and French cafés; I breakfasted every morning at the same French café near my guesthouse, eating croissants and drinking café au lait in the same chair and table on the second floor with a view to all the activity on the street.

Bùi Viện Road also had several CD shops loaded with pirated music of every genre, DVDs, computer software, and video games for PlayStation 2. The prices for these CDs were very low. So low that Happy Tours, a travel agency on Bùi Viện Road, gave all of its customers a voucher to pick up a free CD at one of these shops; the tours they sold were priced at no more than $5 or $6. I met a group from New Zealand who had bought 36 DVDs for less than $40. This is one example of the "same, same, but different" economic philosophy of Vietnam, a country that was politically Communist, but had a full functioning mixed economy since the mid 1980s thanks to the Đổi Mới Policy.

Vietnam was–by far–the cheapest country I had traveled through in Southeast Asia. I could stay in a beautiful hotel room with a television set, air-conditioning, and a refrigerator for $10 a night. I bought cans of Coke for less than 40 cents apiece. I ate massive and delicious pizzas for less than two or three dollars. I drank a pitcher of beer for about a dollar. And these were the prices for foreigners! The prices for locals were much lower. For example, I learned today from my waitress at a restaurant where I had dinner that she made about US$1 a day (GDP per capita in 2004 for Vietnam was US$606.90[1]) thus she, along with many others, could not afford genuine commercial goods such as a DVDs, CDs, books, or scooters from developed nations, which translated into increasing demand for pirated goods. U.S., European, and Japanese brand goods are unaffordable to the average Vietnamese worker. But thanks to Western pop culture being broadcasted worldwide via television, films, and the Internet, Vietnamese consumers want the brand name goods they see nonetheless. In order to have what they see the average American or European enjoying the Vietnamese make products that are the "same, same, but different." Pirated DVDs look almost no different from the genuine article. It is the same … yet different. And books. There are millions of books that you could buy that have been photocopied page by page from an original. I bought a few books such as *In Retrospect: The Tragedy and Lessons of Vietnam* by Robert S. McNamara here that were the "same, same, but different." I am sure that Western multinationals such as Penguin Books, Sony, and The North Face are up in arms with the fact that Southeast Asia has a vibrant, massive, and growing market for the pirated versions of their products.

Vietnam, Cambodia, Laos, and Myanmar are poor developing nations. In addition, they are countries that have been bombed and torn apart by the greedy, economic, and geopolitical interests of developed countries such as the U.S., Japan, and France. These impoverished Southeast Asian nations are still suffering from the long-term effects of the wars waged within their borders by wealthy foreign oppressors. Members of rural families in Cambodia, Laos, and Vietnam are still killed every year by unexploded bombs (UXBs) that the U.S. or France had littered all over their country throughout the 1950s, 1960s, and 1970s.[2,3,4] I saw several people in Vietnam who had lost their hands, arms or legs to an unexploded ordnance (UXO). And I saw photographs of Vietnamese babies that had been born with the most horrific deformities imaginable as a result of the herbicidal warfare program the U.S. waged in Vietnam (I will later discuss the horrendous effects Agent Orange has had–and continues to have–on the children of Vietnam).

Since the U.S. did not clean up the mess of unexploded ordnance that they had left behind in Laos, Cambodia, and Vietnam, one can understand why the people of these Southeast Asian nations do not care whether or not media conglomerates from the developed world are losing millions to billions of dollars to piracy in the region. The Vietnamese cannot afford high priced Western brand goods. But they–along with most consumers around the world with access to Western media–want these consumer goods. Perhaps the people of Southeast Asia deserve access to those goods (CDs, DVDs, books, and clothing) through acts of piracy.[5] It is the least that profit maximizing multinationals, tax revenue making governments, and citizens enjoying social services from the developed world can do after–directly or indirectly–supporting the exploitation and destruction of the resources and people of Southeast Asia over the past few decades.

Another example of this "same, same, but different" economic philosophy that I saw on Bùi Viện Road were the low-end galleries selling hand painted fakes of well-known works by Leonardo da Vinci, Gustav Klimt, Salvador Dalí, Pablo Picasso, and Joan Miró.

Scooters present another example of the rampant illicit trade in Vietnam. I learned from a few expats that five years ago the streets of Saigon were not littered with the quantity of speeding motor scooters that I now saw in 2004. With a GDP per capita of US$606.90[6] the average Vietnamese national is unable to afford a car (thus there are few to be seen roaming the streets of Saigon) so the only affordable option is the motor scooter. Cheap scooters manufactured in China that have been designed to look like their expensive Japanese counterparts have been flooding the Vietnamese market by the tens to hundreds of thousands per year. Jeffrey W. Alexander explains in his book *Japan's Motorcycle Wars: An Industry History* that although "Chinese motorcycle manufacturers had an annual production of over 20 million units" their domestic sales "totaled approximately 11 million units per year."[7] The low consumption in China is in part due to limitations enforced by municipal governments and bans in major cities that seek "to curb traffic congestion, noise pollution, and exhaust emissions."[8]

> As a result, Chinese motorcycle firms were "forced to pursue aggressive export strategies" to sell the excess production to "large developing countries like Indonesia, Vietnam, Argentina, and Brazil. Chinese makers have been less successful in India, Thailand, Malaysia, and the Philippines, however, because those countries'

governments fear that inexpensive (and often illegally copied) Chinese imports will damage their domestic motorcycle industries. In China itself, Honda Cub-type motorcycles are not as popular as scooter and sport models, but due to the popularity of the Cub-type in Southeast Asia, particularly in Indonesia and Vietnam, most exports from China are illegal copies of Japanese Cub-type models. In 2001, Indonesia granted import licenses to eighty-seven new motorcycle brands, fifty-seven of which came from China. The quality of these Chinese exports, however, was often very poor."[9]

I saw entire Vietnamese families piled on these "Cub-type models" speeding from one direction to the other while not adhering to traffic lights that were few and far between. In addition, I saw men transporting large objects, such as refrigerators, that were strapped to the back of their motor scooters! I also saw couples parading their motorized status symbol at the roundabout located at the intersection of Trần Hưng Đạo and Lê Lợi Street. And near this roundabout there was a park where I saw young couples congregate at night to whisper sweet nothings while holding each other as they sat on their scooters. Young Vietnamese men often joke that the key to picking up a beautiful Vietnamese girl is baiting them with an expensive looking knock off scooter … this pick-up technique, among others, reinforces the materialistic stereotype that people from Hanoi have of those from Saigon.

The Củ Chi Tunnels & The Vietnam War

According to political scientist Guenter Lewy (1978) there were 1,353,000 total deaths in North and South Vietnam during the 1965-1974 war period of which 627,000 were North and South Vietnamese civilian deaths.[10] Political scientist R.J. Rummel (1997) estimated that U.S. forces committed 5,500 democidal killings (defined by Rummel as "the murder of any person or people by a government, including genocide, politicide, and mass murder"[11]) during the 1960-1972 period,[12] and a 1995 demographic study stated that the number of North Vietnamese civilian deaths caused from U.S. bombings was in the range of 50,000-65,000;[13] U.S. bombings in Cambodia is estimated to have killed anywhere between 50,000 and 150,000 civilians.[14]

In comparison to the excessive number of Vietnamese civilian casualties, 58,318 U.S. combatants were killed during the Vietnam War.[15] How many civilian and combatant lives will be lost in Iraq when the U.S. finally departs from the Southwest Asian nation (500,000 deaths from 2003 to 2011[16])? Why did the U.S. invade Iraq in 2003? Weapons of mass destruction? Yes, that was the rationale stated in the Authorization for Use of Military Force Against Iraq Resolution of 2002 that was made into public law by the U.S. Congress.[17] Wait a minute ... there were no WMDs in Iraq.[18] So, can someone–particularly George W. Bush and Tony Blair–please explain to me–in extreme detail–why the U.S. and the U.K. went to war with Iraq?

My sarcasm, frustration, and embarrassment are the result of seeing with my own eyes the adverse, long-term social, economic, political, and environmental impacts of U.S. foreign policy during the Vietnam War on the poor developing nations of Laos, Cambodia, and Vietnam. After witnessing how the people of these Southeast Asian nations continue to suffer–nearly three decades after the end of the Second Indochina War–I find it difficult, as a U.S. citizen, to find a strong enough reason to support any war or conflict since World War II.

The U.S. government employed just over 9,087,000 active duty military personnel during the Vietnam War period from 1964 to 1975 of which 2,594,000 served "within the border of South Vietnam"[19] leading to 58,318 U.S. casualties.[20] According to the Department of Defense (DOD) the U.S. government spent "168 billion (worth around $950 billion in 2011 dollars) ... the United States spent approximately $168,000 for an 'enemy' killed. However, $168 billion was only the direct cost. According to Indochina Newsletter of Asia Resource Center, the United States spent from $350 billion to $900 billion in total including veterans' benefits and interest."[21] Imagine the number of public schools, universities, and hospitals (along with investments in medical research) the U.S. could have provided instead.

To support the U.S. military, Australia sent over 60,000 of their citizens to serve in the war "including ground troops and air force and navy personnel ... 521 died as a result of the war and over 3,000 were wounded."[22] South Korea, New Zealand, Thailand, the Philippines, and several other nations also sent troops to Vietnam to fight with U.S.

troops.[23]

In a paper published in the *British Medical Journal* (2008), researchers provided a new estimate of war deaths in Vietnam stating "3.8 million Vietnamese died in the protracted fighting in Vietnam, mostly from 1955 to 1975, compared to previous estimates of … 2.1 million."[24] Again, compare that number to the 58,318 U.S. combatants that were killed during the war.[25] Of the 3.8 million Vietnamese deaths, how many were infants, adult civilians, and combatants?

According to the Vietnamese government (1995) civilian deaths totaled two million during the 1955 to 1975 period.[26] Although we may question the reliability of that number due to its source (in the same way the Vietnam government will question figures reported by the U.S. government), the U.S. killed such a high number of civilians in part due to the difficulty military personnel had in accurately identifying the enemy. A South Vietnamese friend by day could be a Viet Cong fighter by night, as a result U.S. military campaigns indiscriminately destroyed villages and killed hundreds of thousands of villagers.

One infamous example is the My Lai Massacre in which U.S. Army soldiers killed 504 "unarmed men, women, children, and babies" on March 16, 1968: "women were gang raped; Vietnamese who had bowed to greet the Americans were beaten with fists and tortured, clubbed with rifle butts and stabbed with bayonets. Some victims were mutilated with the signature 'C Company' carved into the chest."[27]

Another example was reported in October 2003 by Michael D. Sallah and Mitch Weiss in the Toledo, Ohio, newspaper, *The Blade*, detailing atrocities perpetrated by a long-range reconnaissance patrol unit nicknamed Tiger Force that killed over 1,000 Vietnamese[28] in the Song Ve Valley committing the following war crimes: the "torture and execution of prisoners";[29] the intentional practice of "killing unarmed Vietnamese" men, women, children, and elderly villagers;[30] the regular "practice of cutting off and collecting the ears of victims";[31] the regular "practice of wearing necklaces" made of "human ears";[32] the regular practice of "collecting the scalps of victims";[33] "an incident in which a young mother was drugged, raped and then executed";[34] an incident in which "a soldier killed a baby", killed the mother, and then decapitated the baby.[35]

Agent Orange—a chemical herbicide that was manufactured by Monsanto (a U.S. multinational agricultural biotechnology corporation) from 1965-1969 and supplied to the U.S. military[36] to be used as a defoliant in Operation *Ranch Hand* as part of its chemical warfare program to destroy vegetation at targeted areas in Vietnam from 1962 to 1971–led to the destruction of 5.5 million acres of "forest and cropland, an area roughly the size of New Jersey."[37] In total, about 20 million gallons of the herbicide was sprayed over tropical landscapes in Vietnam, Cambodia, and Laos.[38] Crop destruction was the predominating objective of the operation with the rationale being that a diminishing food supply would weaken the Viet Cong,[39] but in reality its most immediate impact was against hundreds of thousands of civilian villagers that faced a resulting famine and malnourishment.[40]

Agent Orange not only poisoned 20 percent of the tropical forests of South Vietnam with recovery taking decades,[41] but seeped into the ground water and food supply of the people living along the Hồ Chí Minh Trail and other targeted areas. This chemical weapon caused a variety of health problems such as skin diseases, cancers, and birth defects both in the short and long term[42] for the Vietnamese population. The government of Vietnam claims that "3 million of its 84 million people have birth defects or other health problems related to the dioxin"[43] whereas the Vietnamese Red Cross has estimated that "as many as one million people in Vietnam have disabilities or other health problems associated with Agent Orange."[44] Above average levels of the dioxin found in breast milk has resulted in horrific birth defects.[45] At the War Remnants Museum in Saigon I saw many pictures and video footage (at times extremely difficult to look at or watch) of adults and children born with deformities that had left them blind (due to being born with no eyes), with enlarged or elongated heads, or with deformed limbs or facial features. I encourage you to Google "agent orange deformities" and see with your own eyes these physical deformations the U.S. government, military, and chemical companies are directly responsible for and ask yourself whether or not it is a war crime. Unfortunately, a class action lawsuit by an association representing millions of Vietnamese victims of Agent Orange that claimed that "American chemical companies committed war crimes by supplying the military with the defoliant" was dismissed in 2005.[46] Thus the moral obligation by U.S. citizens to provide aid, support, and relief to those still affected by Agent Orange falls predominately–and unfairly–upon nonprofit and nongovernment organizations.

Today, ultrasound is used to detect whether or not an unborn Vietnamese infant has a birth defect (most likely due to the lingering effects of Agent Orange). If an unborn child is detected to have severe deformities it is aborted.[47] Long-held fears of birth defects and child deformities caused by Agent Orange in Vietnam is perhaps one of several factors to explain why the country has the highest abortion rate in Asia, and one of the "highest in the world," where "40 percent of all pregnancies ... are terminated each year."[48]

On May 27, I went to the Củ Chi tunnels, which were located about an hour outside of Saigon. As I was to discover, the tunnels were practically in the backyard of a former U.S. Army and Army of the Republic of Vietnam (ARVN) base where thousands of soldiers had been stationed at the height of the war. It was here that the Viet Cong had dug some of the most sophisticated tunnel systems to evade detection.

The Củ Chi tunnels covers a 165-square kilometer area and is 121 kilometers long.[49] According to my guide (a former South Vietnamese Army (SVA) soldier), during the war there were approximately 300,000 Vietnamese residing in the tunnels (which I questioned), but from that number 44,145 had been killed by the war's end.

Logistically speaking, Viet Cong soldiers–again, according to my Vietnamese guide–were better equipped than their U.S. counterparts. The Viet Cong used the AK-47 as their standard assault rifle whereas U.S. soldiers used the M16. The AK-47 (Mikhail Kalashnikov finished his design of the rifle in 1947[50]) was fabricated in the Soviet Union, but supplied to the Viet Cong via communist China. The AK-47's detachable magazine could hold 30 rounds or it could be fed by a 20 or 40-round box magazine,[51] and it could also fire M16 rounds. The M16's detachable magazine could only hold 20 rounds. Just by the type of standard firearm supplied during the Vietnam War the U.S. soldier was at a disadvantage.

My guide went on to explain that the Viet Cong soldiers who dug and fought in the Củ Chi tunnels received their supplies from North Vietnam at the southern end of the Hồ Chí Minh Trail. He said that the Viet Cong were essentially composed of poor (the soles of their shoes were made from car tires), determined volunteers; they were never paid whereas U.S. and South Vietnamese soldiers were paid for their armed service.

The irony, according to my guide, was that during the war many U.S. bases in South Vietnam hired South Vietnamese women to cook, clean, and maintain the base. These women worked from 8 a.m. to 4 p.m. and made about $300 a month. After work many of these women would return to their villages supplying information about the layout of the base to the Viet Cong or they were themselves Viet Cong. And every so often, under the cover of darkness, Viet Cong soldiers would sneak into targeted U.S. bases with explosives and blow up buildings and supplies.

The guide then informed my tour group that since it was often feared that pilots serving within the South Vietnamese Army could possibly be Viet Cong a hidden camera was attached to the bombers they flew, and if upon return it was discovered that the pilot had bombed U.S. troops instead of Viet Cong targets he was immediately shot without trial.

Many unexploded bombs (UXBs) were dropped over Vietnam; "the Vietnamese government estimates that around 14m tonnes or ordnance ... was dropped on Vietnam between 1959 and 1975. Between 10% and 30% of it failed to detonate."[52] A portion of these UXBs were then scavenged by the Viet Cong, reworked, and inserted into cars or trucks that were set to explode when they were driven into a U.S. base or government building.

Our guide highlighted that many of the Viet Cong soldiers serving in the Củ Chi tunnels joined the fight against the U.S. after members of their families had been killed by cluster bombs dropped by the B-52 bombers. In addition, he explained that the Viet Cong–in an effort to encourage more women to help in the cause against the U.S.–awarded medals to Vietnamese girls and young women and recognized them as "American Killer Hero".

Since the majority of the Củ Chi fighters were farmers they used inexpensive animal trapping techniques against U.S. combatants; one infamous example was the punji stake: a camouflaged pit filled with sharpened, vertical bamboo sticks designed to impale the feet and/or legs of American soldiers.

My guide explained the following information by utilizing a large, upright diorama encased in glass of the Củ Chi tunnels. The tunnels were divided into three levels: the first and second levels were used for fighting, and the third level provided basic living, cooking, and sleeping quarters. The first level was located three meters below the surface, the second level was six meters below, and the third level was ten meters below the surface. The second level was typically used as a transit tunnel that allowed the Viet Cong to move from one area or level to another; this level was also loaded with booby traps in the event that U.S. troops discovered and invaded the tunnels. The Củ Chi fighters that lived in the tunnels slept in hammocks that could absorb the shock waves that rocked the tunnels during bombing raids. Smoke from the kitchen chambers would flow into several compartments and then release above ground at a location far from where the labyrinth of tunnels was located.

The tunnels were made by hand with the use of small shovels and baskets to collect and dispose of the dirt, and they had groundwater wells that allowed rebel fighters to take a bath three times a day.

Ventilation was provided by air holes that were made by digging into the ground and placing a hollow bamboo stick that was long enough to reach the first level; over time the stick would decay leaving only the long shaft of the air hole.

War Remnants Museum

A visit to the War Remnants Museum is a must for anyone traveling to Saigon. It can be argued that the museum is politically biased, which was evident in the exhibits that detailed events to conform to government propaganda, but it was interesting to see how the Vietnamese portrayed the French, the United States, and the Vietnam War; the museum is their side of the story, in the same way the U.S. has its history books, films, and museums laced with their perspectives, biases, and propaganda. It is important for us to see both sides of historical events to find the truth somewhere in-between.

After Hồ Chí Minh as Chairman of the Provisional Government of the Democratic Republic of Vietnam declared Vietnam's independence (a proclamation modeled to an extent after the United States Declaration of Independence) from France on September 2, 1945, the U.S.–in alignment with the Truman Doctrine of containing communism–provided France with over $1.3 billion dollars from 1947 to 1953 to continue their war effort in Vietnam.[53] And "by the time French forces surrendered to the Viet Minh in mid 1954, Washington had invested almost $3 billion in 'saving' Indochina from the spectre of communism."[54] U.S. President Dwight D. Eisenhower would go on to speculate in 1954–in what would become known as the "domino theory"–that if Vietnam fell to communism so would other neighboring Indochina nations.

A good portion of the museum was dedicated to the victims of Agent Orange: the toxic herbicide and defoliant chemical that was sprayed from U.S. Army helicopters and low-flying military airplanes to destroy targeted tropical vegetation in Vietnam. The toxins from the U.S. Military's herbicidal warfare program from 1962 to 1971 known as Operation *Ranch Hand* caused deformities in the hands, arms, legs, and feet of the Vietnamese.[55] Children born from parents who had been exposed to Agent Orange had facial deformities such as overgrown heads or unusual growths in and around their bodies. Many were born blind and some were born with no eyes or flesh covering their eye sockets.

Coconut Tree Prison

The museum also had an exhibit educating viewers of the brutality of a 40,000 square meters prison that was built by the French from 1949 to 1950 on Phú Quốc, which is the largest island in Vietnam. The prison was designed to hold no more than 14,000 prisoners, but throughout its use during both the First and Second Indochina War it housed between 30,000 and 40,000 Vietnamese inmates.[56]

The torture techniques used by the French colonists in the prison varied: pins were stuck into fingertips, snakes placed into women's trousers, electric shock was used, and beatings with the use of clubs and hammers. Some prisoners were beaten so severely that they left with arms or legs that were completely paralyzed.

Prisoners ate insufficient quantities of food composed of decayed fish, vegetables, and meat. Only half a can of drinking water was given to prisoners each day. Very little water was given to female prisoners during their menstrual cycle. Howard Zinn mentions in his book

A People's History of the United States that "Red Cross observers found continuing, systematic brutality at two principal Vietnamese POW camps—Phu Quoc and Qui Nhon, where American advisors were stationed."[57]

On display, outside of the museum, was a life-size model of the infamous "tiger's cage" that was used specifically for political prisoners. During the hot, tropical summer season five to 14 prisoners were placed within one of these small, enclosed cages where their ankles were shackled to a long, iron bar, which limited their movement within the cell.

I have typed as much as I can about the Củ Chi tunnels, Agent Orange, and the War Remnants Museum. If you are interested in learning more please search the Internet for more information, visit your local library, or go to your nearest bookstore.
Posted by The Legacy Cycle at 2004-05-31T02:32:00-07:00

Monday, June 7, 2004

Final Thoughts on Saigon

What I had forgotten to mention in my account of Saigon were the women and what they (or their society) considered to be beautiful. Beauty is purity, which in Vietnam translates to purity of the skin.[58] The lighter the skin the more desirable the woman to a Vietnamese man. If I could speak Vietnamese I could ask and find out for myself whether or not men in Vietnam really obsess over the lightness of women's skin color or if it is just some false cosmetic belief that women adhere to. But the advertisements here—as in the Western world—further reinforced the belief; the Vietnamese models depicted on billboards, magazines, and television commercials, as well as Vietnamese actresses and popstars, all had very light skin.

This obsession for light skin has led nearly every Vietnamese woman—from adolescents to those in their fifties and sixties—to cover up as much of their body (limbs, head, and face) before venturing out into the oppressive glare of the tropical sun. The heat and humidity in Vietnam are intense; and although I have been walking around in shorts and a T-shirt I need to take two to three showers a day. The women here wear pants, and if they wear a short-sleeved shirt they put on full-length evening gloves that cover their hands, forearm, elbows, and biceps. To keep the sun from tanning their face they wear a hat, sunglasses, and a lightweight scarf tied at the back of their head to cover everything below their eyes. I saw thousands of women riding scooters on the streets of Saigon completely covered up. It was rare to see the face of a Vietnamese woman. It made me wonder if these women would not prefer to wear a burqa. I also came across skin whitening creams sold in local markets that promised to maintain and/or further enhance the lightness of a woman's skin.

This fixation among Vietnamese women to protect their skin from the sun to maintain a cosmetic status quo may seem ridiculous, but the practice occurs to some degree in all societies. There are those of us who are quick to do anything to adhere to what society deems as beautiful and attractive: some go to the gym not for the benefits it provides in terms of health, but to enhance our physique; we–in developed nations–go to tanning salons because tanned skin represents one's wealth and ability to travel to tropical locations; and we buy cosmetic goods, teeth whiteners, and fashionable clothing to keep up with the latest fast fashion trends.

So, the question remains. What is beauty? What is beauty as defined by our culture or society? There are many facets to a person's beauty. There is physical beauty, the beauty of one's character, of one's skills and abilities, and of one's thoughts and perspectives. But as stated in the previous paragraph it seems that physical beauty is tied, in some sense, to wealth.

Women in Vietnam and Thailand are perplexed by North American and European women who–from their perspective–want to spoil their "white" skin by lying out in the sun for hours on tropical beaches. Perhaps here we may understand the difference in what Eastern and Western cultures regard as beautiful in regards to what is considered to be a sign of wealth.

A woman from the Netherlands that I met in Saigon was on her way to Indonesia. She explained to me: "There is no way I can go back to my country after such a long vacation without a tan. I am going to Indonesia to relax after all this time backpacking to get a nice tan before returning home."

In the West, it could be argued that getting a tan is a status symbol, which represents one's financial ability to travel to exotic locations. In essence, a tan is beautiful in the West because it is equated with wealth.

In Thailand, Vietnam, and throughout Southeast and East Asia, it is believed that only the rural poor do backbreaking work in the heat of the sun as they tend their paddy fields. The rich are those who work within the shade and comfort of a store or office. This urban class of workers, managers, and entrepreneurs are rarely out in the sun and thus have lighter skin. So, we can see that beauty in many Asian countries, such as Thailand and Vietnam, are equated with a perception of wealth.

The Slums of Saigon

An aspect of Saigon that I was shocked to discover were the slums. My initial impression of the city was little different than from the cities I had traveled through in Malaysia and Thailand. All cities have their tourist sites, business districts, commercial areas, and ghettos, but the slums that I saw at a distance in Saigon were the worst I had seen in Southeast Asia. I have not been to Manila, but the slums that I saw in Saigon reminded me of the pictures I had seen of the slums in and around the Philippine capital.

The slums were located at the point where districts one, four, five, seven, and eight intersect; it was where the Kinh Đôi and Kinh Tế Canals, the Bến Nghé River, and the Rạch Ông Lớn stream converged. At this intersection, the color of the water in the canals was black as a result of heavy urban and industrial contamination. Along the banks of these canals I saw hundreds to thousands of squalid shanty houses made from discarded sheets of metal and plywood piled on top of each other. It was a sad and frightening sight to know that adults and children lived in such an unsanitary place.

Bus Trip to Nha Trang
Sunday, May 30 to Monday 31, 2004

This was to be the first of several amusing bus trips that I took as I traveled north through Vietnam. My bus departed Saigon at eight in the evening, but it was not just a vehicle that transported people and luggage, it also doubled as a truck transporting goods. On my bus windsurf boards had been placed between nearly every seat; an obvious hazard in the case of an emergency because the boards made it almost impossible for passengers to get from one end of the bus to the other. But Vietnam does not seem to be a very litigious society so this "hazard" was of no concern to the bus company.

The ride to Nha Trang took about 10 hours so we arrived bright and early the next morning. I exited the bus, grabbed my bag, and hired a tout to take me by scooter to a hotel that he recommended, which faced the beach. I entered the hotel and found that it was cheap and clean. I checked-in, went up to my room, took a shower, turned on the air conditioner, and went to bed. I woke up at noon and decided to take it easy since there were no significant sights that I was interested in seeing; Nha Trang is essentially a beach resort town. Although I did not go to Mũi Né, I had heard from many backpackers that the town and its beaches were far more pleasant than Nha Trang.

Thus, on May 31, I essentially ate, walked, rested since I was sick with a cold, got caught up on emails, and updated this blog.

Posted by The Legacy Cycle at 2004-06-07T00:23:00-07:00

Tuesday, June 1, 2004

A Day at the Table

Nicholas found refuge from the tropical Saigon heat—and the endless scores of scooters and mopeds that crisscrossed and weaved through the streets with little regard for pedestrians—in the quaint room of his guesthouse that was located on the top floor of a four-storey, narrow building. The room was clean, pleasant, and most important of all, it had air conditioning. He paid six dollars a night for the room.

A door adjacent to his bathroom opened to a small balcony; it was so small that he could only stand on it, to sit in a chair was not possible. Although he never used the balcony, he loved the fact that he had one. And when given the chance, he would brag to fellow backpackers that his room had a balcony while never mentioning its size.

Most nights he arrived to his guesthouse at just past midnight. The family that ran the establishment was usually in bed, asleep, at that hour. He would have to ring the doorbell and wait. A head with tired eyes would pop out a window from one of the floors above just to see who was ringing in the middle of the night. Moments later the side door to the guesthouse would open, and Nicholas would enter taking off his shoes while apologizing to the head of the household who had unlocked the door.

Since he had a television in his room, Nicholas watched a program about forensic crime scenes on the Discovery Channel each night before falling asleep. He preferred the BBC or CNN to find out what was happening in the world, but his guesthouse did not subscribe to those channels.

On the morning of May 13, Nicholas woke up at 6:10; he had a breakfast date, two in fact. He had to first meet Estelle, a beautiful and young French woman of Laotian and Vietnamese descent, at 7:00, and at 10:00 he planned to meet Carmen and Zaira from Barcelona, and Jacky from South Africa.

Struggling to get out of bed, and regretful that this morning was to be his last in Saigon, Nicholas sat up. He noticed that his throat felt raw, the air conditioner had dried out the air, and he prayed that it would not develop into a sore throat.

After showering, putting on a black, faded T-shirt and black athletic shorts, and obsessively checking the locks on his bag for the third or fourth time, Nicholas left his room and descended three floors. He passed the living room on the ground floor of the guesthouse, said hello to the Vietnamese family that ran it, and took out his worn-down Adidas Samba shoes from a cupboard turned shoe rack before stepping out into an alley just off from Bùi Viện Road. He put on his shoes while looking into the living room of the home across the alley from him seeing children watch television as they ate their breakfast.

The café where he was to meet Estelle was located less than a minute walk from his guesthouse. He walked out onto Bùi Viện Road and saw Estelle dressed in a black, spaghetti strap shirt and a brown patterned sinh–a traditional Laotian tube skirt–rushing to be on time. She did not see him. She crossed the street, and he called out to her. She looked back, smiled, and waved hello.

"I'm sorry I'm late," Estelle greeted Nicholas.

"No, no, don't worry. As you can see, the café is just now opening."

They walked into the two-storey French café and approached the glass display of the counter, but Nicholas was disappointed to see that there were barely any pastries. He wanted Estelle to have a fine selection of French pastries to choose from, but it appeared that the day's pastries had yet to be delivered to the café. Nicholas expressed his disappointment, but Estelle explained that she was not feeling well, and that all she wanted to eat was yoghurt. She ordered in French at the counter while Nicholas looked over the few pastries that had been left from the previous day.

After ordering, they both walked up the steps leading to the second floor and sat at a table that overlooked the early morning activity of Bùi Viện Road.

The first and last time these two travelers had seen each other was in Luang Prabang, Laos. And then, more than two weeks later, the two ran into each other while on a separate tour of the Mekong Delta. They agreed to meet for breakfast, and thus this is how they came to find themselves enjoying an early morning meal in Saigon.

They asked each other questions of the personal facts and details that they had remembered from their previous meeting in Laos. The conversation was quiet and pleasant. Anything more than that would have been too much for such an early hour.

After breakfast, Estelle explained that she was going to the Reunification Palace. Nicholas knew the way and had more than an hour before his second breakfast meeting. He decided to walk with her to the destination.

He enjoyed her company as they walked, particularly her sweet

French accent. The exotic curiosities of Saigon—such as street vendors setting up their makeshift shops to sell handicrafts or food—appeared along the streets catching their attention. And soon enough they had reached the palace, and it was time to say goodbye. If and when they would ever see each other again ... the gods only knew.

Nicholas walked back to Bùi Viện Road with a slight skip in his walk. He was happy. He had about twenty minutes before the clock struck ten so he decided to check his email at an Internet café with—as he was to discover—a terribly slow connection. Twenty-five minutes at the cybercafé came and went, and Nicholas was not able to open a single email. He paid the bill for the worthless Internet connection and rushed to meet Carmen, Zaira, and Jacky outside the Southern Hotel.

He arrived and apologized for being late. Carmen who was wearing a dark brown tank top that revealed the black thin straps of her bra and a patterned skirt of horizontal lines told him not to worry. Zaira and Jacky shook their heads in agreement. Nicholas then noticed that Zaira was wearing a black tank top and a colorful red, yellow, and pink patterned skirt that reached her feet and that Jacky—who had her dark blonde hair pulled back—was wearing a pink T-shirt and blue shorts. He then led them to the same French café where he had breakfast with Estelle; the café now had a large variety of French pastries on display. Carmen and Zaira ordered in French croissants and cups of café au lait. Jacky ordered the same meal as did Nicholas.

They carried their trays up to the second floor and sat at a table that provided a view of Bùi Viện Road. And there they were, an American gent, a South African lady, and two princesses of Spain. The hours passed as if they were minutes. Nicholas loved the animated gestures of Carmen and Zaira. He loved seeing their relationship. They were friends. But they behaved as if they were a couple. They could read each other. They understood one another. They knew each other's mind, heart, and spirit. They possessed between them what many married couples dreamed of and strived for, but never achieved. They were free within their relationship to simply be who they were without bending too far out of shape. They had found a pleasant space; a space that permitted them to act like spirited children again—joking with each other and with the world around them. Through them Nicholas and Jacky found hope that yes, *indeed*, two individual souls could find each other, fall into one another, support each other, and interdepend. They were hope. Yes, indeed. They were hope.

The afternoon sun rose high into the sky and hunger began to pelt their stomachs. They called the waitress over and ordered their afternoon meal. The conversation between the four travelers continued; as did the laughter they shared. And all the while Nicholas thought of his past and what his future would bring.

He could feel it, a part of himself beginning to die and making room for something new, something he had never known before. And he welcomed this death with sadness, and a smile. He felt old and tired at the age of twenty-seven; solitude so often his friend. So much had he done only to come home to the quiet of the night. He could sense that this long journey through the ancient heart of the "Old World" would be his last alone. Somewhere, over the ocean that would take him back to the place of his birth, would he find his new life with his future wife ... *whoever she may be.*

Posted by The Legacy Cycle at 2004-06-01T02:11:00-07:00

Monday, June 7, 2004

Overnight Bus to Hội An
Tuesday, June 1 to Wednesday 2, 2004

I woke up early on the first day of June to the intense light of the sun, got up, showered and dressed, and took a stroll along the beaches of Nha Trang. When noon approached I entered an Indian restaurant and ate a decent curry with bland tasting naan bread. After lunch, I returned to my hotel, washed up, and checked out. I had a few hours before the bus for Hội An picked me up from the hotel. To pass the time I went to an Internet café to clean out my email and update this blog.

It was a relaxing and uneventful day. The bus ride to Hội An was also uneventful.

Posted by The Legacy Cycle at 2004-06-07T01:15:00-07:00

Monday, June 7, 2004

Hội An
Wednesday, June 2, 2004

Hội An is a charming town that provides a break from the ridiculous number of noisy, gas-guzzling motor scooters that surge through Saigon's paved veins. The town is situated along the Thu Bồn River and is small enough that I walked through most of it within a few hours.

After checking into my hotel, and leaving my bag in my room, I walked down Phan Đình Phùng Street while swatting away requests from locals who tried to pressure me into following them to their tailor shop; Hội An is a popular stop for tourists who want to buy a tailor-made suit or dress. I was not interested in getting a tailored suit, and even if I was interested I did not have enough time to get one because I was only going to be in Hội An for 24 hours. But this did not stop the locals from trying to convince me that they could measure, cut, stitch, finish, and iron a suit in such a limited amount of time.

I turned right along Lê Lợi Street and headed toward the river. Along the street I saw a row of old French colonial buildings. The paint was fading on the majority of these buildings and their exterior walls had splotches of dark mold. Most of the buildings doubled as shops and homes with the ground floor serving as a commercial space and the living quarters located above.

Bạch Đằng was the road that ran along the Thu Bồn River, which had a few charming Vietnamese restaurants that catered to foreign travelers. As I walked east along the river I noticed a variety of floating vessels: semi-large wooden ships, small boats that could hold fifteen people, and circular basket boats that could only hold one or two people. I saw men fishing along the river and as I walked further east I happened upon the Hội An Central Market.

After two months of traveling I am now very close to being exhausted of seeing, exploring, and photographing food markets; I nearly veered away from the central market, but I ultimately decided to check it out. The section of the market located near the river logically sold fish. The market ran from north to south so after seeing and smelling the fish portion of the market, I walked north and found that the goods being sold changed from meats to vegetables to lettuce to roots to herbs and spices to tools and home appliances. Again—within the market—locals badgered me to follow them to their tailor shop to get a suit. From that moment on this was what I said repeatedly: "No … No thank you … I don't need a suit … because I don't need a suit … because I'm a musician and I don't need a suit … no I don't need a rock-and-roll suit … please leave me alone … For the love of God—LEAVE ME ALONE!"

Desperately seeking to escape the constant selling pitches of the locals I decided to cross the Cẩm Nam Bridge to get to the Cẩm Nam village. To get to the bridge I had to walk down Hoàng Diệu Street, which—as I neared the bridge—had shops dedicated to footwear. And, again, I repeated to touts: "No … you see those things on my feet … they are shoes … no I don't need another pair of shoes … yes, my shoes are ugly, but I'm backpacking so I don't care … please go away … Please—for the sake of my sanity—LEAVE ME ALONE!"

I spent about two to three hours walking around Cẩm Nam village. There really was not much to see, but it was quiet and no one verbally harassed me to buy something, although people did stare at me. But the children I encountered were cute, and at times I would hear a tiny little voice say, "hello." I would turn to face the voice and find an adorable Vietnamese girl or boy. Amazing to see that the people of Hội An teach their children English at the earliest age possible so that when they grow up they too can charge down the streets of their town and torment tourists until they buy something.

In the afternoon, I returned to my hotel and rested. In the evening, I went out and had a small meal in a poorly lit coffee shop. As I waited for my food a woman, whose husband owned the coffee shop, approached me. She seemed very nice and genuine, but as soon as I let my guard down she passed me her tailor shop business card. I told her I was leaving the next morning and that there was no possible way for her to make me a suit in such a short amount of time. She insisted that I stop by her shop after I finished my meal. I reluctantly agreed. She also insisted that I have breakfast at the coffee shop in the morning before I left for Huế. I just nodded my head.

After dinner, I walked to the tailor shop, and as soon as I

stepped into the shop there was a commotion of activity. Two men came up to me and I asked for the woman. One of them ran up to the second floor to get her. She came down (she had been washing her hair) and greeted me. She then began showing me all the clothes and suits in the shop. I conceded that it was all very nice. She pointed to some night robes for men and said that I should buy one. Although they were nice I did not want to carry an article of clothing that I did not actually need for the rest of my journey. I explained over and over to her that I did not want to buy a thing. I soon left.

I walked around town to get a feel for its nightlife. I came across a Chinese temple that was in the midst of a festival celebration. There were many people of all ages walking into and out of the temple. I walked into the temple and saw a stage that had been set up with a statue of a child Buddha complete with neon lights flashing all around it. There was traditional Vietnamese music blasting from speakers and an announcer who publicized each dancing and singing act. I stood and watched a few acts of young Vietnamese women in traditional dress dancing an ancient style that enchanted me along with nearly every male in the audience; except for the young children who could have cared less. There seems to be nothing more sensual than the sight of a woman dancing with ease and grace.

Many people around me soon began giving me an odd look; I was the only foreigner in the temple. I tried to pass it off by smiling to the children, but they hid their faces behind the legs of their parents.

When I had seen enough, I left and walked back to my hotel. Along the way I looked into the homes of families who all kept their front doors wide open. I often saw children or adults watching television. And in every home, I saw a shrine on the wall before the main entrance. The sizes of the shrines varied from small to large; a few were so tall that from the floor they touched the ceiling.

It was here in Hội An that I was beginning to feel the strong cultural influences of China.

Posted by The Legacy Cycle at 2004-06-07T01:25:00-07:00

Monday, June 7, 2004

Morning Bus to Huế
Thursday, June 3, 2004

I took a morning bus from Hội An to Huế. The ride was six hours. On this bus, several boxes were piled in the aisle at the center of the bus making it impassable for the passengers who sat in the back.

I sat in the back of the bus with a Vietnamese family who had an eight-year-old Vietnamese girl who sat one seat away from me. Behind us there were backpacker backpacks that were piled so high that they completely covered the rear window.

The view that we saw along this journey was spectacular. We drove up a series of small mountains and saw down below deserted beaches and a turquoise colored sea. Most of the tourists in the bus were quick to pull out their cameras to take photos. I decided against the idea for a specific reason.

About an hour prior, I took out my MiniDisc player to listen to some music. The Vietnamese girl noticed and communicated that she wanted to listen to the device. Being nice (and an idiot) I gave her my headphones. She took the headphones and then pointed to the MiniDisc protective case signaling that she wanted to open it. I told her no. But she asked again and again. I said no repeatedly. She settled down and listened to the player's music, but when I was not looking she took the liberty to open up the case and look through the other three MiniDiscs that I had. I turned my head and saw what she was doing, but instead of taking it away from her I let her investigate while keeping a close eye. She pulled the MiniDisc player out of a protective cloth and began pressing its buttons. She found the eject button, took out the MiniDisc, and put in another one. From that point on she would listen to one MiniDisc for about 12 seconds, eject it, and put in another one. She did this for about 30 minutes without getting bored. When it became apparent that she could go on forever like that I finally took the MiniDisc player away from her.

I pulled out a book to read. She wanted to read it too! Never mind that she could not read in English, she wanted to read it. I said no to her and she became upset. I then took out a mechanical pencil (I always read with a writing utensil to take notes), she then began grabbing at my pencil. I had to fight her off—nearly beat her off. All the while her mother simply ignored her and the torture she was putting me through.

By the time we arrived to the spectacular views of the beaches from high up in the mountains I decided that it would be a horrible idea to pull out my digital camera because I knew that this evil Vietnamese girl would attack me to get her hands on it.

In the early afternoon, we arrived to Huế, and as one of the many get-as-much-money-out-of-the-foreigner schemes that existed in the tourism industry here, the bus took us to a hotel for us to "have a look." Too tired to go on a hotel hunt I decided to simply stay at the hotel recommended by the bus driver and leave it at that.

After taking a shower it was time to eat, and with an English couple that I had met way back in Cambodia we set out for some food. We ended up at a café where we ran into Aaron Brumo. I first met Aaron (an architect who had been traveling around the world on a fellowship from the University of California, Berkeley) in Saigon.

When we finished eating we made our way to the Forbidden Purple City. In order to do so we had to cross the Trường Tiền Bridge, which was built over the Sông Hương River.

The Forbidden Purple City is located within the Imperial City, which is enclosed within a citadel that is surrounded by a moat that is 10 kilometers in length.[59] Construction began on the walled palace in 1804 by Emperor Gia Long to serve as his public and private residence. In front of the citadel's southern interior gate I saw a 37-meter-tall, but unimpressive, flag tower; I later discovered that it was the tallest flag tower in Vietnam. The construction style and interior design of the buildings and palaces within the citadel seemed to be influenced by traditional Chinese art and architecture. Unfortunately, there was not much to see within the Imperial City as only 10 structures out of more than 150 remain as a result of the bombardments and fighting during the Battle of Huế in 1968.

After exploring the Imperial City, the English couple and I (Aaron decided to stay) decided to take two Vietnamese cyclos (three-wheeled bicycle taxis) back to our hotel.

In the evening, we met Aaron at his hotel and crossed the Sông Hương River again to have dinner at the Lạc Thạnh Restaurant, which had a large sign out front that read: "The Food is Awesome!" We sat on a small balcony on the second floor with an overlooking night view of the river and a street corner that was active with speeding scooters and pedestrians.

After dinner, we walked south, crossed the Phú Xuân Bridge, and returned to our hotels.

The Boat Tour of the Royal Tombs
Friday, June 4, 2004

By this point in the journey I had become burnt out on sightseeing temples and tombs, and going on tours. Whether or not it was a good idea to go on this boat tour to see the imperial tombs of the Nguyễn dynasty (1802-1945), I don't know. But I did it. To sum up the experience the tour was a typical "you buy, you buy" tourist trap that included a discriminatory entrance fee that required foreigners to pay 55,000 VND while Vietnamese residents only had to pay 20,000 VND.

Posted by The Legacy Cycle at 2004-06-07T04:44:00-07:00

Monday, June 7, 2004

Hanoi Notes & Final Thoughts on Vietnam
Saturday, June 5 to Monday, June 7, 2004

My blog entries during my time in Vietnam have been rushed or have not focused on recounting historical events prior to the 20th century; this is especially true for my accounts of Nha Trang, Hội An, and Huế.

I am experiencing a degree of travel burnout; after about two months of backpack travel I am beginning to lose interest in visiting more cultural sites. If and when this happens the best thing to do (I am told but veteran travelers) is to stay in one place for a few days, build a routine, rest, and clear the head.

Since I was spending no more than 24 hours in Nha Trang, Hội An, and Huế, I was pushing the limits of my ability to see, discover, and digest; I had become a numb traveler that was trying to get from point A to B with little desire to take notes or research the historical significance of the sites I was visiting.

I have been in Hanoi for three full days, and I feel better. Tomorrow, I fly to Hong Kong where I will stay for three days and two nights to prepare for my travels through China.

Before I describe my time in Hanoi I would like to discuss my perception of Vietnam as a whole. Vietnam is the first country in this journey where the people have completely exhausted me mentally, physically, and emotionally. The GDP per capita of Vietnam is $606.90 U.S.[60] thus making it nearly impossible for the average Vietnamese citizen to afford traveling outside their own country. But for foreigners–such as myself–traveling in Vietnam is extremely cheap. As a result, the Vietnamese enviously see foreigners as wealthy, and thus begins their persistent tactics to extract as much cash out of the tourist automated teller machine.

One Vietnamese boy who badgered me to buy one of his postcards or illicit, photocopied books finally said: "Look, just give me ten thousand dong. It is nothing for you. You are rich. You come from a rich country. I have nothing. Give me some money so that I can go to school and learn more English. So that I can buy some food and have a place to sleep."

"Look!" I replied, "I have heard that story every day from a hundred different people. I am not rich. And I won't give you ten thousand dong because I don't want to! You expect me to give you money–everyone in this country expects me to give money. Yes, ten thousand dong may be nothing to me, but I can't give it to everyone so I'm sorry–LEAVE ME ALONE!"

The boy left me alone. But what he said summed up how the Vietnamese view foreign tourists. They do not care why you have come, what country you have come from, or what you may think of Vietnam. All they want is your money. And they will follow you, bother you, pester you, and ask you "friendly" questions to skim a buck off you.

Every day men on motor scooters kept calling out and asking me: "Moto?" I tried to ignore them, but the moment we made eye contact they quickly explained that they could take me anywhere around town for a "small" fee. This black-market taxi service was everywhere, and they never left me alone as I walked the streets of the Vietnamese capital. I heard–at least every 10 seconds–the following sales pitch: "Moto? Where you go? Go to museum? I take you–five thousand dong, cheap for you." This constant badgering drove me to the point of fantasizing about buying a gun to threaten the next motor scooter driver that said, "Moto?"

I had tried various ways to politely, and kindly, say no to these pestering motor scooter drivers. It did not work. By my last day in Hanoi I had become so angry, tense, bitter–and so close to losing my sanity–that I simply stared passed them shouting, "NO!" In those moments of standing on the very edge of lucidity, I had fun with the drivers telling them all sorts of lies.

Scooter Driver: Moto?

Domenico: NO!

Scooter driver: Where you go?

Domenico: Alaska!

Scooter driver: You come.

Domenico: How much?

Scooter driver: Ten thousand dong.

Domenico: Really! That is amazing. You will take me to Alaska for ten thousand dong?

Scooter driver: Where you from?

Domenico: Uzbekistan.

Scooter driver: Uz–Uz–Uz–

Domenico: Uzbekistan. Central Asia. South of Kazakhstan.

Scooter driver pointing to my ring: How much?

Domenico: One hundred trillion Turkish dollars.

Scooter driver: Come, you come. I take you.

Domenico: No–for the love of God and Buddha and whoever else–NO!

Due to my expertise as a trained anthropologist I have deciphered the true meaning of frequent questions made to tourists by Vietnamese motor scooter touts.

- "Where are you from?" really means "I want to know which country you came from so that I have an approximate idea of how much money I can rip-off from you."
    - If you answer the question by explaining that you are from a nation with a high GDP per capita income—such as the United States, Japan, or the United Kingdom—it is simply over for you. You will immediately be targeted by the tout as a wealthy tourist. I recommend that you answer the question with an obscure country with low per capita income, such as Uzbekistan, Armenia, or Burundi.
- Touts pointing to a traveler's jewelry (such as a necklace, bracelet, or watch) frequently ask, "How much is that?" Translation: "By learning how much you spend on jewelry I can approximate your level of affluence."
- "Which hotel are you staying at?" Translation: "By learning how much you spend on a room in a hotel I can calculate your disposable income level."
- "Where are you going?" Translation: "If I can find out if you are going to an area of the city where people shop for particular goods or services I can determine what you want to buy and take you to a place that sells it 'cheaper' so that I can get a kickback from your purchase."
- "Moto?" Translation: "I have no taxi license, but since I have a motor scooter I can take you where you want in the city for a price that is four times greater than the regulated taxi prices."
- "What's your name?" Translation: "I want to learn your name so that I can call you by it in an attempt to make you believe that I am your friend when all I really want is your money."

These questions cover the basics of what the Vietnamese will routinely ask travelers.

Although Vietnam is beautiful and enchanting, I did not like being constantly reminded by every single Vietnamese man, woman, and child that I was a living, breathing, walking automated teller machine. I am sure the people I met across Myanmar, Laos, Cambodia, and Thailand also saw me as a wealthy foreigner that they could skim money from, but they hid their intent a hell of a lot better than the Vietnamese.

I need to run and grab some dinner so that I can watch about 100 pirated DVDs tonight in my hotel room ☺.

P.S. I will write about Hanoi in a day or two.

Posted by The Legacy Cycle at 2004-06-07T05:23:00-07:00

Tuesday, June 8, 2004

I have found my ideal travel writing atelier. I found a quiet, dimly lit, and air-conditioned Internet café with a high-speed connection in Hong Kong, which means that I'll be writing a lot while I am here.

Today, I flew from Hanoi, Vietnam, to the Hong Kong Special Administrative Region of the People's Republic of China. Although Hong Kong is technically a part of China it feels like a city-state that has very little to do with the communist mainland. As a result, I will count Hong Kong as country number nine on the growing list of countries I have visited on this trip.

1. South Korea
2. Singapore
3. Malaysia
4. Thailand
5. Myanmar
6. Laos
7. Cambodia
8. Vietnam
9. Hong Kong

And in a few days, I'll be in China.

Hanoi – "The City of Lakes"
Saturday, June 5 to Tuesday, June 8, 2004

The comparison often made by those from the East Coast of the United States that have traveled the entire length of Vietnam is that Saigon is New York and Hanoi is Boston. Hanoi is a small, quiet, and quaint city that is not heavily oriented toward the entrepreneurial, capitalist spirit of Saigon. What I most enjoyed about Hanoi were the small, scenic lakes peppered throughout the capital; their sight would instantly elicit in me a feeling of calm.

I stayed in the Old Quarter of Hanoi, which used to be (and still is to an extent) a commercial center with zigzagging streets each dedicated to vendors of a particular manufacturing or retail trade. Navigating through the Old Quarter was almost like walking through a maze of streets that veered right and left according to an urban plan designed only to confuse newcomers; the strategy I used to cross from one part of the quarter to the other was by developing market knowledge of the types of goods sold on particular streets. Hàng Quạt Street had an abundance of mom-and-pop shops that sold altars and other religious items for home ancestor worship along with items and trinkets needed for funeral rites. Lương Văn Can was an urban haven for eyewear. Need food? Go to the Đồng Xuân market, which is divided into specialized sections by more streets. If you go east on Hàng Chiếu Street you will find the seafood section: live crabs, shrimp, prawns, fish, fish, fish, and more fish, frog skins, and frog legs? The meat section is located further down, and is complete with large, blood dripping slices of pork and beef hanging from hooks in the tropical summer heat.

The Old Quarter is littered with mom-and-pop shops; the ground floor of these shops served as the commercial space while the area behind the store or on the floors above the shop provide a residential space for the store owners. It was amusing to walk past these shops and see the owners eating lunch with their families right in the middle of their shop. I felt like I would be intruding if I walked in to buy something, and so I did my shopping in the morning and evening so that I did not disturb them while they ate their lunch.

I saw the following goods sold in the Old Quarter: iron bars, grills, and steel products for the home; toys, eyewear, altars and shrines for ancestral veneration purposes; Eastern and Western medicine; pirated CDs, DVDs, and computer software; shops selling trinkets and shirts for tourists; clothing shops dedicated to each gender and all ages (one street only sold women's clothing whereas another street only sold children's clothing), shoes, and so on.

The Internet café is about to close so I will have to stop. I will write more about Hanoi tomorrow.

Posted by The Legacy Cycle at 2004-06-08T06:27:00-07:00

Wednesday, June 9, 2004

Hồ Chí Minh
Sunday, June 6, 2004

On June 6, I began my tour of seeing the preserved corpses of dead communist leaders. The Hồ Chí Minh Mausoleum faces the Hanoi Citadel. I wanted to walk through the citadel via Cửa Đông Street, but was deterred by Vietnamese soldiers that were guarding one of its entrance gates. As a result, Frederick (a blond, blue-eyed young Swede I had met in Saigon and was currently rooming with at the hotel) and I walked south on Lý Nam Đế. Along this street I saw a several examples of Hanoi architectural charm. The street (as most streets in the Old Quarter of Hanoi) was lined with tall, beautiful trees. A few of the trees on Lý Nam Đế had grown dangerously close to a few apartment buildings, and in a couple of cases trees had grown straight into a few balconies and buildings. These intruding trees had not been viciously cut down by the city of Hanoi or by the residents of the affected buildings. Thus, there was a satisfying trade-off between the structural damage done by the tree branches that had grown into the balconies and the added sense of harmony between man-made linear structures and the curving, organic nature of urban trees.

As we continued to walk and stare at the trees that had merged into the buildings I began to think of what Hanoi would look like if human beings disappeared from this place and nature retook the city. After seeing the glorious jungle temples of Angkor in Cambodia I wondered if Hanoi would one day be forgotten to be rediscovered centuries later. What would be left of it if the trees of the Old Quarter were already reclaiming it? The city's narrow roads would be further torn up by scores of emerging, thick tree roots while legions of tree branches weaved into the cracks of buildings pushing apart their walls until they came crashing down.

It is curious to think that perhaps centuries from now Hanoi would be deserted, later rediscovered, and visited by tourists and apathetic school children who would rather be doing something else than see the famed "Ruins of Hanoi." Would future historians and archaeologists be able to piece together the social, political, and economic details of how the Vietnamese challenged the imperial might of France and the United States in the 20th century? Of how the Vietnam War divided American society? Perhaps not … this simply goes to show that all things must end and be forgotten. No matter how glorious the feat or accomplishment, no matter how significant the win or loss in war, no matter how many lives had been lost, no matter how wealthy or powerful the government, nation, or corporation … it is all temporary, and ultimately holds little meaning over vast stretches of time.

It was my first time to a mausoleum. I expected something grand. But the Hồ Chí Minh Mausoleum of grey granite and red, polished stone appeared small, sad, dark, and morbid. Although I was impressed by the thousands of Vietnamese men, women, and children who were waiting patiently in line to see the embalmed body of the man who had fought for over two decades to establish an independent Democratic Republic of Vietnam. Thirty-five years after his death there were still so many people paying homage to a man who stood against two powerful Western nations: France and the United States.

Frederick tried to find the end of the line, but neither he or I succeeded. After checking in our cameras at a security checkpoint and buying a brochure–that we were told was an entrance ticket, but was not–Frederick and I ran in search of the end of the snaking line. When we thought we had found the end we were disappointed to discover that the line continued around a corner and extended further and further. Luckily, foreign visitors were given precedence, and we were allowed to cut into the middle of the line.

The line moved swiftly like a conveyor belt. Thirty minutes later we entered the mausoleum; I was relieved to feel cool, air-conditioned air, which provided a needed break from the Hanoi heat. The antechamber leading to the central hall looked like the bland entrance of an unimpressive corporate office building. We followed the moving line to the left of the antechamber and continued up a ramp that led into the darkly lit central hall where Hồ Chí Minh's body rested within a glass case that had a soft, orange light illuminating his face. I could not believe how well preserved the body had been kept. It was as if Hồ Chí Minh had been frozen in time. I stared for a moment as his characteristic white beard that flowed graciously from his chin to chest and admired the serenity of his appearance. Four guards dressed in white uniforms were located at each corner of the glass case. And on the wall behind and above the body there were the communist symbols of a red star and the sickle and hammer. I must confess that after witnessing this unusual communist tradition of preserving the body of a dead political leader—for all to see for decades—that I was surprisingly impressed.

After exiting the mausoleum, Frederick and I walked and then rested at an outdoor drink shop where we both had some freshly squeezed sugarcane. A Vietnamese tout—as expected—approached and offered to drive us around town for a small fee. I warned the tout that he was getting no business from us. He ignored my warning, and so I sat there making up answers to his questions that led to his escalating sales pitch. We left after 20 minutes. The tout was upset and expressed his anger that he had wasted his time without making a dime from us. Not my problem.

We walked south to the Temple of Literature, but we did not enter it because I was still suffering from acute temple burnout. We then walked looking for the Hanoi Railway Station. We eventually found it and Frederick got the schedule and fare information he needed for trains departing for China. We continued to the Friendship Cultural Palace, had lunch at a restaurant, walked north to the Hoàn Kiếm Lake, and later arrived to our hotel.

In the evening, we met up with two other blond and blue-eyed Swedes (friends of Frederick) who were in their mid to late twenties.

We had dinner on the second-floor terrace of a pleasant backpacker joint. I had two orders of a massive tuna sandwich. The beers were only thirty cents each so we loaded up on that as well. Since the alcohol content of the beer was very weak the Swedes took out a circular, flat, aluminum can of moist powder tobacco called snus, which I did not hesitate to try. The tobacco was wrapped in a small packet that they taught me to place under my upper lip. After about 10 minutes I felt the kick from the product, but after 20 minutes I had had enough and took it out. As for the Swedes who had grown up on this stuff they kept it under their lips for the entire night.

After dinner, we walked back to our hotel, but along the way we stopped at several pirated CD and DVD shops; pirated DVDs sold for just under one dollar each.

The next day Frederick bought about 20 DVDs and since we could rent a DVD player at our hotel reception desk we decided to simply run errands on June 7 and watch as many DVDs as we could in the evening.

Posted by The Legacy Cycle at 2004-06-09T20:21:00-07:00

HONG KONG & MACAU

Wednesday, June 9, 2004

Hanoi, Vietnam to Hong Kong
Tuesday, June 8, 2004

I took a Vietnam Airlines flight from Hanoi to Hong Kong yesterday. And although I enjoyed the rustle and bustle of traveling by bus and train in Southeast Asia, I admit that it was a wonderful luxury to travel by plane.

I sat in an aisle seat during the flight, which hindered my ability to see Hong Kong as we descended into the city. Any modern political map will display Hong Kong and Macau as a part of the Chinese mainland, but since China practices a "one country, two systems" policy where both Hong Kong and Macau are treated as special administrative regions (SAR) it was hard for me to consider these two capitalist, autonomous territories as part of socialist China. The special administrative region classification that Hong Kong and Macau fall under has conveniently allowed the government of the People's Republic of China to treat these two regions as politically and economically separate so that strict mainland government rules and regulations do not stifle its free market vitality and economic growth.

Case in point: I have a Chinese visa. Originally, I was going to travel by bus and train from Hanoi into southern China, which would have activated my visa. But I learned before booking my train ticket that if I wanted to go to Hong Kong from China then my Chinese visa would expire, and I if I wanted to return to the Chinese mainland from Hong Kong I would have to apply for another Chinese visa. *What the hell?* I thought. *Is Hong Kong a part of China or not?* Since my Chinese visa did not include Hong Kong then as far as I was concerned Hong Kong was not a part of China, and thus it *is* its own separate state.

Hong Kong = 3 Parts Tokyo + 2 Parts New York

The Hong Kong International Airport and Airport Express train system was a marvel to experience. The airport was sleek, clean, and efficient, and the Airport Express rivaled that of any Japanese train system. After collecting my bag from the baggage claim area and placing it on a baggage cart I made my way to the Airport Express. Initially, it seemed unnatural to walk through the sterile environment of the airport after spending weeks traveling through the rough and unpredictable terrain and conditions of Myanmar, Laos, Cambodia, and Vietnam. The airport, the express train, and Hong Kong itself–as I was about to discover–worked like a fine timepiece where nothing too unexpected was to be expected. Life in Hong Kong it seemed–and in the capitalist developed world in general–was built on being stable, predictable, and safe. Thus, something had been lost. Life in the developed world now appeared mundane and tame to me.

    I bought my express train ticket at a ticket vending machine by pressing a few selections on a touch sensitive screen. I then walked to the train platform where an immaculately dressed uniformed employee lifted my bag off the cart, took the cart and parked it, and waited. When the train arrived he then took my bag into the train and placed it into a luggage holding area. Now *that* is what I call service. I thanked the employee and sat down noticing that the backside of the headrests of all the seats had a computer monitor that displayed the train's location on a digital map that showed all the stops it would make from Lantau Island to Kowloon to Hong Kong. The train, which was cleaner than any Tokyo train I had ever been on, soon exited the terminal and began to travel so fast that my ears popped every time it traveled through a tunnel. I gained my first glimpses of Hong Kong from this speeding train; my immediate thoughts were that I wanted to live in this impressive Asian metropolis as I had never seen so many pristine skyscraping apartment buildings standing so close together, and propped up against the lush and steep mountainous slopes of Lantau.

After making an error as to which stop to get off, I arrived at Tsim Sha Tsui (the shopping and nightlife district of Kowloon; the name translates to nine dragons); it was considered by many people I had met from HK as the decrepit part of the city because it was crammed with massive, low-income apartment buildings, sketchy camera and electronic shops, legions of men from Bangladesh and India desperately trying to persuade potential customers into their tailor shops, working girls enticing men, and suspicious sauna and massage parlors that advertised their services with flickering neon signs in Chinese, English, and Japanese along streets and alleys.

As soon as I exited the Tsim Sha Tsui Station, a Bangladeshi tout approached and explained that he could take me to a guesthouse in the Mirador Mansion. The infamous Mirador Mansion was one of two colossal apartment complexes (the other was Chungking Mansion) at the southern end of Nathan Road that was chock-full of inexpensive guesthouses for travelers on a budget, lowlifes, cheap souvenir and porn shops, dodgy electronic shops, and people shouting.

I followed the Bangladeshi tout to a small shop that sold cheap artwork within the Mirador building (the shop was a front for the guesthouse) and noticed that the walls of the common area on the ground floor were caked in dirt and grime, and stained by spilled food and drink. After grabbing some keys from a bored looking guy sitting on a stool inside the small store, the Bangladeshi man led me to the elevators. We entered one of four elevators, ascended to the eighth floor, stepped out, and walked to the door of an apartment. He unlocked the door and swung it open to reveal that the apartment had been renovated to accommodate five individual rooms. I chose the $20 per night room with a window at the end of the corridor.

My room was small; there was only enough space for a lofted bed and a bathroom; the bathroom was smaller than the washrooms on a commercial airplane. In fact, the bathroom was so small that when I took a shower the next morning I was nearly standing in the toilet.

But the view from my room provided a cityscape scene reminiscent of the film *Blade Runner*. The apartment building across the street was an enormous concrete block of soot and filth. Hundreds of air conditioners that were decades old extended out from nearly every brown tinted window on the building. It appeared as if I was in the Chinatown of New York City in the year 2049.

After figuring out how to use the air conditioner and relaxing a bit on my short and elevated bed I left the apartment to go for a walk. But before descending from the eighth floor via the stairwell I looked down the light well at the mass of rusted buckets and piled up metallic junk cluttered between the large ventilators and machines that powered or cooled the building. I then observed the activity on the floors below: each floor a blend of sweatshops, tailor shops, dry cleaning, guesthouses, and apartments for low-income families from Bangladesh, India, Pakistan, or an African nation. Although the Mirador was designed to be an apartment complex it was more often used by entrepreneurs on the low end of the economic spectrum for small-scale industries.

I descended the stairwell, exited the Mirador, and took a long stroll down Nathan Road. I headed north into the guts of Kowloon. The road was lined with shops, shops, and more shops. From where I started there were many designer clothing stores, but the farther north I traveled the less I saw of them. Instead I saw more and more Chinese restaurants, massage parlors, inexpensive clothing shops, game centers, and large neon signs that hung from buildings over pedestrian walkways and streets.

I was especially amazed to see bamboo scaffoldings along the walls of buildings that were either being renovated or in the process of being constructed.

Hong Kong had the look of Tokyo: the red and white Toyota town car taxis in Hong Kong were similar to the black Toyota town car taxis in Tokyo; the myriad number of neon signs that stuck out from the sides of buildings to advertise all things imaginable; and the lustrous corporate skyscrapers that lit up the night sky. Hong Kong also had the feel and sound of New York: people shouting, car horns being honked repeatedly, and decades-old, weathered brick buildings. In Japanese cities like Tokyo, prefabricated homes and buildings have a life span of about 30 years, at which point they are torn down so that new residential or commercial structures can be built; thus, Tokyo is in a constant state or renewal; rarely did I see an old building in Tokyo that was more than a third of a century old.

At night, I walked to Star Ferry Pier and saw the most spectacular city skyline I had ever seen in my life. I sat and stared at the towering works of steel and glass architecture across Victoria Harbor and all the corporate logos that competed for my attention: AIA, Sanyo, Sharp, Sony, Panasonic, Epson, TCL, Nikon, LG, Hitachi, Olympus, Allianz, Philips, Canon, Onward, Marriott, CMG, Principal, Renesas, Citigroup, and Cosco.

Posted by The Legacy Cycle at 2004-06-09T21:15:00-07:00

Sunday, June 20, 2004

The Hand that Touched the Concrete Hand of Jackie Chan

I spent the morning reading in Kowloon Park before heading south to the Victoria Harbor waterfront to walk along the Avenue of the Stars, a promenade modeled after the Hollywood Walk of Fame to honor celebrities of the Hong Kong film industry like Bruce Lee, Jet Li, Jackie Chan, and Chow Yun-fat with plaques, statues, and handprints in concrete.

Northeast of the promenade I took a five-minute ferry ride across Victoria Harbor to Hong Kong's Queen's Pier where I disembarked and walked on Lung Wo Road passing Hong Kong City Hall. I crossed Connaught Road and walked through the Cenotaph (a 1923 war memorial where British servicemen held daily ceremonies until 1997 to raise and lower the British Royal Navy and Union Jack flags, and the colonial flag of Hong Kong).[1] I soon arrived in front of the HSBC Building (The Hongkong and Shanghai Banking Corporation headquarters), which—architectural speaking—looked like a vertical version of the U.S.S. *Cygnus* space exploration vessel from the 1979 film *The Black Hole*. When the building was completed in 1985 it was the world's most expensive building costing approximately US$668 million. But as I stared at the monstrosity I could not fathom as to why it was so expensive—it is not tall at 178.8 meters or visually impressive.

Eventually, I found myself at St. John's Cathedral where I rested for an hour: the first 30 minutes in silence reading and looking through my *National Geographic traveler: China* book, and the last 30 minutes listening to a live piano recital.

After the recital, I had lunch, walked to the Peak Tram terminal, and took the tram up—ascending at times at a 45-degree angle—to Victoria Peak.

The terminal at Victoria Peak was within a shopping mall full of gimmicks for tourists and a tacky wax museum, but the view of the Hong Kong cityscape on the northern slope of the peak was impressive. In contrast to the urban landscape of towering skyscrapers the view from the southern slope of the peak provided pristine, lush, untouched forest and vegetation that stretched all the way down to the sea. I spent about an hour or two walking along the roads of Victoria Peak admiring the natural surroundings and the multi-million-dollar residential properties.

After taking the tram back down, I walked northwest along Upper Albert Road in search of Lan Kwai Fong—a popular hangout area for expatriates to drink and eat after work. I believe I found aspects of the area while passing several posh Tibetan antique shops, but did not see much of a gathering as it was before the time that most Hong Kong residents clocked out of work.

After my failed attempt to find Lan Kwai Fong, I ascended (a 20-minute journey) via the escalators near SoHo, which collectively is the longest escalator in the world,[2] to the Mid-Levels reaching Conduit Road. I then made my way back down and found a market selling fish and meats; it was the cleanest outdoor food market I had come across on this trip.

Hong Kong Notes

1. Massage parlors, saunas, and karaoke bars: many if not most of these businesses are fronts for prostitution. Kiosks sell comic book pornography.
2. Traffic lights: the walking alarm bell sounds like percussive cowbells being struck in a sixteenth note pattern.
3. Cell phones: I saw several cell phones that were of a sleek plas-

tic bar design that were attached to the ears of passing pedestrians, which freed both hands. I did not see this cellular phone technology in Japan.
4. City public buses: these public vehicles were clean double decker busses with several interior computer monitors that advertised a variety of consumer products.

Kowloon
Thursday, June 10, 2004

I took it easy today in Kowloon. I shopped for a few articles of clothing and went to see the movie *The Ladykillers*, which I enjoyed—"hippity-hop."

Posted by The Legacy Cycle at 2004-06-20T22:09:00-07:00

Sunday, June 20, 2004

Macau
Friday, June 11, 2004

I traveled to Hong Kong from Kowloon with the intention of going to Man Mo Temple, but I changed my mind and took a ferry to Macau from the Hong Kong Macau Ferry Terminal instead. I was only in Macau for about five to six hours.

Going through customs in Macau, and on my return to Hong Kong, revealed the concern both territories had in regards to the SARS epidemic that had struck in 2003. I had to fill out a Health Declaration Card, and when an immigration officer reviewed the answers on my card an infrared camera on his workstation panned up and down detecting my body temperature.

In the limited time I had in Macau, I walked quickly and saw as much as I could of the former Portuguese colony. I traveled south from the Macau Ferry Terminal along Avenida da Amizade toward the

Sands Macao casino. I entered the casino after passing through the metal detectors and immediately felt like I was in Las Vegas with the only difference being that all the patrons were of Asian descent. Ideas began to flood my mind for *Book III – Tribe* of the *Dark Legacy* series. While there I could only think of my father and the many times I went to Las Vegas with him as a child.

After the casino, I continued down Avenida da Amizade until I arrived to Dr. Carlos d'Assumpção Park; a promenade lined with banyan trees. There were a few benches along the promenade where elderly Chinese men and women sat and gossiped to pass the time. At the end of the water-side park stood the 20-meter high Kun Iam golden statue, which was located on a small, man-made island that could only be accessed from a causeway. The statue is dedicated to the Chinese Buddhist goddess of mercy and stands on a white, lotus-shaped dome.[3]

I walked west along Avenida Dr. Sun Yat-Sen and around the long curve of Rua da Praia do Bom Parto until it intersected with Avenida Dr. Mário Soares. I followed the street south to a traffic circle where I saw the famous Casino Lisboa.

Casino Lisboa

The first floor was crammed with so many people that there was nearly not enough space between the gambling tables to pass. At times, I needed to squeeze through the doors to get from one crowded room to the other.

The second floor was for smokers. The air was thick with cigarette and cigar smoke and the carpet was peppered with cigarette burns while the accumulating ash of cigars and cigarettes could be seen in the corners of every room.

The third floor was for casino members and VIPs only.

The Casino Lisboa was dumpy and poorly designed. It was crammed and not impressive since the carpets and walls were old and fading.

After the casino, I had a bite to eat before I went on a run to see the facade and ruins of the 17th century church of St. Paul, which had been destroyed by a fire caused by the havoc of a typhoon in 1835.

Interesting enough the church was designed by an Italian Jesuit, built by Japanese Christians in exile, and attended by the Portuguese.[4]

I then walked through the Camões Gardens and to the Old Protestant Cemetery where Royal Navy captain Henry John Spencer-Churchill (the great-great-grand-uncle of Winston Churchill) and US Naval Lieutenant Joseph Harod Adams (grandson of John Adams (second president of the U.S.) and nephew of John Quincy Adams (sixth president of the U.S.)) were buried.

In the northern section of Macau, I walked down Avenida do Coronel Mesquita to visit the Kun Iam Temple, but it was closed. And from the temple I walked all the way back to the Macau Ferry Terminal to return to Hong Kong.

Thoughts on Macau

In the casinos, I saw masses of Chinese, Hong Kong, and Macau men and women of nearly every social level represented. The VIP sections were reserved for the high rollers who could not be seen mingling with the commoners. But at the Sands Macao casino it appeared that the dominant clientele was upper middle-class individuals who were from mainland China and Hong Kong. The Casino Lisboa on the other hand was mainly populated by local residents some of whom—or most of whom—seemed to be lower middle-class addicts of card games; more of a rough crowd when compared to the Sands Macao.

Macau as a whole was unique and surprising. It had the look and feel of Lisbon, Portugal, but with Chinese habitants (Portuguese residents in Macau make up about one to two percent of the population).

The streets of Macau curved, twisted, and turned in almost nonsensical directions providing an inefficient street plan making it absolutely necessary for me to use my map as I navigated through the autonomous territory.

And strangely, the Chinese residents seemed to have acquired a bit of the social values and mannerisms of the Portuguese. They seemed relaxed and dedicated to family in an almost Mediterranean sense. I would often see retired Chinese men sitting on park benches or on plastic chairs along sidewalks watching with adoring eyes young children go by.

On the darker side, it was apparent that Macau served as the sex fantasyland for Hong Kong and Chinese mainland men (prostitution is legal in Macau,[5] and has become "a destination for the trafficking of women and girls from the Chinese mainland, Mongolia, Russia, Philippines, Thailand, Vietnam, Burma, and Central Asia for the purpose of commercial sexual exploitation."[6] Go to the Hong Kong Macau Ferry Terminal and you will see many, many sex tourism vendors offering hotels, casinos, and strip club deals that include a night or more with a prostitute.

Macau is famed for its triads (Chinese transnational organized crime groups) who run prostitution rings, traffic drugs, engage in money laundering, gambling, extortion, and robbery.

In an article entitled "Triad Organized Crime in Macau Casinos: Extra-Legal Governance and Entrepreneurship" published in the *British Journal of Criminology*, sociologist T. Wing Lo concluded that "triads are now … forced to work beyond Macau's borders, collaborating with mainland officials and syndicates. Rapid economic growth in the mainland 'has induced triads to move away from the rigid territorial base in Macau to develop flexible, social and entrepreneurial networks with mainland officials, junkets, whales [high rollers], investors and criminals.' "[7]

> In addition, it should be noted that according to the U.S. Department of State's *2012 Trafficking in Persons Report* that Macau "is primarily a destination and, to a much lesser extent, a source territory for women and children subjected to sex trafficking and possibly forced labor. Victims originate primarily from the Chinese mainland, with many from inland Chinese provinces who travel to the border province of Guangdong in search of better employment. Sex trafficking victims in Macau also include women from Mongolia, Vietnam, Thailand, and Russia. Many trafficking victims fall prey to false advertisements for jobs in casinos and other legitimate employment in Macau, but upon arrival, are forced into prostitution. Foreign and mainland Chinese women are

sometimes passed to local organized crime groups upon arrival, held captive, and forced into sexual servitude. Victims are sometimes confined in massage parlors and illegal brothels, where they are closely monitored, forced to work long hours, have their identity documents confiscated, and are threatened with violence. Chinese, Russian, and Thai crime syndicates are believed to be involved in recruiting women for Macau's commercial sex industry. Macau made no changes to the immigration regulation structure which renders foreign migrants vulnerable to forced labor; those foreign migrants who are fired for cause or quit must wait 6 months to obtain another work permit. In one documented case, Macau also has been a source territory for women who are subjected to sex trafficking elsewhere in Asia."[8]

Posted by The Legacy Cycle at 2004-06-20T22:35:00-07:00

Sunday, June 20, 2004

General Observations of Hong Kong

1. The number of air-conditioners jutting out from the four to five to nine to 10-storey high apartment complexes was probably equal to half the population of Hong Kong for I saw an unfathomable number of air-cons sticking out from the apartment windows of buildings all along Nathan Road dripping water on the sidewalks leaving a wet line; at times the drops fell on my head, shoulders or glasses.

2. The teenage girls in Hong Kong dressed up to the same pop, punk fashion as the girls in Tokyo, causing me to continually speculate if the girls I saw on the street—or in coffee shops— were Japanese or residents of Hong Kong. In nearly all cases the girls were from Hong Kong; I was able to tell by watching their mannerisms or the way they spoke: Japanese girls speak softly, hold an upright posture, and do not wave their hands

around whereas Hong Kong and Chinese girls talk excitedly, slouch, and use a lot of exaggerated hand movements.

3. There are many narrow alleys in Kowloon. Although the main streets are wide and building complexes large, alleys are narrow as well as staircases of two to three-storey buildings. Walk down any street that is perpendicular or parallel to Nathan Road and you will find mom-and-pop shops with narrow staircases leading up to the living quarters.

4. I walked north on Nathan Road for about 45 minutes before exploring the side streets where I discovered areas that were dedicated to a specific product or industry. For example, I found a street dedicated to the sale of fabric.

5. Kowloon was noisy, busy, gritty, hectic, and oversaturated with businesses engaged in some aspect of the shadow economy, whereas Hong Kong was sterile, legal, and well-run. I preferred Kowloon as it had more character than Hong Kong.

6. Women and men in Hong Kong are loud and aggressive compared to the Japanese. In one case, I saw a street cleaning woman screaming at her male co-worker. But it turned out that she was actually telling her story in such an excited manner that she was yelling. This is very un-Japanese behavior. Use of loud or aggressive language in public is a big no-no in Japan.

7. The Mirador Mansion was full of oddities: backpacker guesthouses, tailor shops, sliding cage doors, men and women's undergarments hanging to dry from washing lines in the light well that were within reach from the hallways and staircases, and sketchy Indian and African men hanging out at the main entrances.

8. Poultry shop windows and eateries displayed defeathered, dead chickens and ducks hanging by their heads from hooks; intimidating butcher knives were used to hack them apart. And when I ate at a chicken restaurant, I spent more time trying to rid my meal of chopped bones than eating and enjoying it. I also came across a turtle soup, fast food restaurant.

Posted by The Legacy Cycle at 2004-06-20T21:00:00-07:00

THE MIDDLE KINGDOM: PART I

Tuesday, June 15, 2004

Internet Censorship

Please be informed that it will be difficult for me to update this blog on a daily basis because certain websites and blog sites—such as the one I am currently using—are prohibited in China (Internet censorship). Regardless, I will keep a written journal of my travels in China and will later publish them online sometime after July 10 (my date of exit from the People's Republic of China).

Posted by The Legacy Cycle at 2004-06-15T21:15:00-07:00

Sunday, June 20, 2004

Hong Kong to Guangzhou, China
Saturday, June 12, 2004

Guangzhou and Shenzhen are typically listed in the top 10 most competitive cities in the category of financial capitals of China by the Chinese Academy of Social Sciences.[1] I had mistakenly assumed prior to entering China that only Hong Kong, Beijing, and Shanghai were the financial capitals of the Middle Kingdom, but for a country with a population exceeding 1.3 billion it made sense that there were several competing financial centers.

Guangzhou is the third largest city in China with a population of over eight million (14.2 million in 2018), and it is the largest city in the Guangdong province.[2] If I had not seen the signs and billboards with Chinese script throughout the city I would not have believed that I was in China. Although China has just over one-sixth of the world's population it boasts space. Unlike Japan, the Chinese can afford to build wide roads, large hotels, and massive commercial and residential buildings.

As I sat in my taxi on the way to Shamian Island and looked out beyond my moving window, I felt no initial cultural shock in realizing that I was now–for the first time in my life–in China. From what I could see, Guangzhou was a big capitalist city filled with urban conveniences. I felt at home.

I arrived to the Guangzhou Youth Hostel on Shamian Island, checked into a pleasant and spacious room, washed up, and went for a walk exploring the Qingping Market and the Jade Market on Changshou Lu before returning to the hostel to rest.

Notes on the Qingping Market

The shops facing Liu Er San Lu (road) were dedicated to Chinese herbal remedies. Sacks and jars filled with dried roots, snakeskins, mushrooms, starfishes, seahorses, deer antlers, skinned deer legs, and turtle shells lined the shelves and floor of each shop.

I took an alley north through the market and passed a long line of mom-and-pop shops selling dried fruits and figs, vegetables, incense sticks, beans, giant bags of packed and dried leaves, chili, red peppers, and sausages.

I saw men playing mahjong: a tile-based game that was always accompanied by the sound of players slamming their tiles on the table. I then came across a very clean public toilet that was maintained by a man who sat in front of it as if he was guarding it. I later saw a Chinese woman coughing up and spitting phlegm on the ground.

Di Shi Fu Lu was a pedestrian shopping street lined with female store attendants standing outside their respective stores clapping and calling out to potential customers.

Shamian Island

The sandbank island was a quiet refuge of parks, trees, neoclassical buildings, children's boutique shops, and children. The island was a concession gained jointly by the British and French in the 1860s after the Second Opium War,[3] thus becoming a sort of "mini-colony" until 1949.[4]

I walked up and down Shamian Street enjoying the shade provided by the trees that lined the boulevard as well as the gardens and playgrounds while noticing that there were bronze statues of children at nearly every corner.

The Children of Shamian Island

The White Swan Hotel is a block away from the U.S. Consulate and was filled with Chinese babies and young children when I entered it. I soon discovered from an interracial American couple I had met in the lobby that the hotel was also referred to as the "White Stork Inn" or the "Baby Hotel." They explained that hundreds, perhaps thousands, of couples from the U.S. and other nations come to Shamian Island each year to finalize the last bureaucratic procedures in the adoption of a Chinese child.

Notes on Chinese Adoption

1. There are direct flights from Los Angeles to Guangzhou, China.
2. Many couples from the U.S., Germany, and Spain adopt Chinese children through the Chinese Center for Adoption.

3. The White Swan Hotel accommodates many couples that are adopting Chinese children because it is located next to the U.S. Consulate.
4. The application process to adopt a Chinese child takes about 18 months and costs about US$18,000.
5. With open adoption in the U.S. there is no guarantee that the adopting couple—even after spending time and money with the pregnant mother who wants to give up the child—will be able to keep the child after its birth.
6. The majority of Chinese children offered for adoption are girls, which was a result of China's one-child policy that was instituted by Deng Xiaoping in 1979 to curb the nation's population growth rate. Due to the social and cultural pressures on Chinese couples to ensure that their first and only child is a boy it is not uncommon for the couple—in both rural and urban areas —to abandon or murder their first-born if it is a girl, which has led to what is now termed gendercide. It was estimated in 1990 by Indian economist Amartya Sen that approximately 100 million women were missing in the world population as a result of either being "aborted, killed, or neglected to death."[5]
7. The date of birth for most of the adopted children is unknown. Many of these children were left in bamboo baskets in locations where they were sure to be found.
8. Adopting parents are typically not allowed to go to the Chinese orphanage where the child they will adopt is residing.
9. The Chinese government pairs couples with a child.

Posted by The Legacy Cycle at 2004-06-20T23:13:00-07:00

Sunday, June 20, 2004

Shanghai
Monday, June 14, 2004

I checked into the Pujiang Hotel (established in 1846 and formerly known as the Astor House Hotel) located at 15 Huangpu Lu and spent nearly a hundred dollars for a two-night stay in a spacious late Victorian room on the fifth floor; it was not wise financially, but I thought I would treat myself to a bit of luxury.

Famed people who had stayed at the Astor House included Charlie Chaplin, U.S. Presidents Ulysses S. Grant (who stayed in room 410 in 1879) and William Howard Taft, and Albert Einstein who stayed in room 304 in 1929.

Shanghai Blues
Thursday, June 17, 2004

My first impression of Shanghai was that it was a sad place. I arrived on Monday when it was cloudy and full of industrial gloom.

I walked down Nanjing Dong Lu, the main pedestrian shopping street of Shanghai, and felt depressed. I had yet to feel or experience any essence of traditional Chinese culture. I reflected that although I had traveled to Hong Kong, Macau, Guangzhou, and now Shanghai, they all looked, tasted, and smelled of Western capitalism to such an extent that the Chinatowns of Chicago and New York felt more like what I had expected to see and experience in China than these cities. It was selfish of me to be disappointed with China as a result of the inner conflict between what I expected to find and what I really discovered. Hong Kong and Macau had lived up to my expectations. I knew nothing about Guangzhou. But in the end, after all this mental complaining I realized that these cities—as trading seaports—were exactly what they were (Occidental and capitalist) as a result of Western imperialistic and semi-colonial economic and military ambitions that overran the country from the 19th to the first half of the 20th century.

I picked up the book *Shanghai* by Harriet Sergeant while in the city to learn more about its history and the impact Britain, France, Germany, Russia, Japan, and the U.S. had on the its development while also learning about the First and Second Opium Wars (and how victorious Britain forcibly gained the right to drug China into submission) and the factors that led to the weakening of the Qing dynasty.

British merchants sold English textiles to India, shipped Indian cotton to China and Chinese silk, tea and porcelain back to the United Kingdom. The policies of the Manchu government ensured the East India Company, Britain's sole representative in the East until 1834, sold less than it bought. The British exchequer had to make up the balance with previous hard currency in the form of silver bars until they discovered the one commodity the Chinese wanted: opium. In the 1760s China imported 1,000 chests a year, each one weighing 133 pounds. By 1838 the total had risen to 40,000 chests and the addicts could be counted in their millions. Opium, grown in India and sold in China, had saved British trade in the Far East and created fortunes for British and American merchants. Taxes on opium made up one-seventh of the revenue of the British government in India while the tax on tea, now paid for by opium, accounted for one-tenth of the total revenue of the United Kingdom.

China's desire to call a halt to 'an infamous traffic', as Gladstone called it, coincided with British determination for greater trade opportunities. In 1840 the First Opium War broke out between the countries which ended in defeat for China two years later.[6]

Shanghai Timeline

Here is a list of important dates concerning the modern history and development of Shanghai (unless otherwise stated the information below is from Harriet Sergeant's book *Shanghai*).[7]

1839 – The First Opium War begins (U.K. vs. Qing dynasty).

1842 – "The Opium War ends with the signing of the Treaty of Nanjing",[8] which results–among many other concessions–with Shanghai being opened to British subjects for their "Mercantile pursuits".[9]

1850 – "Outbreak of the Taiping Rebellion".

1853 – Occupation of Shanghai by Taiping rebels.

1864 – Taiping Rebellion ends.

1894-5 – The First Sino-Japanese War (Empire of Japan vs. Qing Empire); Japan wins resulting in the first factories being built in Shanghai.

1904-5 – The Russo-Japanese War (Empire of Japan vs. Russian Empire); Japan wins.

1911 – "The Chinese Revolution, inspired by Sun Yat-sen, results in the overthrow of the Manchu [Qing] dynasty".

1912 – "Yuan Shikai is elected President of the Republic of China".

1920 – "Civil war breaks out in China between various warlords".

1921 – "The first National Congress of the Communist Party is held in Shanghai".

1925 – "A general strike by Chinese workers against Britain and Japan begins after a demonstration on May 30th in Shanghai"; "Sun Yat-sen dies".

1926 – The Nationalist army led by Chiang Kai-shek sets out from Guangzhou to reclaim China from the warlords.

1927 – "Chiang Kai-shek splits from his Communist allies in Shanghai".

1928 – Nanjing becomes the capital of the Republic of China.

1931 – The Empire of Japan invades and occupies Manchuria.

1932 – Japanese imperial forces invade Shanghai.

1937 – The Second Sino-Japanese War (Empire of Japan vs. Republic of China) begins; Nanking Massacre takes place (an estimated 40,000 to 300,000 Chinese men, women, and children were raped and slaughtered by Japanese imperial troops);[10] Chinese Nationalists and Communists unite to fight the Empire of Japan.

1945 – End of the Japanese occupation of China.

1949 – "Shanghai falls to the Chinese communists".

Shanghai had been a city of particular economic importance to European and Japanese imperial powers from approximately the mid-19th to the mid-20th century; by the 1930s it had become "the largest port and industrial centre of the Far East."[11] Its location at the end of the Yangtze River and its access to ports in Japan and Southeast Asia were prime reasons as to why it rose to become the most important city in the Orient during the industrial period.[12] Due to a series of wars and treaties with a weakening Qing dynasty that were favorable to the interests of Western imperial powers, Shanghai quickly became a magnet for European, American, and Japanese merchants (along with refugees, missionaries, gangsters, drug dealers, criminals, international arms dealers, and artists[13]) who could develop and expand their trading operations with no taxation paid to China "other than maritime customs dues and the land tax".[14]

After reading Harriet Sergeant's book, I understood why Shanghai looked like Chicago, New York, or London in the 1920s. Essentially, Shanghai was a city that had less to do with traditional Chinese history and culture and more to do with the shadow of Western imperialism. As Harriet explains: "By the 'twenties and 'thirties Shanghai was as much a Chinese as a Western creation … Architecturally, Shanghai recalled a city in northern Europe or America. Neo-Grecque skyscrapers and department stores lined the business centre. Fake Tudor houses and Spanish-style villas filled the suburbs."[15] Harriet's book highlights through the history of Shanghai the understandable rising tension between China and the West, which ultimately explained to a degree China's rejection of Western political capitalism and embrace of communism.

With the end of the First Opium War, and the signing of the Treaty of Nanjing, the Qing dynasty was forced by the United Kingdom to open Shanghai along with "four other ports" to foreigners.[16] This marked the first time in China's "four-thousand-year history" that it was unable to expel invaders.[17] Soon after "France, Belgium, Sweden, Norway and Russia put forward their demands while setting up businesses in the Treaty Ports."[18] The United States also sought to gain concessions from China thus President Tyler sent "Massachusetts politician, Caleb Cushing," resulting in a treaty in 1844 that provided a clause placing "Americans in China under consular jurisdiction."[19] As a result, "the Chinese had no power over foreigners of the 'most-favoured-nation' variety … They could only be tried in their own courts and by their own consulate … For the next hundred years it ensured the safety of foreigners, his property and his business. China and its troubles could not touch him."[20] Shanghai ultimately became "a state within a state" in China representing to "both foreigner and Chinese" of "their unequal relationship: an insult to China and confirmation to the West of its superiority."[21] There is, to this day, an undying myth that prior to 1949 there was a "sign placed in Shanghai's Huangpu Park that allegedly read: 'Chinese and Dogs Not Admitted.'"[22] Historians agree that such a sign never existed (instead there were regulations in 1903 that stated "No dog or bicycles are admitted" and "No Chinese are admitted, except servants in attendance upon foreigners")[23] but the legend continues to thrive as it symbolically embodies to the Chinese the insulting inequality experienced as a result of Western imperialism.

As can be imagined, at that time, the impoverished Chinese–who lived near and far from Shanghai–had come to envy and hate the Westerners who were exploiting their country. This resentment led to and fueled the Boxer Rebellion (1899-1901), nationalism as led by Sun Yat-sen and Chiang Kai-shek, and Mao Zedong's communist movement.

It is of no surprise then that the movements to reclaim China from Western imperialism began in Shanghai by Western-educated Chinese men such as Dr. Sun Yat-sen. These educated Chinese who had grown up in Shanghai knew that the only way for China to take back what was rightfully theirs had to be accomplished by Western means. Driven individuals like Mao Zedong took Western ideologies such as communism as an antidote to Western capitalism.

Shanghai was the cradle of the revolutionary movements that had taken China to where it is today, a nation–of over a billion people–ruled by the Chinese Communist Party (CCP).

The Future of Shanghai & China

Today, China is striving to develop and return Shanghai to its former economic glory. It is said by some that in the future Shanghai will overcome Hong Kong and Tokyo in economic importance, that it will be the top financial hub of East Asia.

Do I agree? To be honest, I do not. Shanghai, in my opinion, is a couple of decades away from overcoming Hong Kong and Tokyo. China's communist political system will slow Shanghai's capitalist ambitions for greater integration into the world economy because it would require a liberation of the Internet, which at the moment is not tolerated by the Communist Party of China (CPC). But one thing is certain, communism's days in China are numbered. I believe that as the middle class grows in China over time, the tight political grip of the Chinese Communist Party will be eroded by the demands of an affluent population. Shanghai, Hong Kong, and Guangzhou are the capitalist engine cities that are driving China's economic growth. These cities (particularly Hong Kong) will lead the "revolution" (or transformation) that will ultimately end political communism in China. Thus, as the Chinese Communist Party continues to invest and develop Shanghai to become the next big financial center in East Asia, they will–at the same time–be planting the seeds of their own destruction.

For those who have been to Tokyo, Seoul, Hong Kong, and Shanghai you will agree that Shanghai has a long way to go to overcome the economic powerhouse cities of Japan, South Korea, and China's special administrative regions. I do not think the generation of China today will lead Shanghai to any form of economic glory in the near future. But perhaps it will be the next generation. I say this because the members of China's middle class that I had come into contact with possessed a more provincial and uniform outlook. Although they were very educated, it seemed that they mostly thought and dressed the same. I found little original reasoning, creativity, or innovative perspectives in our conversations. If China is to grow to become a dominant economic power then it needs to foster both freedom of expression and a greater diversity of ideas among its population.

Dwelling on these thoughts, I must confess that I am not impressed with what I have seen in China. I have found more ambition, imagination, and inventiveness from the people of Southeast Asia,

South Korea, and Japan than in China. For example, the interior design for nearly every restaurant I passed or ate in consisted simply of white walls devoid of pictures or paintings. I could say the same for the majority of the stores, hotels, and homes I saw in China. In addition, I saw little to no advancements made in the fields of art and design. How can China grow economically without thriving, creative, and innovative ideas expressed through the mediums of art, design, engineering, and architecture?

One reason economists cite China as the next big economic power in the global economy is that it will soon have a middle class of over 300 million,[24] which translates into an enormous consumer market for Western goods. This massive middle class that is essentially the size of the entire U.S. population will buy clothing from the Gap, eat at fast food restaurant like KFC and McDonald's, take out car loans to buy vehicles from GM, Toyota, and Renault, and buy electronic devices from Sony and Apple. China will most definitely become one of the largest consumer markets in the world.

Although software and record labels from Europe, Japan, and the U.S. will find it very difficult to make profit in China. Anything digital that *can be* burned off a CD or DVD *will be* in China. Microsoft as well as U.S., European, and Japanese music labels will continue to lose billions of dollars to rampant piracy in emerging markets.[25,26] So forget selling software and making a buck in China and Southeast Asia.

If China does not encourage independent thinkers and entrepreneurs to create companies that can compete globally then the nation will fall victim to simply being a manufacturing haven and consumer market for the West.

What does China produce and export to the West under the logo of its own multinational corporations? Name one Chinese company that is a legitimate rival to Honda, Toyota, Nissan, BMW, Microsoft, Apple, Sony, Nokia, Vodafone, or Samsung. It is a nation that under the brand of its own domestic firms makes cheap, low quality products that are exported to Southeast Asian nations (consider the Chinese motorcycle manufacturers example I provided in my chapter on Vietnam). How can China become a powerhouse economy in its own right by selling to a Southeast Asian market that has very little purchasing power?

In my opinion, Japan will continue–for at least another decade–to be the economic power of East Asia until its aging and shrinking population begins to diminish its macroeconomic potential. But I hope that I am wrong for China's sake.

Posted by The Legacy Cycle at 2004-06-20T23:49:00-07:00

Saturday, July 3, 2004

Shanghai's Barbershop Brothels
Wednesday, June 16, 2004

In Shanghai, I saw barbershop brothels for the first time after having heard about them in Thailand. The area north of Yan'an Xi Lu and Yan'an Zhong Lu was littered with them.

Wuding Xi Lu Notes

Wuding Xi Lu had a few barbershop brothels on every single block, and in some cases, there were several brothels lined on a single block.

I discovered, as I walked through the city, that not only were brothels disguised as barbershops, but there were others disguised as massage parlors and karaoke bars. It seemed clever for a brothel to be weakly camouflaged as a barbershop (dull pink light bulbs–in some rare cases blue–illuminating the barber's pole (some of which had hearts on them) usually gave them away) because brothel owners could potentially gain customers who entered with the intention to have their hair cut; most of the barbershop brothels that I saw in Shanghai were located next to or near legitimate barbershops. The store windows of the barbershop brothels all had the Chinese written characters for beauty and hair as well as the number 60 and minutes, obviously what kind of barbershop charges by the hour?

When I looked into the barbershop brothels through the windows I could see that it was darkly lit in a soft pink glow with mirrors and chairs set up much like a traditional barbershop, but it was plain to see that it had been years since it had–if ever–been used for the purpose of cutting hair. I could also see Chinese women scantily dressed lounging around in boredom. In some cases, windows of barbershop brothels were heavily tinted preventing me from seeing anything other than a hazy pink glow.

      In terms of clientele, these barbershop brothels were for locals as they did not advertise to foreigners or sex tourists. Some of the brothels were so rundown and dilapidated that it was clear that they serviced lower-class, blue-collar Chinese men (perhaps migrant workers from the countryside). In addition, these barbershop brothels were far west of the Bund in an area not frequented by tourists.

Posted by The Legacy Cycle at 2004-07-03T21:15:00-07:00

Saturday, July 3, 2004

Last Day in Shanghai
Friday, June 18, 2004

Today will be my last day in Shanghai. It is another dreary day; I have yet to see the city bathed in sunlight.

Comic Store

Yesterday, I went to the General Post Office Building and then into town in search of English bookstores. During my quest I found a comic bookstore that sold Japanese comics in English that were imported from the U.S.? And the store's clientele were Chinese men and women? There was a second floor to the establishment full of tables where patrons could sit down and read comics, much like a manga café in Japan. The comics were expensive (one copy sold for more than US$10) and the selection was not vast leaving me to wonder how a niche shop such as this could stay in business.

The Shanghai Museum

I went to the Shanghai Museum; it was clean, efficient, and modern in design. I spent a lot of time looking at the bronze vessels from China's Bronze Age (4,000 BC). Some of the vessels were large cauldrons that were most likely used to burn offerings; the cauldrons were similar to the ones I had seen in front of the Temple of the City Gods in the Old City of Shanghai. My main critique of the museum was that the cultural objects on display were presented out of context. I had to read a small caption that detailed the date of the object and its purpose or use. Perhaps placing these objects within an exhibit that showed how these objects were used would have been more interesting.

One vessel had an engraved depiction of a scene in a temple that illustrated devotees ascending steps to an altar where a priest awaited to greet them. This is the type of context where vessels such as this one was used.

After seeing in Myanmar the amount of money and gifts given as tribute by the people to the stupas all over the country, it was easy to understand how important the temples were in ancient times and also the need by royal families or warlords to control these religious centers to legitimize their power while also gaining revenue.

After the bronze vessels, I visited the hall dedicated to the history of Chinese porcelain. I also saw Chinese coinage, stamps (strictly used by bureaucrats), jade ornaments, and tribal clothing of the various Chinese ethnic groups.

After exiting the museum, I was approached by several middle-aged Chinese men who wanted to take a picture with me in front of the Shanghai Museum. It was odd, but I entertained their request. In the evening, I had dinner in a shopping mall that looked no different from any mall in the U.S.

The Communist Dynasty

A man in my dorm room (after my two nights in a single bedroom I stayed in the hotel's attic where they had rows of beds for backpackers) explained to me that China had always been ruled by powerful feudal dynasties that propagated the hierarchal and rigid class structures that kept the masses in place for 4,000 years. Farmers stayed farmers as royal families maintained their royalty. But he also explained that there had also been a meritocratic tradition starting in the sixth century AD in which anyone with the financial means to study for and pass civil service exams could move up the social ladder, but this mobility could never be passed on to offspring.

This all changed in 1912 when Sun Yat-sen ended 4,000 years of dynasty rule by ending the Qing dynasty and establishing the Republic of China, which gave way to the conflicting interests of the Nationalists and the Communists.

Although Mao preached egalitarianism and communism to workers and peasants all over China to form his Red Army that ultimately pushed the Nationalist to Taiwan, it seemed that he simply reinstated–through the Communist Party–the dynastic tradition of the masses abiding by the political will of a one-party state. What is the difference between the Communist Party of China and the dynasties that ruled before 1912? Nothing. China has not changed.

Posted by The Legacy Cycle at 2004-07-03T21:17:00-07:00

Saturday, August 14, 2004

On the following pages, you will find the first short story I wrote for my blog while traveling through Asia. I began writing this steampunk, espionage tale in the lobby of my hotel in Shanghai on a dreary, grey day. The work is fiction, but the events, conversations, and ideas have their place in reality.

Posted by The Legacy Cycle at 2004-08-14T13:17:00-07:00

DOMENICO ITALO COMPOSTO-HART

The Astor House of Old Shanghai

DOMENICO ITALO COMPOSTO – HART

DRAGON BONE BOOKS

CHAPTER 1

He laid the rolled, silk scroll on his hotel bed and took a step back. The wood floor creaked. He looked down at his old, beaten leather boots and thought again about why he liked the Chinese painting. It was the utter loneliness. *Yes, that is it.*

The cool night winds from the long open window caressed his neck causing him to shiver. He rubbed his arms feeling tired. It had been a long day, and he knew that tomorrow would not be as peaceful as today. A foghorn then sounded into the night. He took a deep breath feeling the faint scent of the sea in the winds. He decided to rest and get ready for bed. But again, he desired to look at the painting. Slowly and carefully he unrolled the scroll and positioned it so that its rectangular shape was symmetrical to the borders of the bed. He took another step back and saw clearly why the painting had appealed to him. He felt like that small, dark figure standing at the edge of a long, thin, and black sandy shore before the magnificent power of crashing waterfall waves. He then stepped toward a circular table by the open window, took a short glass of anise London dry gin on the rocks, and grabbed the arm of a finely sculpted, colonial sofa chair; he pulled the chair closer to the bed, and sat down.

Thoughts and memories began to fill his mind like faint, clattery raindrops hitting an old, copper roof. He did not want to think too much, and so he kept distant from those thoughts by observing them. He smiled as he observed while staring at the painting. But soon the smile faded. He thought of her again, and with her came the not too distant events of the day.

* * *

He arrived to Shanghai in the evening, under dark grey clouds, by a steam locomotive from Guangzhou. Dismal and sad were his first two impressions of the bustling city.

He bought the week's issue of the *North China Herald* at the railway station and then hired a rickshaw man to take him to his hotel. He was unshaven, wearing a dirty, mid-length leather coat of calf suede, a Sinclair club collared shirt, wrinkled canvas field trousers, and muddied mid-calf boots. He knew that his appearance would not be appreciated in the lobby of what many considered to be the best hotel in Shanghai, but he also knew that many Western guests would simply pass him off as another foreigner back in from the "bush".

When he arrived to the hotel he paid his ride, took his leather packsack, and walked up the red, carpeted steps of the main entrance. Two sleek and well-dressed Chinamen smiled, bowed, and opened the two main entrance doors. He bowed his head back to them and entered the lobby quickly able to distinguish between the American, British, French, German, Japanese, and Russian guests who were seated or standing throughout the grand Victorian room in their finest attire while speaking, observing, smoking, reading, or drinking. Many European heads turned to swiftly observe and dismiss him as some lost messenger. As for the Americans in the room, there were only two, and they were too busy drinking their whiskey to pay him much attention.

He approached the check-in desk and requested their best room; it had been too many weeks of sleeping in low-cost, filthy old guesthouses throughout southern China. He believed that he deserved a treat to feel like a gentleman again. The receptionist explained that there was one room left on the fifth floor for fourteen pounds. He hadn't spent that kind of money in an entire month. Regardless, he took the room for two nights.

A Chinese servant standing beside the check-in desk offered to take his packsack, but he declined the offer and simply asked where the lift was located. "Up these steps and at the end of the hall," the receptionist replied. He thanked the receptionist, walked up the steps, and approached the liftman that was already opening the lift cage for him. "Fifth floor," he requested as he stepped into the lift.

And as the lift ascended he reviewed the newspaper article on the third page; the article detailed what two sources believed would be the new foreign policy doctrine of the McKinley administration in regards to its increasingly aggressive approach to China. The article went on to discuss U.S. Secretary of State John Hay as the mastermind behind the policy and that perhaps by the end of the year the policy would be officially communicated to European nations. The lift stopped, the liftman opened the lift cage, and he walked out into a long, dark corridor. "To the end of the hall, sir," the liftman said before he closed the cage. He walked to the end of the corridor, turned to his left, and saw the door to his room. Room 502.

He entered and found the room very much to his liking: high ceiling, large windows allowing the grey light of the dreary day to illuminate the bedroom and bathroom, wood flooring, a master bed, and an oak desk against the wall facing a large, hanging mirror.

He approached the central window of the bedroom and looked out at a view of the Huangpu River that was filled with the traffic of both wind and steam powered cargo ships, the Waibaidu Bridge, and the Bund, which was lined with strolling, well-dressed Europeans, various types of horse drawn vehicles, and surprisingly one Benz Patent-Motorwagen that was catching the attention of nearly everyone it passed. He then turned away from the window, dropped his packsack and newspaper on the bed, wound his watch, and decided to take a shower.

After shaving and getting dressed in fresh but wrinkled clothes he decided to take a walk. He took the stairs down to the lobby, exited the hotel, crossed the Waibaidu Bridge, and walked south along the Bund. At Nanking Road, he turned right. Now walking west, he thought, *West is home. Where I belong*; it had been eight years since he had been to the land of his birth.

"Excuse me, sir," a young woman began with a sweet, Cantonese accent. "But, we have a gallery on the third floor. Would you like to come and see it?"

She was his first tout in Shanghai. He had traveled throughout southeast Asia and had grown bitterly numb to the elaborate stories and lies he had heard day after day from touts in Rangoon, Bangkok, Phnom Penh, Saigon, Hue, Ha Noi and countless other cities and towns. But she was a woman: young, not forceful, and unaware of her seductive powers. *So much does she have to learn*, he thought remembering his long-ago military training days.

"It's just this way," she said pointing to the revolving entrance door of an old, colonial styled building. "Where are you from?"

Where are you from? How many times had he heard that question in the past seven months? "I'm originally from Chicago."

The girl gave a quizzical look.

"In the United States."

She nodded her head with a smile. "Where in the United States is it?"

"Well–"

"Is it near New York?" she interrupted.

"No. God, no. What an awful place. No, Chicago is on the west coast of a large lake called Michigan."

The girl smiled. It was then that he noticed her pearl earrings. He immediately thought of the women he had known in the seaport city of Valparaiso, Chile. Shaking his head slightly to rid his mind of those memories he looked into her eyes and could see that she still had very little idea of where Chicago was located.

"What kind of gallery?" he asked, changing the subject.

"We have Chinese calligraphy–do you know calligraphy?"

He nodded.

"And we have traditional Chinese paintings–and modern too."

He loved art. When he was in boarding school he had two very good friends who were artists. He did his best to encourage them. But that was now years ago. *It actually feels like decades.*

"Please, please come," she asked.

Deciding that it was best to take a break from the stench of horse manure, urine, and rotting waste that littered the street he nodded and said, "Yes, let's go."

She gave another smile and escorted him into the old building. Inside a small and dark entrance hall, and to their left, she pointed to an open lift expecting him to enter, but he waited for her to enter first. Pleased with his small act of kindness she walked into the lift. He then followed.

The gallery was on the third floor and was simply a room that was neither large nor small. Scroll paintings were hanging on all the walls, and upright stacks of oil canvas paintings were on the floor leaning against two of the walls. There was a table in the center of the room that was covered with piles of smaller paintings; beneath the table were stacked green boxes that he assumed were used to pack the scrolls once they were bought and rolled.

"Are you an artist?" he asked.

"Yes, I am—well, I only do calligraphy."

"Oh, do you have some of your calligraphies here?"

"Yes, just over here."

She led him to the opposite side of a wall partition in the room. He then saw several hanging calligraphy paintings.

"Can you read any of them?" she asked.

"No, only bits and pieces. Like that kanji—I mean character. That means school, does it not?"

"To study. That is the meaning."

"School—to study. I was almost right."

"Yes, perhaps." She pointed to one of her paintings and explained, "This means plum and this is tea. These two characters give a peaceful sense. This calligraphy is meant to relax. Rest the mind. Do you know what this means?" she asked pointing to a large, single calligraphy that he had never seen before.

"No, I don't know what it means," he said enjoying her sweet voice and small movements.

"It means love."

"Oh," he said slightly taken aback. He then thought of the Japanese character for *great liking*, which was far different in appearance than the Chinese character for love. He took a good look at the individual parts that composed the character and said, "That means heart and that means friend."

"Yes," she said impressed that he could identify the individual characters that composed the entire character for love.

"But, I don't know that character."

"It means house or home."

He wanted to impress her by drawing the Japanese character for *great liking* and to then explain to her that it was composed of the Japanese characters for woman and child. He rehearsed in his mind what he would say; *there is no greater, and purer a form of love than that between a mother and her child*. But he said and did nothing.

"Where did you learn to read characters?" she asked.

"In Chicago, and later in Japan."

"In Japan?" she said with dislike in her eyes.

"I used to live there."

"Really?"

"Yes, and while I was there I learned quite a few Japanese characters."

"Chinese," she said sharply. "The Japanese stole this from us."

He had nothing to say in reply.

"Over here we have more paintings. These are more traditional," she pointed to four paintings framed on silk scrolls hanging on the wall. "Each one represents one of the four seasons: spring, summer, fall, and winter. In China, we often liken the seasons to our lives. Spring is for the child; summer is youth and strength–vitality; fall for settling down, having a family; and winter, for rest in the old age."

"Interesting."

"Yes, and here we have another four seasons, but this is more modern. The colors are more vibrant in these paintings."

"Yes, I like these very much." He took a long moment to admire the summer painting that was composed of a lively, green color. "How much is this one?"

"The summer one? Well, it is part of a set. I can't sell you only one. For all four it is one thousand two hundred yuan."

"Oh," he said disappointed.

He then looked to a series of paintings of warriors armed with tightly pulled bows riding on horses. "I like these. Particularly this one."

"This is by a more famous painter. They are Mongolian riders hunting."

"How much is this one?"

"Four hundred yuan."

"Oh," he said, "that isn't so bad."

"You should buy it. It's meaning is success."

He instantly thought of his deceased father and decided that he would buy it. But before declaring his decision, he decided to continue looking for he wanted to spend more time with the girl. Then he saw it. It was a painting that was far different from all the others. He took a closer look and saw that the painting was of what appeared to be an enormous, cloudy sky hovering above the tiniest tree at the edge of a thin and bare cliff. It was a sad painting that was full of loneliness. "This is a tree," he said.

"No, it is of a famous Chinese poet. That crashing down above him is a waterfall–from the Yangtze River. He is walking along the edge of a sandy floor. Those tiny, curved lines are birds. The poet wrote about the insignificance of himself in all the vast space of the universe. That is why he is so small and insignificant in the painting."

He was now more drawn to the painting. The story behind it was tragic. But he loved it, this painting of vast nothingness. He took a few steps away from the painting to admire it some more. He then noticed that half of it was in shadow. "Can you move it? I want to see it in the light."

"Yes," she answered as she grabbed a pole to lift the painting to then place it on a wall with more light.

He looked at the painting now in the light. The light bleached the painting. He could see that the painting's effect on him was enhanced when it was hanging in a dark place.

"Yes, I like it. I like it very much. But it looks better in shadow, not in the light."

Although he had made up his mind to buy the painting, along with the other for his deceased father, he wasn't prepared to leave the young girl. He quickly fished for questions to ask her and spoke:

"Are you from Shanghai?"

"Inner Mongolia ..."

"When did you leave?"

"Three years ago, ..."

"Which do you like better, Shanghai or Beijing?"

"Shanghai ..."

"Do you have brothers and sisters?"

"One younger sister ..."

"What kind of paintings—or styles—do you prefer?"

"Impressionism ..."

When he finally left the gallery, he had bought a total of three paintings. The third was for his future wife, whoever she would be. It was a traditional Chinese landscape painting with vibrant splashes of pink for the leaves of the cherry trees. Although it could have, the painting did not remind him of Japan in the spring.

And as he took the lift down to the first floor with the girl he felt the urge to ask her out for a drink when she finished work at the gallery. But ultimately, he decided against it. He knew that in the immediate end everything that attracted him to her—her sweet voice, small movements, and smile—would lose their luster and appeal, and that he would find every reason why he did not like, or perhaps, could not stand her.

* * *

There was the painting on his bed. He leaned toward it from the chair; the floorboards creaked again. He took another sip of gin from the short glass in his hand savoring the taste upon his lips and pulled the painting closer toward him. Distant voices called to him. He could hear the men, their screams as gunfire hailed upon them. He gripped his drink. Dark, shadowy images of children clinging to their mothers appeared while cavalry stormed in to crush them. Swords in the gun smoke were raised to the sky reflecting the faint sun, and brought down in swift strokes to cut the innocent down. He clenched his jaw and stared. The darkly lit room began to fade, and to his dark eyes there was only the painting.

* * *

"Sir, would you like to come in and see some paper cuttings?"

"No, no thank you," he said in the bazaar of the Chinese quarter of Shanghai.

She approached him. He was standing on the side of the street. "Where are you from?"

"From Canada," he lied. "Toronto."

"Oh, yes. I know it. We've had many customers from there. Would you like to come in?"

"No, no. I've already bought a few paintings today."

"But, these are traditional Chinese paper cuttings–very cheap. For your girlfriend–do you have a girlfriend?"

"No," he blushed as he walked further into the street.

"You should get a Shanghai girl. They are very nice. Very good for you."

He did not reply. *What does she mean I should get a Shanghai girl? Are they for sale too?* he thought with a sarcastic grin.

"Why are you smiling?"

"No, nothing."

"Please, come in. Just looking. You don't have to buy anything."

"Look, I'm wasting your time. I'm not going to buy anything."

"Are you waiting for a rickshaw?" she asked finally noticing that he was standing in the street.

"No, I want to take a picture of this street," he said as he pulled out a folding pocket Kodak camera.

"Oh, go ahead. I wait."

He looked behind to make sure that no horses or horse drawn vehicles were approaching and then stepped toward the center of the street. He framed the street in a way he found pleasing to his eye, made an adjustment to the lens, took two pictures, and walked back onto the sidewalk.

"Now you can come in." She took his hand and pulled gently; he enjoyed being touched by her. He looked at her and decided to go into her shop.

"These are all handmade and unique. No two are alike."

He looked at the many works of paper cuttings that were framed on the walls. There were animals, images of Empress Dowager Cixi, as well as Chinese children in traditional dress. He could see the price tags on the pieces and agreed that the paintings were indeed cheap.

"Do you like this one?"

"Which one?"

"This one. I thought you were looking at this one?"

"Oh, no."

"Do you know its meaning?"

"No, I don't." *Obviously*, he thought.

"It's my favorite one; it was made by my mother. Most of these are hers. This is her shop."

"Oh," he was now intrigued.

"It is called, *Love is like a Bird*."

He looked at the *Love is like a Bird* paper cutting and tried to understand how that meaning could be derived from it. All he saw was a young woman with flowers all around her and a white dove flying above her head.

"Do you like it?"

"Yes," he lied again.

"My mother says love is always on our minds. We may try to distract ourselves to not think about it. But in the end the thoughts of love keep coming back to us. Like a bird that we free but soon returns."

"Oh," he said. He liked the story, in fact he liked it more than the paper cuttings itself.

"Do you want to buy it?"

She then ruined the moment for him. He found his slight attraction to her disappear in an instant. He realized that he was just another sale and decided that the story she had just explained to him was probably false.

"No. I told you that I wasn't going to buy anything." He began to walk to the door.

"We have many more. You don't need to buy anything for your girlfriend?" she rushed to say.

"I already told you," he began disappointed that she had forgotten what he had previously explained, "I don't have a girlfriend."

"I know. I didn't mean that. Your friends?" she asked eagerly.

"No," he answered and left.

And as he walked away he thought about the story and agreed that love was always on our minds.

* * *

The painting stared back at him. He looked and found a strong understanding with the old poet in the painting. He knew what it felt like to be completely alone, and to be reminded of it by the vast spaces found in nature: standing in a desert at night or when watching the distant setting sun dip into an unending ocean. He wondered if he would ever marry and how difficult it would be for him to settle into giving up his long-time affair with solitude.

He looked at the vastness of the waterfall that overpowered the poet in the painting. And then he thought again of her. Yes, her; still there, lingering in his mind. She was far from him, perhaps now nestled in her home in London. He didn't know her, not at all; they had only spent a couple of days together in Saigon discussing their travels through the Orient. He now felt that his mind was too old and worn to fantasize and dream about a future with her that would never be. It was then that he knew that for the rest of his journey he would be condemned to think about her. She would haunt him. Yes, she would haunt him until the end. *If only there was some way to reach her.*

And so, he stared at the poet in the painting, sitting alone, in room 502, in the Astor House of old Shanghai.

There was a sudden knock at the door.

He immediately shook his head of his thoughts, "Yes, who is there?" and went to his packsack that was on the floor by the bed, reached into it, and pulled out a loaded Smith & Wesson Model 3 Schofield revolver, which he had modified by attaching an optical gun sight onto the barrel.

"No need for the weapon," the voice on the other side of the door announced.

How the hell does he know I have a gun? he thought concerned that perhaps the U.S. military police had tracked him down.

"I strongly suggest that you open this door. We do not want to attract too much attention."

The voice was British. He was relieved for a moment that the man was not American. Regardless, Americans could still be there behind this individual waiting for him to open the door to rush in and grab him.

"And why should I open this door?"

"I know who you are, what you have done, and how soon the military police will be here. Believe me when I tell you this. You have no other option than to listen to what I have to offer you."

He turned to look out the window to see if he could escape.

"Do not think it. You cannot escape. There are two sharpshooters who have you within their sights so again, open the door. You have ten seconds."

He checked his revolver to confirm what he already knew, that it was loaded.

"Checking your Schofield will do you no good. Drop the weapon and open the door. Five seconds."

How does he know? He went to the desk, placed the revolver on it, and approached the door. He cracked the door open and saw a man impeccably dressed but whose face was concealed by the darkness of the hall. He was wearing a white wing tip shirt with a black silk puff tie and pearl tie tack; a red dragon vest with a silver pocket watch chain hanging from its top button; a black swallowtail coat, black pinstriped trousers, and he was holding a black Victorian top hat in his left hand.

"Winters, Nicholas Winters, I presume," he said with a smile and slight bow.

"How do you know my name?"

"May I come in?"

"Is that a question or a command?"

"I am British, Mr. Winters. Please excuse the oddity of the circumstances, but when I can, I try to be polite and courteous."

"Are you god damn joking with me?"

"Pardon me, Mr. Winters?"

"You heard what I said."

"Mr. Winters, believe me when I tell you this, we do not want to attract too much attention. Now, I have asked you politely, but if need be I will enter your room by force. I suggest you let me in now."

Nicholas saw the sudden intensity in the stranger's eyes. He stepped back from the door allowing the gentlemen to step into his room.

Once he had entered into the dim light of the bedroom he turned to face Nicholas and said, "The name is Kell. And it is a pleasure to make your acquaintance."

Nicholas then noticed that Kell was wearing what appeared to be a mechanical earpiece of tiny gears with a radio antenna the length of a toothpick sticking up from it.

"How do you know my name?"

"There is quite a lot that we know about you, Mr. Winters."

"We?"

"Yes, 'we', but I will not explain to you who *we* are just yet. Time is of the essence, Mr. Winters. So, I will make this short," he then placed his Victorian top hat on the bed near the painting. "We have been tracking you since your escape from the MP prison in Manila as a favor to our American counterparts—quite an impressive escape. Our agents caught sight of you while you were in Burma and then again in French Indochina, and although there were a couple of months—here and there—when we lost track of you, for the most part you were predictable. Not a good thing, Mr. Winters, to be predictable."

Nicholas, uncomfortable, made his way toward the desk where he had placed his revolver.

"Ah ah ah, Mr. Winters. I would not do that if I were you," he smiled as he took out a pair of goggles with dark red tinted lenses from his coat pocket, put them on, rotated the lenses as if trying to focus them on something, and began scanning the room.

"What are you looking for?"

"It is none of your concern for the moment," he walked toward the circular table by the open window and poured anise London dry gin into a clean, short glass. He took a moment to smell the aroma of the gin and took a sip while he looked out into the night enjoying the view of the city and its lights. "Naturally, you are here in Shanghai. And naturally you are here at the Astor Hotel," he paused to take another sip. "Your taste for luxury has remained, Mr. Winters. You were born in Chicago–1867, a post-Civil War child; and born into tremendous wealth. Your father profited greatly during the war, didn't he? Humph, well, regardless your parents were killed in the Great Chicago Fire leaving you, as sole heir to their fortune. Their loyal and most trusted manservant, a man by the name of Yao Xi Wang, raised you and placed you, as your father would have wanted, into a New York boarding school. You attended New York University, graduated, and then pursued a degree in law for one year, but dropped out. In your desire to see the world you joined the U.S. Navy and rapidly rose in rank to then join the Marine Corps in 1891 where your platoon was involved in combat against Chilean nationalist rebels. You were then stationed throughout the Pacific with considerable time spent in Japan before you were deployed to serve in repressing the Filipino insurrectionists in the aftermath of the Spanish-American War–"

"So what the hell do you want from me?" Nicholas, now very tense, interrupted.

"It is simple, Mr. Winters. The Americans have seized all of your bank accounts in the U.S. and we know of your three accounts in Great Britain. Work for us and gain continued access to your funds. We simply need an insider. Have you heard of the Righteous Fists of Harmony or, in the native tongue, Yìhétuán?"

He shook his head.

"I am disappointed, Mr. Winters."

"Well, I just arrived this evening," he said bitterly. "And I do not feel the need to stay on top of currents events, especially events here. I'm just passing through."

"Nothing could be farther from the truth. You will be intimately involved in the workings of this place."

"That is only if I accept whatever you are offering."

"We are not offering, Mr. Winters. You will do what we require of you."

"Or what?"

"We are," he paused to take off his goggles and placed them back in his pocket. "We are, at times, compelled to share with our American counterpart sensitive information, Mr. Winters. Your location would be greatly appreciated by the U.S. Consulate. And we have two military police officers on stand-by waiting for us to … as you Americans say, give them the okay."

"Then call them. Have them arrest me. Take my money. Why should I do whatever it is you want me to do?"

"Citizenship, Mr. Winters. You are a man without a country. Great Britain is there, with open arms, waiting to receive you, a lost American soul."

"The United States is my country, sir."

Kell began to laugh. "The United States," he continued laughing, "the United States is your country?" His face then turned gravely serious. "The moment you are discovered *your country* will hang you. You are a traitor to your nation, Mr. Winters—"

"I am not! I did what was just and right—"

"Murdering members of your company?"

"It was not murder!" he exclaimed. "What was I supposed to do? Stand there and watch the slaughter of innocent men, women, and children?"

"Rebellion is not a pretty thing, Mr. Winters. Of course, you Americans know all about rebellion. Your *former* nation was founded on it. But your nation is not what it pretends to be any longer. The United States is an empire. You have Cuba, Puerto Rico, Samoa, Hawaii, and the Philippines." He took a moment to sit down in the other colonial sofa chair by the round table. When he was comfortable he continued, "Gone are the days of republican idealism, Mr. Winters. The United States is now the perpetrator. How pathetically sad it is to see a nation constantly declaring itself as a defender of the people's right to self-government, when at the same time they are preventing such a right for the Filipino people, the Cuban people, the people of Hawaii, Samoa, et cetera. You know all about that, Mr. Winters, you have seen it for yourself.

"But we are happy to see the U.S. align itself in such a way with the British Empire. It is inevitable, Mr. Winters. There will always be empire."

"So what the hell does this all have to do with me?"

"How did it feel to see so many innocent men, women, and children butchered by your countrymen?"

"We were at war," he answered with clenched fists.

"You call that war?" he laughed again. "I call it massacre—a murderous slaughter! It has been estimated that in the province of Batangas, from a population of three hundred thousand, that U.S. guns, disease, and famine has killed off a third of the population. So horrible is the killing that I have just learned that members of the 24th Infantry have deserted to join with the Filipino rebels to fight against the country of their birth."

"Who are you to place judgment on my country? A subject of the British crown lecturing me on the immoralities of the American empire?"

"You are right, Mr. Winters. You are quite right. We have strived to learn our lesson. Violence begets violence. Thus, it is in the interest of the crown to steer clear of conflict and war with the people of the lands we are occupying. Lives can be saved, Mr. Winters. And you can help us save those lives here, in this place. Otherwise, history may repeat itself. A case in point, what was it that provoked the Spanish-American War?"

"The destruction of the USS *Maine*. Two hundred and sixty-six navy men died in that explosion."

"Thus, tipping the balance among the American populace, the McKinley administration, and the Congress to finally seek war with Spain. *'Remember the Maine, to hell with Spain!'* Was this not one of the many slogans among the American people pressuring their government to seek war? How convenient for the war hawks of your country to have had such an event as the sinking of the USS *Maine*."

"What are you getting at?"

"Come here, Mr. Winters," he stood up from the sofa chair with his drink. "Stand with me before this view."

Nicholas, suspicious, did not move.

"Come, believe me, I do not bite. Come and look at the magnificence of the scene before us."

Nicholas took a few steps toward the open window.

"There before us is the most magnificent, multinational city on this side of the globe. Look how we took a sleepy, little old fishing town and turned it into this glorious site. Just look at the scene before you, Mr. Winters. There is the future of China. Trade with the outside world, advancements in technology, education, the further expansion of rail lines, factories built, jobs created. We can do all of this peacefully. But there are agents out there seeking to destroy that future; all it would take is one, singular event, and war is at hand. Just like the *Maine*. Lives lost. The innocent killed. Children orphaned."

Nicholas looked down for a moment as he thought of his childhood.

"In six weeks' time," Kell continued, "we will launch for all to see, here in Shanghai, a British prototype rigid airship based on stolen designs from both David Schwarz and Ferdinand Graf von Zeppelin. It is a message to the Germans that we are winning the race for air superiority. But as you can imagine there is great need among our enemies to ensure that the launch ends in failure; and failure, Mr. Winters, of an airship filled with hydrogen means an explosion. I can just see it now, this view of Shanghai at night and the destruction of a British airship crashing down into the Bund killing hundreds of onlookers.

"Who will be blamed? The British will blame the Germans and thus begins our war here. But it is not the Germans that are striving to do this, Mr. Winters. It is the Chinese. We believe that the Righteous and Harmonious Fists are planning to do this, and if they succeed then there will be war. An airship crashing down upon the Bund will end British, German, French, Russian, American, and Japanese lives. European nations and the U.S. will call for war and they will rain down upon the Chinese a hailstorm of gunfire taking everything that they desire: the coalmines, iron mines, land, waterways, et cetera. Tens of thousands of lives will be lost." Kell paused to take another sip of gin from his glass.

Nicholas contemplated Kell's words as he looked out at the night scene before him. He then took in a deep breath and asked, "And you want me to help you prevent this?"

Kell smiled and turned his head slowly to Nicholas, "Yes, of course, Mr. Winters."

"And you will provide me with British citizenship and continued access to my funds?"

"British citizenship and access to your accounts I can guarantee–"

"And I want safe passage to London after I complete my mission here," he interrupted.

"London?" Kell asked with a furrowed brow. "London," he whispered as he turned to analyze the Chinese painting on the bed. "Travel may have to wait for there is much to do here. But really, Mr. Winters, what your ambitions are in regards to your future destinations are none of my concern."

"Fine then, how is it that I can help you prevent this future war?"

"Good, Mr. Winters, good," he said with a sly grin as he placed his glass on the round table. "The Righteous and Harmonious Fists are boxers, but you know the fighting styles of this land as taught to you by your manservant, Yao Xi Wang."

"That was long ago."

"You have a sufficient understanding of Mandarin, do you not, Mr. Winters?"

He laughed, "I understand maybe twenty percent of what is said."

"You are able to read Japanese, and thus, Chinese characters."

"Yes, but no more than any novice."

"These are all fine, Mr. Winters. You see we want you to be kidnapped by this secret society and you have already, unwillingly, made contact with one who could bring you to them."

"Who?" he asked puzzled.

"The girl from the calligraphy gallery. The gallery is a front. She is there to bring in foreigners from the Astor House, gain their friendship, or love, and get whatever information she can regarding their political, military, or economic intent in Shanghai.

"She already believes you to be of very high social standing considering the room you are able to afford at this hotel."

"She knows which room I am in?"

"Yes, of course, Mr. Winters. This hotel employs so many Chinamen. They observe and report."

"And you want me to do the same, report from their end?"

"Exactly."

"And how will I report back?"

"We have the technology that will enable you to communicate with us through Morse code. But, we will get to that later. For now, we want you to report back on the obvious: their leaders, their numbers, their locations, their networks, their weapons, and so forth, but we want you to pay particular attention toward this energy source called *Chi* or *Qi* that is supposedly being utilized by the master fighters among them. If you ask me, it is silly superstition emanating from the imagination of a people feeling the adverse effects of opium. But there is concern that if these Qi masters are able to accomplish what they say they can—super human strength, skin resistant to strong cuts, bodies resistant to bullets—then their numbers could obviously overwhelm ours. Again, it is foolishness, much akin to the Ghost Dances of the Sioux Indians, but my superiors want to know more. Perhaps if this Qi energy can be harnessed it can be used to power our machines and gone are the days of steam," he quickly scoffed at the idea. "In any case, it is late, Mr. Winters. For now, we are watching you and you are safe. Rest for tomorrow there is much to discuss, and much to do."

He took his Victorian top hat from the bed and made for the door, but before he made his exit, he turned to face Nicholas and said, "Since you are now one of us, Mr. Winters, a *shadow man*, the name is, Vernon; Vernon George Waldegrave Kell." He bowed his head and said before he closed the door, "I bid you good night."

And as Kell made his way down the dark hall toward the lift he smiled at how easy it was to turn Nicholas to their side and whispered, "If he only knew that it was us who destroyed the *Maine*."

THE MIDDLE KINGDOM: PART II

Saturday, July 3, 2004

International Refugee Day & the Rape of Nanjing
Sunday, June 20, 2004

I arrived to Nanjing on June 19 by train (hard seat) from Shanghai to another cloudy day.

On the two-hour train journey, I saw scores of rice fields (some stretching to the horizon) and an increasing number of factories and smokestacks belching the black, toxic fumes of burnt coal (the cheapest and most abundant fossil fuel in China[1]). In some areas I saw large, bleak industrial factories surrounded by moat-like canals filled with black liquid. Dotted between the rice fields and factories I saw two to three-storey dull, grey, concrete, and cinderblock communist-era apartment buildings that lived up the ideals of brutalist architecture.

The train arrived to Nanjing Railway Station, and when I exited the station I received many stares (it seemed that foreigners did not frequent the city).

The Touts

The touts inside and outside the station quickly approached me showing brochures loaded with hotel pictures. Most of the touts could say nothing more than "hello" in English. Due to the language barrier, the touts were not effective nor persistent in convincing me to accept their offers. I simply shook my head saying, "no, no, no," and one by one the touts gave up and walked away. Generally speaking, I found most of the touts in China to be passive compared to the very aggressive touts that spoke several languages in Southeast Asia.

Following the map in my pirated *Lonely Planet: China* guide I walked to Nanjing University and checked into a single dormitory room. I washed up, turned on the television and watched a few minutes of famed investor Jim Rogers consistently shoot down a Chinese academic who insisted that the stock market was rigged, locked up my belongings, and went for a walk looking for something to eat.

I spent the afternoon and evening in Nanjing walking east within the city until I passed the ruins of the Heavenly Gate and the Eastern Gate of the old Ming City Wall (at 32 kilometers it is the longest wall ever built to fortify a city[2]). From the wall, I walked back to Nanjing University, and on the way, I saw five barbershop brothels for low income to middle-class men. These brothels, like the ones in Shanghai, were next to legitimate barbershops, and they didn't have touts trying to lure me in. The women stayed inside waiting; some were sleeping.

Invasion of the Bland Restaurants

The interior design of the restaurants I saw during this walk was the same: an open room with off-white walls, and uniform tables and chairs complete with porcelain plates. There were few to no paintings on the walls. I did not see any degree of creativity put into decorating these restaurants. They were all dull and uninspiring.

It should be noted that the buildings in Nanjing—and most cities in China with the exception of Shanghai and Beijing—were the same in architectural design: concrete, drab, unstimulating, and uniform. As

I continued my walk I found the urban environment to be increasingly dreary. I saw no signs of creativity on the streets (not even a single work of graffiti), in the people, or in the buildings. Everything was colorless, tame, and almost lifeless; the result, perhaps, of a society decades under a communist regime that had strived to flatten and remake its people in accordance to egalitarianism. It seemed that inventiveness and originality as expressed through the mediums of art, architecture, clothing, music, dance, and so on, which did not serve the interests of the Chinese Communist Party, had been stamped out (the impact and legacy of the Cultural Revolution). I saw few to no signs or indications on the streets of Guangzhou, Shanghai, and Nanjing of China's once rich "five thousand years of history" and culture.[3] The Chinatowns of Southeast Asia were a greater tribute to the traditional culture of China than China itself.

It is important to note that China is not "a nation with a five-thousand-year history", instead "The Shang dynasty (founded around 1600 BC) of the Yellow River valley in northern China is as far back as we have solid archaeological evidence and positive proof of the first written records."[4]

Teaching Kids for 10 Minutes

Today I walked into a community center for children. I went up to the second floor to watch the ballet classes, but I accidentally looked into an English class for elementary school children. The teacher quickly invited me into the class to observe. I sat at the back of the room and observed. The teacher was very good; I was impressed with how much fun the kids were having, how much they knew, and how eager they were to learn.

The teacher then asked me to teach the class for 10 minutes! I froze. The children turned and stared at me. I quickly thought of an easy lesson to teach from my English teaching days in Japan. I went to the front of the class, yelled, and taught in a comedic fashion. I'm not sure the kids learned anything, but they laughed their heads off. I guess they had never seen a teacher break so many Chinese teaching taboos. I left the class with all of them following me and screaming, "Goodbye teacher!", but for doing so the other teachers reprimanded them.

The Nanjing Massacre Museum

On December 13, 1937, the Imperial Japanese Army sacked the capital city of Nanjing and slaughtered between 40,000 to 300,000 civilians in six weeks.[5]

The Memorial Hall of the Victims in Nanjing Massacre by Japanese Invaders is a memorial museum preserving evidence of the mass murder and mass rape committed by Japanese soldiers, which today is still not fully acknowledged in Japanese government authorized history textbooks.[6] I had come to Nanjing for the explicit purpose of visiting this museum. In Japan, I had read Iris Chang's non-fiction book *The Rape of Nanking: The Forgotten Holocaust of World War II* and was shocked to discover that irrefutable historical evidence regarding the massacre in Nanjing was either whitewashed or deleted from the pages of history books provided to Japanese students at the secondary educational level. This inability by the Japanese government to recognize and apologize for the massacre continues to fuel the political tension between China and Japan.

The museum stands on part of the execution pit called Jiangdongmen (pit of 10,000 corpses) where I saw on the ground–within a sheltered area–the skeletal remains of thousands of Chinese that had been slaughtered. I could see that some of the bones had bullet holes and bayonet cut marks. The mass grave is composed of seven layers of bodies piled on top of each other, which suggests irregular deaths and hurried collective burials. I saw the skull of a six-year-old child whose head was severed from its body before burial. There were the remains of a woman whose upper and lower jaws had been forced apart, suggesting that something had been shoved into her mouth. I saw rusted nails embedded into skulls, pelvises, and limb bones. I also saw hairpins, copper coins, buttons, snail shells, and bullet casings scattered all over the mass grave.

Museum labels in the memorial hall explained that before arriving to Nanjing the Japanese–from their base in Shanghai–invaded and massacred civilians from several towns:

> Massacre at Jingshanwei: Japanese 10th Army landed on Hangzhou Bay and killed 351 innocent peasants.

Massacre at Suzhou: in the town of Changshou 3,000 civilians were killed and 374 Chinese women raped.

Massacre of Xuxi: 2,000 people were killed and then the Japanese set fire to the city after looting and occupying it.

Massacre at Changzhou: the Japanese Imperial Army killed 4,000 refugees. Groups of Chinese women were escorted to the headquarters of the Japanese troops to be insulted, gang raped, and shot to death.

Massacre at Jiangyin: 1,000 people were killed.

Massacre at Zhengjiang: the Japanese shot people at random with machine guns. They raped, looted, and burned.

Prior to the capture of Nanjing, two Japanese officers of the 16th Division, Toshiaki Mukai and Tsuyoshi Noda, held a contest to see who could kill 100 people with their swords. The contest was publicized in the *Tokyo Nichi Nichi* and *Osaka Mainichi* newspapers. But because it was unclear during the contest as to who had reached 100 first the competition was begun again and the goal was raised to 150.[7] Both soldiers were later tried by the International Military Tribunal for the Far East, convicted, and executed in January 1948.

The Nationalist government led by Chiang Kai-shek moved the capital from Nanjing to Chongqing on November 20, 1937. One hundred thousand Chinese troops then evacuated Nanjing leaving the civilian population to fend for themselves. Imperial Japanese troops then took the city on December 13 and began a six-week slaughter.

According to the Chinese Military Tribunal for War Crimes in Nanjing, "more than 190,000 Chinese prisoners of war and civilians were shot with machine guns in large groups by the Japanese Army and their bodies were incinerated … In addition, more than 150,000 people were killed in small or scattered groups, and their bodies were collected and buried by charity organizations. Altogether, more than 300,000 people were murdered."[8] There are horrific accounts of Chinese corpses being thrown into the Yangtze River and civilians being buried alive. The International Military Tribunal for the Far East estimated that there were over 20,000 cases of rape in Nanjing by soldiers of the Japanese Imperial Army;[9] girls, the elderly, and pregnant women were not spared. And in many cases victims were disemboweled or left on the roadside to die. Many girls who survived the countless incidences of gang rape contracted venereal diseases. Captain Gunkichi Tanaka, one of only four Japanese army officers tried during the Nanjing War Crimes Tribunal, claimed to have decapitated over 300 individuals at Nanjing in one day.

John H. D. Rabe, a German citizen and Nazi Party member, and other foreign residents who stayed in Nanjing established the Nanjing Safety Zone, which protected 250,000 Chinese civilians from the mass slaughter. Rabe's account of the atrocities are documented in the book, *The Good Man of Nanking: The Diaries of John Rabe*.

The trial of the International Military Tribunal for the Far East in Tokyo brought 28 Class-A Japanese War Criminals to justice. They were all sentenced to death and were hung on December 22, 1948 in Tokyo.[10]

I should also mention that in 1938 troops of the Nationalist government under the command of Chiang Kai-shek broke the levees of the Huang He River in an attempt to stop the advancement of Japanese troops. Although effective, the strategy resulted in the deaths of nearly one million Chinese peasants.[11]

Posted by The Legacy Cycle at 2004-07-03T21:55:00-07:00

Tuesday, July 13, 2004

Xi'an & the Terra Cotta Warriors
June 22 – 24, 2004

I took an overnight, hard sleeper train from Nanjing to Xi'an on the night of June 21. This was my first journey by hard sleeper (I took a soft sleeper from Guangzhou to Shanghai) and it was very comfortable and safe. The hard sleeper car consisted of open compartments of six beds (three stacked on each side) whereas the soft sleeper consisted of closed compartments of four beds (two stacked on each side).

I threw my bag onto my assigned bed (it was the middle bed of the three), hopped up, stretched out, and used my bag as a pillow. Facing the window, I looked out into the darkness between concentrated hours of reading. There was also a television for each open compartment. The programs were all in Chinese so it did not distract me while I read. Although I did put my book down to watch a comedy talk show. The host was interviewing a Chinese hip-hop star. It was ridiculous to see this Chinese teen spit out lyrics that mixed English with Chinese. He then went on to show the host different hip-hop mannerisms that he had learned by studying hip-hop music videos from the U.S.

This Chinese pop star—I assumed—knew little of the history and culture of African American hip-hop music; a musical genre that emanated from and reflected the harsh realities of low-income, inner-city areas. It could be argued that a hip-hop artist who has not grown up in these marginalized, urban neighborhoods is simply imitating what he thinks that culture may be about. I find it comical, after having lived in Japan or while traveling through China, to see Asian pop stars imitate American hip-hop culture through their lyrics, lingo, style of dress, and behavior. But since the 1990s, hip-hop culture has become mainstream and cool for middle-class, privileged American, Japanese, and Chinese teenagers. This demographic now tries to speak, act, or dress in the same style as their favorite hip-hop artist, but within the safe confines of their suburban community. What would happen if a Japanese hip-hop pop star, wearing his dope, hip-hop clothes and attitude, walked into South Central, L.A. or the Cabrini-Green public housing project in Chicago. How would those from an urban ghetto in the U.S. respond to a Chinese hip-hop star trying so desperately to be something they are not?

There is a band in Japan that I respect called Love Psychedelico. Their singer is fluent in Japanese and English (she lived for a number of years in San Francisco) and her lyrics are a mix between the two languages, which worked well because she had a strong understanding of both cultures and languages. But what I could not stand to see in Tokyo were Japanese pop artists spitting out English lyrics that they could not pronounce or perhaps didn't even understand. It seemed as if their music producers or label had forced them to shout out a few words in English to add a superficial layer of "cool" to their music.

On the morning of June 22, a tout approached me as soon as I got off the train and led me to a halfway decent hotel not too far from the Xi'an railway station. When I checked in I signed up for the Terracotta Army tour for the next day.

After resting in the hotel, I decided to explore the city. I walked south down Jifeng Lu and passed several massage parlor brothels that lined nearly an entire street block; these brothels were located relatively close to the railway station. The brothels were small and extremely dirty. The women sat in plastic chairs by the doorway awaiting their next customer. As soon as I walked passed them they began shouting: "Massage? Massage?" I shook my head repeatedly until one woman ran up to me, grabbed my arm, and tried to pull me into her establishment. I yanked my arm back and ran away. This was the first time I had experienced such an aggressive tactic by prostitutes in Asia, although I have heard stories of aggressive women in Thailand, Cambodia, and Vietnam.

When I arrived to Dong Dajie ("Eastern Avenue"), I turned right and walked west until I saw the Bell and Drum Tower at the intersection of Nan Dajie and Xi Dajie. The Bell Tower was located at the center of a traffic circle with the Drum Tower located next to it. Around the traffic circle there was a shopping mall, a posh hotel, and plenty of Chinese restaurants catering to tourists. I headed to the Drum Tower, took a look around it, and walked under it to reach the Muslim Quarter of Xi'an.

Xi'an marked the "eastern departure point of the Silk Road".[12] Muslims from Central Asia migrated into China along the route. It is in Xi'an where Islam, Christianity, and Buddhism were first introduced into China.[13] Along the streets of the Muslim Quarter I saw Chinese men wearing white taqiyahs (Muslim skullcaps) and Chinese women wearing white shawls to cover their hair. The restaurants here served a mix of traditional Chinese and Muslim dishes. The highlight was the Great Mosque that was hidden behind narrow streets that were lined with vendors selling an assortment of souvenirs (I bought two old copies of Mao's *Little Red Book*). Although the open-air areas of the Great Mosque were open to the public, the prayer hall was prohibited to non-Muslims.

Today was the Dragon Boat Festival in China, which explained why all the main streets in the Muslim Quarter were lined with vendors selling food and candies. It was quite festive.

In the afternoon, I walked south down Nan Dajie to the impressive South Gate; Xi'an is yet another city in China that was fortified by a several kilometers long city wall. The moat around the city still exists, as does most of the old wall that was originally built in the 14th century. I later took a taxi to the Taoist Temple of the Eight Immortals, which was built during the Song dynasty (960-1279 AD).[14] Within the temple I found several halls dedicated to specific Taoist gods and a newly painted series of plaques describing a story of a particular Taoist god.

After the temple, I walked north along a street that was a market for the locals. One part of the market that held my attention for 30 minutes was an open-air, mom-and-pop shop that sold live birds, chickens, and fish. There were several stacks of cages filled with chickens, ducks, or other various birds, and buckets and large styrofoam boxes filled with live catfish and eels. Customers simply pointed to the chicken, duck, bird, or marine life that they wanted and the shopkeeper would then grab the animal, kill it, and prepare it so that it could be taken home in a plastic bag.

Death of a Chicken

A customer pointed to one of several chickens in the old, dirt stained wooden cage that was stacked on two other cages. A 12-year-old boy, who worked in the open-air poultry and seafood shop, slid the cage door open and grabbed the chicken by the neck. The chicken ruffled its feathers and called out in alarm as the boy took a pair of industrial scissors and cut its neck open. The chicken fluttered more, but the boy threw the bird into a metal vat of hot water, placed a lid over it, and waited as the blood rushed out of the fowl's trashing body. When the chicken ceased to move the boy removed the lid, lifted the dead bird, and threw it into a feather removing machine. He turned the machine on; it shook violently as it plucked the feathers out. After a minute, the boy turned the machine off, took out the plucked chicken, threw it into a plastic bag, and gave it to the customer.

Death of a Catfish

A customer pointed to the catfish that swam in a plastic bucket that was crowded with marine life. A 12-year-old boy, who worked in the open-air poultry and seafood shop, grabbed the catfish and threw it on the ground. The fish wriggled and twisted on the floor as the boy took hold of a hammer. The fish squirmed and gulped air. The boy began bashing the head of the fish until it was bloody and dead. He then put down the hammer, grabbed a fish scale remover, and began scraping off its scales. When he finished he threw the fish into a plastic bag and gave it to the customer.

The Terracotta Army
Wednesday, June 23, 2004

I was part of a tour group. The majority of people on the tour were Chinese except for a couple from New Zealand and a woman by the name of Nao from Japan. The tour bus took us to a museum and a few tacky tourist shops before taking us to a 76-meter-tall tomb mound where Qin Shi Huang, the first emperor of a unified China in 221 BC, was buried.[15] The mound has yet to be excavated, but its size and height was impressive; Chinese legend tells that Qin Shi Huang ordered 700,000 laborers to construct his tomb. But modern scholars such as British historian John Man have claimed that the number of laborers needed would have been in the tens of thousands.[16]

After ascending and descending the mound, we ate lunch and were then led to the Terracotta Army. The site consisted of four pits with more pits likely to be discovered in the future. The most famous pit was Pit 1 where I saw terracotta horses in the first row—there was an empty space behind them revealing in the earth the imprints of the chariot wheels that had decomposed over a 2,000-year period— followed by 6,000 life-size terracotta warriors facing east and lined along 11 corridors that were two-and-a-half meters wide. The pit was sheltered under what looked like a hangar. Originally these terracotta soldiers were each hand painted. And every single warrior was unique, they were not produced from a mold. The soldiers were all armed; archaeologists have uncovered more then 40,000 swords and weapons.

In Pit 2 chariots, cavalry, infantrymen, and archers in standing and kneeling positions were discovered; it will be several years or decades before the entire pit is excavated. In this pit, I saw the imprints of wooden beams in the earth that had supported a wooden roof, which covered the terracotta figures.

Pit 3 was a small pit that consisted of 68 high ranking soldiers and a war chariot. The outfits of these high-ranking soldiers were more elaborate than the ones I saw in Pit 1.

Pit 4 was empty.

The Museum of Qin Terra-cotta Warriors and Horses displayed the best examples of the weapons that had been found in the four pits along with the two incredibly detailed bronze chariots that were discovered near the tomb of Qin Shi Huang, who, in addition to being the first emperor of a unified China, also ordered construction of the defensive wall that would be the precursor to the Great Wall of China.

I must confess that the sight of the Terracotta Army was absolutely fascinating and became one of the highlights of my travels through China.

Posted by The Legacy Cycle at 2004-07-13T19:27:00-07:00

Thursday, July 15, 2004

Culture Shock Blues in the Middle Kingdom

He was sitting at a table on the fourth floor of a Beijing shopping mall. And he was angry. He was so full of anger that any confrontation with an aggravated Chinese citizen would have provoked a fight, perhaps ending with his arrest by the Beijing police.

What caused this rage? A combination of factors: Chinese government bureaucracy and the rules and regulations concerning the exchange of Chinese RMB for U.S. dollars. It took him all afternoon and evening, and all morning and early afternoon of another day, to find the means to buy U.S. dollars with the large stack of Chinese RMB that he had withdrawn from a Citibank ATM. He had accomplished the task illegally. He sold his RMB by soliciting newly arrived foreigners who were standing in line at one of three Chinese bank tellers at the Beijing Capital International Airport. As he sold his RMB he dared to be arrested for committing the act of creating a black market to buy and sell foreign currencies. He wanted to be provoked into an argument—a fight—to vent and release all of his traveling angst. The police at the airport, if they had inquired into his illicit trade, could have been the trigger to detonate him; he had little concern of being dragged into a Beijing prison. He did not care; he was foolish, reckless, apathetic, and livid.

Another factor that fed his rage came from a series of discomforts and annoyances since his departure from Xi'an, which he complained about to backpackers he met along the way. In addition, he confessed to those willing to listen that he had yet to experience Chinese "culture shock," but it was apparent to those he spoke to that his complaints and irritations were a sign that he *was* in a state of severe "culture shock."

He then reflected back to the seven-hour train journey on a hard sleeper to Luoyang. After his arrival, in his tired state, he walked from the train station and followed the map in his poorly photocopied and pirated guidebook to a recommended hotel. Unable to quickly find the hotel he cursed his book and the gods. Eventually, he found the hotel; it was spacious, but worn down, and upon close inspection, grimy; ultimately, it was unimpressive. Essentially the hotel represented everything he was beginning to dislike about China. You could say that after his three-and-a-half years in Japan he was seeing China through the eyes of one expecting and accustomed to Nippon efficiency and cleanliness. In his mind China was a filthy place where men and women loudly hacked up and spat out phlegm regardless of whether it was in a public or private space.

After taking a shower in his room he decided to make a list of all the things he found incredibly foul in China.

The List

1. Dried snot on the hotel room walls. What the f*&k? Why is it not possible for people here to use a handkerchief instead of blowing out the insides of their nasal passages into the air, floor or walls of my hotel room?

2. The ground is a garbage bin. Everyone throws his or her trash on the ground, into the street, and on the floor (carpeted or not). Bus drivers throw their empty plastic bottles out the window. Pedestrians throw their plastic bags and leftover food on the ground. Men in hotels spread their cigarette ash all over the carpet; carpets in all buildings are peppered in cigarette burns, they are filthy and disgusting. People blow their noses straight onto the ground. Kids wearing split pants urinate and defecate in all directions.

3. Maintaining and cleaning indoor surroundings does not seem to be a priority. The interior of many hotels and buildings that I entered were in disarray: filthy elevators, dirty floors, sticky tables, and stained walls. How often are these public spaces scrubbed and cleaned?

4. Too many people in China are chain smokers. Yellow stained teeth caused by excessive smoking is a common sight.

5. Brothels are everywhere; especially near train and bus stations. Small shops sell sex devices in plain view of children. I found a freaking water balloon condom in the drawer of my hotel room! Prostitutes call my hotel room at all hours of the day and night.

6. The people of China are loud. They yell. And taxi and bus drivers are repeatedly honking their horns.

Observations

1. People (mostly men) playing cards, checkers, or mahjong are a constant sight.

2. I often see men, and sometimes women, carrying and drinking

from a glass jar filled with water and tealeaves.

3. People in China do not know how to wait patiently in line at bus and train stations. Instead, as a collective mob, they attack the teller to buy a ticket.

4. The vast majority of the Chinese population is unable to speak a word of English. And that is a good thing because touts quickly walk away after only one attempt at trying to sell something to foreigners like me. Chinese touts are not nearly as aggressive or innovative in selling souvenirs to tourists as the touts I experienced in Southeast Asia.

Luoyang
Thursday, June 24, 2004

He strolled the streets of Luoyang for miles in search of an Internet café. Unable to find one after two hours, he decided to search for any cultural light that would brighten his thoughts. Instead he passed row after row of insipid buildings. But at the center of the city he gazed at the hypermodern corporate buildings that seemed out of place in the industrial, urban grey of Luoyang. He then noticed an unfinished, five-star hotel that stood next to a series of low-income, brick buildings with walkways that had been littered with garbage (most likely by the residents). Seeking to avoid this scene of modern wealth on the doorsteps of the poor he walked toward an Olympic stadium that had a bleak, bronze statue of two fútbol players: one running and the other sliding to gain control of a ball. He snapped a picture of the statue while locals walked by wondering why.

It began to rain. *Great*, he thought, *perfect!* He walked east hoping to find a restaurant that had an inviting sign in English because he had not eaten all day. Instead, he found a fish market within an enclosed lane that was lined with rusty and rundown shops. As he walked down the lane he saw men and women inside each shop lounging around watching programs on their black and white television sets. When he exited the fish market he saw several seafood restaurants. But he was too embarrassed to walk into any of them because he did not want to go through the hassle of trying to communicate what he would like to eat. So, he chose to be stubborn and hungry, and continued on toward the river.

The river was wide, and on its northern bank there was a park. He walked toward and through the park to reach a concrete kiosk where he sought shelter from the rain. He stood under one of the corners of the kiosk that had a projecting canopy; near him there was an adolescent Chinese couple. He could see that the girl had been in an accident, which had caused the scarring on her neck and lower jaw. She was simple in appearance and had difficulty speaking, but she had a boy by her side that cared for her deeply. The couple soon left to sit beneath the long, protective branch of a tree that was next to the river. He was beginning to feel lonely again. He was beginning to feel sad.

Once the rain had stopped he decided to walk east along the river. It was quiet and the grass was very green.

An hour later he passed a Taoist temple and continued east down a ragged street lined with aged, uniform homes and barbershops.

So many barbershops in this country, he thought. *Why? All the people that I have seen have the same hairstyle.*

He looked into each barbershop to see if they were indeed a barbershop or a brothel; a few were brothels.

At the end of the street he stopped and bought a bag of fresh, rubbery bread from a vendor. He walked north and came across the 1,400-year-old gate entrance into the Luoyang Old Town District. After buying a drink for more than it was worth and passing a vendor who was selling roasted rats he walked through the gate.

Upon entering the complex, he saw towers and fortified town walls that were lined with old homes, shops, and restaurants; Chinese women dressed in uniforms called out to the passing pedestrians to enter and buy. At the far end of the main avenue there was another ancient gate. As he walked toward the gate he looked into every open door seeing long corridors that revealed mothers tending to their children.

And as the sun began to set, he walked back the entire length of the avenue until he exited the ancient gate to take a taxi to his hotel.

Posted by The Legacy Cycle at 2004-07-15T01:50:00-07:00

Thursday, July 22, 2004

The Longmen Caves
Friday, June 25, 2004

It took me over an hour to reach the Longmen Grottoes by bus from Luoyang. The caves are located along both sides of the Yi River, and there are 1,400 caves housing nearly 100,000 statues of Buddha, bodhisattvas, demons, and warriors along with 2,800 inscriptions.[17] The caves were created over a 600-year period with the first of the caves carved in 493 AD.[18]

It took me two hours to see all of the largest caves, although it felt much longer since the beating of the afternoon sun had worn me down. The most impressive cave was the Ancestor Worshipping Cave. The central Buddha statue was about "55 feet (16.5 m) tall and flanked by bodhisattvas and a ferocious guardian figure."[19] The Cave of Ten Thousand Buddhas actually had 10,000 Buddha statues no bigger than my thumb carved into the cave's limestone walls.

Most of the caves were high up along the slopes and cliffs of the Xiangshang and Longmenshan mountains; they were accessible by staircases. Unfortunately, most of the caves had been damaged and defiled; many of the Buddha and bodhisattva statues were headless. Antique collectors, anti-Buddhists, Japanese soldiers during the Second Sino-Japanese War, and communists had cut or slashed the heads and faces of many of the most prominent statues.[20,21] It was sad to see that these wonderful works of religious devotion had suffered from varying forms of sacrilege during the 20th century.

Dengfeng & the Shaolin Tourist
Saturday, June 26, 2004

I was happy to leave Luoyang; it was another example of a city that had been wiped of its traditions, culture, and history by the Cultural Revolution. I have been consistently disappointed with each city I traveled through in China with the exceptions of Shanghai and Beijing.

All the other cities were devoid of any visible creative urge: restaurant interiors were typically static, people seemed to dress the same, and although there was a plethora of barbershops and hair salons everyone's hairstyle was also the same. You would think that with the vast number of small businesses dedicated to hair maintenance that there would be a certain degree of hairstyle variety. But–no–everyone had settled for the same, tasteless hairdo.

I left my hotel in Luoyang, went to the bus station across the street, and bought my bus ticket for Dengfeng. While searching for my bus I saw a sleeper bus with steel framed bunk beds stacked inside to allow long distance travelers to slumber. Unable to find my bus in the outdoor platform area, I asked a bus station employee to help me. He kindly led me to my bus. I thanked him, boarded the bus, and settled into my seat.

The journey was three hours. I was the only foreigner on the bus and as expected I attracted a few stares and speculative thoughts. Since I was headed to Dengfeng (a country-level city located near the famed Shaolin Temple), I was sure that a few people on my bus assumed that I was headed to see the many kung fu academies around the city. The true purpose of my journey was to pay my respects to the legendary beginnings of the Zen Buddhist tradition.

After graduating from Boston University, I lived at the Shim Gwang Sa (Mind Light Temple), a Korean Zen Buddhist temple in Boston, for nine months. I lived as a monk while pursuing the art of Zen sword. This unique Buddhist tradition of combining a meditative and compassionate religion with the martial arts began in the Shaolin Temple in the 6th century AD.[22]

My Zen master at the Shim Gwang Sa was taught by Zen master Dae Soen Sa Nim (Seung Sahn Haeng Won), the 78th Patriarch of a lineage that traced back to Bodhidharma, the Indian sage (and 28th Patriarch) responsible for founding Zen Buddhism in East Asia.[23]

The bus dropped me off just outside the city of Dengfeng. I hailed a taxi, which pulled up right next to me, entered, and showed the driver the Chinese characters in my guidebook that represented the guesthouse I wanted to go to. The driver nodded and called out an overpriced fare that I was too tired to argue against. After a five-minute journey, we arrived to the guesthouse, but I could see that the building had been abandoned; and for the rest of my journey in China

I would discover more guesthouses listed in my *Lonely Planet* guidebook that had gone out of business or disappeared. The driver then took me to the lavish Shaolin International Hotel. I entered the hotel, went to the check-in desk, and asked how much one night would cost. The answer: US$35 a night. Although the price would be a budget buster for me I decided to take the room since it did not seem that there were many other options in town. I went outside to pay the driver and returned to the check-in desk.

While I filled out some forms a bus arrived unloading a small army of overweight martial artists from the U.S. Chinese guests in the lobby were amused by the sight of obese Americans who had placed more emphasis on size and muscle than on speed and dexterity.

I received my key card and took the elevator up to my floor. I walked to my room door, entered, and discovered an opulent space with a view of Mount Song: one of the Five Great Mountains of China.

After I washed up and rested, I returned to the lobby and requested a taxi. What I got was a minivan driven by a Chinese woman who charged 20 RMB for the trip to the Shaolin Temple. As we drove toward the temple she kept pointing to printed pictures of sights around Dengfeng. I agreed to see one temple that was supposed to be the first nunnery in China.

After we pulled up to the temple, I exited the minivan, bought my ticket, and went into the unimpressive nunnery. I walked from one small temple to the next finding in each a depressed Buddhist nun who was busy either jamming her finger into her nose or looking at the nostril ooze at the tip of her index finger. I tried to find something of interest in the nunnery, but I overheard several British travelers complaining: "Another temple? When the bloody hell will we see Shaolin?" I decided to leave the nunnery and go directly to the Shaolin Temple.

The driver took me to Shaolin, but she charged me an extra 20 RMB for the nunnery excursion when we arrived. I paid her and got out. After I had bought my ticket to enter the Shaolin Temple I saw my driver waiving at me to get into her minivan again. It seemed that she wanted to drive me past the gates to the various locations that surrounded the Shaolin Temple. Like an idiot I decided to hop back into her minivan. We drove past the gates into a parking lot where she parked the taxi. She then led me to an auditorium where I saw children rehearsing through unbelievable fighting feats of kung fu. I immediately wanted to see the show and went to the box office, but as soon as I pulled out a 50 RMB bill to pay for a 20 RMB ticket the driver grabbed my money and my hand and pulled me from one box office employee to the other while jabbering in Chinese. I realized that she was trying to negotiate with any of the ticket box employees to cheat me out of my 50 RMB. I snatched my money from her and walked away. She followed me, but she realized that I was so angry that she stayed away.

That fiasco, along with discovering the grounds of the temple to be a tacky tourist haven, ruined my experience at Shaolin. Again, it felt like no aspect of traditional Chinese culture was sacred; it appeared that any element of China could be sold for a lousy buck. All around the Shaolin Temple I saw souvenir stalls with shelves of tasteless trinkets and martial arts students giving live demonstrations. I began to wonder what the abbots from centuries past would think of this circus. Would they be shocked to see the once long kept secrets of kung fu on open display to photo taking tourists in plaid Bermuda shorts? How sad. I do not recommend the Shaolin Temple to any traveler. Instead, rent a stupid kung fu movie.

To get away from the ridiculousness of Shaolin I hiked up the mountain that according to legend Bodhidharma ascended when he arrived to the Shaolin Temple from India in 527 AD and was refused entry. Near the top of the mountain the Indian sage entered a small cave, sat facing the wall, and meditated for nine years.[24] After witnessing this achievement, the monks of Shaolin invited Bodhidharma into their temple so that they could learn from him. He taught the monks a series of physical and meditative exercises that developed into the art of kung fu.

The climb up to Bodhidharma's cave was exhausting; it took me an hour. But I was very happy to sit inside the cave with the permission of a young man who was the guardian of the site and pay my respects to Bodhidharma's legacy.

When I returned to the base of the mountain, I befriended several Chinese adolescents who were studying kung fu. They led me to the Forest of Dagobas, a cemetery of over 200 brick pagodas for Shaolin monks. While in the cemetery these young men and I posed in various kung fu positions for tourists who took pictures of us.

On the taxi ride back to Dengfeng, I saw thousands of young

339

martial artists training in unison in the courtyards of their respective kung fu academies.

Zhengzhou: another freakin' Chinese town
Sunday, June 27, 2004

After breakfast, I went for a walk around Dengfeng in the hopes of finding a China International Travel Service (CITS) agency. But I could not find one within walking distance.

I checked out of my hotel, took a taxi to the bus station, and bought a ticket to Zhengzhou. The bus I took was clean, meaning no one had spat on the floor. The ride was three hours.

After arriving in Zhengzhou, I walked to the train station to buy a hard sleeper train ticket to Jinan, but the only tickets available were for hard seats. I decided not to buy the ticket because of what I had read in my guidebook concerning gangs robbing passengers in the hard seat carriages of overnight trains.

Using my guidebook, I tried to find a hotel that was supposed to be in front of the train station, but I never found it. Instead I ended up in a hotel that was on the third floor of a dilapidated building: the ceiling of the dark hallway that led to my room was falling apart and the carpet was wet and moldy. My hotel room was dingy and the bathroom was illuminated by a flickering light bulb. There was a TV in the room that did not work and there was no air conditioner.

Not wanting to spend too much time in my room, I went out to explore Zhengzhou. I walked for a couple of hours in this city of about eight million people, but I could find no significant cultural sights. I found myself wondering: *China, a land of over 5,000 years of history [really, 3,600 years of history[25]], but where the hell is all the history?*

Not wanting to spend more time than necessary in this city, I went back to the train station and bought a hard seat ticket for Jinan. I was not looking forward to the seven-hour overnight experience of sitting on a hard seat in a crowded train, but it was better than spending a night in the worst hotel in Zhengzhou.

The train departed at nine in the evening. The hard seat carriage was very crowded, but I had a seat. I sat down and looked at the individuals and families who were standing in the aisle wondering how they were going to endure the night journey to their destination.

An hour after departing I knew that I was in good company in the hard seat carriage (people were friendly), which was a relief from my fear of being robbed by bandits. I spent most of the journey speaking to two Chinese men who sat across from me. One of the men decided to read my palm: "Yes ... work is good ... work is good. You will do very well in your career. Yes ... yes ... your health. Take care your health. Eat more vegetable than meat. Don't eat meat–only a little. Yes ... you have pain in your knees and your lower back. Take care. Yes ... your health. Take care of your health. You need to sleep more. You sleep little. Sleep eight hours. Nine hours. Yes ... you get angry. A lot of anger comes out of you ... perhaps once a month this anger comes out."

I agreed with most of what he said, but I was surprised to hear the comment about my anger. To confirm the reading, my explosive rage reared its ugly head the next morning.

Arriving to Tai'an
Monday, June 28, 2004

The two Chinese men I had been speaking to on the train explained that it was better that I get off at Tai'an than at Jinan if I wanted to climb Mount Tai. The advice saved me an hour off my train journey. I arrived at Tai'an very early in the morning.

As soon as I exited the train station a young taxi driver approached me. I followed him, entered his taxi, took out my guidebook, and pointed to the guesthouse that I wanted to go to. He kept shaking his head explaining in Chinese that the guesthouse was closed. I pointed to my eye signaling that I wanted to see the guesthouse to verify if it was closed or not. I did not trust the man. In fact–after three weeks in China–I did not trust anyone.

He drove me to an abandoned building and said that that was the guesthouse. I erupted into a storm of yells and curses. I could not remember the last time I had vented so much anger at someone. The taxi driver was scared. He pleaded that he was not lying. I calmed down, looked carefully at the Chinese characters on the building, and realized that indeed it was the guesthouse I had wanted to go to and that it was closed. Again, my guidebook failed me.

I apologized to the driver. He drove me to a hotel, but it was too expensive. He took me to another hotel and negotiated a lower price for me with the lady at the reception desk. After I agreed to stay at the hotel he asked for his fare and left. I checked in and went to my spacious and clean room seeing that I received a bargain. I felt guilty for having given the driver such a hard time.

I went to sleep and woke up before noon. I took a shower, dressed, and went first to a bank to change my Japanese yen for Chinese RMB. I then walked looking for a restaurant listed in my guidebook, but I could not find it. Instead I went to a Chinese restaurant, but because I could not read the menu I walked with the waitress to the tables of other customers and pointed to the dishes that seemed appealing.

Twenty minutes later I received several plates and bowls of food. I ate as much as I could, but I did not come close to finishing everything that I had ordered. When I was done I asked for the bill and paid it; it was cheap.

With a full stomach, I tried to find an Internet café that was recommended in my guidebook, but when I found the location I could see that the café had closed down months ago. I then went to the Taoist Dai Temple to seek blessings for my next morning ascent of Mount Tai. Although I could not see the mountain because it was a cloudy day, I enjoyed the temple's gardens and the ancient cypress trees.

Posted by The Legacy Cycle at 2004-07-22T09:05:00-07:00

Thursday, July 22, 2004

Taishan
Tuesday, June 29, 2004

When I was in high school, and learning the craft of the drums and percussion, Rush, a Canadian progressive rock group, became the band that I aspired to emulate. I idolized Neil Peart, the drummer for the band, as not only a skilled percussionist, but as a master lyricist and world traveler. There began my desire to write and travel.

The music of Rush and Neil's lyrics became an anthem for my own beliefs and philosophical outlooks. Inspired by Neil I sought to travel, read, and write. By his example, I realized that I did not want to only be a drummer, I wanted to be a philosopher, a poet, a nomad, and a source of inspiration for others.

It was from hearing the Rush song "Tai Shan" that my interest in East Asian culture grew. As the years passed, I dabbled more and more in Zen Buddhism, Chinese philosophy, and the martial arts, particularly the art of the Zen sword and the way of the samurai.

It had been a long desire of mine to climb Mount Tai and pay homage to Neil Peart who had made the ascent in the 1980s. And so, on the morning of June 29, I woke up to fulfill this adolescent dream.

I began my climb at 6:11 a.m. and arrived to the summit by 8:30. I expected the conquest to take me four hours, but I did it in just over two. The brisk summit had a few temples and tawdry tourist shops, which I avoided by retreating to a quiet peak where I could take in the cloudy, alpine landscape. There I meditated. There I prayed to the spirit of my grandfathers and members of the Hart and Composto clans. I thanked God for the life I lived in Japan and for my travels through Asia. In a way, I said goodbye to the East. Climbing Taishan represented the end of my four years in Asia.

Mount Tai: A History Lesson

Mount Tai is the most sacred of the five Taoist mountains in China. A climb to the top is considered to be a spiritual journey–a pilgrimage–by the Chinese. Taishan is 5,000 feet high with 6,660 stone steps to aid in the ascent.[26,27] The ascent of the mountain is required of all devote Taoists.[28] And it is said that those who reach the summit will live for a hundred years.[29]

At the base of the mountain, I came across an army of elderly men and women who had made it their daily morning routine to climb perhaps a tenth of the mountain.

During the ascent, I came across teenagers, families, and couples, but it was odd to see older men and women pursuing the climb in near formal attire. Everyone was sweating and panting on the way up. Middle-aged men rolled their dress pants up to their knees and hiked their button up shirts above their plump stomachs.

Ze Train to Beijing
Wednesday, June 30, 2004

I had a lot of time to kill today. My train for Beijing did not depart until half past ten at night. I spent the day trying to find an Internet café, but had no luck. So, I walked around town finding more dreary buildings and a market in an abandoned industrial warehouse. It would have been perfect to see a movie today, but I could not find a suitable movie theater. Pirated DVDs seemed to have killed the movie-going culture here.

In the late evening, I returned to my hotel and read a book. When it was time to leave, I called a taxi and went to the train station. Along the way I saw an Internet café! The café was near a corner I had passed repeatedly while in Tai'an. I cursed myself for not walking down that street; I could have accomplished a lot of writing on this blog.

Arrival in Beijing
Thursday, July 1, 2004

I arrived to Beijing on a cold and somber morning. After exiting the train station, I walked to a large hotel that also–according to my guidebook–had a hostel. I went into the hotel, but the staff informed me that the hostel had moved. I left the hotel and headed in the direction of another hostel, but an old man riding a cycle rickshaw offered to take me to where I was going. I told him the name of the hostel and he said that he knew where it was. I hopped into the rickshaw and away we went. We eventually stopped at a guesthouse, but it was full. The rickshaw driver peddled to another guesthouse, but it was too pricey. I asked the rickshaw driver to take me back to the first hostel. We then began to argue. He asserted that he had already taken me to the hostel, but I did not believe that the hostel he had taken me to was the one I had pointed out in my guidebook. I paid him and jumped into a taxi, and as we drove north I saw a sign for the hostel that I had wanted to go to and I realized that the rickshaw driver had indeed taken me to it. He was right, I was wrong.

The taxi driver and I drove around Beijing for an hour trying to find a cheap hostel; he kept running out and back into his taxi asking random people on the street about the location of certain places to stay. We finally ended up at the International Youth Hostel just behind the five-star Great Dragon Hotel. I took my bag and ran into the hostel to see if they had room. They said they did not know. I decided that I would wait until they figured out if they *did* or *did not* have room, but first I ran out to pay the taxi driver and saw that he was gone. I asked the guard to the hotel about the taxi and he explained that he had left. I could not believe that I had received a free one-hour taxi ride in Beijing. I felt horrible. Of all the hellish taxi drivers that I had experienced in China, this one was the nicest. He deserved his fare and a handsome tip. But he left before I had the chance to pay him.

Tomorrow I will sit down and write about Beijing. I was there for about nine days.

Posted by The Legacy Cycle at 2004-07-22T11:06:00-07:00

Friday, July 23, 2004

Beijing
Thursday, July 1 To Friday, July 9, 2004

What a relief it was to arrive in Beijing after two weeks of town and city hopping. I was more than happy to see and be surrounded by foreigners at the hostel. For the two weeks that I traveled from place to place within central China I–for the most part–was the only foreigner. Rarely did I see another traveler from Western lands.

Beijing is not China. It did not represent in any shape, way or form the types of people or income brackets that I came across in the rest of the country. Beijing is an immense, cosmopolitan city. And it is growing.

During my first morning, at the hostel, I became friends with Rob, a thirty-year-old American from New York City. It was his fourth time to Beijing, and this time he was here to stay. We had breakfast at a Chinese Islamic restaurant and talked mostly about politics.

I discovered through my conversation with Rob how much Beijing had changed over the past four years, and how much it was going to change in the years ahead. When he first arrived to the Chinese capital four to five years ago he said that there was no car traffic. Instead, there were tens of thousands of people riding bikes in all directions. But today you hardly see people riding bikes. In fact, more than 400,000 cars were added to Beijing's streets in 2003, "a nearly 25 percent increase."[30] In 1995, "the number of registered vehicles (including cars, vans, buses, and trucks)"[31] on the road in China was two million.[32] In 2004 the number hit 20 million[33] (62 million in 2009, with an expectation of over 200 million by 2020).[34] China's growing, affluent middle class of 300 million (essentially the entire population of the U.S.) is driving the demand for gas guzzling cars and SUVs.[35] As a result, U.S., European, Japanese, and South Korean car manufacturers are all eager to gain a stronger foothold into the Chinese car market (China became the world's largest car market in 2009).[36] With the current lack of regard for the environment and atmosphere, China will be the number one emitter of carbon dioxide, putting the U.S. in second place (in 2006 China became the biggest emitter).[37]

Western car manufacturers, the Chinese government, and Chinese consumers seem not to care–for the moment–about how these vehicles impact the air they breathe. What will China's environment, and the health of its people, be like when the majority of the nation's billion plus population enters the middle class? In a 2007 World Bank report, entitled "Cost of Pollution in China", it was stated that "up to 760,000 people die prematurely each year in China because of air and water pollution."[38] In addition, "air pollution in China's cities leads to 350,000-400,000 premature deaths."[39]

Rob expressed his disbelief in how many new corporate office buildings had been constructed in the year and a half that he was away;

a visible sign that multinational corporations were moving in to get a piece of the Chinese RMB pie.

On July 2, I spent time relaxing with Rob and his Canadian friend, GQ–a nickname reflective of how he was habitually dressed in the latest of men's fashion. While we sat outside a Starbucks sipping coffee they recounted how they met at the International Youth Hostel in 2001, and of their nightlife misadventures in Sanlitun (an area of Beijing that is famed for its bars, restaurants, dance clubs, and international shops).

In the evening, I joined Rob, GQ, and a group of American travelers from the youth hostel for a round of beers in Sanlitun where we saw fashionable Beijing women, wearing designer sunglasses and clothing, strut their stuff up and down the streets. I found myself wondering if these women were Japanese because for most of my journey through the interior of China I had never seen Chinese women dressed with such style. But the undying Chinese art of spitting gave them away. I was disturbed to see and hear these Beijing women dressed with such appeal to then cough up a mouthful of phlegm and spit it on the ground.

As for Beijing men, it did not seem that they spent too much time on their appearance. Instead, they enjoyed smoking from cigarettes packaged in elegant red boxes with gold trim.

I spent nearly every evening during my stay in Beijing in the television lounge of the hostel where I watched pirated DVDs to catch up on films that I had missed such as *Spider-Man 2*, Michael Moore's *Fahrenheit 911*, *The Human Stain*, *The Italian Job*, *The Last Samurai*, and *Along Came Polly*.

The Great Wall
Saturday, July 3, 2004

I decided to sign up for the Great Wall tour offered at the hostel. I met a wonderful group of people in the three-hour minivan journey to the wall. The most notable was an American teacher who was traveling with his two kids.

The most popular section of the wall for tourists to see was Badaling. Do not go there. Backpackers who had visited Badaling explained that the wall was not original and looked more like a Disneyland Epcot version of the Great Wall.

We were dropped off in a remote farming village near the 19-kilometer section of the wall called Simatai. Curious, poverty-stricken locals walked up to us eager to sell us Great Wall T-shirts and hats. We followed our guide and hiked up through the thick vegetation of the surrounding hills until we could see the Great Wall. Although parts of the wall were crumbling, it was impressive. We continued up, entered the wall through an opening, arrived to the top, and hiked east. I moved quickly, and after a half-hour I had lost sight of my group. I traveled the remaining length of the wall alone.

There were watchtowers every 500 meters or so on the wall. The steps to ascend the towers were very steep, but they provided views of the surrounding countryside from their narrow arrowslits. Some parts of the wall were in complete ruin as a result of centuries of erosion.

As I traveled along the wall I tried to imagine the hundreds of thousands of soldiers, and conscripted (enslaved) men and women who worked to build the wall (according to historical records nearly one million laborers worked on the wall[40]). A reminder that human labor in China was–and still is–plentiful and cheap.

Cheap labor seemed to be the strongest pillar to China's glorious dynastic past, and its economic growth in the present. The manufacturing plants and supply chains of many companies from developed nations are rushing to China to utilize the nation's vast army of poor, unskilled, and low-cost laborers (in 2003, GDP per capita incomes in China was $1,288.64,[41] but also note that in 2016 per capita incomes had risen to $8,123.18 thus "China's most prominent global competitive advantage" is weakening[42]).

After hiking, sweating, and trying to outrun a tout or two selling ice-cold bottled water and postcards I rested near a wire-cable suspension footbridge.

As I waited for the remaining members of the tour group to arrive, I spoke with a Canadian married couple that were near the end of their year-long trip around the world.

Once back in Beijing, a few of the guys that I had met from the Great Wall tour group and I went out for dinner to eat honeyed Peking duck and drink Chinese beer. It was a festive evening of indecent jokes and the occasional burp.

The Starbucks inside the Forbidden City
Monday, July 5, 2004

Monday morning, I went to Tiananmen Square and the Forbidden City with two friends I had met at the hostel. Although we had left early to get in line for the Mausoleum of Mao Zedong, we discovered that the mausoleum was closed. Being sarcastic, we proceeded north through one of the world's largest city squares in search of the memorial dedicated to the Tiananmen Square Massacre of 1989. We looked, but of course there was no memorial to the unknown number of casualties ("declassified files reveal" ... "that at least 10,000 civilians were killed"[43]) because the Chinese Communist Party had whitewashed the event. We passed the Monument to the People's Heroes and proceeded toward the southern gate of the Forbidden City where hangs the famed portrait of Mao Zedong.

The Forbidden City was built from 1406 to 1420 AD and covers 72 hectares.[44] There are 980 buildings within the palace complex, and, according to myth, there were 9,999 rooms because only the celestial emperor could have 10,000 rooms.[45,46]

I could have spent a lifetime exploring all the buildings, chambers, and 8,000 plus rooms in the Forbidden City. It was simply too large to cover in a day. But it was strange not to see any trees or vegetation in the vast open stone courtyards of the palace; I could not even find a single blade of grass growing between the stones of the courtyard. We saw several throne chambers and temples, and each had a large sign that provided historical information in Chinese and English. But the bottom of every sign read: "Brought to you by American Express".

And if American Express corporate sponsorship was not

enough there was actually a Starbucks inside the "587-year-old Forbidden City"![47] Had the Chinese sold their cultural soul for a lousy U.S. buck? I found the site of this coffee shop in the heart of Chinese imperial history very upsetting.

Eventually, we walked into a few enclosed areas within the Forbidden City that had beautiful gardens.

After exiting the Forbidden City from its northern gate, we walked up to Jingshan Park, an "artificial hill" made from the earth that had been dug to create the moat that surrounds the Forbidden City.[48] The view from the temple at the top of the hill provided a scenic view of both the Forbidden City and Beijing.

After the park, we decided to hire a cycle rickshaw driver that had been pressuring us to employ his service. We bargained the driver down to a suitable price and then we squeezed into the backseat of the rickshaw. The site of three healthy young men sitting nearly on top of each other in the back of a frail cycle rickshaw that was peddled by a nearly dead elderly man was absurd.

Mao Zedong
Tuesday, July 6, 2004

A couple of friends from the hostel and I woke up early to beat the lines for the Mausoleum of Mao Zedong. We took a bus and a subway to Tiananmen Square. Although the subway in Beijing was suitable and cheap, I was surprised to discover that the number of subway lines were not extensive for a city with a population of over 12 million.[49]

When we arrived to the southern end of the mausoleum we were shocked by the number of people waiting in line. We approached the line and followed it looking for the end, but as we walked and walked and saw no immediate end we decided to run until finally, after five minutes, we came to the end of the line. We waited in line for about an hour and 15 minutes amazed to see that 28 years after Mao's death there were still thousands of people lining up every day (except Mondays) to pay their respects.

We saw the body of Mao Zedong covered with a communist flag inside a glass coffin within a spacious room that was well illuminated. I found the experience of seeing Hồ Chí Minh's body that was guarded by four soldiers within a darkly lit room more striking than this experience.

Refer to "Culture Shock Blues in the Middle Kingdom" Journal Entry
Wednesday, July 7, 2004

I wanted to go to the Summer Palace today, but I needed to first withdraw Chinese RMB from Citibank so that I could exchange it for U.S. dollars before traveling to Mongolia and the Russian Federation. Unfortunately, I discovered that to convert Chinese RMB to dollars was nearly impossible. I could go on for pages about this upsetting discovery, and bureaucratic banking bullsh*t experience, but I will not because I covered it in my "Culture Shock Blues in the Middle Kingdom" blog entry [I discuss it anyway in the next section]. I spent the entire day running all over Beijing trying to find a way to exchange my Chinese RMB. At the end of the day, I had failed in my quest and I was not able to see the Summer Palace.

The RMB Drama Continued
Thursday, July 8, 2004

I needed U.S. dollars for my Trans-Mongolian rail trip; I could not buy Mongolian tugrik or Russian rubles in China so I needed plenty of dollars to last me well into my journey across the Gobi Desert and Siberia. As a result, I spent the morning and early afternoon walking from one Chinese bank to another in a desperate attempt to convert my RMB to the U.S. currency. It was repeatedly explained to me by every bank teller I encountered that I could not make the exchange without a specific form that I should have been given when I first bought RMB. But since I had withdrawn my RMB from automated teller machines I did not have the form. In a last-ditch effort, I took a bus to the airport where again I found that I could not legally change my RMB for U.S. dollars at the currency exchange booths.

I was left with only one option. I became an illegal money changer. I solicited new arrivals in the airport that were standing in line in front of the currency exchange offices. I sold my RMB at an unbeatable rate, and I was not caught or arrested by the police.

After illegally exchanging all my RMB at the airport, I ran to see the Temple of Heaven.

The Temple of Heaven

The Temple of Heaven is located far south of Tiananmen Square in an expansive park. It was at this temple that Chinese emperors "conducted the most significant ceremonies and rites of the year," which "established the divine link between Heaven (tian) and the Son of Heaven (huangdi), channeling eternal law to the Earth."[50]

I walked from one temple to the other watching families and travelers pose for photos. I found a pleasant spot within a stone doorframe and watched a Chinese woman go through the subtle movements of qigong, which is the ancient practice of cultivating qi (vital life energy) into your body for healing purposes.[51]

The Last Full Day in Beijing
Friday, July 9, 2004

I spent the day stocking up on provisions of dried food and bottled drinks for my train journey to Mongolia. I also had some time to go to an Internet café to get this blog up to date.

Posted by The Legacy Cycle at 2004-07-23T07:04:00-07:00

MONGOLIA

Friday, July 23, 2004

The Trans-Mongolian Rail: Beijing to Ulan Bator
Saturday, July 10, 2004

There is nothing more relaxing and pleasant for a traveler than an overnight train. On a train, a backpacker does not feel guilty spending more hours than needed to sleep, read, and stare out the window.

In the early morning of July 10, I took a taxi with an Australian man from my hostel–who was also taking the 8 a.m. Mongolian rail–to the Beijing railway station. Once we arrived to the station, we saw a horde gathered in front of it.

We each made our way through the crowd, entered the station, found our train, and boarded our respective passenger cars. I moved through the crowd of people who were either searching for their compartment or trying to store their luggage and found my sleeping compartment, which I shared with a nearly retired German couple and a young Mongolian man who told me that he preferred flying to Ulan Bator than taking a train. I jumped up to my lofted bed and got comfortable for the journey by taking off my shoes and getting a book out of my bag. The train left on time. I took turns between reading a few pages and looking out the window, but after an hour the rocking motion of the train caused me to doze off. I woke up in the late morning, took out a few snacks and a drink, ate, read, and spoke to the German couple.

Nightfall came around eight in the evening and although we had traveled for nearly 12 hours we had yet to arrive to the border.

The landscape during the journey was flat and barren. There was only endless land and sky. There was nothing man-made that could be seen outside other than the utility poles that ran alongside the train tracks. There were no animals or birds. Never had I seen so much open and untouched terrain. I had entered God's Country.

The Gobi Desert
Sunday, July 11, 2004

I woke up at half past five in the morning, looked out the window, saw the Gobi Desert, and went back to sleep.

At half past seven I woke up again, sat up, and ate some crackers and tuna from a can. When I finished I stepped down from my bed, looked outside, and saw the unending desert terrain with scattered patches of grass.

Out there, beyond my window, was the vast expanse of land and sky.

In the distance, I saw Mongolian yurts and herds of sheep and horses; I also saw–every so often–a rabbit dart away from the train.

By afternoon the land became hilly and green, which reminded me of the landscapes I had seen in Ireland.

Once the train neared Ulan Bator, the number of trees and flowers I saw increased.

A Mongolian woman in her early thirties by the name of Altai and her driver met me at the train station in Ulan Bator. They worked for Tsolmon Travel, which was also associated with White Nights Travel (the travel agency I used to plan the Mongolian and Russian portions of my trip). Altai was very nice and informative, but she kept apologizing that I would have to take the train to Russia a day later than what I had originally planned; I insisted that she did not have to worry because I was quite happy to spend an extra day in her country.

After changing some money at a currency exchange office that had a plainly dressed guard with a gun tucked into his pants, we drove to the National Sports Stadium to see the wrestling events that were taking place on the first day of the famed Nadaam Festival.

The Nadaam Festival celebrates "the three games of men"[1]: wrestling, horse riding, and archery. This celebration dates back to the age of Genghis Khan about 800 years ago,[2] but the Nadaam Festival is now linked to commemorating the 1921 revolution that led to Mongolia declaring its independence from China;[3] but from 1924 to 1990 Mongolia was heavily supported and influenced by the Soviet Union.[4] Legend tells that in the centuries before Genghis Khan, the warriors of differing Mongolian tribes would compete in these three sports before or after battle.[5]

While I watched the wrestling events in the stadium, I noticed that the Mongolian crowd of men and women were assertive and pushy; they would stick out their hand or arm and shove people out of the way. And when we left the stadium, I saw a drunken man urinating in front of a large group of people. I also saw open bottles of alcohol littered around the grounds of the stadium and several drunken, old men stumbling. It became apparent that if China had a very strong tobacco culture, Mongolia had a very strong alcohol culture.

Altai and I jumped back into her company car and headed for Gorkhi-Terelj National Park. While we drove east of Ulan Bator we could see from the north the approach of rolling storm clouds. Within moments heavy rains fell, but it only lasted for 20 minutes. On the way to the national park we stopped at the yurt of a Mongolian family to buy kumis (fermented mare's milk). I was able to take a peek into the yurt and saw the mother of the family preparing dinner by dunking the entire head of a skinned goat into a vat of boiling broth. As for the mare's milk, it was fizzy—just like the palm wine (toddy) I had in Myanmar—but it smelled like vinegar and sour dough. After we finished our drinks, we returned to the car, and continued our drive.

Thirty minutes later, we arrived to the yurt camp where I would spend two nights; it was located between rocky hills and picturesque mountains. I took my bag and followed Altai up a gradual slope to a large, permanent, wooden lodge designed like a yurt where she helped me check-in and translated information from the receptionist such as the times that breakfast, lunch, and dinner would be served. She then escorted me to my private yurt (one of 35), which was further up the hill. As we walked hearing the faint sound of cattle moans in the distance, she pointed to a wooden building to our right and explained it had toilets and shower rooms. At the door of my yurt, Altai explained the time she would pick me up in a couple of days and a few other details, and left me to get settled and rest. I opened the door to my yurt and saw a simple, but comfortable, looking bed to the left, a wood burning stove at the center of the room, and behind the stove a short, wooden table with a green thermos (filled with water) and two stools. I unpacked my bag, rested on my bed, and read a few pages from the *The Travels of Marco Polo*. I then decided to go out and explore.

I hiked through the tall grasses of a steep hill seeing grasshoppers jump away from me with each step that I took. And although I rarely saw birds flying in the sky, I always heard them chirping.

I reached the top of the hill and continued until I could no longer see the camp. I sat down on a rock and looked at the rolling hills of the grassland that surrounded me. The land seemed to be untouched by man. It was pure and heavenly.

Notes on Mongolia
Monday, July 12, 2004

At the summit of a mountain, east of my camp, I found a terrain of boulders, skinny trees, grasses, and flowers. Speckles of pollen stained the knees of my pants as I walked through the grassland.

During my ascent, I saw scores of grasshoppers jumping away from my path. They were all uniquely camouflaged to the environment. Some were as green as the grass they were hiding in whereas others were pink or black making them nearly indistinguishable from the eroded granite rocks that were covered in dried moss.

The only sounds that I heard were the horseflies. Yes, even in the most remote of locations there are flies. The horseflies were about the size of my thumbnail.

I was surrounded by the glorious makings of nature. There were no signs of man. No footprints or discarded rubbish. There were only butterflies and the constant creaking of critters within the grassland.

I was totally alone—and at long last! There was no Internet, no television, and no jabber of human tongues. There were no commercials, no stores, no buildings, or streets.

I was far from the makings of people. This was paradise. I was blessed. Sitting there on a rock, I could only think of those that I had met and seen during my journey. Many were sad, depressed, lost, suffering, and hungry. Many were striving for food, money, and a superficial, Western consumer ideal that had invaded their mind through the constant barrage of advertisements and television images that paraded objects that no one really needed.

The horseflies continued to swarm around me. I watched them as they explored my ankle or foot. They had probably never seen anything as unusual as me. They hopped onto the pages of my journal wanting to explore the white sheets of paper.

I realized that everything material back in the developed world meant very little to me. Prestigious offices, designer suits, cars, and electronics were—in the end— rubbish.

All the answers that I sought could be found here in the lands of Mongolia.

God protects this place for it is a holy frontier.

Posted by The Legacy Cycle at 2004-07-23T08:42:00-07:00

Saturday, July 24, 2004

Buuveit Ger Camp to Ulan Bator
Tuesday, July 13, 2004

I rose from bed and looked out from the wooden door of my private yurt to see a mystical morning fog receding from the valley that the camp was located in. I did not want to leave.

I took my towel and soap bar, exited my yurt, and walked to the camp's washroom cabin that was 30 meters away; I had difficulty walking as my inner thighs and buttocks were sore from horseback riding the previous day.

During the afternoon of July 12, I went horseback riding. I did have a guide, but he kept some distance so that I would have a more private riding experience. Although the last time I had gone horseback riding was in high school I still knew how to steer my horse. But I had no control over the pace of the animal.

My horse ate grass every moment he could, but I would pull back on the rein to bring his head up. We trotted toward the mountains, but suddenly my horse took off at a dead run. It was an exhilarating experience that was not forgiving to my inner thighs.

I wanted to see a site called Melkhii Khad (Turtle Rock), but when I saw storm clouds approaching from over the northern mountains I realized that it was not a good idea. But my horse kept running, and I sang to the beating rhythm of the hooves stomping on the ground. And then it began to rain. I looked back for my guide, but could not find him. My horse then stopped to eat some more. I pulled its head up with the rein again, but he would only walk a few steps and eat again. The horse and I were at odds. The horse did not care that I wanted to find the guide. All he wanted to do was eat in the rain. So, I gave in. He defeated me, and there I was, unable to do much, but sit on my grazing horse in the hard, cold rain. Seven minutes later my guide found me, rode up beside me, took my rein, and led my horse to a nearby yurt camp.

At the camp, we got off our horses and tied the reins to a horse stable fence that had a few horses within it. We then went to the door of one of the yurts and knocked. We were greeted and permitted in, which allowed me to see the interior of a Mongolian family home. Within the yurt there were two Swedes that had also been caught out in the rain, three Mongolian men who were busy watching wrestling matches from the Nadaam Festival on a black and white television set, and three Mongolian women: a woman in her thirties and two teenagers. The Swedes and I were served a variety of traditional Mongolian dairy foods. I tried a little bit of everything that was offered to me while washing the food down with fermented mare's milk.

The door of a yurt always points south. Marco Polo even described this fact 700 years ago in his travelogue *The Travels of Marco Polo*. Inside the yurt I saw beds on wooden frames; women typically sleep on the bed that is aligned along the eastern curving wall of the yurt. There was a stove at the center of the yurt that faced east. The beds for the men were located on the western side of the yurt and the family shrine was located along the northeastern side.

The yurt was warm as a result of the felt insulation and the heat from the stove. But during the hot summer months the felt that typically touches the ground is rolled up and tied so that air can freely flow through the yurt from the ground and up through the opening above the stove.

After taking a shower, getting dressed in my yurt, and eating breakfast, I began getting my bag ready for my return to Ulan Bator. At 10:45 a.m. I was ready and waiting at the check-out desk, and at 11 a.m. an employee of Tsolmon Travel picked me up.

To save money, I arranged with Tsolmon Travel to stay in the home of an elderly Mongolian woman who spoke Mongolian, Russian, and some English. Her apartment was located on the south side of the longest bridge in Ulan Bator in one of a series of standardized apartment buildings of the Soviet era. The woman's apartment was clean, and the decor reminded me of my grandmother's home in Chile.

In the afternoon, I went out to explore the city. On my way north, I ran into an English student by the name of Clive who was actually on my train from Beijing to Ulan Bator. We decided to have lunch together before heading south to see the Winter Palace of the Bogd Khan. It was within this complex that the eighth Jebtsundamba Khutuktu–Mongolia's eighth living Buddha and last king–lived for 20 years. Although the grounds of the complex were not well maintained, the palace housed several beautiful Tibetan Buddhist temples. On display within the palace were the clothes, furniture, and toys of the king.

Sükhbaatar Square

Clive and I walked from the palace to Sükhbaatar Square. The square reminded me of Tiananmen Square, but on a much smaller scale. At the center of the square stood a low-quality statue of the 1921 revolutionary hero Damdin Sükhbaatar riding gallantly on a horse.

Located at the northern end of the square was Sükhbaatar's Mausoleum, which housed the tombs of Damdin Sükhbaatar and Khorloogiin Choibalsan, communist leader of Mongolia's government from 1939 to 1952. The mausoleum was not open to the public.

Clive and I then tried to find Millie's Café, a popular spot among travelers and expatriates, but although we followed the map in our guidebook we were unable to find it because it had changed locations.

For dinner, we went into a bar and restaurant called the UB Jazz Club. I had a mutton dish and a dark Mongolian beer.

Ulan Bator
Wednesday, July 14, 2004

I suffered from a bad case of diarrhea. It was the mutton that made me sick. This was the first time that I had been sick on this trip since Myanmar. I took some medicine–it was the medication I received from the hospital in Bangkok–and made my way to an Internet café in town. But I could not really focus on updating my blog since I spent most of my effort trying to hold down my stomach.

At one in the afternoon, I went to Sükhbaatar Square to meet Stina Märtson, an Estonian friend I had met backstage in Tokyo before performing with a band I was in called Favorite Underdog. She was a professional vocalist who made a living in Japan as a singer and a model. She also worked on a few movies: she was a stand-in in the movie *Lost in Translation*; if you watch the making-of segments on the DVD you will actually see her sitting next to Bill Murray in one of the restaurant scenes. She used to work with my friend Toshi who was a music producer and the rhythm guitarist for Favorite Underdog. Toshi introduced us. At that time, she was just a week away from moving to Mongolia with her Mongolian husband (who she had met in Japan), and I was just a month or two away from beginning this trip. I told her that I would be traveling through Mongolia, we exchanged contact details, and thus there we were in Sükhbaatar Square.

She took me to one of her favorite restaurants in the capital, which she confessed did not have great service, but did have great food and a lot of expatriates as regular customers.

I had some more mutton dishes (probably not the best idea considering the state of my stomach) and a Mongolian tea that looked more like soup because it had bits of mutton in it. The food was very good.

After a long lunch, she drove me in her car to the Zaisan Memorial, a memorial dedicated to the Mongolian and Soviet soldiers killed in World War II. The memorial was located on a hill that provided a panoramic view of the capital, but I could see a haze hanging over the city caused by the pollution that was trapped by the surrounding mountains.

After the memorial, we drove to the UB Guesthouse to pick up Roni; she was an Israeli young woman with dark blonde and curly hair that I had met on the train from Beijing, and although she was of Russian descent she had grown up in Kazakhstan. The three of us headed to the National Academic Theatre of Opera and Ballet of Mongolia to see a show displaying traditional Mongolian costumes, dances, acrobatics, music, and throat singing. One of the traditional costumes that I saw was the inspiration for one of Padmé Amidala's headdresses for the film, *Star Wars: Episode I – The Phantom Menace*. A few of the dances gave the illusion of horse riding. The throat singing was the most remarkable; I was amazed that the human body could produce such deep, reverberating tones.

After the show, we went for drinks at a nearby bar and restaurant. I had chocolate milk. Stina's husband later joined us.

We talked about the homeless children in Ulan Bator. I saw in many of the streets of the capital homeless Mongolian boys and teenagers. Stina and her husband explained to me that most of these children had chosen to live on the streets as an alternative to experiencing domestic violence. They said that alcoholism was a major problem in Mongolia that had resulted in countless cases of drunken men beating their sons, daughters, and wives.

The homeless children that I had seen were harmless. They approached me on a few occasions for some pocket change or to collect my empty, plastic water bottle, which they could redeem at a recycling center for some money. I should mention that Clive and I were nearly attacked the previous day by a drunken man who demanded money. The experience caused a sudden, violent adrenaline urge in all of us, but a Mongolian boy held the man back; the boy was most likely the son of the drunken man.

According to the National Center Against Violence (NCAV), "one in three families in Mongolia are affected by domestic violence".[6] In addition, "Alcoholism, according to a 2006 study by the World Health Organization, affects 22 percent of men and 5 percent of women in Mongolia."[7]

The following is an excerpt from an article entitled "Living in a manhole" that was published in *The Economist* in 2000 regarding street children in Mongolia's capital.

> ... a manhole between the Hard Rock Club and the Ulan Bator Hotel, has half-a-dozen children living in it. Last year, one child stabbed another to death here. A second child died in an alcohol-induced coma.
>
> During the day, the girls from this manhole offer themselves to men for $5 a time. That is good money, if they get it. On a recent day, they had money and only one of the children, a boy of 14, came up the ladder to greet Father Gilbert. The others, he said, had been drinking vodka and had passed out. With a grin, the boy took the food and went below again.
>
> The manholes, in which many of Ulan Bator's nearly 3,000 street children live, are fetid places that lead either to the sewers or to the city's heating system. Underground life does nothing to reduce the high incidence among the children of scabies, tuberculosis, urinary infections and sexually transmitted diseases. But at least it is warm. Ulan Bator is the world's coldest capital city, with winter temperatures that can dip below -30°C. By leaving the covers open, the government acknowledges that the manholes have become life-savers. Indeed, aid workers say that deaths from hypothermia are

more common in the summer, when a cold snap can catch the homeless off guard.[8]

Thursday, July 15, 2004

Today, Roni and I met up with two Israeli backpackers who had traveled throughout India, Southeast Asia, and China. They told us a story about a backpacker they had met in Ulan Bator who had been assaulted after dark and that another traveler had been beaten by five Mongolian men and stripped of nearly all his clothing.

Roni and I later went to Gandantegchinlen Monastery, which was considered to be the largest and most important Tibetan-style Buddhist monastery in the country; there were about 150 monks in residence dressed in the robes of a lama. The monastery was spared from the religious purges of the 1930s that resulted in the deaths of 15,000 lamas[9] and the destruction of nearly every religious building.

Before I approached the monastery, I spun the bronze Tibetan Buddhist prayer wheels that had mantras inscribed on them. I prayed for a safe journey and thanked God for all the wonderful blessings that I had experienced in the countries I had traveled to.

That night I took the Trans-Mongolian train to Siberia.

Posted by The Legacy Cycle at 2004-07-24T01:07:00-07:00

RETURNING
TO THE LAND OF PLENTY

DOMENICO ITALO COMPOSTO-HART

RUSSIA

Saturday, July 24, 2004

Siberia by Train

I shared my train compartment with two British college students and a Russian Mongol man. Our train carriage did not have air conditioning or a fan so we kept the window cracked open to allow for a breeze. The landscape changed as we traveled north from green rolling hills to desert.

On July 16, our train sat at the Mongolian-Russian border from 6 a.m. to 10:30 a.m. The air outside was hot and dreadful. We sat in our compartment bearing the heat and unable to use the washroom (the train attendants locked the washrooms before, during, and after arriving to each station so that no human waste could collect on the tracks).

At 9 a.m., Mongolian immigration officers came to our compartment and asked for our passports. About an hour and a half later the train departed, but again on the Russian side of the border the train stopped so that Russian immigration officers could inspect the cargo and passengers. The wait there took about four hours. Once we had cleared Russian customs we were allowed to get off the train to wash up, change money, and eat some food in the train station.

I went to change my U.S. dollars for Russian rubles, but the process took about 20 minutes as backpackers from my train and I had to wait in line for an exchange that took longer than necessary.

With my rubles, I went to a store inside the train station that looked like a small grocery store from the 1920s. I bought some drinks and food from the shop owner who used an abacus to calculate the transaction.

The Russian border was the destination for the Russian Mongol in our compartment so for the rest of the journey it was just the British students and I. The train continued for most of the day with a few stops until we arrived to Ulan-Ude, which was where the students disembarked. I walked around the station to stretch my legs before the train continued for Irkutsk. Although, on the map, the distance between Ulan-Ude and Irkutsk seemed short (not really, as it was approximately 450 kilometers away), it took eight hours to get there. Since I had the compartment all to myself I stretched out and enjoyed the passing scenery into the evening and night until I fell asleep. Later that night, I woke up after feeling raindrops hit my face from the open window, but I was too tired to do anything about it so I went back to sleep.

Irkutsk & the Storm of the Century
Saturday, July 17, 2004

I arrived at the Irkutsk railway station early in the morning. A Russian college student who worked for Baikalcomplex (a tour operator that was associated with White Nights) met me at the station, led me to a car, and drove me to the Angara Hotel Complex where I was able to change some more money.

While driving through the city the student explained to me that a strong storm had hit Irkutsk during the night and killed four people, which explained the countless number of felled trees and broken branches that littered the sidewalks and streets. He went on to explain that Irkutsk was a college town that attracted the youth of Siberia.

We drove for about an hour southeast to Listvyanka–a town on the shores of Lake Baikal–to the home of a modest Russian family where I would spend one night.

The father of the family was strongly built and wore a faded New York Giants jersey; the mother was large and loving; and their skinny teenage son was aloof. I stayed in their son's room, where there was a world map from the Soviet era.

I had a quaint breakfast with the father who spoke the best English in the family. He said that he had lived in Mongolia for two years during his military service for the Soviet Union. He then told a story of how he would go fishing with his friends, and how the Mongolians were perplexed to see them do that. I pointed to the jersey he was wearing and asked if he liked American football. He gave me quizzical look. He had no idea that the jersey he was wearing—and had worn for countless years—was of a U.S. football team.

After breakfast, I spent most of the day walking up and down along the shores of Lake Baikal.

Lake Baikal

Lake Baikal is the deepest rift lake in the world.[1] It is 1,642 meters deep,[2] 636 kilometers in length, and has a width that runs anywhere between 27 to 80 kilometers. It has 23,615.39 cubic kilometers of fresh water[3] and possesses 22 percent of the world's fresh surface water.[4] There are 3,500 species of plants and animals to be found in and around the lake[5] of which 2,600 are endemic.[6]

The smell of the lake and the smooth stones that lined its sandy shores reminded me of Lake Michigan with the only difference being that the lake's water was crystal clear; I could actually see thirty meters deep into the water.

At the end of a thin strip of beach along the lake I sat and watched locals drink, suntan, and bathe in the nearly ice-cold water. The large physical size of the older Russian men and women struck me, especially after years of living in Japan, and months of traveling through Asia where most of the people were thin. Older Russian men were large and brawny while older Russian women were large and big breasted. As for the younger Russian men and women, they were thin and attractive. While sitting on the beach a drunken Russian man approached me and asked where I was from. I answered that I was from the U.S. He then said with a thick Russian accent, "Welcome! Drink Russian beer." He poured me a cup and I drank as he chugged on his bottle. He later went swimming to alleviate his inability to stand.

I walked back down along the lake to a port where I paid for a boat ride tour. I sat with an American woman who was in her sixties. She explained to me that she had lived for most of her life in different countries teaching English. She had even lived in Afghanistan for 11 years! She said she was there, "before, during, and after the Russian occupation." She was a bit too opinionated–for my tastes–as she talked about all the amazing places she had been to in Siberia and how sad it was that I had chosen not to see them.

After the boat ride, I walked back to the home of the Russian family in the rain and had a Russian feast for dinner that was complete with wonderful little pastries displayed on a small, silver platter.

Sunday, July 18, 2004

A van driver from Baikalcomplex picked me up at eleven in the morning to take me to the train station. In the van, there was a Dutch couple and an American couple from Indiana. At the train station, we dropped off our bags, but I took a taxi into town with the American couple since we had some time before the train would depart.

I spent the next few hours with the couple. They had been married for over 40 years and were nearing retirement. In their years together, they had traveled or sailed to over 100 countries. The husband was very energetic and talkative, but he would always watch over his wife. I could see that he cared deeply for her. They made my day grand. It was wonderful to see a couple so much in love and off to new adventures.

I liked Irkutsk. It was a small city that was home to the descendants of artists, academics, officers, and aristocrats that had been exiled to Siberia after the 1825 Decembrist revolt. These cultured exiles developed Irkutsk into a university town of pastel colored buildings and old wooden homes.

Posted by The Legacy Cycle at 2004-07-24T01:07:00-07:00

Saturday, July 24, 2004

Trans-Siberian Rail to Moscow

The legendary Trans-Siberian Railway (the longest running railway in the world) was the vehicle that carried me away from the East and back to the West.

I shared my train compartment with Monty and Ben, two young men approaching their mid-twenties. Monty was from New York, and he was working as a tour guide for Sundowners Overland. Ben was from Australia, and he was training under Monty to become a tour guide for the company. Monty explained to me that Sundowners Overland was an Australian travel company that took groups on exotic journeys throughout Central Asia.

It was a pleasure to spend my four-day train journey with Monty, Ben, and the people in their group. As young bachelors often do, we told stupid jokes and talked about stupid movies while playing different card games.

In one instance, two Russian girls who were probably in middle school asked to play cards with us. But we ended up playing card games that only they knew how to play. As time went on, more and more people from the Sundowners group came into our compartment trying to help us understand the rules of the game. We slowly began to realize that as soon as we had figured out the rules, the girls would change the game to another, thus leaving us with the task of trying to comprehend the rules all over again.

In a fit of frustration, I grabbed all the cards and told the girls that they had to play one of our card games. Of course, they had no idea what they hell I said since they did not speak English and we did not speak Russian. We ended up playing poker. A competitive atmosphere arose between the youngest Russian girl and I. Every time I beat her I would rub it in her face with a mean adolescent laugh. She would respond by beating my arm with her fist. At one point she turned to me, ran her index finger across her throat, and shouted, "Kaput!" Monty, Ben, and I began laughing hysterically. Of all the words she said, we definitely understood that one. Yes, she wanted me dead.

The train journey was a vacation. All I did was sleep, eat, sleep some more, read a book, sleep, talk, play cards, eat, talk, and then sleep again. But by the fourth day, I was more than eager to arrive to Moscow to stretch, walk around, and take a shower.

Moscow
Wednesday, July 21 to Saturday, July 24, 2004

A silent employee of White Nights Travel picked me up from the train station and drove me to the Izmailovo Hotel (at 5,000 rooms, it is the largest hotel in Europe, and it was the world's largest from 1980 to 1993[7]). The hotel was built to accommodate the athletes that came to compete in Moscow for the 1980 Summer Olympics (the U.S. along with 64 other nations boycotted the sporting event in protest of the 1979 Soviet-Afghan War). Just within view of the hotel was the largest urban park in the world. There were a lot of "in the world" accomplishments in Moscow. For example, the Cathedral of Christ the Saviour was built on what was once the world's largest open-air swimming pool.[8] The Rossiya Hotel, located near Red Square, was once the world's largest hotel before the Excalibur Hotel and Casino in Las Vegas took that title in 1990.

After arriving to the hotel and checking in, I decided to take it easy and relax. I went up to my room, showered, and then proceeded down to the lobby to find a place for dinner and to check my email. After that I returned to my room and went to bed.

The Moscow Metro
Thursday, July 22, 2004

I woke up at half past six, got dressed, ate an early breakfast, and went to the nearest Moscow subway station.

The Moscow Metro is a tourist destination. I could have dedicated a couple of days to just riding from one station to the next in an attempt to explore each of the 120 uniquely designed and ornate stations (as of 2018, there are "over 180 metro stations"[9]). The first stations dated back to 1935 and was dug so deep that they also served as bomb shelters during World War II.[10]

It was initially intimidating to navigate through the Moscow rapid transit system because all the signs were in Russian, but I gradually gained my bearings and had little difficulty arriving to each destination. I was able to see several subway stations beautifully designed utilizing a range of art styles to promote the ideals of Socialist realism, which, for example, utilized socialist themes such as men and women marching with firearms or tools of industry to define paintings or bronze statues. As for the subway trains, they were old and rickety, and the brass lights that lined the ceiling occasionally flickered on and off.

I was particularly impressed to see that the trains came into each station nearly every minute or two, which made this metro system more frequent that the Tokyo subway system. Some of the escalators to exit or enter the stations were old, but so fast that it made me dizzy several times.

It was nice to see the passengers on the trains reading; I had escaped the cell phone, comic book reading culture that occupied the time of subway passengers in Japan, South Korea, and China. Russians read. And at most subway station kiosks, books were sold.

Lenin

In the late morning, I saw the body of Lenin inside the mausoleum that bears his name in Red Square.

Compared with the mausoleums of Hồ Chí Minh and Mao Zedong there were few to no Russians in line to see Lenin's corpse. Most of the people in line were tourists. I waited in line for about 45 minutes while talking with a group from Mexico and two beautiful blonde university students from Switzerland.

After seeing Lenin's body, I spent the day with the two women from Switzerland who were a day away from beginning their journey to Beijing via the Trans-Mongolian Railway. We explored Red Square and the 500-year-old Saint Basil's Cathedral.

Earlier that morning, I had entered the Cathedral of Christ the Saviour and witnessed middle-aged women who had their heads covered with a shawl constantly making the sign of the cross on their forehead, chest, and right and left shoulders while bowing incessantly. I also saw two women get onto their knees and lower their heads to the ground. I wondered if the Russian Orthodox tradition of bowing the head to the ground had been influenced by any Oriental tradition.

There were no seats for devotees in the cathedral. Everyone had to stand to observe the priest sing and go through the religious rites. The priest would disappear every so often behind a wooden wall decorated with darkly painted icons of Mary and Baby Jesus.

The layout of the 16th century Saint Basil's Cathedral–and the cathedrals inside the Kremlin–did not accommodate many worshippers. There was only enough room for the priest and a few devotees in the space provided in front of the main shrine and rite area. The cathedral was a labyrinth of small chambers and rooms located between spiraling stairways and curved walls of frayed red bricks.

After Saint Basil's Cathedral, we walked through the GUM (formerly known as the State Department Store during the Soviet period), which faces Red Square. The late 19th century building was elegant and had about 150 shops, cafés, and restaurants (although "in its original form it housed more than 1,000 shops"[11]). Unable to afford anything to eat inside the GUM the two Swiss women and I went to the Alexander Garden–located along the western wall of the Kremlin–to eat a few sandwiches. The garden was full of Muscovites who were reading, taking a nap, or eating on its well-manicured lawn.

After lunch, we walked south to the State Tretyakov Gallery to see the largest collection of Russian fine art.

In the evening, I found the largest Internet café in Eastern Europe and sat down to get this blog up to date. By the time I finished, it was night and I walked around Red Square to take a few more photos.

The Moscow Kremlin
Friday, July 23, 2004

The Moscow Kremlin–the center of the Russian political universe–was exactly what the Russian word implied, a fortress. It was behind those walls that the Russian Orthodox Church had been based since 1326

AD;[12] it was beyond those walls that Joseph Stalin lived and terrorized the people of Russia; it was within those walls that Mikhail Gorbachev declared the dissolution of the Soviet Union in December 1991.

As a child who grew up during the last decade of the Cold War, I never thought that I would have been able to walk inside the walls of the Kremlin. How many British and American spies have tried to breach its walls and gain access to its strategic secrets? Inside the fortress there were four Russian Orthodox cathedrals, two churches, the Kremlin Senate (where the President of the Russian Federation resides), the Kremlin Palace of Congresses, the 15th century Palace of the Facets (a building that contained the formal reception hall of the Tsars), the Kremlin Arsenal, and the Kremlin Armory. Lined up along the south wall of the Arsenal building were over 800 cannons that had been captured from Napoleon's retreating Great Army in 1812. I also saw the cracked, six-meter-tall Tsar Bell (the largest bell in the world); it weighed approximately 202 tons and was cast in the 1730s, but was never rung.[13]

Open Bottles of Beer all over the Place

Whether it was on the shores of Lake Baikal, the streets of Moscow, or in the subway, Russian men and women always seemed to have an open bottle of beer in their hand (even when reading a book). Every kiosk in this country had windows that were covered from top to bottom with an extensive selection of beer. I had thought that Russia was a paradise for vodka lovers. No, it seemed to be a paradise for beer aficionados.

So, if you are a beer devotee, and enjoy drinking in public, then the Russian Federation is where you need to spend your next holiday.

Afterthoughts on Moscow

I wish I had more time to explore Moscow. I was initially afraid to come to this city. I had heard stories from travelers of Russian organized crime groups and corrupt policemen harassing tourists to gain access to their wallets. But that was not the case for me, luckily. Moscow was a marvelous, cosmopolitan city of gourmet cafés and restaurants with streets lined with designer clothing shops and parked exotic cars.

Muscovites were pleasant, warm, to the point (they said nothing more than what needed to be said), and proud of their long and trying history.

I know that I will return to Moscow. And if I could ever afford to do so, I would like to buy a small flat in the heart of the city.

Posted by The Legacy Cycle at 2004-07-24T03:01:00-07:00

ESTONIA

Monday, July 26, 2004

"Rääkimine hõbe, vaikimine kuld"
Sunday, July 25 to Monday, July 26, 2004

"**R**ääkimine hõbe, vaikimine kuld," is an old Estonian saying that translates to "speaking silver, silence gold." It is an appropriate proverb to describe the capital of Tallinn and its people. The city has a population of nearly 400,000, but walk through its cobblestone streets and it feels like a quiet town of 30,000. The fortified Old Town of the city is a UNESCO World Heritage Site, which boasts 13th century medieval architecture, orthodox churches, and a 1.9-kilometer-long defensive wall.

I spent two days in the city, but I was able to see most of the Old Town in an afternoon. The Old Town was quaint, quiet, and full of boutique shops, restaurants, and cafés with wooden decks full of tables, chairs, and people sitting, talking, eating, and drinking. There were young Estonian women every few blocks holding postcards and calling out, "Estonia's best post cards!" to break the silence of the town.

It is said that the people of Estonia like their neighbors to be no closer than a kilometer away. I believe it. Tallinn was nearly a ghost town. If it had not been for the tourists that paraded on the streets near Raekoja plats (the plaza where stands the only surviving 14th century gothic town hall in Northern Europe), I would have believed that the capital had been abandoned. Most Estonians flock to their summer cottages in July and August to get away from the tourists that invade their city.

I walked south of the limestone hill of Toompea and the Toompea Castle into an area that felt like a secluded and soundless northern suburb of Chicago.

Tallinn was charming, safe, and—as I mentioned—quiet. Tomorrow I leave for Helsinki, Finland, by way of a three-hour boat ride across the Gulf of Finland.

The Ethnic Groups of Estonia

According to Estonia's 2000 census, the population is 68 percent Estonian, 26 percent Russian, and about 3 percent Ukrainian and Belarusian.[1] When Estonia joined the European Union in May of 2004 a large percentage of the Russians residing in the country were rendered stateless. The "long and difficult" naturalization process requires that any resident seeking Estonian citizenship to pass a language exam.[2] Due to the exam, many Russians have not been able to claim Estonian citizenship or refused to do so to avoid conscription into the Estonian army or out of loyalty to their culture, language, and homeland.[3]

And now that Estonia is part of the EU, these Russians continue to have no citizenship: they are not legally recognized as Russian or Estonian citizens. They are unable to "vote in national elections or stand for a seat in Parliament."[4] Although they can vote in local elections they "cannot be members of a political party or work in public offices and in some other positions."[5] In addition, "for many jobs, including the private sector, the law requires fluency in Estonian, via a certificate of language proficiency, shrinking further the number of jobs noncitizens can apply for."[6]

Ultimately, what will become of these stateless Russians living in Estonia? Younger generations not living within isolated Russian towns near the border will integrate and learn the Estonian language, but older generations may resist out of a patriotic loyalty for their Russian heritage or simply not feel the need.

Posted by The Legacy Cycle at 2004-07-26T10:43:00-07:00

SUOMI

Thursday, July 29, 2004

Helsinki, Finland = Utopia?
Tuesday, July 27 to Thursday, July 29, 2004

The ferry ship to Helsinki from Tallinn went without incident. Up on deck I fell asleep on a bench to soothing Baltic winds and the sight of a seagull hovering over the sea.

I woke up about an hour later and stayed on deck although the temperature began to drop. As the ferry neared the Finnish capital, I saw a few rocky islands covered with vibrant green grass and deciduous and coniferous trees. More and more islands appeared; one island in particular had a series of white industrial cylindrical structures. The ferry soon entered Eteläsatama (South Harbor), the largest passenger harbor in the country.

I disembarked, walked two blocks from the harbor, and checked into the Eurohostel, which turned out to be one of the best hostels I had ever stayed in. The hostel reflected the country. It was extremely clean and organized. Every morning the hostel restaurant provided a buffet style breakfast of healthy foods with a staff that seemed dressed more for a four-star restaurant than for a hostel. The personnel at the reception desk were always happy and eager to help. The hostel's laundry machines actually cleaned and dried my clothing (as opposed to other laundry machines I had used throughout my trip that did not wash and dry). There was a communal sauna room and spotless dormitory style showers and toilets. The rooms were plain, but they were immaculate and had lockable closets. The hallways looked like the corridors of a naval ship.

After locking up my bag and washing up, I ventured out to explore Helsinki. The first thing to strike me was how clean and pristine the city appeared. There was no garbage littering the sidewalks and roads. I assumed that the people of Finland had been well trained to dispose of their rubbish in the public garbage bins. But I could only find one garbage bin or two in the entire capital. How did this city stay so clean?

I found the people to be very well educated, pleasant, and quiet. They rarely spoke out loud and they were all able to speak in perfect English.

The city reminded me of Boston on a smaller scale. I was able to walk around most of the city in about two-and-a-half hours. There was no shortage of public and private transportation systems. There were green trams similar to Boston's Green Line, a subway system, and plenty of taxis. As I traversed the city it seemed that there were public buses and trolleys along every street, and entrances to subways at every corner. I felt that for a city where most locations were within walking distance there was an excessive supply of public transport systems. Perhaps for a country that is continually ranked as one of the least corrupt in the world[1] the result is excess provision of public transport services. Now, who would not mind living in a country like that?

Is Helsinki a living model of a social, economic, and political Utopia? It was a perfect city of beautiful, centuries-old buildings, and cobblestone streets with hidden public speakers playing the soft sounds of birds chirping.

All the shops, movie theaters, museums, streets, and markets that I saw were impeccable in appearance; the people of Finland rival the Japanese in their cleanliness.

There was a pristine esplanade that reminded me of the Boston Common between the streets Pohjoisesplanadi and Eteläesplanadi where I heard the soothing sounds of classical music played by young men and women on violins, cellos, acoustic guitars, and a marimba. I sat down at one of the cafés along the esplanade to sip from a cup of gourmet coffee while listening to sweet, hypnotic melodies.

I walked northwest from Kaivopuisto Park and found a residential area that reminded me of Beacon Hill in Boston.

Senaatintori (Senate Square) was where I saw the Government Palace, the building that housed the largest gathering of least corrupt politicians.

SpåraKoff: the pub tram

Riding along the tram tracks of Helsinki was the SpåraKoff, a red tram that had been converted to serve as a moving bar and restaurant! Passengers could travel to work or home drinking their favorite brew. It is the only tram in the world to offer such a service. This leads me to the only nuisance I discovered in Helsinki: the occasional drunken man.

Finland vs. Russia

It is a political and geographic joke that Finland (ranked in the Corruption Perceptions Index as one of the least corrupt countries in the world) is located in the northwest corner of the Russian Federation (one of the most corrupt nations in the world).

I shared my room at the hostel with a twenty-something American from California who was living in St. Petersburg; he was in Helsinki on a visa run. His wife, who he met in college, was Russian.

He explained to me that Russia was an extremely corrupt country. Obtaining a visa was an example of that corruption. It was a hassle to acquire a Russian visa through the government, thus the easiest and fastest means to procure one was through a Russian travel agency. He said that most of these travel agencies were owned and run by ex-Russian police officers that had easy political access to getting a visa. When would the bureaucracy to attain a Russian visa without the use of a travel agent end? According to my roommate, as long as there were ex-cops extracting cash by supplying visas faster than the Russian embassies and consulates there would continue to be a corrupt system.

Oligarchs

The Soviet Union ended on December 25, 1991. In its wake, the Russian Federation and its president, Boris Yeltsin, arose. The 1990s was marked by a dangerous race between the communists seeking to regain political control of the nation and the aggressive market liberalization reform movement pushed by Yeltsin, Anatoly Chubais, Yegor Gaidar, the Russian oligarchs (the business elite that used their political influence to accumulate tremendous wealth via the privatization of firms and state assets in the 1990s), the U.S. Treasury, the International Monetary Fund (IMF), the World Bank, Jeffrey Sachs, and the Clinton administration.

In 1992, "the Russian government issued vouchers to every Russian citizen" as part of its privatization program.[2] Russians could then "acquire shares in specific companies (or the company in which they worked), exchange them for shares in mutual funds, or sell them."[3] Markets soon formed for the buying and selling of these vouchers. Unfortunately, the majority of "Russians did not easily grasp the true significance and potential of stockholding."[4] Thus "in the hungry months that followed price liberalization," (rising unemployment, rapidly falling GDP, rising suicide rates, and hyperinflation) "many found no better use for the vouchers than to sell them."[5] Ultimately, vouchers provided to approximately 144 million Russians[6] "converged into the hands of the few, who ended up owning considerable shares of privatized enterprises" creating an elite new class of savvy businessmen known as the Russian oligarchs.[7]

As wealth concentrated within the hands of the oligarchs, "public disapproval deepened"[8] for Yeltsin's privatization program, and by the 1995 Russian legislative elections it appeared that the Communists had made a comeback by gaining 139 out of 450 total seats. In addition, Yeltsin's popularity dropped to "5 percent by early 1996."[9] For the oligarchs, this political resurgence of the Communist Party of the Russian Federation meant a likely loss of their newly gained wealth as the privatized firms they owned through their shareholdings would be nationalized. What to do? A deal, known as the loans for shares scheme, was struck between Yeltsin and the oligarchs in which the oligarchs would provide loans to Yeltsin's administration and 1996 presidential election campaign in return for shares in state-owned natural monopolies.[10] Yeltsin won the election gaining 54.4 percent of the votes. Soon after, Yeltsin fulfilled his promise and began selling off–at rock-bottom prices–government assets to the oligarchs. One example was the sale of "Norilsk Nickel–losing money but with annual revenues of $1.5 billion–for $180 million" to Vladimir Potanin;[11] a man who essentially became a billionaire overnight.

The political uncertainty of the 1995 and 1996 elections resulted in the oligarchs taking their money out of the country and investing it abroad, which negatively impacted Russia's balance of payments where outflows of financial capital exceeded inflows.[12,13,14] This in turn, along with falling GDP and oil prices, and unsustainable government deficits (the government spending more than what it collected in taxes), placed tremendous downward pressure on the Russian currency.[15] To support the rubles peg to the dollar, the Central Bank of the Russian Federation "used its foreign exchange reserves to buy" the excess supply of rubles in the foreign exchange markets.[16] Investors and "speculators could see how much in the way of reserves was left, and as reserves dwindled, betting on a devaluation became increasingly a one-way bet."[17] In response, "the IMF approved an $11.2 billion loan"[18] on July 20, 1998 to assist the central bank of Russia to maintain their overvalued currency; a loan that required Russia to borrow "more in foreign currency and less in rubles."[19] In addition, "the World Bank was asked to provide a $6 billion loan."[20]

> According to Nobel Prize winning economist Joseph Stiglitz who was Chief Economist at the World Bank at the time: "Many thought that the IMF was making it easier for the government to put off meaningful reforms, such as collecting taxes from the oil companies. The evidence of corruption in Russia was clear. The Bank's own study of corruption had identified that region as among the most corrupt in the world. The West knew that most of those billions would be diverted from their intended purposes to the families and associates of corrupt officials and their oligarch friends …[21]

> "In spite of strong opposition from its own staff, the Bank was under enormous political pressure from the

Clinton administration to lend money to Russia."[22]

Not surprisingly–other than the speed to which it occurred–to economists at the World Bank, "three weeks after the loan was made, Russia announced a unilateral suspension of payments and a devaluation of the ruble."[23] As a result, by January 1999, the ruble "declined in real effective terms by more than 75 percent from its July 1998 level."[24] The devaluation of the ruble, the Russian government defaulting on its expanding debt (nine percent of GDP),[25] and the spillover effects of the 1997 Asian financial crisis led to the 1998 Russian financial crisis. Keep in mind that an objective of the loan was to sustain the overvalued Russian ruble. How is it then that weeks after a multi-billion-dollar injection to the central bank the ruble crashed? The answer, the oligarchs bled "the money out of the country" leaving Russian citizens to pay off the rising public debt derived from IMF and World Bank billion-dollar loans denominated in foreign currencies.[26] Essentially, "the billions of dollars that it [the IMF] had given (loaned) Russia was showing up in Cypriot and Swiss bank accounts just days after the loan was made".[27] The oligarchs stole government funds and loans while struggling Russian citizens were left to foot the bill. Thus, I cringe to see reminders of this stolen wealth when I see European fans sporting Chelsea football jerseys. Russian oligarch Roman Abramovich was able to buy the Chelsea Football Club in large part to the billions he stole from the Russian people during this period.

This dog-eat-dog economic game widened the gap between the rich and poor.[28] Many of the newly impoverished were nearly retired to retired elderly who possessed obsolete skills who then–in a desperate effort to revitalize their dreams of what could have been–poured whatever savings they had left into slot machines, gambling dens, or bars where they drank away their sorrows. It was not uncommon for me to see on the streets of Moscow old women trying to sell trinkets to make ends meet.

> Joseph Stiglitz explains in his book, *Globalization and its Discontents*: "While the size of the national economic pie was shrinking, it was being divided up more and more inequitably so the average Russian was getting a smaller and smaller slice. In 1989, only 2 percent of those living

in Russia were in poverty. By late 1998, that number had soared to 23.8 percent, using the $2 a day standard. More than 40 percent of the country had less than $4 a day, according to a survey conducted at the World Bank. The statistics for children revealed an even deeper problem, with more than 50 percent living in families in poverty."[29]

Fire & Ice

I did not have the chance to go for a drink at the Arctic Icebar where the temperature was -5°C (cold enough to keep the ice walls, tables, and bar from melting). Instead, I experienced a Finnish sauna on two occasions at my hostel. I also learned that most apartment buildings in Finland have at least one communal sauna.

Tonight, I take a 16-hour ferry to Stockholm, Sweden.

Posted by The Legacy Cycle at 2004-07-26T10:43:00-07:00

THE OPEN-MINDEDNESS OF THE SWEDES

Monday, August 2, 2004

Stockholm, Sweden
Friday, July 30 to Monday, August 2, 2004

It is said that the Swedes are the most open-minded people on the planet. And after spending a few days in Sweden, I would have to agree. There was a dramatic difference between the ethnic makeup of the population of Stockholm versus Helsinki. The people of Helsinki were homogeneous (about 93.4 percent of the Finnish population is Finnish followed by 5.6 percent Swedes), but in Stockholm I saw a cosmopolitan mix of Swedes, Indians, North Africans, Africans, Southwest Asians, and Chinese. For example, when I explored the Royal Palace in Stockholm one of the royal guards that I saw dressed in a gleaming blue uniform was Chinese. Although the sight was something unexpected for me, it was not for the Swedes and their open-door policy toward immigrants.

Sweden is a country where binational marriages are increasing[2] and where under 20 percent of the population was born abroad.[3] I strolled the streets of Gamla Stan, the Old Town, and saw a group of Chinese, Indian, Thai, and Swedish girls who were speaking and giggling with each other in Swedish.

The nearly half a million foreign nationals among Sweden's

population of 8.4 million,[4] and 15 percent of Greater Stockholm's 2 million residents, are foreign-born.[5] But there is segregation in Stockholm. I traveled to the outer fringes of the city and saw ghetto-like neighborhoods.

As I had mentioned, the population of Helsinki was homogeneous. And it may lead one to think that a homogeneous population may lean more toward racism. I did see one young man in Helsinki wearing a T-shirt that read: "Thank God I was born White." And the only country I had ever experienced racism was in Japan, a country with an extremely homogeneous population. But I do not want to rush toward unfair judgments about Finland as a whole. On the ferry ship to Stockholm I met a 19-year-old Finnish man by the name of Lauri. He had just begun his backpack trip through Europe. He was very eager to see and learn all that he could about the nations that he would be visiting. And he exuded this excitement by jumping on any opportunity to speak and practice the many languages he had been studying. In the time that I spent with him walking through the streets of Stockholm I heard him speak Spanish, Italian, Swedish, English, and his native Finnish. He spoke five languages! And he had studied the modern history of most European countries; he explained to me in incredible detail the history of Finland and Sweden and their political relationships with Russia and Germany.

"Welcome to Sweden!"

I approached a vendor who had a hot dog cart in a park near the Vasa Museum. He took my order in Swedish, but when he realized that I did not understand him he switched to English. After I paid and took my food he asked me: "Where are you from?"

I answered, "The U.S."

He replied: "Welcome–welcome! U.S.A. Welcome. Welcome to Sweden."

"Where are you from?"

"Iraq," he said with pride.

My eyes widened. I was surprised that he was happy to see me, an American. He explained that he was pleased that the U.S. overthrew

Saddam Hussein. I told him that I did not like George W. Bush. But he did not care. He liked Bush. He said that his parents and extended family were still living in Baghdad. When I was about to leave he took my hand, shook it, and said again: "Welcome, welcome to Sweden!"

I felt good after that. As an American traveler, I had been constantly met with the resentment that people had for the country of my birth. But here was an example of someone praising the military deeds of my nation. Deeds that I did not support.

The Rainbow Flag

The flagpoles that lined the eastern entrance of the Royal Palace had several rainbow flags waving with the winds in support of the Stockholm Pride festival that was held yesterday.

And throughout the city I saw many restaurants and cafés that catered specifically to the LGBT community; another reminder of Sweden's progressive open-mindedness.

The City of Peace

The Nobel Banquet (the annual banquet held after the Nobel Prize ceremony) is held at the Stadshuset (Stockholm City Hall), a fortress-like brick building designed in the national romantic style with a prominent tower that provides a panoramic view of Stockholm from its summit.

Stockholm was one of the most beautiful national capitals I had visited on this journey, which, coupled with its tradition of tolerance, made it a utopia in my eyes.

The Swedish Tradition of Travel

During my journey through Southeast Asia and East Asia I had met a large number of Swedish travelers. Whether I was in Malaysia, Thailand, Cambodia, Vietnam, Myanmar, China, or Mongolia, I kept running into Swedes. Sweden only has a population of just over eight million. It was remarkable that for such a small population there were so many Swedes exploring the globe.

Vasamuseet

The Vasamuseet (Vasa Museum) was a spectacular maritime museum dedicated to the nearly intact 17th century ship that sank on her maiden voyage in 1628 during the Thirty Years' War. The ship was to join the Baltic fleet of Swedish King Gustavus Adolphus to secure seaports along the coastline of Poland.

Due to the abundance of freshwater that drains from the surrounding coastlines into the Baltic Sea its salinity is significantly lower than that of other oceans and seas. This condition—along with the fact that the water of Stockholm's ström was toxic until the late 20th century—did not provide a suitable environment for shipworm and microorganisms to thrive and break down the wooden vessel. As a result, the *Vasa* ship was very well preserved considering that it had been beneath the sea for over 300 years.

In 1956 Anders Frazén, an amateur archaeologist, presented evidence of the location of the *Vasa* ship. Soon after work was under way to excavate and raise the vessel to the surface. In 1961 the ship was raised and stored in a temporary warehouse where archaeologists worked to conserve the structural integrity of the ship while also excavating it to uncover a wide variety of archeological treasures: clothing and shoes of sailors, one of the sails, spoons, forks, plates, pitchers, tool boxes, coins, cannons, and so on.

Catching Up with Old Friends

I took a one-hour bus ride on the first day of August to the college town of Uppsala to meet Frederick, Malin, and Marcus; three Swedish friends that I had met in Vietnam.

They picked me up from the bus station and explained that Uppsala University (founded in 1477 AD) was the oldest university of the Nordic nations, and that the late 13th century Uppsala Cathedral was also the tallest church of the Nordic countries. They took me into the cathedral and showed me the final resting place of Swedish monarch Gustav Vasa and his three wives.

As we explored the town, the three of them detailed their plans for the future: Malin would be going to Great Britain to pursue her studies in film and television; Frederick would begin his first year at Uppsala University; and Marcus was going back to work for the Carlsberg brewing company.

They later drove me four kilometers north to Gamla Uppsala to see the three "royal mounds" where—according to legend—the gods Thor, Freyr, and Odin were buried; the mounds reminded me of the royal burial mounds that I had seen in Gyeongju, South Korea. They then took me to see a 12th century church that served as the office of the archbishop until 1273 AD.

Posted by The Legacy Cycle at 2004-08-02T10:43:00-07:00

OSLO, NORWAY

Wednesday, August 4, 2004

Land of Vikings & The Unaffordable Sandwich
Tuesday, August 3 to Wednesday, August 4, 2004

I arrived to the Oslo Bus Terminal at about six in the morning with an aching neck and back caused by sleeping on a stiff bus seat. After getting off the bus and putting on my backpack, I walked seven minutes to the Albertine Hostel, but when I arrived the staff informed me that I could not check in until three in the afternoon. I had a tremendous amount of time to kill. I threw my bag into the baggage room of the hostel, washed up, and left in search of breakfast.

At this point in the journey, I was very tired and simply in need of a place to stay with no want to explore another city. I had burnt out. I was now looking forward to going to Hamburg where I could to stay with my uncle Joachim and his family to relax, recover, and prepare for further travels.

In that state of mind, I walked through the center of Oslo content to see that it was a small city. From the Oslo Cathedral, I walked west until I found a café that was open at half past seven. I bought a sandwich, a carton of milk, and sat down. When I finished my sandwich, I read a book.

Since I had a lot of time before I could check into the hostel and take a needed shower I decided to explore Oslo. I left the café and walked west to the Royal Palace, which was located at the top of a hill. There was a delightful park around the palace where I took a stroll.

I later made my way to the bay where I explored the Akershus Fortress. The fortress was not impressive from within, but it provided a view of the Oslo skyline. There were two museums inside the fortress; I decided to check out the Norway's Resistance Museum, which chronicled the resistance movement against the Nazi occupation of the country during the Second World War. The museum was disappointing. The dioramas appeared to have been made by elementary students and I learned more from overhearing an American talk to his friends about the stories he had heard from his Norwegian father about his involvement with the resistance movement than from the museum itself.

From the fortress, I walked past the Oslo City Hall and continued walking until I could finally check into the hostel. At three o'clock I checked in, took a shower, and fell asleep. I did not wake up until the hostel fire alarm went off at three or four in the morning (I had slept for 12 hours straight). When I woke up I found that there was a German traveler in my dorm room. Together we exited the hostel and waited with everyone else for the police and fire department to arrive. The fire alarm was a false one and we all returned to our rooms. Soon after, three young Italian men entered the room and we chatted a bit about Oslo. I then went back to sleep.

On Wednesday, August 4, I visited the National Gallery to see the famous Edvard Munch painting, *The Scream* (less than three weeks later on August 22, 2004 the painting was stolen by two masked men), as well as works by Claude Monet, Pablo Picasso, and self-portraits by Vincent van Gogh. After the gallery, I walked to a pier near Oslo City Hall and took a seven-minute boat cruise to the Bygdøy peninsula to visit the Viking Ship Museum.

Vikingskipshuset på Bygdøy

The museum has three original 9th century Viking ships in its collection: Oseberg, Gokstad, and Tune. The three ships were excavated from large burial mounds in three different locations between 1867 and 1904. Archaeologists found a woman and her slave (a girl) buried in the Oseberg ship whereas in the other two ships they found men. During the Viking Age from 800 to 1050 AD it was customary to bury the dead in boats.

The following are notes I took from the exhibits of the museum.

> The dead were buried in a burial chamber in the stern of the ship. Bodies were buried with a supply of food, drink, horses, dogs, and useful and decorative objects.
>
> When the ships were excavated it was discovered that they were robbed of their precious items. Regardless, an array of fantastic finds was found. Clothes and objects made of wood were found preserved. This was in part due to the fact that the ships were buried in blue clay and covered with stones, clay, and turf.
>
> The Vikings came from Norway, Sweden, and Denmark and they traded furs, bird down, walrus ivory to their European counterparts as well as iron that was produced in Norwegian mountain hamlets.
>
> Vikings usually took to the seas to trade and settle new lands.
>
> Vikings, as merchants, sold goods in towns and marketplaces and established trading colonies in Ireland and Russia and settled Iceland and Greenland, and were the first Europeans to reach North America. They sailed the coasts of Europe into the Mediterranean, the rivers of Russia into the Black and Caspian Sea.
>
> During the Viking Age, Norway consisted of smaller chiefdoms, later it was unified under a single king.

Viking Class Structure

The ships found in the museum were for the upper class. Yeoman farmers formed the backbone of society, and they were free men who held the right to bear arms. Slaves were the lowest class; they were the property of owners, held no legal rights, and were usually foreigners who had been taken prisoner on a raid.

Norsemen plundered churches, monasteries, and towns.

Viking Ship Building & Long Sea Journeys

Viking shipwrights did not use plans or drawings; all measurements were taken by eye … Sails were made of woolen cloth.

The crew of a Viking ship had to row and bail, operate sails, rigging and steer the ship. Conditions on the ship were not pleasant for there was no shelter from the cold and rains. There is no evidence that food was ever cooked on board and so while at sea it is believed that they ate dried foods and drank water. They often sailed in coastal waters during the day and then parked their ship upon a beach to sleep on land by night.

With the single square sail of the ship they could sail with and against the wind … and could hit speeds of 12 knots (24 km/hr).

The Vikings did not use maps or compasses. They used coastal waters and man-made landmarks to navigate … and in foreign lands they found new signs and landmarks … and in the open sea they navigated to wave patterns and the prevailing winds. Logic told them that the mid-day sun shown in the south and that sea birds were a sign for land.

The Norwegian Subway

The Nordic nations have a reputation among travelers for being expensive. I agree. And I found Oslo to be the most expensive city in Scandinavia. For example, I spent over US$10 on a foot-long Subway sandwich that did not come with a drink or a cookie. I found myself hesitant to buy anything in Norway and eager to cross the border.

But I would like to return to Scandinavia and spend a month or two camping, hiking, and bicycling through the mountains of Norway and the unspoiled forests of northern Finland. But that would all depend on my ability to afford such a luxury.

Posted by The Legacy Cycle at 2004-08-04T10:43:00-07:00

COPENHAGEN, DENMARK

Monday, August 9, 2004

Thursday, August 5 to Saturday, August 7, 2004

I am now in the home of my uncle Joachim in Hamburg, Germany. Here I have found a warm and pleasant place to rest and prepare for a couple more months of travel; and most importantly I have given my weather-beaten backpack a good scrub down and wash.

Instead of describing this city I will simply post on this blog photos that I took in Copenhagen.

Posted by The Legacy Cycle at 2004-08-09T05:28:00-07:00

Photos can now be viewed via Instagram @thelegacycycle

BERLIN, GERMANY

Friday, August 13, 2004

My state of mind has changed during this leg of the journey. Asia still lingers in my thoughts. But I am now here in Europe traveling through the land of my ancestors.

There is a lot that is going through my head now: thoughts of the past, the present, and the future, thoughts of life and death, and thoughts of love and solitude.

These feelings need an outlet. And so, from this point forth, until I return to my home in the land beyond the Pillars of Hercules, I will share with you a story that I had been working on while traveling. A story playing on the theme of loneliness with an element of mystery, magic, and hope.

I hope you will enjoy the story as much as I have enjoyed writing it. I will post this story entitled, *The Astor House of Old Shanghai*, in the next day or two (please note that this steampunk short story begins on page 301 of this travel book).

Posted by The Legacy Cycle at 2004-08-13T13:17:00-07:00

A NOTE FROM BRATISLAVA, SLOVAKIA

Sunday, August 22, 2004

I have a lot to catch up on with this blog. I have been to Hamburg and Berlin as well as to Warsaw and Krakow, Poland. I am now in Bratislava, Slovakia. I have been taking a break from the Internet, but I will return with tales from this part of the journey. As to where I am going, here is my planned itinerary:

>Vienna, Austria
>
>Budapest, Hungary
>
>Belgrade, Serbia
>
>Transylvania and Bucharest, Romania
>
>Sofia, Bulgaria
>
>Skopje, Macedonia
>
>Tirana, Albania
>
>Sarajevo, Bosnia
>
>Zagreb, Croatia
>
>Ljubljana, Slovenia
>
>Vaduz, Liechtenstein
>
>Switzerland
>
>Lyon and Marseille, France

Tunis, Tunisia
Sicily
Sardinia
Barcelona, Spain

It will be in Spain that this journey will end. And it will be in Barcelona where I will find home again.

With Love,
Domenico

Posted by The Legacy Cycle at 2004-08-22T13:17:00-07:00

THE ART OF BURNING OUT & FINDING SALVATION IN BARCELONA

Friday, September 3, 2004

I was in Belgrade, Serbia last week and it was there that I realized that I was completely burnt out on backpack travel. I decided to go to Barcelona to decompress, rest, and stay in one place for a while.

And that is where I am now. I just moved into an apartment in Plaça Reial; I'm renting a room and living with university students from Italy and Argentina. I will return to the United States sometime in November.

In the meantime, I will be in my cocoon preparing for my return to the U.S. by working again on my first book, *Dark Legacy: Book I – Trinity*.

Until next time,
Domenico

P.S. In regards to the salvation aspect of arriving to Barcelona, well, yes, I have found it. To elaborate on that I will not. Some sacred treasures are meant to be kept hidden ... like an enchanted temple deep within a lush jungle.

Posted by The Legacy Cycle at 2004-09-03T05:46:00-07:00

CATALUNYA

Wednesday, July 19, 2006

I have not updated this blog for two years. I am near the end of completing the final draft of my first science fiction and fantasy novel, *Dark Legacy: Book I – Trinity*.

I have begun to think more about of the story and details that will comprise *Book II – Travels* of the series. My 2004 journey from Japan to South Korea, and through Southeast Asia, China, Mongolia, Siberia, Scandinavia, and Eastern and Western Europe will find their way into the storyline for *Book II*. I will revisit and take what I have written during my travels and perhaps prepare it for publication.

That aside, I am content. When I was a boy I dreamed of embarking on a great adventure in search of fortune or love. I embarked on that adventure back in 2004. And yes, along that road I did find a great love. We were married on midsummer of this year. But that is another story.

With Love from Barcelona,

Domenico Italo Composto-Hart

Posted by The Legacy Cycle at 2004-07-19T01:21:00-07:00

WHITE LION RISING

DOMENICO ITALO COMPOSTO-HART

CHAPTER I

He hit seventh gear and rapidly approached the motorcycle's maximum speed of three hundred and thirty-nine kilometers per hour.

"White Lion Two-Six, keep it steady," Junichi cautioned Lleónart through his helmet's radio receiver. "Túnel de Vallvidrera in twenty-five seconds. Target is now headed toward the old Agbar Tower—take Diputacío—arrival time in five point forty-two minutes."

Lleónart checked the speed, rpm, and fuel holographic digital gauges that appeared at the base of his tinted helmet's visor. He wanted to see the GPS map displaying his location and the location of the target. Instantly, the digital gauges were minimized on his visor's screen and a real-time satellite map maximized before his hazel eyes. He analyzed the pulsating red line that charted the path to the shattered tower trying to discern an alternate route other than the one chosen by the NAV.

"Don't waste your time," Junichi, the chief navigation engineer, said with irritation. "Always second guessing the machine. Have some faith in the damn thing."

"Only in me," Lleó replied as he leaned the bike through a smooth corner on the dark, desolate toll-way. "Machines are predictable—"

"Not when they're manned by pilots—" Junichi corrected.

"Suspend unnecessary talk," Xavi, commander of the operation, demanded of Junichi and Lleó. "Keep this channel clean. We're picking up drone chatter."

Lleónart saw the Túnel de Vallvidrera come into view through the night-vision setting of his visor and tucked his elbows, knees, and body into the bike to reduce unnecessary wind friction and maximize speed. He minimized the GPS map on the screen with a thought and pulled up the destination counter seeing the numbers descend from five, four, three, two, one; he was now in the absolute dark of the tunnel traveling at three hundred and thirty-nine kilometers per hour.

In the quiet of the long tunnel, where he was out of radio contact, his mind thought of the incident that brought him to the center of the covert putsch planned by his neo-renaissance patron, Takagawasan.

* * *

Lleónart kicked the bike up from fourth, to fifth, to sixth gear on the straightaway after the ninth corner hitting two hundred and seventy-two kilometers per hour before briskly shifting down to brake into corner ten.

"Brake deeper into corner ten," Xavi, the CX GP Motorcycle team crew chief, urged in Catalan with his deep, raspy voice. "Damn it–brake deep!" Xavi shouted as Lleó hit the first and then the second apex on the corner. "Son of a bitch, in-and-out. Keep it wide. Good–that's it!" he nervously scratched the mole beneath his brown, right eye and then rubbed his dry, rough fingers against the facial stubble along his right cheek. "You know what to do on eleven–and in-and-out on corners twelve-thirteen." His eyes squinted at the center screen that was suspended above him at the entrance to the team's pit-box and watched the aerial images of the riders approaching the next corner.

Lleó passed corners eleven, twelve, and thirteen and gear shifted up from third, to fourth, to fifth, and back again to fourth, and third gear reducing speed to one hundred and seventy-one kilometers per hour on the nearly right-angle curve of corner fourteen. At corner fifteen he down shifted to second gear and then up to third and fourth gear punching the bike up to two hundred and twelve kilometers on corner sixteen.

Now on the front straightaway he shifted up to sixth gear. He spotted his team's digital signboard reading "+0" and "1" and sped through the Grid at seventh gear reaching three hundred and nineteen kilometers per hour seeing–in an instant–out of the corner of his right eye–his pit-box where members of his team were either analyzing the lap times, corner speeds, engine temperature, rpm, and gear position data streaming from his bike's computer to the screens that hung above the entrance to the garage or watching live video feed of the MotoGP World Championship Montmeló Circuit race. "He's still on my ass."

"Two laps to go," Xavi informed. "This is it—moment of truth." He adjusted his noise canceling, dual-muff radio headset.

A sudden rush of anxiety overcame Lleó at the prospect of being minutes away from winning the championship and claiming the first victory for the Federation of Catalan City-States on the twenty-fifth year anniversary of their independence and the twenty-year anniversary of the completion of the Sagrada Família basilica.

"Your heart rate is climbing, Lleó. Stay focused," Xavi said. "Race what's in front of you—forget the Terracotta Kid."

Lleó shifted down to fourth and then third gear and sped through the chicane of corners one and two at a speed of one hundred and eighty-eight kilometers before shifting up to fifth gear reaching two hundred and thirty-five kilometers per hour for corner five.

"That's it, keep it wide," Xavi commented.

"He's not taking the bait," Lleó expressed referring to the Chinese pilot directly behind him.

"And he won't. He's going to use your tail wind for this lap. He's going to make you do all the work."

"Shit!"

"Focus," he instructed in Catalan. "It's all you now."

Now headed toward corner four he down shifted from sixth to third gear seeing on his visor the G-force holographic gauge reading -2.2 as he hit one hundred and fifty kilometers per hour.

"You need to carry better corner speed. You must hit two-five-nine," Xavi stressed as he scratched the mole beneath his eye again. "Take it down from fourth to second gear on five and keep it wide."

Lleó ran through corners six, seven, and eight and took the bike up to fifth gear on the straightaway leading to corner nine. His speed gauge read 246 km/h before immediately descending down to 230 km/h and then up again on the next straightaway to 272 km/h.

"Find your marker and break deep on corner ten—don't let this son of a bitch pass you now." His hands tensed into fists.

He shifted down to seventy-four kilometers per hour as soon as he passed the red and white lined curbstones on the inside of the track that served as his braking marker, but the Terracotta Kid quickly overtook him on the outside and slid into the inside position, cutting him off, and forcing him to brake further.

"Shit!" Lleó exclaimed, "god damn it—"

"Shut it," Xavi interjected as he pressed the earmuffs of his radio headset to his head. "Focus and catch that Xi'an Real Madrid supporter."

He shifted up riding right up against the Terracotta Kid's red and yellow bike on corners eleven, twelve, and thirteen desperately seeking to drive in on the inside and pass him, but on all three corners he was shut out.

On the short straightaway between corners thirteen and fourteen he gear shifted up from third, to fourth, to fifth, and back down again to fourth and third gear hitting one hundred and seventy-two kilometers per hour on the sharp curve of corner fourteen; he rode his front tire right up to the Terracotta Kid's rear hard compound tire. At corner fifteen he down shifted and then shifted up to fourth gear punching the bike up to two hundred and twelve kilometers per hour on corner sixteen. Now on the front straightaway he shifted rapidly up to sixth gear trying desperately to close the gap between him and his opponent.

"Last lap, Lleó. Remember—only fourteen on this one," Xavi said with unease.

"Got it," Lleó replied as he took in a short, deep breath to center himself mentally for a fourteen corners lap as he passed rapidly through the Grid and the Main Grandstand.

Entering into the speed trap of the straightaway in seventh gear at three hundred and twenty-two kilometers per hour, Lleó slowed down as he rode near the red and white lined curbstones on the left side of the track directly behind the Terracotta Kid who began moving toward the inside of the track to shut him out of the first corner.

The Chinese pilot maintained his lead into corner two by continuing to ride on the inside of the track.

"Open the gas early on corner three to get a good drive out," Xavi advocated.

Lleó rode directly behind his competitor into the apex of corner three at two hundred and forty-four kilometers per hour but found no opportunity to pass him. But now—on the straightaway to corner four—he rode close behind the Kid using his slipstream to his advantage.

"He's not closing the door!" Xavi shouted; his fists tightened.

Lleó advanced instantly into the inside of the track passing the Kid but he braked too deep into the corner making him run wide leaving the door open for his Asian adversary to regain first position by riding on the inside of the track to pass him.

"Shit–fuck–fuck!" Lleó cursed in Catalan as he chased after the Chinese biker who was riding from the middle to the inside of the track on the next corner giving no opportunity for him to make a pass.

"Line him up," Xavi demanded pointing at the screen. "Line that son-of-a-bitch up and make another pass."

Shifting up out of corner five from fifth to sixth gear he rode directly behind the Terracotta Kid and tried to use his slipstream to build up his own bike's momentum to overtake. After hitting two hundred and seventy-five kilometers per hour, he shifted down to third gear for corner seven leaning the bike so close to the track that his left knee and elbow were scraping the pavement. Then into corner eight, he shifted up to fourth gear trailing directly behind the biker trying desperately to keep the gap between them as short as possible on the straightaway to corner nine. Braking deep into the corner in fifth gear the Chinese pilot ahead maintained his position on the inside of the track and sped away into the next straightaway. Lleó immediately shifted up to sixth and then seventh gear seeing his competitor ride into the middle of the track while he positioned himself on the outside.

"He's shutting the door." Xavi shook his head in frustration.

As they rapidly approached corner ten, Lleó stuck his left leg out in the old Rossi fashion to give him more corner speed, and right at the apex of the corner his front hard compound tire was nearly side to side with the rear tire of the Terracotta Kid's bike.

But the Chinese rider shut Lleó out of corner eleven by riding close to the inside as a flurry of red and white lined curbstones passed them.

"Time is running out–fight damn it!" Xavi shouted and punched the air with his right fist.

Lleó did not respond. He stayed focused feeling the world beyond the track fade to grey as he chased his rival into corner twelve riding right up behind him knowing that it would be impossible to pass him now, but not in corner thirteen. They rode into the next corner– the Terracotta Kid maintained the inside position–and Lleó rode directly behind him, but coming out of the corner the Asian rider kept to the outside of the track. *There it is*, Lleó thought. He moved to the right side of his competitor's bike shifting up and slamming the gas to finally make his pass. "Holy shit!" he heard Xavi roar while hearing his teammates in the background hollering in joy and disbelief. He aimed for the inside of corner fourteen in fifth gear blocking his opponent who now rode directly behind him and shot his bike straight across the final straightaway shifting up and passing through the finish line.

"You did it—you son of a gun!" Xavi bellowed as he jumped up and grabbed his closest teammate to embrace him. "You god damn did it!"

Lleó sat up in the bike's seat feeling a torrential wave of relief, disbelief, and excitement consume the whole of his mind and body as he pumped his fists into the air. "I can't believe it ... I can't believe it," he cried in his native tongue with a quivering voice.

"Believe—*macho*! Believe it!" Xavi boomed in broken English knowing that the world was now listening to their radio frequency; he ran out of the pit-box and onto the pit lane to join the rest of his pit crew who were celebrating by grabbing each other, singing, breaking open bottles of cava, and dancing. "Take your lap and get your ass over here!"

Lleó pulled on his front tire brakes almost lifting the rear wheel up into a stoppie and looked back to the finish line seeing his competitors speeding, approaching, and passing him. He turned his motorcycle around and rode his way back to the starting Grid seeing the crowds in the Main Grandstand up on their feet cheering for him and waving hundreds of yellow and red striped Catalan flags. The remaining riders began passing through the finish line and Lleó rode toward the inside of the track to avoid them. Once he reached the inside of the track he stopped and stared at the crowds in the Main Grandstand while waving to them.

Suddenly, someone began patting and hugging him from behind. Frightened, he turned and realized that it was an excited teenaged spectator who had found a way onto the racetrack. Lleó then saw three security personnel running toward them from the pit-lane.

"Take this!" the spectator shouted in Catalan as he tried to shove into Lleó's gloved hands a hollow steel pole with a large, faded Catalan pro-independence flag fluttering from it. "Take this and take your lap!"

Lleó nodded and pointed to the back of his motorcycle.

The teenager, who was dressed in heavily worn blue jeans and a white and black CX team T-shirt, began looking for a way to insert the flagpole safely into the mechanical workings at the rear of the bike. Unable to find a way to attach the flagpole before security arrived he grabbed Lleó's arm and placed it firmly into his hand, "Take it—parade it for your country!" He then ran away along the track toward corner one.

Lleó tightened his grip on the flagpole and began to rev his motorcycle's engine; the three security officers ran passed him in pursuit of the fast-moving teenager.

"Take your lap," Xavi instructed. "Everyone is waiting for you to take the lap."

Lleó looked back down the pit lane and saw Xavi and his team in front of their pit-box laughing, smiling, gulping cava from large bottles, and hugging each other while the crews of the other teams approached to congratulate them on their victory.

"We got the cava—we're missing you, so hurry up!"

Lleó stopped revving the engine and began to shake. Disbelief gave way to the reality of his surroundings. All that he saw confirmed in his mind what he had fought so hard, and for so many years to accomplish. He had won. He had won in Catalonia defeating his greatest opponent, the Terracotta Kid. It was more than just a victory in a game. It was a political statement. A declaration of a rise among European city-states, federations, and confederations to unite once again and provide a much-needed balance of power to the international, geopolitical arena, which, for so long, had been dominated by the Chinese Empire, Russia, and their allies in the Middle East, North and Sub-Saharan Africa, and South America. It would mark, among many, the beginning of Europe's Neo-Renaissance. He began to weep.

Xavi could hear Lleó crying on the other end of his radio headset, "Take it easy, cumpà. When you're ready, take the lap, cool down, and we'll be here waiting for you at the parc fermé."

"Thank ..." he could not finish the sentence. He let out and began to cry.

Xavi signaled to Aleix, the short and stocky radio frequency engineer seated at his computer terminal that consisted of several large and small flat screens near the rear of the pit-box, to jam Lleó's radio signal so that no one could hear him shed tears.

Lleó bent over his bike and bowed his head as his body shook. He felt weak; his stomach felt empty, and his heart faint. He wanted to take off his helmet and breath the air of the track: the smell of diesel, burnt rubber, and bike exhaust. These were the smells of his childhood. For so many years he trained and trained on this very track with the support of his corporate patron, Takagawasan. Although Takagawa had adopted him, provided for him, pushed him to his limits by way of his CX team to become what he was, he had never met him. So much gratitude did he feel for Takagawa, but he was a distant, almost ghost-like, guiding entity. He received digital messages from Takagawa throughout his life: messages of advice, strategy, satisfaction, or disappointment. Those messages were a constant reminder that although Takagawa remained physically elusive, he was always there, observing, watching, and keeping a detailed eye. He was, to Lleó at least, a guiding, digital father figure.

He coughed feeling phlegm rise up to the top of his throat and shook his head. Enough, it was time to take his lap. He gathered himself and straightened his back to wave at the crowds in the Main Grandstand. Security cars and heavily armored Mossos d'Esquadra vans began lining up along the Main Grandstand to serve as an additional barrier between the animated crowds and the track.

"Better get over here before things get out of hand," Xavi warned.

"You got it." Lleó revved the engine and then pulled the bike's front brake and slammed on the gas simultaneously to burnout. The rear wheel spun rapidly against the track, causing the tire to heat up and produce white smoke. The acrid smell of burning rubber filled the air. He began to turn the bike to face corner one as the rear tire screeched and produced an arced mark on the track. He then released the brake and set off leaving behind his signature "fish hook" skid mark.

"You got to hear this," Xavi said. "You'll love to listen to this as your take your corners!"

Gripping the flagpole in his left hand Lleó rode into corners one and two hearing only radio static after Xavi's comment, but then he heard his radio pick up a Catalan GP announcer shouting over the cries and hollers of loyal CX Team supporters who were celebrating around the press box, "This is it–this is it! You can hear … you can hear it–the people are motivated, inspired by this victory.

"For the first time–for the first time since the dissolution of the European Union in 2034, a European rider has finally won the MotoGP World Championship!

"Yes–yes, over successive waves of Chinese, Indian, Russian, and Brazilian victories a Catalan has won for Europe's cause! Those sounds out there–the calls of the people, it is a statement–a declaring statement for support of the European cause over the encroaching political and military might of China!"

"I don't know if I want to listen to this," Lleó said with concern as he raced down the short straightaway between corners eight and nine.

Xavi looked beyond his team's celebration in the pit lane that now included out-of-tune renditions of old national songs and careless, nearly drunken dancing, and saw Aleix typing frenetically at his keyboard. He suddenly stopped typing, leaned back, turned his head, and confirmed to Xavi with a nod that he had a secure radio channel. "They will rally behind you," he warned. "Taka foresaw this."

"What are you talking about?" Lleó asked as fear began to grip him. He lowered the flag feeling the pull of the wind against it as he accelerated the bike.

"There is much to discuss, Lleó. This is no longer a game."

"What the hell are you talking about?" he then slowed the motorcycle down. "I do not want people to rally behind me—"

"If the fragmented nations of Europe do not unite now, there will be nothing—nothing to stop the expanding military might of imperial China. Their hawks seek another war. They will strike the final blow to solidify their occupation."

"That's impossible—"

"How is it impossible?" he interrupted. "There is no protection for us. The Great Quakes of 22 and 25 destroyed the already limping economies of Japan and the U.S. There has been no balance of powers since. We've played the diplomatic game for as long as we could with China. But the constant squabbling, and competition between European states, is only encouraging China and their allies to strike us hard and fast again before we gain the sense to unite. Europe must bind and rise—Lleó. Europe must rise."

Nearing corner thirteen, Lleó shook his head in disbelief. "Well thanks for the lesson, Xavi, but—"

"No! This is something more. *You* are something more!" he stressed.

"Xavi! I'm just a pilot—you're my crew chief, and I just want to enjoy this."

Xavi nodded realizing that it was not the moment to discuss such matters. "We're here waiting for you in the box. Come on home, champion," he smiled as he rubbed his fingers again against the facial stubble along his right cheek.

Lleó rounded corner fifteen seeing the Main Grandstand in the distance to his right, and the moving sea of hundreds to thousands of waving red and yellow Senyera and Estelada flags, along with pockets of white and red flags bearing the Cross of St. George. He pumped the flag in his left hand up and down, sped toward corner sixteen, and heard the roar of the crowds increase in intensity and volume.

    The long stretch of the straightaway was before him, and he rode toward the Grid pumping his fists, and the flag, in victory. A sharp pain then surged through his chest. He dropped the flag and bent forward toward the bike's gas tank gagging for air.

    "Lleó!" he heard Xavi shout. "Stay down!"

    The visor of his helmet shattered. He felt his head thrown back by the impact of something that had struck him. Hitting the pavement and sliding across the straightaway, he saw his bike continue forward without a rider. His body rolled and stopped against the grass along the racing lane. He touched his chest with his left gloved hand where he felt the throbbing pain, looked down at his fingertips, and saw the stain of his own blood. Another shot ripped through his right leg. He felt blood and bile begin to fill his throat and lungs. Choking and coughing up blood, he felt its metallic taste swirl around his tongue; he then saw security and medical personnel running toward him from the pit lane. His eyes fluttered until a cold, grey mist consumed his sight. Silence enveloped him. Darkness consumed him.

*   *   *

He could feel his heart beating like a drum, pumping blood through his veins. He opened his eyes, but he could not see. His entire body felt rigid, especially his feet that were unusually cold and numb. A sterile bed sheet covered his body, which he lightly touched with the tip of his right index fingers. He listened to the pulsating beep of machines to his right. He tried to make a sound by opening his mouth, but could not. He tried to move his head, but could not. The tip of his nose was warm. He knew that the room that echoed the rhythmic beeps of the machines off its metallic and glass walls was warm, but he could not understand why his feet felt so cold. Fatigued, he fell back into a dark world of dreams.

    Voices woke him. He was glad to hear them, but he did not understand them. Japanese was the language they were speaking. He was able to understand a word here and there in their conversation. Words he had learned while working with the Japanese engineers of his

Grand Prix team. He did not recognize the voices, but he knew that there were two men and a woman who spoke Japanese with a Catalan accent. *Doctors*, he tried to whisper in their language. The three adults stopped talking and looked at his lips.

"Lleónart, do not strain yourself to speak just yet," the woman said in Catalan as she approached him. "We are working to slowly revive you. Just rest. You are safe."

Her voice was comforting, sensual, and sincere. He relaxed.

"Your muscles are emaciated from so long in this bed, but we are rebuilding them," she explained. "Takagawasan, your patron, has gone to great lengths to bring you back from your deep sleep. You will regain your strength and your senses. Please be patient."

"How long?" he tried to say.

She did not understand him. "Just rest. Soon all will be revealed to you, but for now just rest."

He then slipped away into another deep sleep.

*　　*　　*

He heard the faint buzz from the LED lights that lined the metallic ceiling in his room and the mechanical hum of the medical machines around his ergonomic hospital bed that was inclined forward at a fifteen-degree angle. He felt stronger and more able than the many times he had woken before. He did not know how many weeks had passed since he had first woken to the whispered discussions of the three doctors who were restoring his body surgery by surgery, but he assumed that perhaps two to three months had passed. He opened his eyes and finally, as the doctors had explained to him before his last surgery, he was able to see. But all in the room was a blur and illuminated by the unnatural, cool blue hue of the LED lights. Unable to focus his vision he closed his eyes and then squinted. The thick glass sliding door to his room opened and closed. He could smell the pleasing scent of her perfume.

"Montsy," he addressed her. "I see, but it's all out of focus."

"That's normal," she assured him as she walked toward his bed.

He wanted to finally see her face, but could not make out any of her details as she neared and leaned over his head, opened his right eye with her thumb, and shot a beam of light into his pupil from her medical pen. All that he could see was a white haze around her that he assumed was her laboratory coat.

"Blown pupil," she whispered. "Normal for the type of head trauma you've suffered."

"So, what's next?"

"Another surgery for your eyes to fully restore the iris sphincters."

He let out a deep sigh.

"Soon this will be all over with and you'll be back on your feet and better than new," she assured him.

"Anything else? More shots?"

"Yes, that's right," she answered with a nod as she checked the digital screens by his bed that provided real-time data concerning his vital signs. "Xavi will be coming by today to check on you."

"Good," he replied with excitement.

"You will have a good talk with him. I know that you've been eager to get many of your questions answered, and that we've urged you to be patient. But you must understand that we needed you to be calm throughout this process."

"Yeah ..." he looked down at his chest. "I've followed your rules ... and you've delivered." He looked up to her blurry, oval face. "I've been feeling better, and soon I'll be able to see and make my way around this metal box without the assistance of the staff, trainers, or bots."

"Yes, that's right, Lleó. But when you regain your sight we will have much to explain to you."

"I don't understand why all of this couldn't have been explained to me before. My ears work just fine. I can listen, can't I? But no one wants to talk. Not talking to me—answering my questions—probably stresses me more than telling me what I want to know. You know that, don't you?"

The rhythmic pulse of his heart rate that sounded through the vital signs monitor began to increase.

"Slow down, you're boosting your heart rate and blood pressure," she cautioned him. "Take a deep breath and relax, please."

He inhaled and exhaled.

"Again," she instructed. "Let's bring that rate down."

He took in another deep breath and relaxed.

She reviewed his vital signs on the screen again. "Good, that's right."

"Well, soon anyway ... you guys will tell me what the hell happened. Just relieved that I'll be able to race again–right, Montsy? Right?" he asked her trying to stare into her dark brown eyes.

"Yes, yes, you do not have to worry about that," she assured him. "You'll be able to ride again."

"Good, good ... good," he said relieved feeling his upper body relax and sink into the memory foam mattress of his medical bed.

The sliding glass door opened and closed.

"Lleó, you're looking better," Xavi announced in Catalan as he stepped toward the base of his bed.

"Wish I could say the same about you, but I still can't make out any details. Montsy said that I'll have my sight back to normal after one more surgery in the next day or two."

"Is that so, doc?" Xavi asked in English.

She nodded. "I'll leave the two of you alone. I'll be back after your talk for your shot." She walked toward the sliding door.

"Thanks, Montsy," Lleó said.

"Your welcome," she answered in Japanese.

The sliding door opened and closed. Xavi rolled a medical stool on rollers toward Lleó and took a seat.

"It's good to see you," Xavi greeted in Catalan.

"It's good to see you too," Lleó replied in their native tongue. "Although you're out of focus," he joked.

"Yes, that's why I'm here."

Lleó sensed anxiety in his voice. "What do you mean?"

"You will gain your sight soon, but before that happens I wanted to talk to you because you will find that some people–and things–are different."

"What do you mean?" His brow furrowed.

"We've known each other a long time ... I've known you since what?" He raised his head. "Since you were five? And look at you now. A young man."

"Yeah, we've known each other a long, long time."

"If you could see me now you'd notice that I look different from when you last remembered seeing me."

Lleó squinted his eyes hoping to bring Xavi's face into focus. "How? How different?"

"I'm older than when you last saw me. I've got grey and white hairs now. Still good looking though," he tried to smile.

"What happened to you?"

"It's not something that happened to just me. You will notice that many of those you knew before the accident are older."

"What the hell happened?" he asked with anger.

"You were asleep for a long time, Lleó–"

"What do you mean I was asleep for a long time?" he demanded to know as he sat up in his bed aggravated.

The vital signs monitor sounded his increasing heart rate.

Xavi stood up and placed his hands on Lleó's shoulders. "Relax, Lleó. Relax," he urged. "You don't want a team of doctors running in here and sedating you again."

"Fuck you–Xavi," he swatted Xavi's arms away. "Don't fucking touch me."

"You need to relax."

"What the hell do you expect from me with rubbish like that coming out of your mouth. This isn't funny!" he shouted pointing his finger at him. "If this is one of your damned jokes–I'm telling you now–it's not funny."

"It's not a joke. Believe me, Lleó. It's not–"

"How long then? How fucking long–damn it!"

"Twenty-nine years."

"Twenty-nine? Twenty-nine years?" he said in disbelief. "What? What the hell are you fucking talking about–twenty-nine years?"

The tempo of his heart rate continued increasing.

The glass door slid opened and Montserrat rushed into the medical room with two other doctors directly behind her.

"I knew this was a bad idea," Montsy said as she pushed Xavi aside, grabbed Lleó's right forearm, and injected a sedative into his vein to calm his nerves and accelerating heart rate.

"What ... the," Lleó murmured as the drug made him faint. He collapsed back into his bed; the memory foam mattress conformed to his body allowing him to sink comfortably into it. His head swung from side to side as the blurred images he saw faded. "Twenty, twenty, twenty ..." he whispered until he lost consciousness.

* * *

"Two-Six, come in," Xavi called. "Radio contact reestablished, please confirm."

Lleónart shook his head of all thoughts and checked the holographic digital gauges that were located at the base of his helmet's visor.

"Slow it down," Junichi advised. "Hitting maximum speed of three-five-zero. Tunnel exit in point zero seven, six, five—"

"Exit Ronda de Dalt–Bésos," Xavi interrupted.

"Yeah, no shit," Lleó said annoyed.

He saw the tunnel's exit rapidly approaching through the night-vision setting of his visor and leaned his motorcycle slightly to the right. He bolted out of the tunnel sending out a strong gust of wind that caused roadside litter and debris to spiral up and out from the tunnel. Speeding up the exit ramp, he took the second entrance that sloped downward into another tunnel before braking hard to make the curved left turn that looped under the enclosed and restricted Ronda de Dalt expressway.

"Target is at station–arrival time in three point fifty-five and counting," Junichi informed.

Lleó accelerated into the entrance tunnel curve feeling the pavement just scrape his suit's knee padding.

"Pull it up a bit," Xavi instructed.

"Let me pilot–damn it!" Lleó shouted in frustration as he pulled the cycle up toward his chest. He pulled the bike up to its vertical position, sped out of the entrance tunnel and onto the nearly abandoned and unlit three-lane expressway. Sitting firmly in the cycle's seat he tucked his body into the cycle to reduce wind friction while accelerating rapidly from eighty to one hundred and fifty-three kilometers per hour.

The word "warning" flashed in red at the top of his visor as a sharp blare sounded through his helmet's radio receiver.

"Shit, shit, shit!" Xavi exclaimed.

"What? What is it?" Lleó asked as he shifted the motorcycle up a gear.

"We've got company. Three drones on heading two six, nine, nine, one."

The GPS map maximized on his visor's screen where he could see the three drones closing in on his position.

"How's that *damn* possible?"

"Alert signal came from …" Junichi continued typing on the keyboard of his workstation's power computer releasing several Trojan programs to scour the North African Trade Alliance's Catalan security grid. He looked from one of the six holographic screens before him to the next searching for the source. "Signal came from Vallvidrera tunnel exit."

"Good fucking use this bike's stealth tech is," Lleó complained.

"Watch the language and play it cool," Junichi cautioned as he adjusted the earpiece of his headset. "Keep your head clear and focus."

"Watch my language?" Lleó said in disbelief. "It's my ass out here–alone!"

"Enough!" Xavi demanded. "We need to …" he thought for a moment as he looked with scrutinizing eyes at the real-time holographic satellite images and digital GPS maps projecting from the diverging lenses at the center of the metallic wall at the front of the darkened command center; the center consisted of nineteen workstations that were each manned by Xavi's team of hackers, programmers, technicians, and engineers. "We need to get you off the Dalt and onto the streets."

"No!" Lleó shouted back. "We need to engage the drones *on* the Dalt. It's a narrow corridor–we can draw them in and–"

"Not a chance–the Dalt is going to be our main vein to get in and out of the city. Can't risk having holes blown in there to reveal the grid we've been constructing."

"He's right, Two-Six," Junichi agreed. "NAV is charting new course. Uploading, now."

The pulsating red line on the GPS digital map was altered revealing his new path to the devastated Agbar tower where his target–the largest armored mech battle droid that patrolled the city–was located.

"Any back-up?" Lleó asked. "Can you shoot those drones down with ours?"

"You know we can't," Xavi said shaking his head as he scratched the stubble along his right cheek. "Not part of the plan yet."

"And these drones weren't part of the plan either–time to improvise," he urged.

"No–you'll–" Xavi paused as his eyes narrowed on the three red, digital dots approaching Lleó's position on the real-time holographic map. "Fine," he looked to Junichi who looked back at him with a furrowed brow. "White Lion Two-Six, you will engage, bring the three down, and proceed to target."

"Good," Lleó replied, "let's see what this thing can do–"

"Enclosed corridor ending in time minus point ten," Junichi interrupted as he typed new commands into the keyboard of his power computer. "You'll be out in the open now. Time to engage. Cycle transformation on my mark."

Lleónart increased speed and prepared himself.

* * *

Their soft footsteps echoed down the long, sleek metallic hall. Lleónart, dressed in a two-piece, skin-tight, K-tech, partial-compression white suit with red lines that traced the outlines of his firm pectoral and abdominal muscles, walked alongside Xavi who was dressed in an old, black Marc Márquez 2013 MotoGP Championship T-shirt, Levi's blue jeans, and black and orange Onitsuka Tiger sneakers that he had replicated on a 3D printer the previous night. Lleónart was amazed by what he had learned from Xavi and the engineers concerning the technological advances made by Takoda Industries over the past thirty years in 3D printing as applied to medicine, electric vehicles, robotics, nanotechnology, space technology, exoskeleton technology, and synthetic clothing. Essentially anything could be scanned and recreated to the functioning likeness of the original article. Remembering his favorite pair of VamCats sneakers, he asked the Japanese 3D printing engineer that was explaining and demonstrating the technology to him to recreate the shoes. The engineer pulled up old digital images of the sneakers on his computer from which a three-dimensional model was constructed and colored in red and white to match the skin tights he was required to wear.

He looked down at the pair of VamCats as they walked and was still amazed that a printer had produced them within moments before his eyes.

"We're almost there," Xavi said.

Lleó looked up and saw the end of the corridor, but no door. "It's a dead end."

"Not quite."

He scratched his shoulder and looked down again wondering why only the shoulders and arms of his skin-tight suit was colored in red and if the circular white emblem with a red cross at its center that was located on both of his deltoid muscles represented part of the old flag of Barcelona.

Xavi stopped, as did Lleó, before the polished steel wall at the end of the corridor.

"Now what?" Lleó asked.

"Now you go, and I stay," Xavi answered.

They heard pressurized air released, and the wall began to ascend into the ceiling.

Lleó, frightened, stepped back. "What's beyond?" he asked as he watched the wall rising.

"An old friend?"

"As old as you?" he joked with unease still trying to adjust to the fact that Xavi was nearly thirty years older than his last memory of him.

"Older."

The wall continued rising and Lleó began to see a large, dimly lit room decorated in a traditional Japanese fashion. The floor was no longer white marble, but lined from wall to wall with tatami mats. At the center of the room was a black, polished, short rectangular table with six dark brown cushions along its longest sides. A wooden rack of seven sheathed samurai swords stood in the right corner farthest from him. A dark red samurai helmet and armor appeared to hover to the right of the rack. In the farthest corner to his left there was a juniper bonsai tree that stood to approximately half his height. And on the wall directly ahead of him hung a traditional Japanese painting that was nearly as high and as long as the wall itself.

"Take off your shoes and go in," Xavi instructed.

Lleó looked at Xavi who nodded his head in the direction of the Japanese room, slipped his feet out of his shoes, took one step forward, and then another, and another. He neared the short table and was immediately startled by the sound of the metallic wall descending. He turned and looked nervously at Xavi who whispered in Catalan, "All will be fine."

The wall contacted the floor. He heard pressurized air release again. He looked at the racked samurai swords and devised a quick plan of defense if his safety was compromised. Minutes passed. There was only the sound of his breathing. He stepped forward, walked around the table and cushions, and approached the large painting. The painting depicted a massive ocean wave that was rapidly approaching a small fishing village. Several panicked fishermen in feeble boats below the rising crest of the wave rowed toward or away from it in a futile attempt to escape the watery hand of death as villagers scurried away from the beach seeking higher ground. He looked at each of the villagers seeing mothers grabbing their children, men running and pulling women behind them, and old men and women accepting their death by standing and facing the violent sea.

"The painting is from the 18th century," a voice called out with a grated and guttural tone.

Lleó turned to his left and saw a bald, heavily aged Japanese man with blotched skin dressed formally in a black cotton gi. "Takagawasan," he said in disbelief. Immediately he kneeled to his patron, placed his hands on the ground, bowed his head until it touched the ground, and turned his palms up. Takagawasan took several steps toward Lleó and said, "Rise."

Lleó did as commanded and stood at full attention before Takagawasan noticing that he was barefoot.

"You look to my feet?"

"Yes ... yes, Takagawasan," he nodded.

"An old habit," he smiled. "I like to feel the earth beneath me. Reminds me to stay grounded in truth ... in reality. Tell me, do you like the painting?" He pointed to the artwork.

"Ah ... yes, yes I do," Lleó nodded again.

"You lie," he shook his head with disappointment. "Never lie to me, Lleónart. Never lie to me."

"I'm–I'm sorry, Takagawasan. Truly, my apologies, I did not mean to offend you."

"No, no you did not," he said with a grin. "Too many times have I seen so many, so eager to please me by only offering what they think I would like to hear in vain efforts to ..." he looked up searching for the words, "to gain my favor. But what I need is the brute and honest truth.

"Tell me, Lleónart. What do you think of me?" He looked directly into Lleó's eyes.

"You're ..." he hesitated.

"Tell me!" he shouted with a vitality that could not have been expected from a man of his age.

"Elusive," Lleó blurted.

"Ah," he nodded. "Is that it?"

"And dark," Lleó added.

"Good, good, Lleónart. You see the ancient part of my soul. You sense the shadow there deep in the heart of me," he pressed his right index finger against his chest.

He walked toward the painting and stopped before it. He looked at the villagers scattering away from the great wave and looked down. "You and I have met many, many times."

Lleó's brow furrowed as he gave a confused look to the back of Takagawasan.

"Something you would like to ask?"

"Yes, Takagawasan," Lleó replied.

"Then ask."

"This is the first time we've ever met, Takagawasan."

"Although I have kept a very careful eye on you ever since I acquired you for the track, you are true. This is the first time we have met … in this life," he smiled to himself.

"What … what do you mean?"

"I am a Buddhist, Lleónart. You should know what that means."

"But I am not, Takagawasan. I've never been religious."

"And why should you after the loss of your parents. You are still young. Feelings of invincibility still flow through your veins. Tell me. Why do you race? What type of person puts himself in such a position? Twenty-five pilots raced each year with the expectations that four or more would die in the game. Tell me. Tell me, Lleónart. What drives a person such as you to engage in such a dangerous sport?"

"My father," he blurted. "My father, Takagawasan," he said with respect.

"And what memory do you have of him?"

"I don't remember much. But his legacy as a cycle pilot has always preceded me. When I race, I feel what he had felt. I experience what he had experienced—"

"And what is that experience?" he interrupted.

"The moment … the zone … pure focus and concentration. No thought other than what I am doing. It is a rush to feel the power of speed. To master the control of a machine so that you can dance as one, swinging from one curve to the next."

"And the fear of death?"

"It is always there, Takagawasan. It is always there," he looked down for a moment. "The anxiety and nervousness I feel before every race is what I do not enjoy. You think that these moments may be your last …" He looked up, "that it may be your last race. But once I'm on that bike and the light turns green none of that matters. I attack the fear by rushing three hundred kilometers per hour straight into it."

"You speak like an old samurai," Takagawasan said as he now looked to the fishermen in the painting. "A samurai who treated every moment as if it was his last." He turned around and faced Lleó. "Although you say you are not religious, you have a religious experience every time you are on that track. You live in the moment and rise above death.

"I have always admired men like you, Lleónart. You live on a knife edge. Once, a long time ago, I dreamed of being a pilot. I trained and raced, but was never able to rise above Moto3. I was too afraid, too unwilling to take unnecessary risk. Only those who risk their very lives to dive into a closing gap win the game. I could never do it. So, I turned my attention to mechanical engineering ... and from there rose Takoda Industries," he smirked, "which is something I do have a talent for. But I am old now. And soon my life will come to an end, which is why you are here for there is one last thing that I must do to right the many wrongs I have committed not only in this life, but in all the ones before."

The wall onto where the painting was framed began to rise into the ceiling revealing a lustrous, black glass wall that projected an array of holographic screens that displayed real-time stock, currency, capital, commodity, and bond market data from the Shanghai SE Composite Index, Hang Seng, Mumbai Sensex, Nanjing T-Wan TSEC 50 Index, BM&F Bovespa, FTSE 100, DAX, CAC 40, EBS, Reuters 3000 Xtra, and the Industrial and Commercial Bank of China Capital Aggregate Bond Index.

"These numbers," he waved his hand before the screens, "is where I reside. This—these flashing, ever changing digits—is my domain."

Lleó focused on one of the screens and tried to make some sense of the rapidly changing numbers and letters that were listed with flashing green and red arrows that pointed up or down.

"The world now is so different from the one I was born into," he took a deep and longing breath. "But, of course, nothing lasts forever, as my grandfather had often reminded me when I was a boy growing up in Japan ... in Kawagoe." He pointed to the center screen. The rows of running numbers abruptly changed to display three newscasts that streamed aerial images of the severe urban damage and flooding caused by the Great Quake of 2022. "It all ended that year. Japan so rapidly destroyed by a series of earthquakes that ate at—and tsunamis that nearly washed away—the whole of the island. I came to

Catalonia as a young man, as a refugee—the lone survivor of my family." He bowed his head. "Then the Great Quake of 2025 threw the whole of the Pacific Coast of the United States into the sea." The images on the screen then depicted satellite images of the altered coastline of the western United States. "Still crippled by the Great Recession, strained by the heavy burden of an ever-expanding national deficit, the United States would only limp on for three more years until it ceased to exist as a legal entity. In the shadow of these global, natural disasters arose to primacy the People's Republic of China. The only political superpower left to check this ascending power in the East was the European Union that without the financial and military backing of the United States dissolved as rising nationalism, populism, and xenophobia ripped the political and economic fabric of the confederation apart. And that," he turned around and looked Lleó in the eye, "is the world you were born into."

Lleó looked at the changing video images of civil strife, rebellion, and warfare that spread across the European continent throughout the 2030s.

"Europe fell back into a Dark Age. Unable to defend itself, the Federation of North African States invaded the continent with Chinese military hardware and tactical support with the intent to establish autocratic order. In a phrase … the East—to an extent—had conquered the West." He smiled. "The historical irony of it," he said under his breath.

The Takoda Industries emblem emerged on all the holographic screens. "Crisis brings opportunity, Lleónart. Takoda Industries began receiving industrial contracts from the governments of the North African Federation and the People's Republic to rebuild Catalonia's seaport and infrastructure. I quickly learned that every man has a price. Although we were occupied I found the means—both legal and illegal—to gain more contracts." The corporate logo of Takoda Industries dissolved into collages of video images that displayed industrial parks, petroleum platforms, natural gas pipelines, airports, seaports, highways, tunnels, and underground transit systems that had all been constructed by Takagawasan's corporate conglomerate. "The ports of Valencia, Algeciras, Las Palmas, Gioia Tauro, Genoa, La Spezia, Trieste, Naples, Marseille, Piraeus, Malta Freeport, and more were all rebuilt by Takoda. And with each port my power and wealth grew as I began to control the flow of illicit goods ranging from cigarettes, cocaine, depressants, hallucinogens, heroin, narcotics, and stimulants, to guns, ammunition, missiles, military aircrafts and vehicles, and electronic systems—

ultimately gaining me defense contracts—to a wide variety of counterfeit products and currencies."

Lleó began scratching the base of his neck as he became very uncomfortable with the information being revealed to him.

Noticing Lleó's discomfort Takagawasan added, "Do not think differently of me, Lleó."

Lleónart crossed his arms over his chest and took a step back.

"I ask you who would you want to control the flow of such goods? The vicious, organized crime groups of the Mediterranean who pay homage to their North African and Chinese overlords ... or my corporation?"

"Does it matter?" Lleó asked. "Better not to be part of such things."

"Spoken with wisdom, yes," Takagawasan acknowledged. "But the world I knew—the one I was born into—was much better than the one you were born into. Of course, you do not know. You cannot compare. But I can," he said with anger. He stepped toward Lleó. "There is no perfect world. But I remember a world where there was a belief in the Enlightenment ideals that laid the political foundation of what were once the United States and the European Union. What world do you want to live in, Lleó? This one? One in which you have no right to speak your mind openly against governments and corporations that are actively seeking to gain greater authority over you? This world is one in which *all* live in fear, and out of that fear the people keep their heads bowed and do not even think to whisper their hatred for the authoritarian and corrupted regimes that speak constant lies and false histories as truth. The Communist Party of China learned much from the political experimentations of North Korea. Year by year I have seen our downward slide into this oppressive, occupying, nearly totalitarian state that will stop at nothing to keep us all locked up in cages, slaves to the dictatorial machinery that keeps a small elite in extreme wealth and comfort back in the East."

"So what—" he stopped before he cursed. "What—what does this all have to do with me?"

Takagawasan's shoulders relaxed. "I am pleased you asked." He smiled. The holographic screens dissipated and all that Lleó could see behind the old man was the black glass wall. The lights of the room began to dim more. "Have a seat," Takagawasan offered.

Lleó was not sure if Takagawasan expected him to sit on one of the cushions that lined the two sides of the short table he had seen.

He turned around and was astonished to see that the table and cushions were no longer in the room. Instead, there was a modern sofa chair with a dark grey, padded interior seat and white exterior that outlined its rectangular shape. "What the–what?" He looked at Takagawasan. "Where is the–the–the table I saw?"

"Are you sure you saw a table?"

"Of course, I did."

"Have a seat, Lleó. Please, have a seat," he insisted.

Lleónart, confused and humbled by the sudden disappearance and appearance of furniture in the room, bowed to Takagawasan, thanked him for the offer, and sat down.

The glass wall became a massive screen that replayed the final laps of the Montmeló Circuit of Lleónart's MotoGP World Championship victory in 2056 AD.

"It was good that you had won," Takagawasan began. "Your victory came earlier than what I had anticipated. You had forced several events into motion."

Hearing the unease in his patron's voice Lleó leaned forward.

"The game you had played was not just a game. It was a sport, yes, but you would be naïve to believe that it was simply that. Each team had gone to great lengths to assure an honorable standing every year, but every team had to pay tribute to China. No state–regardless of size–would have risked offending the Chinese Empire by winning the Grand Prix–"

"But, Takagawasan," Lleó interrupted, "please forgive me, but I am not the first to win."

"Yes, you are!" he shouted not appreciating the break in his lecture.

"I apologize, Takagawasan." Lleó placed his hands on his knees and bowed his head low in a very formal manner.

"Every team that had won had done so with the consent of the Chinese authorities. A Chinese corporation–directly or indirectly–sponsored all those winning teams. Sinopec Racing, Sinochem Motoracing, Baosteel Project, Jardine Tech 1 were obvious, but Hindustan Petrol Motorsport, Zee MotoGP, Gazprom Racing, LUKoil Power, and Akella Power Electronics were all provided patronage by the Middle Kingdom. HSBC Race 1, Aramco Team, Vitol Speed, Glencore Rush, Eni GP, and Petrobras Racing were all teams that–to some extent–were independent of Chinese influence, but kept a low profile to maintain face with China. No occupied state wanted to draw greater attention from China when it came to international competitive events such as the Grand Prix.

"To you the Grand Prix was a race. But to those with full knowledge of the intricate political workings of the world saw the Grand Prix as a forum where states, industries, and corporations came together to compete and display their technological abilities. During the Cold War the Olympics showcased the athletic might between the two former superpowers. The Grand Prix served the same purpose with the difference being that all occupied states agreed to allow the Chinese and their allies to win, year after year. But you changed all that." The large digital screen showed Lleó riding and braking hard around corner ten of the last lap of the Montmeló Circuit. "You gave the Federation of Catalan City-States its first victory twenty years after the completion of the Sagrada Família. It was my hope that your victory would inspire an insurgence in Catalonia that would quickly spread across a fragmented Europe against our occupation. It was my hope that those brave enough would rise to unite the European states against our common enemy. But I was foolish." The screen showed–from several points of view–the shots that struck Lleó's head and body as he neared the finish line; images Lleó had seen several times with Xavi and Doctor Montserrat as he recuperated on his medical bed. He watched and saw again his body go limp from the shots, collapse, fall, and slide down the track as his motorcycle veered toward the grandstand and crashed into the wall of the speedway. "Information was leaked. I did not have the foresight to see it. You were eliminated. Takoda Industries was disbanded. My allies and I went into hiding."

"To where?" Lleó asked. "Where could you possibly hide?"

"Here," he said pointing to the ground as if the answer was obvious.

"And where exactly is here? Where am I? Where are we?"

"Deep, deep underground. And above us," he pointed up, "Tibidabo–"

"The mountain?"

"Yes," he smirked. "Provided so many contracts to rebuild Barcelona I had Takoda Industries build a secret and extensive network of tunnels, bunkers, research laboratories and facilities two kilometers under the Collserola mountain range allowing for easy access into and out of the city and the seaport. It was here that we brought your body for neuro–" he paused, "for cryopreservation."

"Cryo what?"

"You were frozen." The large screen showed Lleó's corpse in an advanced technology operating room being prepared by a team of medical technicians and droids. "When our development of medical nanotechnology that could rebuild human tissue at the molecular level had been perfected we began the process to reanimate and resuscitate your brain ... and body in 2085 AD. Thus, your youth has been preserved when those that you knew had aged accordingly to the passing years."

Lleó's stomach pained him. He felt the urge to vomit his morning meal of steamed rice, green tea, and miso soup.

The screen then showed a silent video of his doctor–Montserrat–in a medical research laboratory explaining a new surgical technique. "I am proud to say that my granddaughter had much to do with your revival."

"Your granddaughter?" he blushed. "Montsy–Doctor Montserrat is your granddaughter?"

"Yes, she is," he said with pride as he admired her striking Eurasian features. "Much of my wife do I see in her eyes. I met my wife in Gamla Stan–the old town of Stockholm–while seeking another government construction contract. We met in a café, talked, and carried our conversation into the streets of the old town. She led me into the Storkyrkan–a cathedral–and it was there that I saw the impressive 15th century wooden statue of St. George and the Dragon. As I worked and traveled throughout the occupied territories of Europe I came to understand that the myth and symbols of the 'warrior saint' permeated the region.

"Symbols such as the red cross that you bear on your shoulders," he pointed, "is depicted on the old flags of England and Georgia, as well as on the flags of so many European cities and former provinces such as Milan, Genoa, Padua, Sardinia, Zadar in Croatia, Freiburg im Breisgau, and of course, Aragón and Barcelona. The myth served as a seed of inspiration as I contemplated what could be done in the aftermath of the strike that had been made against you and the European cause."

"Inspired you to do what?" he questioned. "Wait–look, Takagawasan. With all due respect, this is all too much–too much to take in. I thought I was just going to go back to racing and I'm sitting here getting some crazy–no disrespect" he said shaking his head, "history lesson."

Three-dimensional schematics of several different versions of a cutting-edge motorcycle that Lleó had never seen before appeared on the screen. "What? What is that?" he asked with growing curiosity.

"I have your attention, do I not?"

"Yes, Takagawasan. Yes, you do. What—what is that?"

"Those are the concept designs that led to the creation of your new charger. But it is more than just a bike," he smiled with pride. "It is also the most advanced military-grade exoskeleton designed for quick hit-and-run guerilla style urban combat. That is what you will race on. That is what you will fight with."

The schematic designs disappeared and the black glass wall became transparent. Lleó's eyes widened when he saw fully illuminated beyond the glass wall the largest indoor racing track he had ever seen. And there, directly in front of him, stood several engineers, mechanics, and technicians behind a matte silver, heavy armored, ten cylinders, ninety-degree V-type hybrid engine motorcycle designed with sharp edges and angles along its body with wheels that had no spokes and bulletproof, dry racing tires. The glass wall descended. Takagawasan dissolved as his holographic projection faded and ceased.

*   *   *

"Five, four, three—"

"Wait—wait!" Lleó shouted interrupting Junichi's countdown. "Hold cycle transformation. I've got a better plan."

Xavi's eyes widened in disbelief as he shook his head in frustration while watching the three drones on the holographic screen. "Damn it, Two-Six—you're out in the open. Those drones are closing in on your position."

"Good," Lleó replied. "Let them come." He shifted up to seventh gear and shot through the dark and empty Ronda de Dalt expressway at three hundred and eleven kilometers per hour.

"Two-Six!" Xavi exclaimed. "We need cycle transformation now! Jettison the diesel—that damn motor is producing too much noise. The drones are triangulating your position by tracking the frequencies emitted by that engine."

"I thought this bike had attained near silence."

"Not in that corridor," Junichi corrected. "You're shooting down an opened tunnel that is amplifying sound. You know that at seventh gear the sound suppression system cannot muffle—"

"Fine—whatever—doesn't matter," he slammed the bike's brakes and shifted down to fourth gear to make a sharp right turn off the expressway onto the avenue that had once been called Estatut de Catalunya.

"What is he doing?" Junichi asked not realizing that he was gripping the hair around his scalp.

"I don't know," Xavi answered. He took a step back to gain a wider perspective on the holographic map trying to discern Lleó's strategy. He scratched the mole beneath his right eye and advised, "All we can do now is trust and watch."

Lleó shifted the bike back up to fifth and then sixth gear as he swiftly went around a roundabout and continued down the empty avenue toward a second roundabout, which led directly to an unlit, short tunnel that he sped directly into and out of in less than a second. He braked again, shifted down to ease through a curve in the road and sped down the avenue toward the kilometer long Túnel de la Rovira. He shifted the bike up to seventh gear and hit three hundred kilometers per hour through the straightaway of the tunnel. He maximized the GPS digital map with a thought and quickly confirmed the course he was taking to the target. Seeing the end of the tunnel approaching, he minimized the map, exited the tunnel, and slammed on the brakes to make a sharp right turn onto Ronda del Guinardo and then an immediate left on Carrer de Pi I Margall.

Speeding the bike back up toward maximum velocity, he saw the extent of the devastation caused by years of an oppressive occupation that had nearly isolated the city. Dilapidated three and four-storey buildings peppered and scarred by bullets holes, and shrapnel lined the street that was littered on both sides with piles of splintered lumber, rusted piping, rotting garbage, crushed and pulverized concrete that had fallen from the façade of the buildings as a result of heavy gunfire and bombardment, torn plastic bags nearly emptied of their contents, and smashed bottles. He shifted the bike down from sixth to fifth to fourth gear, turned left onto Carrer de l'Escorial, made an immediate right turn onto Travessera de Gracia, and then made a sharp left turn onto Passeig de Sant Joan; a street that he had remembered in his youth as being lined with plane trees. But now, only the stumps of the trees remained for the impoverished inhabitants of the city had cut them down more than a decade ago to provide heat in the night during a long and punishing winter.

He accelerated the cycle toward its top speed not seeing a single street or apartment light activated. The night vision setting of his helmet's visor provided a view ahead of Plaça de Tetuan; renamed Plaça de Tiananmen by the Chinese occupying forces. He focused the lens of his visor by straining his eyes and could clearly see the makeshift garrison that had been constructed with welded iron plating around three People's Liberation Army Type 111 main battle tanks that had fired upon, smashed into, and crushed the Bartomeu Robert monument. He switched his visor's camera to thermal imagining and saw the body heat of seven soldiers within the compound beginning to cluster around the slit openings facing the street he was racing down. Several sparks flared from the garrison's slit openings, and then he heard the chink, chink, chink of their bullets pelting his bulletproof, stealth motorcycle.

"They're on to you," he heard Xavi warn him through his helmet's radio receiver. "No shit!" he replied as he swerved from one side of the street to the other. He flipped the red safety switch on the cycle's right handlebar off and activated the missile guidance system.

"Wait–wait–wait," Xavi exhorted. "What they hell are you doing?"

Lleó locked onto his approaching target and fired one of four anti-tank guided missiles. He slammed on the brakes hearing the continued clink of bullets impacting the front, angular shield of his motorcycle and braced for the shockwave to come. The soldiers scurried. The missile struck and unleashed an explosion of black flame that mushroomed up from the pulverized garrison. He kicked the cycle back into gear and advanced toward the devastated fiery square.

"Congratulations, you ass–I knew it–why don't you damn listen to me!" Xavi exclaimed in Catalan. "All three drones are now heading for Tetuan," he said in English.

Lleó accelerated toward the burning square leaning the cycle closer toward the left side of the dilapidated street. He shot passed Carrer de la Diputació and decelerated deep into the curve of the street that merged into the roundabout before accelerating the cycle back up from second to third to fourth gear. He was now speeding down what was once named Gran Via de les Corts Catalanes and saw–a kilometer away–the towering, mechanical, heavy armor bi-pedal battle tank droid standing on its thick, iron cast hind legs at the center of the Plaça de les Glòries. The battle droid's upper torso began rotating in the direction to which Lleó was riding. He zoomed the binocular lenses of his helmet onto his target and could see the droid's cockpit–tinted, thick glass reinforced by a webbed frame of titanium–at its center. He sighted its two mounted, multiple missile launchers each holding sixteen 183-millimeter rockets and its four sets of fast-firing, six-barreled 24-millimeter rotary cannons. Immediately, the cannon's specifications appeared on his visor's screen highlighting its rate of fire: 8,000 rounds per minute.

    Lleó prepared for cycle transformation. He signaled with a thought to the computer to release the cycle's racing fuel and to begin power transition to its electric generator. He unholstered his handgun, looked back, and fired several rounds at the street behind him until the stream of leaking fuel from his motorcycle lit on fire creating a burning trail that chased after his vehicle.

    "What in God's name are you doing?" Xavi shouted. "You're lighting yourself up!"

    The digital screen projected on Lleó's visor, then flashed in red bold text: Drone Lock On. Lleó accelerated up to seventh gear passing the old bullring that had been razed to the ground by the bombardment of heavy artillery and could see that he had only seconds before the battle droid would be able to target and fire upon him. His screen now read: Drone Missile Launch.

    "White Lion Two-Six–you have one–two–three–I repeat three–Hellfire II missiles deployed with heading one-one-two-nine," Junichi informed with rising anxiety.

    "Cycle transformation on *my* mark," Lleó began the three-second countdown. He increased speed, passed another city block, and prepared himself as he watched the three Hellfire missiles bearing down on his position on the digital map. He leaned the cycle to the left side of the inclining street, fired his boosters, and shot the motorcycle up the street ramp to the elevated roundabout that had been half torn down. Jettisoning the cycle's ten-cylinder, liquid-cooled 20-valve engine in midair, he launched the plasma thrusters as he somersaulted further up into the dark air toward the battle droid's cockpit. The battle droid began firing its rotary cannons tearing up and shredding the four-lane avenue. Instantly the cycle transformed around Lleó's body into a heavily armored exoskeleton. Lleó's body spread open and crashed directly on top of the battle droid's cockpit. He looked down seeing the front wheel of his cycle now attached to his armored left forearm acting as a shield and saw the battle droid's masked pilot looking up at him in disbelief.

*   *   *

A massive explosion lit up the satellite image of Plaça de les Glòries. Xavi's eyes widened as he watched the second and third drone Hellfire missiles strike, explode, and destroy the battle droid releasing a massive mushrooming cloud of fire and ash into the night sky. He collapsed into his padded, metallic command chair and stared at the center screen of the command center dreading the thought that Lleó had been killed. All in the room were quiet as they watched the rockets from the droid's the two mounted, multiple missile launchers ignite, discharge, or launch—sending red lines of fire in all directions around the plaza—and collide into and demolish the windows, balconies, floors, and roofs of several surrounding buildings.

Junichi looked over to Xavi, stood up from his workstation, approached him, and placed his hand on his shoulder to comfort him through the loss of his young friend. Moments passed. A thick, somber air consumed the command center. There were no whispers, no talk, and no thought of what to have made of this first, but failed mission of Lleó Two-Six. Junichi inhaled deep into his lungs and let out the tight air within his chest and watched as the rising smoke from the scene began to clear as a result of a sudden gust of wind from the sea. He listened to the radio only hearing static and saw the data of Lleó's vital signs on another screen frozen from the moment of the first Hellfire missile impact into the battle tank droid. All communication with the exoskeleton cycle's computer had been severed.

But there, at the northeastern exit of Gran Via, a dark object moved. "What? What is that?" he asked as he pointed to the moving object on the center screen.

Xavi straightened his back and looked to where Junichi was pointing. "What? I don't see anything."

Junichi took a few steps toward the screen and pointed directly to the moving object.

"Can we zoom in?" Xavi requested.

"Yes, sir," replied a voice from one of the command center's personnel.

435

The satellite image began to zoom in on the northeastern exit. And there, through the gusts of black smoke did they see several large, burnt metallic sheets and plating that covered a crater being abruptly moved by something beneath. The satellite image magnified the crater that was surrounded by piles of bent and distorted iron beams that seemed to have been thrown about like matchsticks. A seared plate was thrust suddenly from the crater.

Xavi stood up and approached the large screen with squinting eyes trying to make out what was causing the movement within that smoldering crater.

Another plate was lifted up and fell back and away revealing the rear wheel of the cycle attached to the upper armored back of Lleó's powered exoskeleton.

"I can't believe it!" Xavi cried. "That's him! He's alive! That– that crazy bastard," he said relieved as he watched the exosuit, burnt and damaged, begin to step up along the rocky slope of the crater and onto the street. He could see the lights of many apartments all along Gran Via beginning to turn on in the aftermath of the explosion.

"White Lion Two-Six, do you copy, over?" Xavi said into the static of his radio transmitter. "White Lion Two-Six, do you copy, over?" he repeated. "Switch to the satphone and see if we can establish a link," he commanded.

"Yes, sir," another voice called out confirming that he would initiate the request.

"White Lion Two-Six, do you copy, over? White Lion we have visual, over. We have visual. What is your status? Damage assessment requested, we have lost link to exo's COM, over."

"Repeat, over," a young voice called back.

A roar of shouts and applause rang out in the command center as soon as Lleó's voice was heard.

"White Lion Two-Six," he smiled. "This is Red Cross One-Eight. We have lost link to exo's COM. Damage assessment requested, over."

"The exoframe has sustained significant damage," the line then crackled, "but actuator cylinders and servomotors in order. Primary cells–forty percent. COM reads that I can exit station and cycle back, over."

"Exit and cycle to one-one-nine T, over," Xavi ordered.

"Will exit and cycle," Lleó complied. "White Lion Two-Six, over and out."

"Over and out," he said as he looked at Junichi with a grin as he shut off his satphone link. Relieved, he looked down, relaxed his shoulders, shook his head, and muttered, "What he did was impossible."

"Not for a cybernetic," Junichi reminded him.

Xavi's brow furrowed as he thought of the moment when he would need to explain to Lleó the truth of what they had done to him. He walked to his command chair, sat down, took his old, blue mug from the stainless-steel counter, and leaned back into his seat. He took a sip, looked at the center screen, and watched the exoframe transform into a leaner, electrically powered stealth motorcycle. He saw a cloud of white vapor smoke up around the rear tire. The rear of the cycle began to turn toward the center of the wrecked street as more and more white smoke smoldered from the burnout leaving an arced skid mark. The motorcycle then shot forward and sped instantly down a three-lane street that was partially enclosed by a decades old three-kilometer reinforced concrete overhang.

Agitated he scratched the mole beneath his eye and mumbled, "It has begun."

NOTES

SAYONARA 日本
1. Yoel Sano, "The Rising Sun slowly sets," in *Asia Times* online, last modified April 27, 2006,
http://www.atimes.com/atimes/Japan/HD27Dh01.html.
2. Maciamo, "Registered foreigners in Japan and by prefecture," in *Wapedia*, last modified July 31, 2005,
http://www.wapedia.com/gaijin/foreigners_in_japan.shtml.
3. Maciamo, "Registered foreigners in Japan."
4. Keiko Sakurai, *Nihon No Musurimu Shakai (Japan's Muslim Societies)* (Tokyo: Chikuma Shobo, 2003), 33.
5. Sakurai, *Nihon No Musurimu Shakai*, 41.
6. Naoto Higuichi, "Do Transnational Migrants Transplant Social Networks? Remittances, Investments, and Social Mobility Among Bangladeshi and Iranian Returnees from Japan," in *8th Asia Pacific Migration Research Network Conference* (UNESCO, May 2007), 7-8.

AN NYOUNG HA SAE YO SOUTH KOREA
1. "The 5 Palaces of Seoul," in *The Chosun Ilbo* online, last modified January 24, 2012,
http://english.chosun.com/site/data/html_dir/2012/01/24/2012012400190.html.
2. Samuel Jay Hawley, *The Imjin War: Japan's Sixteenth-Century Invasion of Korea and Attempt to Conquer China* (Seoul: The Royal Asiatic Society, Korea Branch, 2005), 490.
3. Nick Easen, "Korea's DMZ: The thin green line," in *CNN* online, last modified August 25, 2003,
http://edition.cnn.com/2003/WORLD/asiapcf/east/08/22/korea.bio.dmz/.
4. Keith L. Pratt, Richard Rutt and James Hoare, *Korea: A Historical and Cultural Dictionary* (Durham East-Asia series, Psychology Press, 1999), 145.
5. Barbara Ann Kipfer, *Encyclopedic Dictionary of Archaeology* (New York: Kluwer Academic/Plenum, 2000), 232.
6. Pratt, Rutt and Hoare, *Korea: A Historical and Cultural Dictionary*, 145.
7. Sarah M. Nelson, *The Archaeology of Korea* (Cambridge: Cambridge University Press, 1993), 250.
8. Alfred Molon, "Orung (Five tombs)," in *Photo Galleries*, last modified August 3, 2006,
http://www.molon.de/galleries/Korea/Gyeongju/Orung/.
9. *World Heritage in Korea*, 길잡이미디어, (Cultural Heritage Administration, Republic of Korea, 2002), 28.

SINGAPORE

1. "Capital punishment and implementation of the safeguards guaranteeing protection of the rights of those facing the death penalty" (PDF), in *United Nation Economic and Social Council: Commission on Crime Prevention and Criminal Justice*, Tenth Session, Vienna (May 8-17, 2001), 18, accessed April 24, 2015, http://www.unodc.org/pdf/crime/10_commission/10e.pdf.
2. "The Merlion is Singapore's New Tourist Image," in *Straits Times* online, last modified August 09, 1972, http://web.archive.org/web/20140910215739/http://www.publicart.sg/?q=book/export/html/326.
3. "The Lion with a Fish Tail is Tourist's Board New Emblem," in *Straits Times* online, last modified April 25, 1964, http://web.archive.org/web/20140910215739/http://www.publicart.sg/?q=book/export/html/326.
4. Heng Wong, "Operation Sook Ching," in *Infopedia – National Library Board, Singapore*, last modified September 29, 1997, http://web.archive.org/web/20080723055935/http://infopedia.nlb.gov.sg/articles/SIP_40_2005-01-24.html.
5. "Did Lee Become PM by One Vote?" in *AsiaOne* online, last modified September 10, 2009, http://news.asiaone.com/News/AsiaOne+News/Singapore/Story/A1Story20090910-166931.html.
6. "Singapore City Hall," in *YourSingapore.com*, accessed July 7, 2015, http://www.yoursingapore.com/content/traveller/en/browse/see-and-do/culture-and-heritage/a-touch-of-history/world-war-heritage-sites/Singapore-City-Hall.html.
7. "Our History," in *Humble Beginnings, Singapore Cricket Club*, accessed July 7, 2015, http://scc.org.sg/about/humble-beginnings.
8. Irene Lim, *Secret Societies in Singapore: Featuring the William Stirling Collection* (Singapore: National Heritage Board, Singapore History Museum, 1999).
9. Lim, *Secret Societies in Singapore*.
10. Lim, *Secret Societies in Singapore*.
11. "Park Experience," in *Night Safari*, accessed July 10, 2015, http://www.nightsafari.com.sg/visitor-info/park-experience.html.
12. "Little Known Facts about the Night Safari," in *Time Out Singapore* online, accessed July 10, 2015, http://www.timeout.com/singapore/things-to-do/little-known-facts-about-the-night-safari.
13. "Leopard Trail," in *Night Safari*, accessed July 10, 2015, http://www.nightsafari.com.sg/walking-trails/leopard-trail.html#content1.
14. "Singapore: Kwan Im Thing Hood Cho Temple," in *Universes in Universe*, accessed July 10, 2015, http://universes-in-universe.de/car/Singapore/eng/ort/kwan/index.htm.

15. "Kwan Im Thong Hood Cho Temple," in *Wikipedia: The Free Encyclopedia*, accessed July 11, 2015, https://en.wikipedia.org/wiki/Kwan_Im_Thong_Hood_Cho_Temple.
16. Thulaja Naidu, "Sri Krishnan Temple," in *Infopedia – National Library Board, Singapore*, last modified December 24, 2004, http://eresources.nlb.gov.sg/infopedia/articles/SIP_276_2004-12-24.html.
17. "38 Residents Left on Pulau Ubin," in *inSing* online, last modified July 16, 2012, http://features.insing.com/feature/residents-pulau-ubin-decrease-38/id-5f563f00/.
18. "GDP per capita (current US$)," in *The World Bank* online, accessed March 9, 2019, http://data.worldbank.org/indicator/NY.GDP.PCAP.CD?locations=SG.
19. "GDP per capita (current US$)."
20. Sean Coughlan, "Pisa tests: Singapore top in global education rankings," in *BBC* online, last modified December 6, 2016, https://www.bbc.com/news/education-38212070.
21. Drew Desilver, "U.S. students' academic achievement still lags that of their peers in many countries," Pew Research Center, last modified February 15, 2017, http://www.pewresearch.org/fact-tank/2017/02/15/u-s-students-internationally-math-science/.
22. Coughlan, "Pisa tests: Singapore top in the global education rankings."
23. Coughlan.
24. Coughlan.
25. Coughlan.
26. Dominic Rushe, "The US spends more on education than other countries. Why is it falling behind?" in *The Guardian*, last modified September 7, 2018, https://www.theguardian.com/us-news/2018/sep/07/us-education-spending-finland-south-korea.
27. Rushe, "The US spends more on education than other countries. Why is it falling behind?"
28. Rushe.
29. Rushe.
30. Rushe.
31. "Singapore: Intolerant Government, Self-censorship," in *Reporters Without Borders*, accessed March 10, 2019, http://rsf.org/en/singapore.
32. "Singapore: Intolerant Government, Self-censorship."
33. "Singapore: Freedom in the World 2015," in *Freedom House*, last modified December 1, 2016, https://freedomhouse.org/report/freedom-world/2015/singapore.
34. "Amnesty International Report 2009: The State of the World's Human Rights" (PDF), in *Amnesty International*, 290, accessed March 11, 2019, https://www.amnesty.org/en/documents/pol10/001/2009/en/.
35. Hans Rosling, *Factfulness* (Hodder & Stoughton, 2019), 33.

36. Rosling, *Factfulness*, 137.

MALAYSIA

1. "Agriculture Sector," in *Volvo Trucks Malaysia*, accessed July 17, 2015, http://www.volvotrucks.com/trucks/Malaysia-markets/enmy/trucks/Truck_by_industry/Pages/agriculture.aspx.
2. Michael Shean, "MALAYSIA: Stagnating Palm Oil Yields Impede Growth," in *Commodity Intelligence Report – United States Department of Agriculture – Foreign Agriculture Service*, last modified December 11, 2012, http://www.pecad.fas.usda.gov/highlights/2012/12/Malaysia/.
3. Marcus Cholchester, Thomas Jalong and Wong Meng Chuo, "Free Prior and Informed Consent in the Palm Oil Sector – Sarawak: IOI-Pelita and the Community of Long Teran Kanan," in *Forest Peoples Programme*, last modified October 2, 2012, http://www.forestpeoples.org/topics/palm-oil-rspo/publication/2012/free-prior-and-informed-consent-palm-oil-sector-sarawak-ioi-pe.
4. "Palm Oil: Cooking the Climate," in *Greenpeace International*, last modified November 08, 2007, http://www.greenpeace.org/international/en/news/features/palm-oil_cooking-the-climate/.
5. "Official Palm Oil Information Source," in *PalmOilWorld.org*, accessed July 17, 2015, http://www.palmoilworld.org/sustainability.html.
6. "Biodiesel – Just the Basics" (PDF), in *U.S. Department of Energy* (2003), accessed July 20, 2015, http://www1.eere.energy.gov/vehiclesandfuels/pdfs/basics/jtb_biodiesel.pdf.
7. "FAQ: Palm Oil, Forests and Climate Change," in *Greenpeace UK*, last modified November 8, 2007, http://www.greanpeace.org.uk/forests/faq-palm-oil-forests-and-climate-change.
8. "FAQ: Palm Oil, Forests and Climate Change."
9. "FAQ: Palm Oil, Forests and Climate Change."
10. Alex Morales, "Malaysia Has Little Room for Palm Oil Expansion, Minister Says," in *Bloomberg* online, last modified November 18, 2010, http://www.bloomberg.com/news/articles/2010-11-18/Malaysia-has-little-room-for-palm-oil-expansion-plantation-minister-says.
11. "Annual Biofuel Demand Forecasted at 51 Billion Gallons by 2022," in *Biomass Magazine* online, last modified February 10, 2014, http://biomassmagazine.com/articles/10002/annual-biofuel-demand-forecasted-at-51-billion-gallons-by-2022.
12. David Crystal, *The Cambridge Encyclopedia of the English Language* (2nd ed. Cambridge: Cambridge University Press, 2003), 109.
13. "CTBUH Criteria for Defining and Measuring Tall Buildings," in *Council on Tall Buildings and Urban Habitat*, accessed August 1, 2015,

http://ctbuh.org/TallBuildings/HeightStatistics/Criteria/tabid/446/language/en-US/Default.aspx.

14. William D. Middleton, *On Railways Far Away* (Bloomington, IN: Indiana University Press, 2012), 236.
15. "Dataran Merdeka (Independence Square)," in *Welcome Kuala Lumpur*, accessed August 31, 2015, http://www.welcome-kl.com/dataran-merdeka-independence-square/.
16. "Dataran Merdeka (Independence Square)."
17. "1.3 Million Mark Thaipusam," in *The Star* online, last modified February 2, 2007, http://www.thestar.com.my/story/?file=/2007/2/2/nation/16758526&sec=nation.
18. "1.3 Million Mark Thaipusam."
19. "List of Longest Bridge in the World," in *Wikipedia: The Free Encyclopedia*, accessed September 14, 2015, https://en.wikipedia.org/wiki/List_of_longest_bridges_in_the_world.
20. "Chap Goh Meh," in *Lonely Planet* online, accessed September 27, 2015, http://www.lonelyplanet.com/Malaysia/peninsular-maaysia-west-cost/georgetown/events/local-festivals-culture/chap-goh-meh.
21. "Jubilee Clock Tower, Georgetown, Penang, Malaysia," in *VictoriaWeb*, accessed September 27, 2015, http://www.victoriaweb.org/art/architecture/penang/01.html.
22. "Cheong Fatt Tze Mansion," in *Tourism Malaysia*, accessed October 02, 2015, http://www.toursim.gov.my/en/my/places/states-of-malaysia/penang/cheong-fatt-tze-mansion.
23. "The Famous Khoo Kongsi Clanhouse/Heritage Buildings/Heritage," in *Tourism Penang Traveller's Guide*, accessed August 8, 2016, http://www.tourismpenang.net.my/index.php/Heritage-Buildings/the-famous-khoo-kingsi-clanhouse.
24. "The Architectural Configuration of the Leong San Tong Khoo Kongsi Complex," in *Leong San Tong Khoo Kongsi*, accessed August 8, 2016, http://www.khookongsi.com.my/the-tour/the-architectural-configuration-of-the-leong-san-tong-khoo-kongsi-complex/.
25. "The Famous Khoo Kongsi Clanhouse/Heritage Buildings/Heritage."
26. "Leong San Tong Khoo Kongsi," in *Leong San Tong Khoo Kongsi*, accessed August 8, 2016, http://www.khookongsi.com.my/.
27. "The Stone Carving and Structure of Leong San Tong," in *Leong San Tong Khoo Kongsi*, accessed August 10, 2016, http://www.khookongsi.com.my/the-tour/the-stone-carving-and-structure-of-leong-san-tong/.
28. "The Spatial Order and Roof Patterns of the Leong San Tong," in *Leong San Tong Khoo Kongsi*, accessed August 10, 2016, http://www.kookongsi.com.my/the-tour/the-spatial-order-and-roof-patterns-of-the-leong-san-tong/.

29. "Religious Beliefs," in *Leong San Tong Khoo Kongsi*, accessed August 10, 2016, http://www.khookongsi.com.my/the-tour/religious-beliefs/.
30. "Religious Beliefs."
31. "Religious Beliefs."
32. "The Stone Carving and Structure of Leong San Tong."
33. "The Murals and Coloured Drawings in Leong San Tong," in *Leong San Tong Khoo Kongsi*, accessed August 10, 2016, http://www.khookongsi.com.my/the-tour/the-murals-and-coloured-drawings-in-leong-san-tong/.
34. "The Murals and Coloured Drawings in Leong San Tong."
35. "The Murals and Coloured Drawings in Leong San Tong."
36. "Malaysia – GDP per Capita," in *IndexMundi*, accessed August 11, 2016, http://www.indexmundi.com/facts/malaysia/gdp-per-capita.

MYANMAR (BURMA) & BANGKOK, THAILAND

1. Charles Kemp and Lance A. Rasbridge, *Refugee and Immigrant Health: A Handbook for Health Professionals* (Cambridge, U.K.: Cambridge University Press, 2004), 98.
2. J. Moe, "Thanaka withstands the tests of time," in *Mizzima News* online, last modified September 17, 2008, http://www.mizzima.com/news/regional/1053-thanaka-withstands-the-tests-of-time.html.
3. Ahmed Shaaban, "Man Arrested for Selling Paan, Supari," in *Khaleej Times* online, last modified August 2, 2013, http://www.khaleejtimes.com/article/20130801/ARTICLE/308019977/1011.
4. "Betel Leaf," in *World Public Library*, accessed October 2, 2016, http://www.worldlibrary.org/articles/betel_leaf#cite_note-WHOCancer-5.
5. Pe Maung Tin, "The Shwe Dagon Pagoda," in *Journal of the Burma Research Society* 24, no. 1 (1934), 1-91.
6. "Shwedagon Pagoda," in *Shwedagon Pagoda*, accessed October 28, 2016, http://shwedagonpagoda.com/index.htm.
7. "Myanmar GDP per Capita / 1998-2016 / Data / Chart / Calendar / Forecast," in *Trading Economics*, accessed October 28, 2016, http://www.tradingeconomics.com/myanmar/gdp-per-capita.
8. "The World Factbook: BURMA," in *Central Intelligence Agency*, accessed October 28, 2016, https://www.cia.gov/library/publications/the-world-factbook/geos/bm.html.
9. David Lazar, "The Monks of Burma," in *Maptia*, accessed November 1, 2016, https://maptia.com/davidlazar/stories/the-monks-of-burma.

10. "Myanmar Passenger Cars per 1,000 People, 1960-201," in *Knoema*, accessed November 12, 2016,
https://knoema.com/atlas/Myanmar/Passenger-cars-per-1000-people.
11. "Mt. Kyaiktiyo," in *Lonley Planet* online, accessed November 12, 2016,
https://www.lonelyplanet.com/myanmar-burma/mon-state/attractions/mt-kyaiktiyo/a/poisig/1044760/1335613.
12. Ryan Bishop and Lillian S. Robinson, *Night Market: Sexual Cultures and the Thai Economic Miracle* (New York: Routledge, 1998), 51.
13. "HIV/AIDS in Asia," in *amfAR*, accessed November 12, 2016,
http://www.amfar.org/around-the-world/treat-asia/aids-in-asia/hiv-aids-in-asia/.
14. "Thailand mulls legal prostitution," in *The Age* online, accessed November 13, 2016,
http://www.theage.com.au/articles/2003/11/26/1069825832486.html?oneclick=true.
15. "Heath Profile: Thailand" (PDF), in *United States Agency for International Development*, last modified March 2008,
https://www.usaid.gov/our_work/global_health/aids/Countries/ane/thailand_profile.pdf.
16. *Annex: HIV and AIDS estimates and data, 2007 and 2001* (PDF), (Geneva, Switzerland: UNAIDS, October 15, 2008), 214, accessed November 13, 2016,
http://data.unaids.org/pub/GlobalReport/2008/jc1510_2008_global_report_pp211_234_en.pdf.
17. Manopaiboon C et al. "Unexpectedly high HIV prevalence among female sex workers in Bangkok, Thailand in a respondent-driven sampling survey," in *International Journal of STD and AIDS* Jan. 24, no. 1 (2013): 34-8, doi: 10.1177/0956462412472300, accessed November 26, 2016,
http://www.ncbi.nlm.nih.gov/pubmed/23512512.
18. Cazzie Reyes, "History of Prostitution and Sex Trafficking in Thailand," in *End Slavery Now*, last modified October 8, 2015,
http://www.endslaverynow.org/blog/articles/history-of-prostitution-and-sex-trafficking-in-thailand.
19. Reyes, "History of Prostitution and Sex Trafficking in Thailand."
20. *A scaled-up response to AIDS in Asia and the Pacific* (PDF), (Geneva, Switzerland: UNAIDS, July 1, 2005), accessed November 28, 2016,
http://data.unaids.org/UNA-docs/REPORT_ICAAP_01July05_en.pdf.
21. *Thailand Recent Economic and Political Developments Yearbook* (International Business Publications USA, 2007), 27.
22. *Thailand Recent Economic and Political Developments Yearbook*, 27.
23. John Berthelsen, "AIDS' Devastating Economic Impact," in *Asia Times* online, last modified July 25, 2003,
http://www.atimes.com/atimes/Global_Economy/EG25Dj02.html.

24. Dulcey Simpkins, "Rethinking the Sex Industry: Thailand's Sex Workers, the State, and Changing Cultures of Consumption," in *Unequal Exchange: Gender and Economies of Power* 12, (1997-1998), accessed November 29, 2016, http://hdl.handle.net/2027/spo.ark5583.0012.005.
25. Simpkins, "Rethinking the Sex Industry."
26. *ILO Global Estimate of Forced Labour: Results and Methodology* (PDF), (Geneva, Switzerland: ILO, June 01, 2012), 13, accessed November 29, 2016, http://www.ilo.org/wcmsp5/groups/public/---ed_norm/---declaration/documents/publication/wcms_182004.pdf.
27. Reyes, "History of Prostitution and Sex Trafficking in Thailand."
28. Louise Brown, *Sex Slaves: The Trafficking of Women in Asia* (London: Virago, 2001), 94.
29. "Ancient Greek Dress / Essay / Heilbrunn Timeline of Art History / The Metropolitan Museum of Art," in *The Met's Heilbrunn Time of Art History*, last modified October 2003, http://www.metmuseum.org/toah/hd/grdr/hd_grdr.htm.
30. Juliette Donatelli, "The History of Fabric Dye," in *Zady*, accessed December 6, 2016, https://zady.com/features/the-history-of-fabric-dye.
31. Mark Cartwright, "Tyrian Purple," in *Ancient History Encyclopedia*, last modified July 21, 2016, http://www.ancient.eu/Tyrian_Purple/.
32. "Fermented and Vegetables. A Global Perspective. Chapter 4," in *Food and Agriculture Organization of the United Nations*, accessed December 6, 2016, http://www.fao.org/docrep/x0560e/x0560e09.htm.
33. "History of Chatuchak Market," in *Chatuchak Weekend Market*, last modified August 30, 2016, http://www.chatuchakmarket.org/news/history-of-chatuchak-market.
34. "Historic City of Ayutthaya," in *UNESCO World Heritage Centre*, accessed December 8, 2016, http://whc.unesco.org/en/list/576.
35. "Historic City of Ayutthaya."
36. Robert Johnson and Gus Lubin, "The 16 Greatest Cities in Human History," in *Business Insider* online, last modified January 20, 2013, http://www.businessinsider.com/largest-cities-throughout-history-2013-1#ayutthaya-took-the-lead-in-1700-ad-with-1000000-citizens-13.
37. "Historic City of Ayutthaya."
38. "Historic City of Ayutthaya."
39. "Attractions: Wat Phra Mahathat," in *amazing Thailand*, accessed December 9, 2016, http://au.tourismthailand.org/Attraction/Wat-Phra-Mahathat--7.
40. Andrea Krystine, "EFF SOURCE Fashion Business Success without Compromise," in *The Ethical Fashion Source*, last modified March 13, 2013, http://source.ethicalfashionforum.com/digital/lotus-flower-fabric-a-new-alternative-to-waterproof-synthetics.
41. "Shinbyu: Rite of Passage from Boy to Manhood," in *Mingalapar – All About Myanmar*, last modified July 13, 2013,

42. *Myanmar Opium Survey 2004* (PDF), in *United Nations – Office on Drug and Crime* (UNODC) (October 2004), 24, accessed December 27, 2016, https://www.unodc.org/pdf/myanmar/myanmar_opium_survey_2004.pdf.
43. Ashely South, *Ethnic politics in Burma: states of conflict* (London: Routledge, 2008), 145.
44. "UN report: Opium cultivation rising in Burma," in *BBC* online, last modified October 31, 2012, http://www.bbc.com/news/world-asia-20150082.
45. "Opium production 'on the rise in SE Asia'," in *Al Jazeera* online, last modified October 31, 2012, http://www.aljazeera.com/news/asia-pacific/2012/10/201210314589154343.html.
46. "A Modern Form of Slavery: Trafficking of Burmese Women and Girls into Brothels in Thailand," in *Human Rights Watch* (1993), accessed December 28, 2016, https://www.hrw.org/reports/1993/thailand/#_1_16.
47. "A Modern Form of Slavery: Trafficking of Burmese Women and Girls into Brothels in Thailand."
48. Joshua Eliot and Jane Bickersteth, *Myanmar (Burma) handbook* (Bath, Eng.: Footprint Handbooks, 1997).
49. Ashley South, *Mon Nationalism and Civil War in Burma: The Golden Sheldrake* (London: Routledge, 2003), 419.
50. "Thailand: Sustaining Health Protection for All," in *The World Bank* online, last modified August 20, 2012, https://www.worldbank.org/en/news/feature/2012/08/20/Thailand-sustaining-health-protection-for-all.
51. Jessica C. Barnett and Edward R. Berchick, "Health Insurance Coverage in the United States: 2016," in *United States Census Bureau* online, last modified September 12, 2017, https://www.census.gov/library/publications/2017/demo/p60-260.html.
52. "Overview of the Uninsured in the United States: An analysis of the 2007 Current Population Survey," in *U.S. Department of Health and Human Services Office of the Assistant Secretary for Planning and Evaluation* online, last modified August 1, 2007, https://aspe.hhs.gov/basic-report/overview-uninsured-united-states-analysis-2007-current-population-survey.
53. "Overview of the Uninsured in the United States: An analysis of the 2007 Current Population Survey."
54. "Health financing profile 2017 Thailand" (PDF), in *World Health Organization: South-East Asia*, https://apps.who.int/iris/bitstream/handle/10665/259645/HFP-THA.pdf?sequemce=1&isAllowed=y.

55. "2017 Health SDG Profile: Thailand" (PDF), in *World Health Organization: South-East Asia*, last modified June 2017, http://www.searo.who.int/entity/health_situation_trends/countryprofile_tha.pdf?ua=1.
56. "2018 Health SDG Profile: Thailand" (PDF), in *World Health Organization: South-East Asia*, last modified July 2018, http://www.searo.who.int/entity/health_situation_trends/cp_tha.pdf?ua=1.
57. "Health financing profile 2017 Thailand" (PDF).
58. "2017 Health SDG Profile: Thailand" (PDF).
59. "2018 Health SDG Profile: Thailand" (PDF).
60. "Health expenditure and financing," in *Organization for Economic Co-operation and Development* (OECD) online, https://stats.oecd.org/Index.aspx?DataSetCode=SHA.
61. "Policy Basics: Where Do Our Federal Tax Dollars Go?" in *Center on Budget and Policy Priorities* online, last modified January 29, 2019, https://www.cbpp.org/research/federal-budget/policy-basics-where-do-out-federal-tax-dollars-go.
62. Bradley Sawyer and Cynthia Cox, "How does health spending in the U.S. compare to other countries?" in *Peterson-Kaiser Health System Tracker*, last modified December 7, 2018, https://www.healthsystemstracker.org/chart-collection/health-spending-u-s-compare-countries/#item-relative-size-wealth-u-s-spends-disproportionate-amount-health.
63. Sawyer and Cox, "How does health spending in the U.S. compare to other countries?"
64. Sawyer and Cox.
65. Sawyer and Cox.
66. Sawyer and Cox.
67. Sawyer and Cox.
68. Ajay Tandon, Christopher J. L. Murray, Jeremy A. Lauer, David B. Evans, "Measuring overall health system performance for 191 countries" (PDF), in GPE Discussion Paper Series: No. 30, EIP/GPE/EQC, *The World Health Report 2000*, World Health Organization, June 21, 2000, https://www.who.int/healthinfo/paper30.pdf.
69. Tandon, Murray, Lauer, Evans, "Measuring overall health system performance for 191 countries" (PDF).
70. Nicole Galan, "What are Medicare and Medicaid," in *Medical News Today* online, last modified November 30, 2018, https://www.medicalnewstoday.com/articles/323858.php.
71. Nicole Galan, "What are Medicare and Medicaid."
72. Galan.
73. Edward R. Berchick, Emily Hood, and Jessica C. Barnett, "Health Insurance Coverage in the United States: 2017," in *United States Census Bureau* online, last modified September 12, 2018,

https://www.census.gov/library/publications/2018/demo/p60-264.html.
74. Sawyer and Cox, "How does health spending in the U.S. compare to other countries?"
75. Sara Boboltz, "Yep, Martin Shkreli's 5,000 Percent Drug Price Hike Is Stil In Effect," in *Huffpost* online, last modified March 9, 2018, https://www.huffpost.com/entry/martin-shkreli-aids-drug-price-the-same_n_5aa3117fe4b07047bec694cb.
76. William T. Cefalu, Daniel E. Dawes, Gina Gavlak, Dana Goldman, William H. Herman, Karen Van Nuys, Alvin C. Powers, Simeon I. Taylor, Alan L. Yatvin, "Insulin Access and Affordability Working Group: Conclusions and Recommendations," in *Diabetes Care* Jun. 41, no. 6 (2018): 1299-1311, doi: 10.2337/dci18-0019, accessed June 30, 2019, https://care.diabetesjournals.org/content/41/6/1299.
77. Ritu Prasad, "The human cost of insulin in America," in *BBC* online, last modified March 14, 2019, https://www.bbc.com/news/world-us-canada-47491964.
78. "Diabetes Drug Intelligence Center 2019: Global Database with Coverage Through 2012–2023 – Insulin Holds the Highest Market Share, and Sanofi, Novo Nordisk, and Eli Lilly Dominate – ResearchAndMarkets.com," in *MarketWatch* online, last modified March 20, 2019, https://www.marketwatch.com/press-release/diabetes-drug-intelligence-center-2019-gobal-database-with-coverage-through-2012-2023---insulin-holds-the-highest-market-share-and-sanofi-novo-nordisk-and-eli-lilly-dominate---researchandmarketscom-2019-03-20.
79. Prasad, "The human cost of insulin in America."

CHIANG MAI, THAILAND

1. "Thailand Travel & Tourism Total Contribution to GDP Total Contribution to GDP – % share, 1988-2015," in *Knoema*, accessed December 30, 2016, https://knoema.com/atlas/Thailand/topics/Tourism/Travel-and-Tourism-Total-Contribution-to-GDP/Total-Contribution-to-GDP-percent-share.
2. "Visitor Statistics, 1998-2015," in *Department of Tourism Thailand*, accessed December 30, 2016, http://newdot2.samartmultimedia.com/home/listcontent/11/221/276.
3. "TOD Advisor's Notebook / Information for Fan-Fiction Writers / R&R and Leave in Vietnam," in *Tour of Duty Info*, accessed January 2, 2017, http://www.tourofdutyinfo.com/Notebook/Essay4-R&R.htm.
4. "Thailand mulls legal prostitution," in *The Age* online, accessed November 13, 2016, http://www.theage.com.au/articles/2003/11/26/1069825832486.html?oneclick=true.
5. "Heath Profile: Thailand" (PDF), in *United States Agency for International Development*, last modified March 2008,

6. https://www.usaid.gov/our_work/global_health/aids/Countries/ane/thailand_profile.pdf.
6. Dulcey Simpkins, "Rethinking the Sex Industry: Thailand's Sex Workers, the State, and Changing Cultures of Consumption," in *Unequal Exchange: Gender and Economies of Power* 12, (1997-1998), accessed November 29, 2016, http://hdl.handle.net/2027/spo.ark5583.0012.005.
7. "Thailand mulls legal prostitution."
8. Manopaiboon C et al. "Unexpectedly high HIV prevalence among female sex workers in Bangkok, Thailand in a respondent-driven sampling survey," in *International Journal of STD and AIDS* Jan. 24, no. 1 (2013): 34-8, doi: 10.1177/0956462412472300, accessed November 26, 2016, http://www.ncbi.nlm.nih.gov/pubmed/23512512.
9. *Thailand Recent Economic and Political Developments Yearbook* (International Business Publications, USA, 2007), 27.
10. *Thailand Recent Economic and Political Developments Yearbook*, 27.
11. Chokechai Rongkavilit, Usa Thisyakorn and Praphan Phanuphak, *Prevention of Mother-to-Child Transmission of HIV: Thai Red Cross Zidovudine Donation Programme* (PDF), (Geneva, Switzerland: UNAIDS, September 2000), 2, accessed January 3, 2017, http://pdf.usaid.gov/pdf_docs/Pnacl383.pdf.
12. *Country Report: Thailand* (PDF), (East Asia and Pacific Regional Consultation on Children and HIV/AIDS Hanoi, Viet Nam 22 – 24 March 2006), 1, accessed January 3, 2017, https://www.unicef.org/eapro/13_thailand.pdf.
13. *Children on the Brink 2002: A Joint Report on Orphan Estimates and Program Strategies* (PDF), (UNAIDS, USAID, UNICEF. UNAIDS, July 2002), 26, accessed January 3, 2017, http://data.unaids.org/topics/young-people/childrenonthebrink_en.pdf.

LAOS

1. "Tales of Saddam's Brutality," in *National Archives and Records Administration*, last modified September 29, 2003, https://georgewhitehouse.archives.gov/news/releases/2003/09/20030929-14.html.
2. Seymour M. Hersh, "Torture at Abu Ghraib," in *The New Yorker* online, last modified May 10, 2004, http://www.newyorker.com/magazine/2004/05/10/torture-at-abu-ghraib.
3. "Hyperinflation under control, Lao minister says," in *The Free Library*, last modified March 23, 2000, https://www.thefreelibrary.com/Hyperinflation+under+control%2c+Lao+minister+says.-a061543946.
4. Jeff Cranmer, Emma Gibbs, Steven Martin and Steven Vickers, *The Rough Guide to Laos* (London: Rough Guides, 2011), 298.
5. "Lao PDR – Population density," in *IndexMundi*, accessed March 12, 2017, http://www.indexmundi.com/facts/lao-pdr/population-density.

6. Bruno Philip, "Laos, south-east Asia's new emerging economy," in *The Guardian* online, last modified November 6, 2012, https://www.theguardian.com/world/2012/nov/06/laos-southeast-asia-emerging-economy.
7. "Royal Palace Museum," in *Asia for Visitors*, accessed March 12, 2017, http://www.asiaforvisitors.com/laos/prabang/museum/.
8. "Wat Wisunalat," in *Renown Travel*, accessed March 13, 2017, https://www.renown-travel.com/laos/temples/wat-wisunalat.html.
9. "Laos: Barack Obama regrets 'biggest bombing in history'," in *BBC* online, last modified September 7, 2016, http://www.bbc.com/news/world-asia-37286520.
10. "Laos: Barack Obama regrets 'biggest bombing in history'."
11. "Laos: Barack Obama regrets 'biggest bombing in history'."
12. "Timeline: North Korea nuclear stand-off," in *BBC* online, last modified April 2, 2013, http://www.bbc.com/news/world-asia-pacific-11811861.
13. Wolf Blitzer, "Search for the 'smoking gun'," in *CNN* online, last modified January 10, 2003, http://edition.cnn.com/2003/US/01/10/wbr.smoking.gun/.
14. Alan J. Parrington, "Mutually Assured Destruction Revisited," in *Airpower Journal* XI, no. 4, (Winter 1997), accessed March 17, 2017, http://www.airpower.maxwell.af.mil/airchronicles/apj/apj97/win97/parrin.html.
15. Bernard Brodie, "The Anatomy of Deterrence," in *Strategy in the Missile Age* (Princeton: Princeton University Press, 1959), 264-304.
16. "Leftover Unexploded Ordnance (UXO)," in *Legacies of War RSS*, accessed March 17, 2017, http://legaciesofwar.org/about-laos/leftover-unexploded-ordnances-uxo/.
17. "Leftover Unexploded Ordnance (UXO)."
18. Jas Rawlinson, "Do you think we'll pay for bad things we've done?" in *news.com.au*, last modified July 4, 2016, http://www.news.com.au/travel/travel-updates/do-you-think-well-pay-for-bad-things-weve-done-revelations-of-aussie-sex-tourists-in-thailand/news-story/a1490ec57bb51253003aa5a2c1547acd.
19. J. Shih, "A plague in prostitution: HIV and AIDS in Thailand" (PDF), in *Rhode Island Medicine* (May 1994), 145-49, accessed March 24, 2017, http://prostitution.procon.org/sourcefiles/a-plague-in-prostitution-hiv-and-aids-in-thailand.pdf.
20. "Percentage of Men (by Country) Who Paid for Sex at Least Once: The Johns Chart," in *ProCon.org*, last modified January 6, 2011, http://prostitution.procon.org/view.resource.php?resourceD=004119.
21. "Laos Corruption perceptions – Transparency International – data, chart," in *TheGlobalEconomy.com*, accessed March 31, 2017, http://www.theglobaleconomy.com/Laos/transparency_corruption/.

22. "Poverty & Equity Data Portal," in *The World Bank* online, accessed March 31, 2017, http://povertydata.worldbank.org/poverty/country/LAO.
23. "Laos: Barack Obama regrets 'biggest bombing in history'," in *BBC* online.
24. "That Dam in Vientiane, Laos," in *Lonely Planet* online, accessed March 31, 2017, https://www.lonelyplanet.com/laos/vientiane/attractions/that-dam/a/poi-sig/414446/356947.

BACK IN BANGKOK

1. "Who is Being Trafficked in Thailand?" in *United Nations Inter-Agency Project on Human Trafficking*, accessed April 5, 2017, https://web.archive.org/web/20150401075408/http://www.no-trafficking.org/thailand_who.html.
2. Lisa Rende Taylor, "Dangerous Trade-offs: The Behavioral Ecology of Child Labor and Prostitution in Rural Northern Thailand," in *Current Anthropology* 46, no. 3 (2005): 411-31, doi: 10.1086/430079. JSTOR 10.1086/430079.
3. Jeremy Seabrook, *Travels in the Skin Trade: Tourism and the Sex Industry* (London: Pluto, 2001), xiii.
4. Ryan Bishop and Lillian S. Robinson, *Night Market: Sexual Cultures and the Thai Economic Miracle* (New York: Routledge, 1998), 159.
5. Bishop and Robinson, *Night Market*, 159.
6. Donald Wilson, "Prostitution in Thailand: Blaming Uncle Sam," (Chiang Mai: Crescent Press Association, December 1994), 4-6.
7. Bishop and Robinson, *Night Market*, 159.
8. Bishop and Robinson, 159.
9. Seabrook, *Travels in the Skin Trade*, 147.
10. Seabrook, 147.
11. Seabrook, 7.
12. Bishop and Robinson, *Night Market*, 8.
13. Charles F. Keyes, *Thailand: Buddhist Kingdom as Modern Nation-State* (Boulder, Colorado: Westview Press, 1987), 113.
14. Seabrook, *Travels in the Skin Trade*, 105.
15. Seabrook, 7.
16. Bishop and Robinson, *Night Market*, 98.
17. Bishop and Robinson, 98.
18. Thanh-Dam Truong, *Sex, Money and Morality: Prostitution and Tourism in South-East Asia* (London: Zed, 1990), 162-63.
19. Bishop and Robinson, *Night Market*, 98.
20. Bishop and Robinson, 98.
21. Bishop and Robinson, 99.
22. Truong, *Sex, Money and Morality*, 179.
23. Bishop and Robinson, *Night Market*, 99.

24. Sanitsuda Ekachai, *Behind the Smile: Voices of Thailand* (Bangkok: Thai Development Support Committee, 1990).
25. Seabrook, *Travels in the Skin Trade*, 13-4.
26. Daniel Yergin, *The Prize: The Epic Quest for Oil, Money, and Power* (New York: Simon and Schuster, 2008), 587.
27. Stephanie Black, "About the Film: *Life and Debt*," in *Life and Debt* (2001), accessed April 21, 2017, http://www.lifeanddebt.org/about.html.
28. Bishop and Robinson, *Night Market*, 99.
29. Catherine Hill, "Planning for Prostitution: An Analysis of Thailand's Sex Industry," in *Women's Lives and Public Policy: The International Experience* Eds. Meredeth Turshen and Briavel Holcomb (Westport, Conn.: Greenwood Press, 1993), 138.
30. Barbara Leitch LePoer, *Thailand, A Country Study* (Washington, D.C.: United States Department of the Army, 1989), 134.
31. Seabrook, *Travels in the Skin Trade*, 6.
32. Seabrook, 81.
33. Louise Brown, *Sex Slaves: The Trafficking of Women in Asia* (London: Virago, 2001), 81.
34. "Who is Being Trafficked in Thailand?" in *United Nations Inter-Agency Project on Human Trafficking*.
35. Bishop and Robinson, *Night Market*, 213.
36. Bishop and Robinson, 160.
37. "Asia Watch Women's Right Project," in *A Modern Form of Slavery* (New York: Human Rights Watch, 1993).
38. Kazuko Watanabe, "Trafficking in Women's Bodies, Then and Now: The Issue of Military 'Comfort Women,'" in *Peace & Change* 20, no. 4 (October, 1995), 501-14.
39. Richard Rhodes, "Death in the Candy Store," in *Rolling Stone* (November 1992), 69.
40. Bishop and Robinson, *Night Market*, 215.
41. Bishop and Robinson, 10.
42. Bishop and Robinson, 10.
43. Bishop and Robinson, 10-1.
44. Bishop and Robinson, 130.
45. Brown, *Sex Slaves*, 74.
46. Ecumenical Council on Third World Tourism, *Caught in Modern Slavery: Tourism and Child Prostitution in Asia* (Bangkok, 1992), 41.
47. Brown, *Sex Slaves*, 54-5.
48. Ekachai, *Behind the Smile*, 177.
49. Bishop and Robinson, *Night Market*, 214
50. Bishop and Robinson, 214.
51. Bishop and Robinson, 9.
52. Ekachai, *Behind the Smile*, 128.
53. Bishop and Robinson, *Night Market*, 213.
54. Bishop and Robinson, 213.

55. Ekachai, *Behind the Smile*, 171.
56. Bishop and Robinson, *Night Market*, 215.
57. Bishop and Robinson, 215.
58. Brown, *Sex Slaves*, 36.
59. Bangladesh National Women Lawyers' Association, *Survey in the Area of Child and Women Trafficking* (Dhaka, 1997), 36-7.
60. Brown, *Sex Slaves*, 39.
61. Brown, 74.
62. Bishop and Robinson, *Night Market*, 229.
63. "Asia Watch Women's Rights Project," in *A Modern Form of Slavery*.
64. Bishop and Robinson, *Night Market*, 8.
65. Bishop and Robinson, 8.
66. Brown, *Sex Slaves*, 4.
67. Brown, 121.
68. Bishop and Robinson, *Night Market*, 8.
69. Seabrook, *Travels in the Skin Trade*, 51.
70. Bishop and Robinson, *Night Market*, 8.
71. Seabrook, *Travels in the Skin Trade*, 74.
72. Bishop and Robinson, *Night Market*, 160.
73. Seabrook, *Travels in the Skin Trade*, 55.
74. Seabrook, 55.
75. Bishop and Robinson, *Night Market*, 160.
76. Bishop and Robinson, 160.
77. Seabrook, *Travels in the Skin Trade*, 136-7.
78. Seabrook, 71.
79. Brown, *Sex Slaves*, 168.
80. Marjan Wijers and Lin Lap-Chew, *Trafficking in Women, Forced Labour and Slavery-Like Practices in Marriage, Domestic Labour and Prostitution* (Utrecht: Foundation Against Trafficking in Women, 1997), 103.
81. Brown, *Sex Slaves*, 195.
82. Wijers and Lap-Chew, *Trafficking in Women, Forced Labour and Slavery-Like Practices in Marriage, Domestic Labour and Prostitution*, 103.
83. Brown, *Sex Slaves*, 195.
84. Brown, 201.
85. Annuska Derks, *Trafficking of Vietnamese Women and Children to Cambodia* (Geneva: International Organization for Migration, 1998), 35.
86. Brown, *Sex Slaves*, 203.
87. "Asia Watch Report," *Double Jeopardy* (January 1991).
88. Brown, *Sex Slaves*, 206.
89. Bishop and Robinson, *Night Market*, 125-6.
90. Brown, *Sex Slaves*, 150.
91. Brown, 150.
92. Brown, 149.
93. Brown, 149.
94. Brown, 147.

95. Peter N. Dale, *The Myth of Japanese Uniqueness* (Croom Helm, 1986), 160.
96. Justin McCurry, "Record numbers of couples living in sexless marriages in Japan, says report," in *The Guardian* online, last modified February 14, 2017, https://www.theguardian.com/world/2017/feb/14/record-numbers-of-couples-living-in-sexless-marriages-in-japan-says-report.
97. Anne Allison, *Permitted and Prohibited Desires: Mothers, Comics and Censorship in Japan* (Boulder, Colorado: Westview Press, 1996).
98. Louise Brown credits Dr. Norihiko Kuwayama of the Department of Neuro-Psychiatry, Yamagata University, who explained to her the psycho-sexual problems of Japanese marriages.
99. Dale, *The Myth of Japanese Uniqueness*, 160.
100. Brown, *Sex Slaves*, 145-6.
101. Seabrook, *Travels in the Skin Trade*, 2.

CAMBODIA

1. *The Cambodia Landmine Museum and School*, accessed May 19, 2017, http://www.cambodialandminemuseum.org.
2. Dan Levin, "China is urged to confront its own history," in *The New York Times* online, last modified March 30, 2015, https://sinosphere.blogs.nytimes.com/2015/03/30/cambodian-historians-call-for-china-to-confront-its-own-past/?_r=0.
3. Rebecca Joyce Frey and Dori Laub, *Genocide and International Justice* (New York: Facts on File, 2009), 83.
4. Craig Etcheson, *After the Killing Fields: Lessons from the Cambodian Genocide* (Greenwood Publishing Group, 2005), 119.
5. Randle C. Deflco, "Justice and Starvation in Cambodia: The Khmer Rouge Famine," in *Cambodia Law & Policy Journal* 2 (2014): 45-84, accessed June 7, 2017, http://cambodialpj.org/article/justice-and-starvation-in-cambodia-the-khmer-rouge-famine/.
6. Deflco, "Justice and Starvation in Cambodia," 45-84.
7. John Li and Sarah Rothstein, "Famine in Cambodia," in *World Information Transfer*, last modified January 28, 2012, http://worldinfo.org/2012/01/famine-in-cambodia/.
8. Jeffrey Hays, "Food in Cambodia," in *Facts and Details*, accessed June 7, 2017, http://factsanddetails.com/southeast-asia/Cambodia/sub5_2c/entry-2890.html.
9. "Cambodians Still Traumatized," in *Radio Free Asia*, last modified August 28, 2009, http://www.rfa.org/english/news/cambodia/trauma-08272009122315.html/.
10. Michael Turtle, "Why Is Cambodia Poor?" in *Time Travel Turtle* (blog), last modified January 2, 2015, http://www.timetravelturtle.com/2015/01/why-is-cambodia-poor/.
11. "Cambodia country profile," in *BBC* online, last modified May 28, 2017, http://www.bbc.com/news/world-asia-pacific-13006539.
12. Turtle, "Why Is Cambodia Poor?"

13. David Nathan, "The truth behind Cambodia's inequalities," in *New Internationalist*, last modified September 12, 2014, https://newint.org/features/webexclusive/2014/09/12/cambodia-economic-inequality/.
14. Daniel Bultman and Sok Udom Deth, "The Afterglow of Hun Sen's Cambodia? Socioeconomic Development, Political Change, and the Persistence of Inequalities," in *Globalization and Democracy in Southeast Asia: Challenges, Responses and Alternative Futures* edited by Chantana Banpasirichote, Boike Rehbein, and Surichai Wun'gaeo (London: Palgrave Macmillan, 2016), 87.
15. E. Luce, "UN blamed for sex boom," in *The Guardian Weekly*, November 14, 1995.
16. "Cambodia: Prostitution and Sex Trafficking: A Growing Threat to the Human Rights of Women and Children in Cambodia," in *Human Rights Task Force on Cambodia*, last modified August 13, 2001, https://web.archive.org/web/20080918233727/http://www.hrsolidarity.net/mainfile.php/1996vol06no04/219/.
17. Marc Askew, "Review: *War in the Blood. Sex, Politics and Aids in Southeast Asia* by Chris Beyrer, in *Contemporary Southeast Asia: A Journal of International and Strategic Affairs*" 20, no. 1 (April 1998), 109, accessed June 8, 2017, http://www.jstor.org/stable/25798412.
18. David Robert Jr., "Cambodia's Hun Sen Is Himself Khmer Rouge," in *The New York Times* online, last modified December 6, 1989, http://www.nytimes.com/1989/12/07/opinion/l-cambodia-s-hun-sen-is-himself-khmer-rouge-722489.html.
19. "Cambodia is Said to Torture Prisoners," in *The Boston Globe* online, last modified June 4, 1987, http://www.highbeam.com/doc/1P2-8013822.html.
20. Nate Thayer, "Dying Breath," in *Far Eastern Economic Review*, last modified April 30, 1998, http://www.nate-thayer.com/dying-breath-the-inside-story-of-pol-pots-last-days-and-the-disintegration-of-the-movement-he-created/.
21. Thayer, "Dying Breath."
22. Christina Wille, *How Many Weapons Are There in Cambodia?* (PDF), in *Geneva: Small Arms Survey* (working paper no. 4) (June 2006), 37, accessed July 12, 2017, http://www.smallarmssurvey.org/fileadmin/docs/F-Working-papers/SAS-WP4-Cambodia.pdf.
23. "Largest religious structure," in *Guinness World Records*, accessed July 12, 2017, http://www.guinessworldrecords.com/world-records/largest-religious-structure/.
24. D. Evans, C. Pottier, R. Fletcher, S. Hensley, I. Tapley, A. Milne, and M. Barbetti, "A comprehensive archaeological map of the world's largest pre-industrial settlement complex at Angkor, Cambodia," in *Proceedings of the National Academy of Sciences* 104, no. 36 (2007): 14277-4282, doi: 10.1073/pnas.0702525104, accessed July 12, 2017,

25. http://www.pnas.org/content/104/36/14277.long.
26. Charles Higham, *Civilization of Angkor* (University of California Press, 2004), 116.
27. "Killing Fields of Choeung Ek in Phnom Penh, Cambodia," in *Lonely Planet* online, accessed July 17, 2017, https://www.lonelyplanet.com/Cambodia/phnom-penh/attractions/killing-fields-of-choeung-ek/a/poi-sig/441632/355881.
28. "DC-Cam, 1995-2005: Yale University Assistance to the Documentation Center of Cambodia (DC-Cam), 1995-2005," in *Yale University: Genocide Studies Program*, accessed July 17, 2017, http://gsp.yale.edu/dc-cam-1995-2005.
29. Bruce Sharp, "Counting Hell," in *Counting Hell: The Death Toll of the Khmer Rouge Regime in Cambodia*, accessed July 17, 2017, http://www.mekong.net/cambodia/deaths.htm.
30. Craig Etcheson, "The Number: Quantifying Crimes Against Humanity in Cambodia," in *Counting Hell: The Death Toll of the Khmer Rouge Regime in Cambodia*, accessed July 18, 2017, http://www.mekong.net/Cambodia/toll.htm.
31. Brent Crane, "Skull by skull, team catalogues KR killings," in *Phnom Penh Post* online, last modified February 24, 2016, http://m.phnompenhpost.com/post-weekend/skull-skull-team-catalogues-jr-killings.
32. Crane, "Skull by skull, team catalogues KR killings."
33. John Morrocco, *Rain of Fire: Air War, 1968-1975 (Vietnam Experience)*, in *Time Life Education* (May 1985), 13.
34. Steven M. Gillon and Cathy D. Matson, *The American Experiment: A History of the United States, Since 1865*, 3rd ed., vol. 2 (Boston: Wadsworth Cengage Learning, 2013).
35. "Landmines UXO and demining," in *Open Development Cambodia* (ODC), accessed July 18, 2017, https://opendevelopmentcambodia.net/topics/landmines-uxo-and-demining/.
36. Peter Zsombor, "Landmine casualties dip below 100 for the first time," in *The Cambodian Daily* online, last modified January 4, 2017, https://www.cambodiadaily.com/news/landmine-injuries-dip-below-100-for-first-time-122921/.
37. Greg Bloom and Nick Ray, *Lonely Planet: Cambodia*, 8th ed. (Oakland, CA: Lonely Planet, 2012), 269.
38. "Cambodia Refugee Crisis: History," in *Forced Migration*, accessed July 19, 2017, http://forcedmigration.ccnmtl.columbia.edu/book/export/html/26.
39. Noam Chomsky and Edward S. Herman, *Manufacturing Consent: The Political Economy of the Mass Media* (London: Bodley Head, 2008), 272.
40. Kenton J. Clymer, *The United States and Cambodia: 1969-2000: A Troubled*

40. *Relationship* (New York: Routledge, 2004), 22.
40. Bertil Lintner, "Dining with the Dear Leader," in *Asia Times* online, accessed July 19, 2017,
http://www.atimes.com/atimes/Southeast_Asia/lC15Ae01.html.
41. Sharp, "Counting Hell."
42. Henri Locard, "State Violence in Democratic Kampuchea (1975-1979) and Retribution (1979-2004)," in *European Review of History* 12, no. 1 (March 2005), 121-143.
43. Ben Kiernan, *The Pol Pot Regime: Race, Power, and Genocide in Cambodia Under the Khmer Rouge, 1975-79* (New Haven: Yale University Press, 2014), 464.

VIETNAM

1. "GDP per capita (current US$)," in *The World Bank* online, accessed July 31, 2017,
http://data.worldbank.org/indicator/NY.GDP.PCAP.CD?locations+VN.
2. George Black, "The Vietnam War Is Still Killing People," in *The New Yorker* online, last modified June 19, 2017,
http://www.newyorker.com/news-desk-the-vietnam-war-is-still-killing-people.
3. "Landmines UXO and demining," in *Open Development Cambodia* (ODC), accessed July 31, 2017,
https://opendevelopmentcambodia.net/topics/landmines-uxo-and-demining/.
4. "UXO Victims," in *Lao National Unexploded Ordnance Programme* (UXOLAO), accessed July 31, 2017,
http://www.uxolao.org/index.php/en/the-uxo-problem/uxo-victims.
5. Kevin Mulqueen, "Meet the pirates of the high streets in Saigon," in *The Telegraph* online, last modified May 17, 2006,
http://www.telegraph.co.uk/expat/4200098/Meet-the-pirates-of-the-high-streets-in-Saigon.html.
6. "GDP per capita (current US$)."
7. Jeffrey W. Alexander, *Japan's Motorcycle Wars: An Industry History* (Vancouver: UBC Press, 2008), 209.
8. Alexander, *Japan's Motorcycle Wars*, 209.
9. Alexander, 209.
10. Guenter Lewy, *America in Vietnam* (New York: Oxford University Press, 1978), 442-453.
11. R.J. Rummel, "Chapter 2: Definition of Democide," in *Death by Government* (New Brunswick, N.J.: Transaction Publishers, 1994), accessed August 2, 2017, https://www.hawaii.edu/powerkills/DBG.CHAP2.HTM.
12. Rummel, "Chapter 2: Definition of Democide."
13. Charles Hirschman, Samuel Preston and Vu Manh Loi, "Vietnamese Casualties During the American War: A New Estimate," in *Population*

and Development Review 21, no. 4 (December 1995): 783-812. doi: 10.2307/2137774.
14. Ben Kiernan and Taylor Owen, "Bombs over Cambodia" (PDF), in *The Walrus* (October 2006): 62-69, accessed July 10, 2018, https://gsp.yale.edu/sites/default/files/walrus_cambodiabombing_oct06.pdf.
15. "3 New Names Added to Vietnam Veterans Memorial Wall," in *U.S. News & World Report* online, last modified May 29, 2017, https://www.usnews.com/news/best-states/washington-dc/articles/2017-05-29/3-new-names-added-to-vietname-veterans-memorial-wall.
16. Amy Hagopian, Abraham D. Flaxman, Tim K. Takaro, Sahar A Esa Al Shatari, Julie Rajaratnam, Stan Becker, Alison Levin-Rector, Lindsay Galway, Berq J. Hadi Al-Yasseri, William M. Weiss, Christopher J. Murray and Gilbert Burnham, "Mortality in Iraq Associated with the 2003-2011 War and Occupation: Findings from a National Cluster Sample Survey by the University Collaborative Iraq Mortality Study," in *PLoS Medicine* no. 10 (2013), doi: 10.1371/journal.pmed.1001533.
17. "Authorization for Use of Military Force Against Iraq Resolution of 2002, Pub.L. 107-243, 116 Stat. 1498, enacted October 16, 2002, H.J.Res. 114," in *U.S. Government Publishing Office*, accessed August 2, 2017, https://www.gpo.gov/fdsys/pkg/PLAW-107publ243/html/PLAW-107publ243.htm.
18. Andy McSmith Charlie Cooper, "Chilcot report: Blair didn't tell truth about WMDs, the deal with Bush or the warnings of fallout – how Britain went to war in Iraq," in *The Independent* online, last modified July 6, 2016, http://www.independent.co.uk/news/uk/politics/chilcot-report-inquiry-tony-blair-iraq-war-weapons-of-mass-destruction-evidence-verdict-a7122361.html.
19. "Vietnam War Statistics," in *International World History Project*, accessed August 3, 2017, http://history-world.org/Vietnam_war_statistics.htm.
20. "3 New Names Added to Vietnam Veterans Memorial Wall."
21. Alan Rohn, "How Much Did the Vietnam War Cost?" in *The Vietnam War*, last modified January 22, 2014, http://thevietnamwar.info/how-much-vietnam-war-cost/.
22. "Vietnam War 1962-75," in *The Australian War Memorial*, accessed August 3, 2017, https://www.awm.gov.au/articles/event/Vietnam.
23. Alan Rohn, "What countries involved in the Vietnam War?" in *The Vietnam War*, last modified January 22, 2014, http://thevietnamwar.info/how-much-vietnam-war-cost/.
24. Will Dunham, "Deaths in Vietnam, other wars undercounted: study," in *Reuters*, last modified June 20, 2008, http://www.reuters.com/article/us-war-deaths-idUSN1928547620080619.
25. "3 New Names Added to Vietnam Veterans Memorial Wall."
26. Philip Shenon, "20 Years After Victory, Vietnamese Communists Pon-

26. (cont.) der How to Celebrate," in *The New York Times* online, last modified April 23, 1995, http://www.nytimes.com/1995/04/23/world/20-years-after-victory-vietnamese-communists-ponder-how-to-celebrate.html.
27. "Murder in the name of war – My Lai," in *BBC* online, last modified July 20, 1998, http://news.bbc.co.uk/1/hi/world/asia-pacific/64344.stm.
28. " 'We killed anything that walked': Vietnam war crimes," in *Socialist-Worker.org*, last modified November 14, 2003, http://socialistworker.org/2003-2/476/476_05_WarCrimes.shtml.
29. Michael Sallah and Mitch Weiss, *The Force: A True Story of Men and War* (Boston: Little, Brown and Company, 2006), 337, 344-345, 349, 353, 370-372.
30. Sallah and Weiss, *The Force: A True Story of Men and War*, 335, 339-346, 350-352, 354-355, 359, 361-362, 367-369, 374-375, 376.
31. Sallah and Weiss, 335-336, 371.
32. Sallah and Weiss, 371.
33. Sallah and Weiss, 346, 374.
34. Sallah and Weiss, 361-362, 377-378.
35. Sallah and Weiss, 360, 363-364, 372-373.
36. "Agent Orange: Background on Monsanto's Involvement," in *Monsanto*, accessed August 4, 2017, https://monsanto.com/company/media/statements/agent-orange-background/.
37. Thomas Fuller, "4 Decades on, U.S. Starts Cleanup of Agent Orange in Vietnam," in *The New York Times* online, last modified August 9, 2012, http://www.nytimes.com/2012/08/10/world/asia/us-moves-to-address-agent-orange-contamination-in-vietnam.html.
38. Fuller, "4 Decades on, U.S. Starts Cleanup of Agent Orange in Vietnam."
39. Wil D. Verwey, *Riot Control Agents and Herbicides in War: Their Humanitarian, Toxicological, Ecological, Military, Polemological, and Legal Aspects* (Leyden: Sijthoff, 1977), 113.
40. Verwey, *Riot Control Agents and Herbicides in War*, 116.
41. Arthur Westing, "Ecological Effects of Military Defoliation on the Forests of South Vietnam," in *BioScience* 21, no. 17 (September 1971), 893-898.
42. "Agent Orange blights Vietnam," in *BBC* online, last modified December 31, 1998, http://news.bbc.co.uk/1/hi/health/227467.stm.
43. Ben Stocking, "Agent Orange Still Haunts Vietnam, US," in *The Washington Post* online, last modified June 14, 2007, http://www.washingtonpost.com/wp-dyn/content/article/2007/06/14/AR2007061401077.html.
44. Jessica King, "U.S. in first effort to clean up Agent Orange in Vietnam," in *CNN* online, last modified August 10, 2012, http://edition.cnn.com/2012/08/10/world/asia/vietnam-us-agent-

orange/.
45. Joe Thornton, *Pandora's Poison: Chlorine, Health, and a New Environmental Strategy* (Cambridge, MA: MIT Press, 2001), 190.
46. "Agent Orange Case for Millions of Vietnamese Is Dismissed," in *The New York Times* online, last modified March 10, 2005, http://www.nytimes.com/2005/03/10/nyregion/agent-orange-case-for-millions-of-vietnamese-is-dismessed.html.
47. Marianne Brown, "Agent Orange still stokes fear in Vietnam's pregnant women," in *The Guardian* online, last modified April 11, 2013, https://www.theguardian.com/global-development/2013/apr/11/agent-orange-vietnam-pregnant-women.
48. Dana Fllek-Gibson, "Vietnam tackles high abortion rates," in *Al Jazeera* online, last modified August 28, 2014, http://www.aljazeera.com/indepth/features/2014/08/vietnam-tackles-high-abortion-rates-2014827131119357230.html.
49. Kaushik, "The Underground Tunnels of Cu Chi, Vietnam," in *Amusing Planet*, last modified July 12, 2012, http://www.amusingplanet.com/2012/07/underground-tunnels-of-cu-chi-vietnam.html.
50. "AK-47 inventor Mikhail Kalashnikov in intensive care," in *RT* online, last modified December 25, 2012, http://www.rt.com/news/mikhail-kalashnikov-intensive-care-826/.
51. "The AK-47 vs. the M16 During the Vietnam War," in *Warfare History Network*, last modified July 14, 2017, http://warefarehistorynetwork.com/daily/military-history/the-ak-47-vs-the-m16-during-the-vietnam-war/.
52. Simon Speakman Cordall, "Landmines still exacting a heavy toll on Vietnamese civilians," in *The Guardian* online, last modified September 18, 2012, http://www.theguardian.com/world/2012/sep/18/vietnam-unexploded-landmines-bombs.
53. Jennifer Llewellyn, Jim Southey and Steve Thompson, "US involvement in Vietnam," in *Alpha History*, accessed August 8, 2017, http://alphahistory.com/vietnamwar/us-involvement-in-in-vietnam/.
54. Llewellyn, Southey and Thompson, "US involvement in Vietnam."
55. Fuller, "4 Decades on, U.S. Starts Cleanup of Agent Orange in Vietnam."
56. "Phu Quoc Prison," in *Phu Quoc Prison*, accessed August 9, 2017, http://phuquocprison.org.
57. Howard Zinn, *A People's History of the United States* (New York: HarperCollins, 2003), 478.
58. Ben Rowse, "White is beautiful in Vietnam," in *ThingsAsian.com*, last modified June 17, 2003, http://thingsasian.com/story/white-beautiful-vietnam.
59. "Imperial Enclosure in Hue, Vietnam," in *Lonely Planet* online, accessed September 15, 2017,

https://www.lonelyplanet.com/vietnam/hue/attractions/imperial-enclosure/a/poi-sig/1154381/357875.
60. "GPD per capita (current US$)," in *The World Bank* online, accessed October 23, 2017, https://data.worldbank.org/indictor/NY.GDP.PCAP.CD?locations=VN.

HONG KONG & MACAU

1. Damian Harper, *National Geographic Traveler: China* (Washington D.C.: National Geographic, 2001), 227.
2. Harper, *National Geographic Traveler: China*, 233.
3. "Kun Iam Statue & Ecumenical Centre," in *Secret Macau*, last modified February 17, 2017, http://www.secretmacau.com/Buddhist-kun-iam-statue/.
4. "Ruins of the Church of St Paul in Macau Peninsula," in *Lonely Planet* online, accessed January 11, 2018, https://www.lonelyplanet.com/china/macau-peninsula/attractions/ruins-of-the-church-of-st-paul/a/poi-sig/364835/1324547.
5. Katie Hunt, "The dark side of Asia's gambling Mecca," in *CNN* online, last modified June 18, 2013, http://edition.cnn.com/2013/06/17/world/asia/macau-dark-side/.
6. "Human Trafficking & Modern-day Slavery – Macau," accessed January 12, 2018, http://gvnet.com/humantrafficking/Macau.htm.
7. Raquel Carvalho, "Shady dealings: triads 'play major role' in high-rolling Macau VIP casino rooms," in *South China Morning Post* online, last modified March 6, 2016, http://www.scmp.com/new/hong-kong/politics/article/1921335/shady-dealings-triads-play-major-role-high-rolling-macau-vip.
8. "Trafficking in Persons Report 2012" (PDF), in *U.S. Department of State*, 228, accessed January 16, 2018, https://www.state.gov/documents/organization/192596.pdf.

THE MIDDLE KINGDOM: PART I

1. Lin Liyao, "Top 10 cities in financial capital in China 2010," in *China.org.cn*, last modified May 18, 2011, http://www.china.org.cn/top10/2011-05/18/content_22588509.htm.
2. "Guangzhou Population," in *World Population Review* online, last modified October 20, 2017, http://www.worldpopulationreview.com/world-cities/Guangzhou-population/.
3. Dean S. Rugg, "Three Phases of History and Land Use on Shamian Island," in *Journal of Geography* 85, no. 4: 154, doi: 10.1080/00221348608979411.
4. Petroc Trelawny, "Europe on the Pearl River: A colonial hangover in

5. "Gendercide," in *The Economist* online, last modified March 6, 2010, https://www.economist.com/node/15606229.
6. Harriet Sergeant, *Shanghai* (London: John Murray, 2002), 15-16.
7. Sergeant, *Shanghai*, 28-29.
8. Sergeant, 28-29.
9. *Treaty of Nanjing* (January 1, 1842), in *USC US-China Institute*, accessed April 20, 2018, https://china.usc.edu/treaty-nanjing-nanking-1842.
10. Samuel Totten, Paul R. Bartrop and Steven L. Jacobs, *Dictionary of Genocide* (Westport, CT: Greenwood Press, 2008), 298-299.
11. Sergeant, *Shanghai*, 1.
12. Sergeant, 13-14.
13. Sergeant, 3.
14. Zhaojin Ji, *A History of Modern Shanghai Banking: The Rise and Decline of Chinas Financial Capitalism* (Armonk, NY: Sharpe, 2003), 28.
15. Sergeant, *Shanghai*, 2.
16. Sergeant, 16.
17. Sergeant, 16.
18. Sergeant, 16.
19. Sergeant, 17.
20. Sergeant, 17.
21. Sergeant, 17.
22. Robert A. Bickers and Jeffrey N. Wasserstrom, "Shanghai's 'Dogs and Chinese Not Admitted' Sign: Legend, History, and Contemporary Symbol," in *The China Quarterly*, no. 142 (June 1995), 444.
23. Bickers and Wasserstrom, "Shanghai's 'Dogs and Chinese Not Admitted' Sign," 446.
24. Helen H. Wang, "Defining the Chinese Middle Class," in *Forbes* online, last modified August 11, 2011, https://www.forbes.com/sites/helenwang/2010/11/24/defining-the-chinese-middle-class/#443193756676.
25. "In China, Microsoft losing out increasingly to free software and piracy," in *South China Morning Post* online, last modified August 12, 2014, http://www.scmp.com/news/china/article/1572339/china-microsoft-losing-out-increasingly-free-software-and-piracy.
26. " 'Chaos' of China's music industry," in *BBC* online, last modified February 21, 2008, http://news.bbc.co.uk/2/hi/asia-pacific/7251211.stm.

THE MIDDLE KINGDOM: PART II

1. Wayne Barber, "Study: Coal power is cheap, abundant – and controversial," in *Electric Light & Power* online, last modified March 23, 2015, https://www.elp.com/articles/2015/03/study-coal-power-is-cheap-abundant-and-controversial.html.

2. Damian Harper, *National Geographic Traveler: China* (Washington D.C.: National Geographic, 2001), 154.
3. John Grant Ross, "5,000 Years of History," in *You Don't Know China: Twenty-two Enduring Myths Debunked* (Manchester, England: Camphor Press, 2014) online, accessed May 15, 2018, https://www.camphorpress.com/5000-years-of-history/.
4. Ross, "5,000 Years of History."
5. Bob Tadashi Wakabayashi, *The Nanking Atrocity, 1937-38: Complicating the Picture* (New York: Berghahn Books, 2009), 362.
6. Tokushi Kasahara, "Reconciling Narratives of the Nanking Massacre in Japanese and Chinese Textbooks" (PDF), in *United States Institute of Peace*, accessed May 10, 2018. https://www.usip.org/sites/default/files/file/kasahara.pdf.
7. Bob Tadashi Wakabayashi, "The Nanking 100-Man Killing Contest Debate: War Guilt Amid Fabricated Illusions, 1971-75," in *Journal of Japanese Studies* 26, no. 2 (Summer 2000): 319, doi: 10.2307/133271.
8. "The Truth about the Nanjing Massacre (22)," in *Xinhuanet* online, last modified November 11, 2015, http://www.xinhuanet.com/english/special/2015-11/11/c_134806674.htm.
9. "HyperWar: International Military Tribunal for the Far East [Chapter 8]," in *ibiblio.org*, accessed May 10, 2018, http://www.ibiblio.org/hyperwar/PTO/IMTFE/IMTFE-8.html.
10. Julian Ryall, "Japan PM dismisses WWII war crimes trials as 'victors' justice'," in *The Telegraph* online, last modified March 14, 2013, https://www.telegraph.co.uk/news/worldnews/asia/japan/9930041/Japan-PM-dismisses-WWII-war-crimes-trials-as-victors-justice.html.
11. Micah Muscolino, "Yellow River flood, 1938-47," in *DisasterHistory.org*, accessed May 10, 2018, http://www.disasterhistory.org/hyperwar/PTO/IMTFE/IMTFE-8.html.
12. "Silk Roads: Dialogue, Diversity & Development," in *UNESCO*, accessed May 15, 2018, https://en.unesco.org/silkroads/content/xian.
13. Harper, *National Geographic Traveler: China*, 96.
14. "Temple of the Eight Immortals (Ba Xian An)," in *Travel China Guide*, accessed May 15, 2018, https://www.travelchinaguide.com/attraction/shaanxi/xian/ba-xian-an-monastary.htm.
15. "Thousands of Animal Artifacts Entombed with Emperor," in *New Historian*, last modified December 2, 2016, http://www.newhistorian.com/thousands-animal-artifacts-entombed-emperor/7648/.
16. John Man, *The Terracotta Army* (Random House, 2010), 238.
17. Harper, *National Geographic Traveler: China*, 119.
18. Harper, 118.

19. Harper, 119.
20. Harper, 119.
21. "The Longmen Grottoes," in *China & Asia Cultural Travel*, accessed May 23, 2018, https://www.asiaculturaltravel.co.uk/the-longmen-grottoes/.
22. Harper, *National Geographic Traveler*, 124.
23. "Dharma Lineage," in *Shim Gum Do – Mind Sword Path*, accessed May 23, 2018, https://shimgumdo.org/dharma-lineage/.
24. Shi Yanzi, "Chan Buddhism of Bodhidharma," in *Buddhism now*, last modified August 17, 2010, https://buddhismnow.com/2010/08/17/buddhism-of-bodhidarma/.
25. Ross, "5,000 Years of History."
26. Harper, *National Geographic Traveler: China*, 129.
27. Harper, 130.
28. Harper, 129.
29. Anniina Koivula, "Mount Tai and the birthplace of Confucius," in *GB Times* online, last modified December 5, 2016, https://gbtimes.com/mount-tai-and-birthplace-confucius.
30. Jim Yardley, "Beijing Journal; Chinese Take Recklessly to Cars (Just Count the Wrecks)," in *The New York Times* online, last modified March 12, 2004, https://www.nytimes.com/2004/03/2012/world/beijing-journal-chineses-take-recklessly-to-cars-just-count-the-wrecks.html.
31. "How Many Cars are There in China?" in *ChinaAutoWeb*, accessed May 25, 2018, http://chinaautoweb.com/2010/09/how-many-cars-are-there-in-china/.
32. "World in the Balance: China Revs Up," in *PBS Digital* (airdate: April 20, 2004), accessed May 25, 2018, http://www.pbs.org/wgbh/nova/transcripts/3109_worldbal.html.
33. "World in the Balance: China Revs Up."
34. "How Many Cars are There in China?" in *ChinaAutoWeb*.
35. "World in the Balance: China Revs Up."
36. Tycho De Feijter, "5 Stunning Facts About the Chinese Car Market You Need to Know," in *Forbes* online, last modified May 16, 2016, https://www.forbes.com/sites/tychodefeijter/2016/16/five-things-you-need-to-know-about-the-chinese-car-market/.
37. Simon Roger and Lisa Evans, "World carbon dioxide emissions data by country: China speeds ahead of the rest," in *The Guardian* online, last modified January 31, 2011, https://www.theguardian.com/news/datablog/2011/jan/31/world-carbon-dioxide-emissions-country-data-co2.
38. "China 'buried smog death finding'," in *BBC* online, last modified July 3, 2007, http://news.bbc.co.uk/2/hi/asia-pacific/6265098.stm.
39. "China 'buried smog death finding'."
40. "How long it took to build the Great Wall of China – 2,000+ years," in *China Highlights*, accessed May 28, 2018, https://www.chinahighlights.com/greatwall/fact/building-time/htm.

41. "GDP per capita (current US$), China," in *The World Bank* online, accessed May 28, 2018, https://data.worldbank.org/indicator/NY.GDP.PCAP.CD?locations=CN.
42. Dmitriy Plekhanov, "Is China's Era of Cheap Labor Really Over?" in *The Diplomat* online, last modified December 13, 2017, https://thediplomat.com/2017/12/is-china-era-of-cheap-labor-really-over/.
43. Kris Cheng, "Declassified: Chinese official said at least 10,000 civilians died in 1989 Tiananmen massacre, documents show," in *Hong Kong Free Press* online, last modified December 21, 2017, https://www.hongkongfp.com/2017/12/21/declassified-chinese-official-said-least-10000-civilians-died-1989-tiananmen-massacre-documents-shot/.
44. Owen Jarus, "Forbidden City: Home to Chinese Emperors," in *Live Science* online, last modified October 29, 2013, https://www.livescience.com/40764-forbidden-city.html.
45. Harper, *National Geographic Traveler: China*, 57.
46. Harper, 57.
47. "Starbucks closes coffeehouse in Beijing's Forbidden City," in *The New York Times* online, last modified July 15, 2007, https://www.nytimes.com/2007/07/15/world/Americas/15iht-starbucks.4.6664994.html.
48. Harper, *National Geographic Traveler: China*, 63.
49. "China: population of Beijing from 1970 to 2010 (in millions)," in *Statista*, accessed May 28, 2018, https://www.statista.com/statistics/466949/china-population-of-beijing/.
50. Harper, *National Geographic Traveler: China*, 74.
51. Roger Jahnke, "History of Qi (Chi) Cultivation," in *Feel the Qi*, accessed May 28, 2018, https://www.feeltheqi.com/articles/rc-history.htm.

MONGOLIA

1. "Naadam, Three Games of Men in Mongolia," in *Diplomat Magazine* online, last modified July 7, 2014, https://www.diplomatmagazine.nl/2014/07/07/naadam-three-games-men-mongolia/.
2. "Naadam, Three Games of Men in Mongolia."
3. "Naadam, Three Games of Men in Mongolia."
4. James Cotton, and D. K. Adams, *Asian Frontier Nationalism: Owen Lattimore and the American Policy Debates* (Manchester University Press, 1989), 130.
5. "About Naadam / History," in *Nadaam Festival*, accessed May 30, 2018, https://www.naadamfestival.com/about-naadam/historical-background.

6. "Mongolia domestic violence: 'I screamed for help, but nobody came'," in *BBC* online, last modified November 25, 2017, https://www.bbc.com/news/world-asia-42050602.
7. Matt McCann, "Way Down and Out in Ulan Bator," in *The New York Times* online, last modified March 7, 2013, https://lens.blogs.com/2013/03/07/underground-and-off-the-radar-in-ulan-bator/.
8. "Living in a manhole," in *The Economist* online, last modified January 20, 2000, https://www.economist.com/node/275428.
9. Urangua Jamsran and Sharaa Munkhtsag, "History of Influence of Buddhism in Mongolian Society," in *Buddhism and Australia: International Conference on Buddhism*, accessed June 6, 2018, https://www.buddhismandaustralia.com/ba/index.php/History_and_Influence_of_Buddhism_in_Mongolian_Society_by_Urangua_Jamsran_and_Sharaa_Munkhtsag.

RUSSIA

1. "Deepest Lake in the World," in *Geology.com*, accessed June 6, 2018, https://geology.com/records/deepest-lake.shtml.
2. "A new bathymetric map of Lake Baikal. Morphometric Data. INTAS Project 99-1669. Ghent University, Ghent, Belgium; Consolidated Research Group on Marine Geosciences (CRG-MG), University of Barcelona, Spain; Limnological Institute of the Siberian Division of the Russian Academy of Sciences, Irkutsk, Russian Federation; State Science Research Navigation-Hydrographic Institute of the Ministry of Defense, St. Petersburg, Russian Federation," in *Ghent University*, accessed June 6, 2018, https://users.ugent.be/~mdbatist/intas/morphometry.htm.
3. Ibid.
4. "Unique Aquarium on Lake Baikal," in *Sputnik News* online, last modified June 23, 2004, https://sputniknews.com/onlinenews/2004062339763495/.
5. "Travels in Geology: Exploring Lake Baikal, the Sacred Sea," in *EARTH Magazine* online, accessed June 6, 2018, https://www.earthmagazine.org/article/travels-geology-exploring-lake-baikal-sacred-sea.
6. "Lake Baikal: Protection of a unique ecosystem: Researchers are investigating how climate change and environmental toxins are impacting on the world's largest and oldest freshwater lake," in *ScienceDaily* online, last modified July 26, 2017, https://www.sciencedaily.com/releases/2017/07/170726103013.htm.
7. "The world's largest hotels (including Mecca's 10,000-room monster)," in *The Telegraph* online, last modified March 8, 2017, https://www.telegraph.co.uk/travel/hotels/galleries/largest-hotels-in-the-world/izmailovo-hotel/.

8. Vincze Miklós, "The Strange History of the Moscow Cathedral That Couldn't Be Destroyed," in *io9* online, last modified February 4, 2013, https://io9.gizmodo.com/5981106/the-strange-history-of-the-moscow-cathedral-that-couldnt-be-destroyed.
9. "A Guide to The Most Beautiful Moscow Metro Stations," in *Vagrants of the World* online, last modified March 20, 2018, https://vagrantsoftheworld.com/moscow-metro-stations/.
10. "A Guide to The Most Beautiful Moscow Metro Stations."
11. "GUM," in *Encyclopaedia Britannica* online, accessed June 6, 2018, https://www.britannica.com/topic/GUM-store-Moscow-Russia.
12. "The Cathedral of the Assumption," in *Moscow.info*, accessed June 6, 2018, https://www.moscow.info/kremlin/churches/cathedral-assumption.aspx.
13. "The Tsar Bell," in *Moscow.info*, accessed June 6, 2018, https://www.moscow.info/kremlin/palaces/tsar-bell.aspx.

ESTONIA

1. "PC222: Population by the place of residence and ethnic nationality," in *Statistics Estonia*, accessed June 8, 2018, https://pub.stat.ee/px-web.2001/Dialog/varval.asp?ma=PC222&ti=POPULATION+BY+THE+PLACE+OF+RESIDENCE+AND+ETHNIC+NATIONALITY&path=../I_Databas/Population_census/PHC2000/08Ethnic_nationality._Mother_tongue._Command_of_foreign_languages/&lang=1.
2. Tacita Vero, "The Gray Zone," in *Slate* online, last modified March 2017, https://www.slate.com/articles/news_and_politics/roads/2017/03/many_ethnic_russians_in_estonia_have_gray_passports_live_in_legal_limbo.html.
3. Vero, "The Gray Zone."
4. Vero, "The Gray Zone."
5. Vero, "The Gray Zone."
6. Vero, "The Gray Zone."

SUOMI

1. "Corruption Perceptions Index 2004," in *Transparency International*, accessed June 8, 2018, https://www.transparency.org/research/cpi/cpi_2004/0.
2. Daniel Yergin and Joseph Stanislaw, *The Commanding Heights: The Battle for the World Economy* (New York: Free Press, 2002), 295.
3. Yergin and Stanislaw, *The Commanding Heights: The Battle for the World Economy*, 295.
4. Yergin and Stanislaw, 297.
5. Yergin and Stanislaw, 297.
6. Yergin and Stanislaw, 295.

7. Yergin and Stanislaw, 297.
8. Yergin and Stanislaw, 297.
9. Yergin and Stanislaw, 298.
10. Yergin and Stanislaw, 298.
11. Yergin and Stanislaw, 299.
12. "Balance of Payments of the Russian Federation for 1994 (Analytical Presentation)," in *The Central Bank of the Russian Federation* online, accessed June 19, 2018, https://www.cbr.ru/eng/statistics/print.aspx?file=credit_statistics/bal_of_paym_an_94_e.htm&pid=svs&sid=pbDK_an.
13. "Balance of Payments of the Russian Federation for 1995 (Analytical Presentation)," in *The Central Bank of the Russian Federation* online, accessed June 19, 2018, https://www.cbr.ru/eng/statistics/print.aspx?file=credit_statistics/bal_of_paym_an_95_e.htm&pid=svs&sid=pbDK_an.
14. "Balance of Payments of the Russian Federation for 1996 (Analytical Presentation)," in *The Central Bank of the Russian Federation* online, accessed June 19, 2018, https://www.cbr.ru/eng/statistics/print.aspx?file=credit_statistics/bal_of_paym_an_96_e.htm&pid=svs&sid=pbDK_an.
15. Ron Rimkus, "Russian Bond Default/Ruble Collapse," in *CFA Institute*, last modified May 5, 2016, https://www.econcrisis.org/2016/05/05/russian-bond-defaultruble-collapse/.
16. Rimkus, "Russian Bond Default/Ruble Collapse."
17. Joseph E. Stiglitz, *Globalization and its Discontents* (New York: Norton & Company, Inc., 2003), 147.
18. Stiglitz, *Globalization and its Discontents*, 148.
19. Stiglitz, 147.
20. Stiglitz, 148.
21. Stiglitz, 148.
22. Stiglitz, 149.
23. Stiglitz, 149.
24. Stiglitz, 149.
25. Rimkus, "Russian Bond Default/Ruble Collapse."
26. Stiglitz, *Globalization and its Discontents*, 150.
27. Stiglitz, 150.
28. Filip Novokmet, Thomas Piketty and Gabriel Zucman, "From Soviets to oligarchs: Inequality and property in Russia, 1905-2016," in *VoxEU.org*, last modified November 9, 2017, https://voxeu.org/article/inequality-and-property-russia-1905-2016.
29. Stiglitz, *Globalization and its Discontents*, 153.

THE OPEN-MINDEDNESS OF THE SWEDES

1. "Finland Demographic Profile 2018," in *IndexMundi*, accessed June 15, 2018, https://www.indexmundi.com/finland/demographics_profile.html.
2. Karen Haandrikman, "Binational Marriages in Sweden: Is There an EU Effect?" in *Population, Space and Place* 20, no. 2 (2013): 177-99, doi: 10.1002/psp.1770.
3. Lena Lundkvist, "Migration results in a younger population," in *Statistics Sweden*, las modified May 2, 2016, https://www.scb.se/en_/Finding-statistics/Articles/Migration-ger-en-yngre-befolkning/.
4. "Summary of Population Statistics 1960-2017," in *Statistics Sweden*, accessed July 4, 2018, https://www.scb.se/en/finding-statistics/statistics-by-subject-area/population/population-composition/population-statistics/pong/tables-and-graphs/yearly-statistics--the-whole-country/summary-of-population-statisitics/.
5. "Stockholm Population 2018," in *World Population Review*, accessed July 4, 2018, http://worldpopulationreview.com/world-cities/Stockholm-population/.

INDEX

1984 (book), 66
1991 Paris Peace Agreements, 200
1997 Asian financial crisis, 35, 146, 178, 384
1998 Russian financial crisis, 384
2012 Trafficking in Persons Report, 282
37 Great Nats, 110
8888 Nationwide Popular Pro-Democracy Protests, 101
Abramovich, Roman, 384
Abu Ghraib, 145
Adams, John, 281
Adams, John Quincy, 281
Adams, Joseph Harod, 281
Affordable Care Act (ACA). *See* Patient Protection and Affordable Care Act (Obamacare)
Agent Orange, 240, 244, 245, 246, 249, 250
Ahka (ethnic group), 126
AIDS (and HIV), 114, 115, 133, 137, 138, 139, 142, 167, 175, 176, 194, 222
Akershus Fortress, 392
Alexander Garden, 374
Alexander, Jeffrey W., 241
al-Qaeda, 22, 24
Al-Qaida. *See* al-Qaeda
Amitabha Buddha, 40
Amnesty International, 194
Amnesty International Report 2009, 60
Anawrahta, King, 127
Andaman Sea, 94
Angkor, 121, 204, 205, 209, 210, 211, 270
Angkor Wat, 121, 204, 208, 209
Anglo-Dutch Treaty of 1824, 70
Anna and the King (film), 77
Aquariums of Pyongyang, The (book), 65
Aranyaprathet, 187, 188
Asia Watch Report, 179
Asian Civilizations Museum, 51
Auden, W.H., 154
Aum Shinrikyo, 22

Authorization for Use of Military Force Against Iraq Resolution of 2002, 243
Ayutthaya, 119, 120, 121, 134, 184
B-52 bombers, 200, 231, 247
Badaling, 348
Bagan, 108, 121, 126, 127
Bago, 108, 110
Baikal, Lake, 368, 369, 375
Baltic Sea, 389
Ban Rom Sai, 137, 138, 139, 140, 141, 142, 143
Bangkok, 96, 97, 98, 105, 113, 114, 115, 119, 120, 125, 128, 134, 138, 161, 162, 163, 164, 165, 166, 170, 172, 174, 176, 178, 183, 184, 186, 187, 189, 190, 191, 202, 360
Bangkok Post, 169, 171, 172, 173, 175
Barcelona, 37, 218, 254, 399, 400, 402
Battambang, 189, 190, 191, 195, 197, 199, 200
Batu Caves, 70
Bayon, 209
Behind the Smile: Voices of Thailand (book), 171, 172
Beijing, 286, 322, 331, 336, 344, 345, 346, 347, 349, 350, 351, 353, 359, 361, 373
Belgrade, 398, 400
Bell Tower (Xi'an), 328
Berlin, 397, 398
Beyond Rangoon (film), 73
Bin Ladin, Usama, 24
bin Mohamad, Tun Dr. Mahathir, 70
Bishop, Ryan, 114, 148, 165, 183
Black Hole, The (film), 277
Black, Stephanie, 168
Blade Runner (film), 275
Blade, The (newspaper), 244
Blair, Tony, 243
Bodhidharma, 56, 337, 339
Bodhisattva Avalokitesvara, 40
Bodhisattva Mahasthamaprapta, 40
Boeung Kak Lake, 224, 225, 235
Bogd Khan, Winter Palace of the, 359

Bokèo Province, 146
Bonaparte, Napoleon, 375
Bonghwangdae, 37
Bowring Treaty of 1855, 165
Boxer Rebellion, 293
Bratislava, 398
British Empire, 53
British Journal of Criminology, 282
British Medical Journal, 244
Brown, Louise, 116, 173, 183
Brumo, Aaron, 262
Bùi Viện Road, 237, 238, 239, 241
Bush Doctrine, 153
Bush, George W., 22, 153, 155, 243, 388
Bygdøy peninsula, 392
Cabinet of Singapore, 51
Cẩm Nam (village), 259
Cambodian Genocide Program, 230
Cambodian Killing Fields, 230, 233, 235
Cambodian People's Party (CPP), 194
Camões Gardens, 281
Campbell, Joseph, 99
Capitalism and Freedom (book), 60
Casino Lisboa, 280, 281
Cathay Hotel (Penang), 73
Cathedral of Christ the Saviour, 372, 373
Cenotaph, 277
Center for the Protection of Children's Rights Foundation (CPCR), 184
Centers for Medicare and Medicaid Services (CMS), 132
Central Bank of the Russian Federation, 383
Central Market (Phnom Penh), 225
Chang, Iris, 324
Changdeokgung Palace, 29, 31
Changi Village, 57
Chap Goh Meh (festival), 74
Chaplin, Charlie, 289
Charoenloet, Voravidh, 178
Chatuchak Weekend Market, 119, 120
Chaukhtatgyi Buddha Temple, 109
Cheah Aun, 78

Cheah Hean, 78
Cheney, Dick, 30
Cheong Fatt Tze Mansion, 75
Cheonmachong (the Heavenly Horse) tumulus, 37
Chiang Khong, 140, 143, 145, 146
Chiang Mai, 115, 120, 134, 135, 136, 137, 138, 155, 170, 184
Chiang Rai, 164, 170
Children's Health Insurance Program (CHIP), 130
China, Great Wall of, 331, 348
Chinese Academy of Social Sciences, 285
Chinese Communist Party (CCP), 293, 294, 323, 349
Chinese Military Tribunal for War Crimes in Nanjing, 325
Chinese Revolution, 291
Chinese secret societies, 53, 83
Choeung Ek, 230, 233
Chol-hwan, Kang, 65
Chongqing, 325
Chow Kit, 70
Chubais, Anatoly, 382
Chungking Mansion, 275
Churchill, Winston, 281
Civilian War Memorial, 50
Civilizations of Angkor, The (book), 209
Clinton administration, 382, 384
Cold War, 375
Colosio Murrieta, Luis Donaldo, 136
Communist Party of China (CPC), 294, 299
Communist Party of Kampuchea (CPK), 193
Copenhagen, 396
Council on Tall Buildings and Urban Habitat (CTBUH), 65
Củ Chi tunnels, 246, 247, 250
Cultural Revolution, 323, 336
Cushing, Caleb, 293
Daeseong-dong, 34
Dai Temple, 342
Danu (ethnic group), 126
Daraprim, 133

Dark Legacy (book), 31, 84, 280, 400, 402
Decembrist revolt, 370
Dengfeng, 336, 337, 338, 339, 340
Deoksugung Palace, 31
Deupree, Aaron, 113, 114
Dhammayazika Pagoda, 127
Diamond Jubilee, 75
Die Another Day (film), 33
Documentation Center of Cambodia (DC-Cam), 230, 235
Đổi Mới Policy, 239
Đồng Xuân (market), 268
Dora Observatory, 34
Dorasan Station, 35
Drum Tower (Xi'an), 328
East India Company, 290
Eastern Yoma mountains, 112
Economist, The, 362
Education Means Protection Of Women Engaged in Recreation (EMPOWER), 184
Einstein, Albert, 289
Eisenhower, Dwight D., 249
Ekachai, Sanitsuda, 171, 172
Eli Lilly (pharmaceutical), 133
Employment of Foreign Workers Act (Singapore), 60
End Child Prostitution in Asian Tourism (ECPAT), 184
Enlightenment, 61
Entertainment Places Act (Thailand), 166
Eteläsatama (South Harbor), 379
EU. *See* European Union (EU)
European Union (EU), 378
Federation of Malaya, 51, 57
Fei River, battle of, 78
Finland, Gulf of, 378
First Indochina War, 249
First Opium War, 289, 290, 292
First Sino-Japanese War, 291
Five Great Mountains (China), 338, 343
Forbidden City, 349, 350
Forbidden Purple City, 262

Foreign Correspondents' Club (Phnom Penh), 225
Forest of Dagobas, 339
Fortune-Teller Told Me, A (book), 65
Frazén, Anders, 389
Freedom Bridge, 33
Freedom in the World 2015, 60
Friedman, Milton, 60
Gaidar, Yegor, 382
Gamla Stan, 386
Gamla Uppsala, 390
Gandantegchinlen Monastery, 363
Genghis Khan, 355
George Town (Penang), 72, 73, 79, 82
Geumgwanchong Tomb, 37
Gia Long, Emperor, 262
Gijeongdong, 34
Globalization and its Discontents (book), 384
Gobi Desert, 351, 354
Golden Rock, 112
Golden Triangle, 114
Good Man of Nanking, The: The Diaries of John Rabe (book), 326
Gorbachev, Mikhail, 375
Gorkhi-Terelj National Park, 355
Grant, Ulysses S., 289
Greenpeace, 64
Guangzhou, 285, 286, 287, 289, 291, 294, 323, 326
Guanyin, 55, 56
GUM (department store), 374
Gustav Vasa, King, 390
Gustavus Adolphus, King, 389
Gwanghwamun Gate, 30
Gyeongbokgung Palace, 30
Gyeongju, 35, 36, 37, 41, 42, 44, 45, 390
Gyeongju Kim clan, 36, 38
Gyeongui Line, 35
Gyerim Forest, 38
Hamburg, 119, 391, 396, 398
Han River, 27, 33
Hanoi, 242, 263, 264, 265, 267, 268, 269, 270, 271, 273
Hanoi Citadel, 269
Hat Yai, 76, 89, 93, 94, 179
Helsinki, 378, 379, 380, 381, 386, 387

473

heroin, 125
Heungnyemun Gate, 30
Higham, Charles, 209
Ho Chi Minh City (Saigon), 191, 232, 237, 238, 241, 242, 246, 248, 250, 251, 252, 253, 258, 262, 268, 269
Hồ Chí Minh Mausoleum, 269, 270
Hồ Chí Minh Trail, 153, 245, 246
Hoàn Kiếm Lake, 271
Hồ Chí Minh, 153, 245, 246, 248, 271, 351, 373
Hobbes, Thomas, 61
Hội An, 257, 258, 259, 260, 261, 263
Hội An Central Market, 258
Hong Kong, 221, 264, 267, 273, 274, 276, 277, 278, 279, 281, 282, 283, 284, 286, 289, 294
Hpaung Daw U Pagoda, 123
HSBC Building, 277
Hua Tuo, 56
Huang He River, 326
Huangpu Park, 293
Huay Xai, 145, 146, 151
Hubback, Arthur Benison, 68
Huế, 259, 261, 262, 263
Huế, battle of, 262
Hussein, Saddam, 145, 388
Hyeokgeose, King Pak, 39
IMF. *See* International Monetary Fund (IMF)
Imjin River, 33
In Retrospect: The Tragedy and Lessons of Vietnam (book), 240
Inbawkon, 123
Indochina Newsletter of Asia Resource Center, 243
Injeongjeon Hall (National Treasure), 29
Inle Lake, 108, 117, 118, 119, 121, 122, 125, 126
Inquiry into the Nature and Causes of the Wealth of Nations, An (book), 61
insulin, 133
Inter-American Development Bank (IADB), 168
International Labor Organization (ILO), 172

International Military Tribunal for the Far East, 325, 326
International Monetary Fund (IMF), 168, 382, 383, 384
International Organization for Migration (IOM), 179
Intha (ethnic group), 126
Irkutsk, 368, 370
Jamalullail, Tuanku Syed Harun Putra ibni Almarhum Syed Hassan, 68
Japan Exchange and Teaching (JET) program, 29
Japan's Motorcycle Wars: An Industry History (book), 241
Japanese Governor General Building, 30
Jayavarman VII Children's Hospital, 221
Jebtsundamba Khutuktu, 359
Jefferson, Thomas, 61
Jiangdongmen, 324
Jin dynasty, 78
Jinan, 340, 341
Jinghpaw (ethnic group), 126
Jingshan Park, 350
Johnson, Lyndon, 166
Johor Strait, 57, 63
Joint Security Area (JSA), 35
Joint United Nations Programme on HIV/AIDS (UNAIDS), 114, 139
Joseon dynasty, 29
Journal of the Indian Archipelago, 74
Kai-shek, Chiang, 291, 293, 325, 326
Kaivopuisto Park, 380
Kalashnikov, Mikhail, 246
Kampuchean People's Revolutionary Party (KPRP), 194
Kandawgyi Lake, 108
Kantha Bopha Children's Hospitals, 221, 222
Kantha Bopha Foundation, 221, 222
Kau Cim, 56
Kaung Daing (market), 122
Kennedy, John F., 166
Keyes, Charles, 166
Khaosan Road, 163, 225, 237
Khmer Empire, 209
Khmer Republic, 193

Khmer Rouge, 192, 193, 194, 195, 199, 200, 230, 232, 233, 234
Khoo Kongsi, 77, 79
Khorloogiin, Choibalsan, 360
Kim Alji, 38
Kim Il-sung, 34
Kim Jong-il, 34, 66, 153
Kim, Chang Sik, 41
King Jr., John, 58
Kissinger, Henry, 222, 231
Klang River, 65, 68
Korean Demilitarized Zone (DMZ), 33, 34
Korean War, 31, 32, 43
Kowloon, 274, 275, 276, 277, 279, 284
Krabi, 89, 93, 94
Krabi coast, 94
Krabi Town, 94, 97
Krakow, 398
Kremlin, 374, 375
Kremlin Armory, 375
Kremlin Arsenal, 375
Kremlin Palace of Congresses, 375
Kremlin Senate, 375
Kuala Lumpur, 57, 63, 65, 66, 67, 69, 70, 72
Kuala Lumpur Railway Station, 68
Kuang Si Falls, 152
Kun Iam (statue), 280
Kun Iam Temple, 281
Kwan Im Thong Hood Cho Temple, 55, 57
Kyaik Pun Pagoda, 110
Kyaikto, 108, 111, 112
Lahu (ethnic group), 126
Lan Kwai Fong, 278
Lantau Island, 274
Lee, Sing Kong, 58, 59
Lee, Thomas, 19, 20
Lenin, Vladimir, 373
Leong San Tong clan, 77
Leviathan (book), 61
Lewy, Guenter, 242
Life and Debt (film), 168
Listvyanka, 368
Lisu (ethnic group), 126
Little Red Book (Mao Zedong), 328

loans for shares scheme, 382
Locke, John, 61
Logan, James Richardson, 74
Lon Nol, 232, 233
Longmen Grottoes, 336
Lost in Translation (film), 360
Luang Prabang, 137, 145, 146, 147, 148, 149, 150, 151, 152, 154, 158, 159, 211
Luoyang, 332, 334, 336, 337
Luoyang Old Town District, 335
Macau, 273, 279, 281, 282, 283, 289
Maha Wizaya Pagoda, 103
Malacca, Kingdom of, 69
Malay Peninsula, 52
Man, John, 330
Mandalay, 106, 108, 109
Mandalay Rum, 125
Märtson, Stina, 360, 361
McNamara, Robert, 166, 167, 240
Medicaid, 130, 132
Medicare, 130, 132
Mekong River, 143, 145, 146, 147, 149, 150, 151, 158
Melkhii Khad (Turtle Rock), 358
Memorial Hall of the Victims in Nanjing Massacre by Japanese Invaders (museum), 324
Merdeka Square, 70
Merlion, 50
Migasiuk, Janusz, 137
Military Demarcation Line (MDL), 34, 35
Ming City Wall. *See* Nanjing Wall
Mirador Mansion, 275, 276, 284
Mộc Bài, 236
Monsanto, 244
Monument to the People's Heroes, 349
Moscow, 371, 372, 373, 374, 375, 376, 384
Mount Kyaiktiyo, 112
Mount Phou Si, 149
Mount Song, 338
Mount Tai, 341, 342, 343
Muang Phôn-Hông, 157
Mũi Né, 253

475

Mukai, Toshiaki, 325
Munch, Edvard, 392
Murray, Bill, 360
Murugan (Hindu god of war), 71, 83
Museum of Qin Terra-cotta Warriors and Horses, 331
Muslim Quarter (Xi'an), 328
My Lai Massacre, 244
Nadaam Festival, 355, 358
Nam Khan River, 149, 150
Nam Song River, 156
Namdaemun Gate (Sungnyemun Gate), 31
Namdaemun Market, 35
Nampan (village), 123
Namsan Mountain, 39, 41
Nana Entertainment Plaza, 120, 164
Nana Plaza. *See* Nana Entertainment Plaza
Nana Tai, 163
Nanjing, 289, 291, 321, 322, 323, 324, 325, 326
Nanjing Massacre, 291
Nanjing Safety Zone, 326
Nanjing Wall, 322
Nanjing War Crimes Tribunal, 326
Nanyang Technological University, 58
Nash equilibrium, 153
nat (spirit), 105, 110, 118
National Academic Theatre of Opera and Ballet of Mongolia, 361
National Center Against Violence (NCAV), 362
National Center on Education and the Economy (NCEE), 59, 60
National Congress of the Communist Party, 291
National Gallery (Oslo), 392
National History Museum (Malaysia), 68
National Institute of Education (Singapore), 58, 59
National Mosque of Malaysia (Masjid Negara), 68
Nattukkottai Chettiar Temple (Penang), 83
Nga Phe Kyaung Monastery, 124

Nguyễn dynasty, 263
Nha Trang, 253, 257, 263
Nichols, Angela, 120
Night Market: Sexual Cultures and the Thai Economic Miracle (book), 114, 148, 152, 165, 167, 183
Night Safari, 54, 55
Nixon, Richard, 222, 231
Nobel Banquet, 388
Noda, Tsuyoshi, 325
Nong Khai, 164
Norilsk Nickel, 383
Norway's Resistance Museum, 392
Novo Nordisk (pharmaceutical), 133
Nyaungshwe, 108, 122
Old Protestant Cemetery (Macau), 281
Old Quarter (Hanoi), 268, 269, 270
one-child policy, 288
Ong Soon Yah, 78
Operation *Menu*, 231
Operation *Ranch Hand*, 245, 249
opium, 53, 125, 290
Organization for Economic Cooperation and Development (OECD), 58, 59, 130, 132
Organization of Petroleum Exporting Countries (OPEC), 168
Orung (Five Tombs), 39
Orwell, George, 66
Osaka Mainichi (newspaper), 325
Oslo, 391, 392, 395
Oslo Cathedral, 391
Oslo City Hall, 392
Padang, 51, 70
Padang Kota Lama, Esplanade, 74
Pagan Empire, 127
Palace of the Facets, 375
palm oil, 63, 64
Panmunjom, 33, 35
Pa-O (ethnic group), 126
Parameswara (king), 69
Partido Revolucionario Institucional (PRI), 136
Patient Protection and Affordable Care Act (Obamacare), 129, 130
Patpong, 163

Patuxai, 160
Peart, Neil, 343
Penang, 67, 72, 73, 74, 75, 76, 79, 80, 81, 82, 83, 85
Penang Bridge, 73
Penang State Museum, 81
People's Army of Vietnam (PAVN), 231, 233
People's History of the United States, A (book), 250
People's Republic of China, 267, 273, 285
Petronas Twin Towers, 65
Pha That Luang, 161
Phayao, 164, 170
Phnom Bakheng, 205
Phnom Penh, 194, 222, 224, 225, 226, 227, 229, 232, 233, 236
Phnom Sampeau, 192
Phongpaichit, Pasuk, 172
Phú Quốc, 249
Plaça Reial, 400
Poipet, 188, 189, 190, 199
Pol Pot, 192, 193, 195, 200, 222, 224
Politics of Tourism in Asia, The (book), 176
Polo, Marco, 358
Poseokjeong, 40
post-traumatic stress disorder (PTSD), 193
Potanin, Vladimir, 383
Power of Myth, The (television), 99
Prasat Trapeang Ropou, 205
Prostitution Suppression Act (Thailand), 116, 166
Psah Chas (market), 204
Public Health Ministry of Thailand, 176, 177
Pujiang Hotel (Astor House Hotel), 288, 289
Pulau Ubin, 57
Pyay, 108, 127
Qin Shi Huang, 330, 331
Qing dynasty, 83, 289, 290, 291, 292, 299
Qingping Market, 286
Rabe, John H. D., 326

Raekoja plats, 377
Raffles Hotel, 54, 82
Raffles, Sir Thomas Stamford, 53
Rai Leh Beach, 96
Rape of Nanking, The: The Forgotten Holocaust of World War II (book), 324
Red Square, 372, 373, 374
Remon, Dan, 185, 186, 191
Republic of China, 291, 299
Rice, Condoleezza, 153
Richner, Beat, 221, 222, 223, 226
Richter, Linda, 176
Robinson, Lillian S., 114, 148, 165, 183
Rousseau, Jean-Jacques, 61
Royal Cambodian Armed Forces (RCAF), 200
Royal Palace (Oslo), 391
Royal Palace (Stockholm), 386, 388
Royal Selangor Club, 70
Ruins of St. Paul, 280
Rummel, R.J., 242
Russian Federation, 351, 375, 381, 382
Russian oligarchs, 382, 383, 384
Russian Orthodox Church, 374
Russo-Japanese War, 291
S-21 prison. *See* Tuol Sleng Genocide Museum (S-21 prison)
Sachs, Jeffrey, 382
Sahn, Seung, 337
Saigon. *See* Ho Chi Minh City
Saint Basil's Cathedral, 373, 374
Sakyamuni Buddha, 56
Sallah, Michael D., 244
Salween River, 125
Sands Macao, 280, 281
Sanlitun, 347
Sanofi (pharmaceutical), 133
Sarkies Brothers, 82
SARS. *See* severe acute respiratory syndrome (SARS)
Scream, The (painting), 392
Seabrook, Jeremy, 167, 175, 177, 183
Sears Tower (Willis Tower), 65
Second Indochina War, 243, 249
Second Opium War, 287, 289

Second Sino-Japanese War, 291, 336
Sen, Amartya, 288
Sen, Hun, 194
Senaatintori (Senate Square), 381
Seoul, 26, 28, 29, 31, 33, 35, 36, 41, 44, 45, 46, 294
Serangoon Road, 48, 49
Sergeant, Harriet, 289, 290, 292
severe acute respiratory syndrome (SARS), 221, 279
sex industry, 114, 115, 116, 138, 165, 167, 169, 170, 178, 180, 183, 184, 283
sex slave trade. *See* sex trafficking
Sex Slaves: The Trafficking of Women in Asia (book), 116, 173, 174, 175, 183
sex tourism, 115, 137, 138, 155, 164, 167, 173, 176, 179, 180, 282
sex trafficking, 116, 125, 282, 283
Shamian Island, 286, 287
Shan (ethnic group), 126
Shan Hills, 118
Shan State, 125, 126
Shan State Army, 125
Shang dynasty, 323
Shanghai, 277, 286, 289, 290, 291, 292, 293, 294, 296, 297, 299, 321, 322, 323, 324, 326, 336
Shanghai (book), 289, 290
Shanghai Museum, 298
Shaolin Temple, 337, 338, 339
Shenzhen, 285
Shikai, Yuan, 291
Shim Gwang Sa (Mind Light Temple), 41, 337
shinbyu (ceremony), 124
Shinjuku, 28
Shkreli, Martin, 133
Shwedagon Pagoda, 103, 104, 105, 112
Siam Square, 163
Siberia, 351, 363, 368, 370, 402
Siddhartha, Prince, 124
Siem Reap, 196, 198, 199, 200, 202, 203, 204, 205, 208, 221, 222, 224, 235

Sihanouk, Norodom (Prince of Cambodia, 233
Sihanouk, Norodom (Prince of Cambodia), 233
Silk Road, 328
Silla dynasty, 36, 39
Silla Kingdom, 36, 39
Silla tombs, 37
Simatai, 348
Singapore, 44, 46, 47, 49, 51, 52, 53, 54, 57, 58, 59, 60, 63, 67, 70, 82, 93, 98, 132, 191, 221, 267
Singapore Cricket Club, 51
Singapore River, 53
Singapore, battle of, 51
Singuttara Hill, 104
Sisophon, 191
Sisowath Quay, 225, 227
Skuon, 224
Smith, Adam, 61
Social Contract, The (book), 61
Socialist realism, 373
Soi Cowboy, 163
Song dynasty, 329
Sông Hương River, 262
Songkran (festival), 97, 101
South Vietnamese Army (SVA), 246, 247
Soviet Union, 246, 355, 369, 375, 382
Soviet-Afghan War, 372
SpåraKoff, 381
special administrative region (SAR), 267, 273, 294
Spencer-Churchill, Henry John, 281
Sri Krishnan Temple, 57
Stadshuset (Stockholm City Hall), 388
Stalin, Joseph, 375
Star Wars: Episode I – The Phantom Menace (film), 361
State Tretyakov Gallery, 374
Stiglitz, Joseph, 383, 384
Stockholm, 385, 386, 387, 388
Stockholm Pride, 388
Straits of Malacca, 52
Sükhbaatar Square, 359, 360
Sükhbaatar, Damdin, 360
Sükhbaatar's Mausoleum, 360

Sukhothai, 120, 121
Sule Pagoda, 101
Summer Palace (Beijing), 351
Sungnyemun Gate. *See* Namdaemun Gate
Ta Prohm, 209, 211
Ta-ang (ethnic group), 126
Taft, William Howard, 289
Tai'an, 341, 344
Taiping Rebellion, 291
Talat Sao (market), 160
Tallinn, 377, 378, 379
Tallinn Old Town, 377
Tanaka, Gunkichi, 326
Tapgol Park, 27, 30, 32
Taungoo, 108, 117
Taungyo (ethnic group), 126
Temple of Heaven, 352
Temple of Literature, 271
Temple of the Eight Immortals (Xi'an), 329
Terracotta Army, 328, 330, 331
Terzani, Tiziano, 65
Tha Phae Gate, 136, 137, 139
Thai Red Cross Aids Research Centre, 184
Thailand: Buddhist Kingdom as Modern Nation-State (book), 166
Thai-Lao Friendship Bridge, 162
Thaipusam (festival), 71, 83
That Dam, 160
Theravada Buddhism, 104, 124, 209
Thingyan (festival), 101
Third Tunnel of Aggression, 33
Thirty Years' War, 389
Thu Bồn River, 258
Tiananmen Square, 349, 350, 352, 359
Tiger Force, 244
Tokyo, 21, 22, 26, 27, 28, 29, 31, 32, 46, 48, 76, 100, 116, 117, 120, 140, 191, 274, 276, 283, 294, 326, 327, 360, 373
Tokyo Nichi Nichi (newspaper), 325
Tomb Raider (film), 210
Ton Sai (beach), 94, 96
Tonlé Sap Lake, 197, 201
Tonlé Sap River, 224, 225

Toompea Castle, 378
Tourist Authority of Thailand, 115, 138, 167
Trans-Mongolian Railway, 351, 353, 363, 373
Trans-Siberian Railway, 35, 371
Travels in the Skin Trade Tourism and the Sex Industry, 167, 175, 178
Travels in the Skin Trade: Tourism and the Sex Industry (book), 183
Travels of Marco Polo, The (book), 356, 359
Treaty of Nanjing, 290, 292
Trink, Bernard, 175
Truman Doctrine, 248
Tsar Bell, 375
Tsim Sha Tsui, 275
Tua Sai Yah, 78
tuberculosis, 222, 232, 362
Tucker, Marc, 60
tumuli (burial mounds), 36
Tumuli Park, 37
Tuol Sleng Genocide Museum (S-21 prison), 230, 233, 234, 235
Turing Pharmaceuticals, 133
Two Treatises of Government, 61
Tyler, John, 293
U.S. Army and Army of the Republic of Vietnam (ARVN), 246
U.S. Department of Defense (DOD), 243
U.S. Treasury, 382
Ulan Bator, 353, 354, 355, 359, 361, 362, 363
Ulan-Ude, 368
UN peacekeeping troops, 194
UNAIDS. *See* Joint United Nations Programme on HIV/AIDS (UNAIDS)
UNESCO. *See* United Nations Educational, Scientific and Cultural Organization (UNESCO)
unexploded bombs (UXBs), 153, 200, 240, 247
unexploded ordinance (UXO), 231, 232

479

unexploded ordnance (UXO), 154, 188, 240
UNICEF. *See* United Nations Children's Fund (UNICEF)
Unified Silla, 40
United Nations (UN), 61, 125
United Nations Children's Fund (UNICEF), 139, 221, 222, 223
United Nations Educational, Scientific and Cultural Organization (UNESCO), 121, 377
United Nations Transitional Authority in Cambodia (UNTAC), 194
United States Agency for International Development (USAID), 139
United States Declaration of Independence, 61, 248
United States Strategic Air Command (SAC), 231
United Wa State Army, 125
Uppsala, 389
Uppsala Cathedral, 390
USAID. *See* United States Agency for International Development (USAID)
Vang Vieng, 154, 155, 156
Vasa Museum, 387, 389
Victoria Harbor, 277
Victoria Peak, 278
Vientiane, 153, 154, 156, 157, 158, 159, 160, 162
Viet Cong, 231, 233, 244, 245, 246, 247, 248
Vietnam War, 32, 138, 153, 154, 166, 187, 188, 200, 243, 246, 248, 270
Viking Age, 392, 393
Viking Ship Museum, 392
Voice of America, 195
Wa people (ethnic group), 126

War Memorial of Korea, 31
War Remnants Museum (Saigon), 245, 248, 250
Warsaw, 398
Wat Phra Mahathat, 121
Wat Phra Si Sanphet, 121
Wat Wisunalat, 151
Weiss, Mitch, 244
Wheeler, Earle, 231
WHO. *See* World Health Organization (WHO)
Wilson, Donald, 165
Wing Lo, T., 282
Wolseong Park, 37, 38
Wongaksa Temple, 30
Wonglah, Moon, 171
World Bank, 129, 147, 166, 167, 168, 194, 346, 382, 383, 384, 385
World Health Organization (WHO), 131, 221, 222, 223, 362
Worldwide Press Freedom Index, 60
Xi'an, 326, 328, 329, 332
Xiaoping, Deng, 288
yakuza, 22, 116, 183
Yangon (Rangoon), 96, 100, 101, 102, 103, 104, 105, 106, 109, 110, 112, 127, 128
Yangon City Hall, 102, 106
Yangtze River, 292, 325
Yat-sen, Sun, 291, 293, 299
Yeltsin, Boris, 382, 383
Yi River, 336
Yi Sun-Shin, Admiral, 30
Yongsan Electronics Market, 32
Yuan dynasty, 83
Yukjonbul, 41
Zaisan Memorial, 361
Zedong, Mao, 293, 299, 349, 350, 373
Zedong, Mausoleum of Mao, 349, 350
Zhengzhou, 340
Zinn, Howard, 249

Printed in Great Britain
by Amazon